Essays on Ayn Rand's
The Fountainhead

Essays on Ayn Rand's
The Fountainhead

Edited by Robert Mayhew

LEXINGTON BOOKS

A division of
ROWMAN & LITTLEFIELD PUBLISHERS, INC.
Lanham • Boulder • New York • Toronto • Plymouth, UK

LEXINGTON BOOKS

A division of Rowman & Littlefield Publishers, Inc.
A wholly owned subsidary of The Rowman & Littlefield Publishing Group, Inc.
4501 Forbes Boulevard, Suite 200
Lanham, MD 20706

Estover Road
Plymouth PL6 7PY
United Kingdom

British Library Cataloguing in Publication Information Available

Library of Congress Cataloging-in-Publication Data

Essays on Ayn Rand's The fountainhead / edited by Robert Mayhew.
   p. cm.
  Includes bibliographical references and index.
  ISBN-13: 978-0-7391-1577-0 (cloth : alk. paper)
  ISBN-10: 0-7391-1577-4 (cloth : alk. paper)
  ISBN-13: 978-0-7391-1578-7 (pbk. : alk. paper)
  ISBN-10: 0-7391-1578-2 (pbk. : alk. paper)
  1. Rand, Ayn. Fountainhead. I. Mayhew, Robert.
  PS3535.A547F69345 2007
  813'.52—dc22   2006023945

Printed in the United States of America

∞™ The paper used in this publication meets the minimum requirements of
American National Standard for Information Sciences—Permanence of Paper
for Printed Library Materials, ANSI/NISO Z39.48-1992.

Contents

Preface

In "The Goal of My Writing," Ayn Rand says: "The motive and purpose of my writing is *the projection of an ideal man*." Howard Roark, the hero of *The Fountainhead*, is her first complete realization of this goal. This collection of essays is an exploration and celebration of *The Fountainhead*, its hero, its underlying philosophy—and its creator.

Part I, which covers the novel's history, begins with Shoshana Milgram's extensive discussion of the creation of *The Fountainhead*: "*The Fountainhead* from Notebook to Novel: The Composition of Ayn Rand's First Ideal Man." Howard Roark and the novel that tells his story were the products of Ayn Rand's creative genius, and Milgram's essay provides us with a window into this act of creation. It also explores the prominence of Nietzsche in the early drafts of *The Fountainhead* and shows that much of the Nietzsche material was removed as work on the novel developed. The next essay—Michael S. Berliner's "Howard Roark and Frank Lloyd Wright"—underscores Ayn Rand's originality. It is often claimed that Roark was modeled after Wright; however, Dr. Berliner demonstrates that although Wright was in certain respects an inspiration for Roark, he was not a model.

Richard E. Ralston's "Publishing *The Fountainhead*" covers the publication history of the novel—a history more interesting than that of any of Ayn Rand's other novels. Michael S. Berliner's second essay, "*The Fountainhead* Reviews," discusses the (surprisingly few) reviews of the novel—with special attention given to the only favorable review Ayn Rand received in her lifetime from the *New York Times*—as well as the reviews of the 1949 Warner Bros. film version of *The Fountainhead*. Jeff Britting's essay, "Adapting *The Fountainhead* to Film," is a detailed study of one aspect of that film's history: the development of the screenplay.

Part II contains essays that focus on *The Fountainhead* as literature and as philosophy. It begins with Tore Boeckmann's "*The Fountainhead* as a Romantic Novel," a detailed discussion of the novel in the context of Ayn Rand's identification of the nature of romanticism in literature and how it differs from two rival schools: naturalism and classicism. Much of the essay serves to underscore the importance of her claim that "the essential attribute of Romanticism" is "the independent, creative projection of an individual writer's values." To illustrate this point, the essay includes a comparison of *The Fountainhead* and Edmond Rostand's *Chantecler*.

In her 1945 letter "To the Readers of *The Fountainhead*," Ayn Rand writes:

> Aristotle said that fiction is of greater philosophical importance than history, because history represents things only as they are, while fiction represents them "as they might be and ought to be." If you wish a key to the literary method of *The Fountainhead*, this is it.

Mr. Boeckmann's second essay, "What Might Be and Ought to Be: Aristotle's *Poetics* and *The Fountainhead*," discusses this "might be and ought to be" principle, demonstrates that it is Aristotelian, and explains how precisely it is "a key to the literary method of *The Fountainhead*."

Shoshana Milgram's second essay, "Three Inspirations for the Ideal Man: Cyrus Paltons, Enjolras, and Cyrano de Bergerac," is an excellent piece of comparative literature that discusses early literary inspirations for Howard Roark: Cyrus Paltons, from Maurice Champagne's *The Mysterious Valley*; Enjolras, from Victor Hugo's *Les Misérables*; and Cyrano de Bergerac, from Edmond Rostand's eponymous play.

Each of the next three essays deals with a topic that spans both literature and philosophy. Andrew Bernstein's "Understanding the 'Rape' Scene in *The Fountainhead*" discusses one of the most misunderstood scenes in the novel—and one of the most misunderstood characters (Dominique Francon). My contribution, "Humor in *The Fountainhead*," examines the humor in the novel and explores in what sense *The Fountainhead* is satirical (whereas *Atlas Shrugged* is not). In her introduction to the twenty-fifth anniversary edition of *The Fountainhead*, Ayn Rand writes that a major reason for the novel's lasting appeal is its "confirmation of the spirit of youth." B. John Bayer's "*The Fountainhead* and the Spirit of Youth" discusses the precise nature of the novel's confirmation of this spirit, drawing on a later essay of Rand's: "The 'Inexplicable Personal Alchemy.'"

The final four essays treat moral-philosophical topics. Onkar Ghate's "The Basic Motivation of the Creators and the Masses in *The Fountainhead*" deals with what creative genius demands and what the "masses" are, and the connected question (to employ the title of a later essay of Rand's) "How Does One Lead a Rational Life in an Irrational Society?" Two of Howard

Roark's major virtues—virtues crucial to being a creator and intimately connected to Ayn Rand's conception of egoism—are independence and integrity. These are the topics of the next two essays: Tara Smith's "Unborrowed Vision: Independence and Egoism in *The Fountainhead*," and Dina Schein's "Roark's Integrity." Finally, Amy Peikoff's "A Moral Dynamiting" discusses moral and legal issues surrounding the novel's climax: Roark's dynamiting of the Cortlandt Homes housing project.

In fall 2005, I interviewed Leonard Peikoff on *The Fountainhead* for more than an hour. I am pleased to include, as an epilogue to this collection, a transcript of that interview, in which Dr. Peikoff discusses, among other things, the characters Ellsworth Toohey, Gail Wynand, and Dominique Francon; the difference in focus between *The Fountainhead* and *Atlas Shrugged*; and what *The Fountainhead* has meant to him personally

*   *   *

In her introduction to the twenty-fifth anniversary edition of *The Fountainhead*, Ayn Rand writes: "Longevity—predominantly, though not exclusively— is the prerogative of a literary school which is virtually non-existent today: Romanticism." Romanticism, she says, "deals, not with the random trivia of the day, but with the timeless, fundamental, universal problems and *values* of human existence." She adds: "I do not mean to imply that I knew, when I wrote it, that *The Fountainhead* would remain in print for twenty-five years. I did not think of any specific time period. I knew only that it was a book that *ought* to live. It did." And it still does. Though it was published more than sixty years ago, it continues to sell; further, it is being taught with increasing frequency in high schools and universities throughout the United States. *The Fountainhead* has become, as it ought to be, an American classic.

Robert Mayhew
Seton Hall University
June 2006

Acknowledgments

I wish to thank Leonard Peikoff (Executor of the Estate of Ayn Rand) for permission to use previously unpublished material of Ayn Rand's, and Jeff Britting (Archivist of the Ayn Rand Archives) for his assistance in accessing this material. Thanks also to Catherine Forrest Getzie and the staff at Lexington Books for their excellent work on this volume, to Neil Erian for preparing the index, and to David Hayes for his helpful comments on the entire collection. I am grateful to Seton Hall University for its continued support of my research, including a sabbatical leave in the early part of which I completed my work on this volume. Finally, many thanks to both the Ayn Rand Institute and the Anthem Foundation for Objectivist Scholarship for grants that supported this project.

Bibliographical Note

Unless otherwise indicated, quotes from Ayn Rand's *The Fountainhead* will be followed by page number(s) in parentheses in the text and not by an endnote. Pagination refers to the Centennial paperback edition (New York: Signet, 2005—published in celebration of the one hundredth anniversary of Ayn Rand's birth), which includes Ayn Rand's introduction to the twenty-fifth anniversary edition and Leonard Peikoff's afterword to the fiftieth anniversary edition.

In some chapters the author quotes from, and refers to, information contained in a series of biographical interviews that Ayn Rand gave in 1960–1961, the tapes and transcripts of which are in the Ayn Rand Archives. References will appear in the endnotes as: Biographical interviews (Ayn Rand Archives).

I

THE HISTORY OF
THE FOUNTAINHEAD

1

The Fountainhead from Notebook to Novel

The Composition of Ayn Rand's First Ideal Man

Shoshana Milgram

The Fountainhead begins in 1922, when Howard Roark is twenty-two; covering eighteen years of the hero's life, it is the longest in time span of any of Ayn Rand's novels. The novel's composition began on December 4, 1935, with Ayn Rand's first notes for a book she planned to call "Second-Hand Lives."[1] She began writing on June 26, 1938; within the next two years, she completed the first of the four parts and six and one-half chapters of the second, and then stopped writing.[2] On December 9, 1941, she signed a contract with Bobbs-Merrill, and she resumed writing two days later.[3] On December 31, 1942, she delivered the completed manuscript.[4] In consultation with Archibald Ogden, whom she considered "a miracle as an editor,"[5] she made cuts and other revisions; the novel was released on April 15, 1943, and officially published on May 10, 1943.[6]

The current article is not a full account of Ayn Rand's life during the composition of this novel. The publication of *We the Living* in the United States and Great Britain, the Broadway productions of *Night of January 16th* and *The Unconquered*, the British publication of *Anthem*, the writing of *Ideal* and *Think Twice*, the Wendell Willkie campaign and other political activities—not to mention the day jobs as reader for RKO, MGM, and Paramount—are subjects for another day. Nor will the scope of this article allow me to include all of her preparations for this novel, from her architectural research to her job with Ely Jacques Kahn. I do not even have room here to consider all the editorial changes—from the omission of extended sequences of events to the editing of passages of dialogue and description—that are evident in the notebooks and the surviving pages of her drafts, or even to describe the entire contents of the notebooks and the drafts. My goal in this article is to describe, with examples, the purposeful editorial principles she applied while writing and revising her manuscript (principles that cohere with her chosen theme), so that I can examine closely (yet still not exhaustively) the decisions she made, from notebook to novel, in projecting—for the first time—her ideal man, in the form of Howard Roark. Her choices—in style and in substance—indicate not only the changes she made in the characterization of Roark, but also, perhaps, some changes in herself.

The notebooks for *The Fountainhead* contain voluminous notes on the theme, characters, and plot, along with summaries of her research, e.g., architectural books and magazines, recommended by a librarian at the New York Public Library.[7] The outlines and notes show the early stages of Ayn Rand's preparatory work: constructing her plots, developing her characters, identifying her themes and ideas.

Her notes, to begin with, present time lines of the architectural and personal development of Peter Keating and Roark, and to their interactions with other key characters. She refers not only to the buildings and relationships we know from the finished novel, but also of events that are not in the surviving manuscript pages (much less in the novel), such as the suicides of a writer and a sculptor, Keating's "romance" with Lois Cook and his marriage to a blonde, Roark's fight with Gail Wynand, the suicide note Dominique gives to Wynand in response to his threats, and Roark's refusal to help the family of a contractor who has gone bankrupt and committed suicide.

She analyzes, at length, the ideas, backgrounds, and features of Roark, Keating, and Ellsworth Toohey. She has lists of possible names for the characters. She occasionally considers characters she later decided to exclude, such as the "Communist—an inhibited, embittered weakling who believes himself an idealist and embraces Communism as the cure for the world's ills."[8]

Regarding her theme, she describes different forms of second-handedness, by contrast with the first-handedness of her hero. Her notes explain how the motives and actions of Toohey, Keating, and Wynand demonstrate their fundamental dependence on others. Initially, it appears, she did not plan for Roark to deliver a speech articulating the principle by which he lived. Her notes indicate that the speech at the final trial was to be given by a distinguished old lawyer.

Although her notes are not always a coherent record of her work—many are undated, and some are cryptic—they show, in detail, how she criticized her prose (e.g., commenting to herself that her first description of Heller was "very bad"), how she decided to make cuts (e.g., noting that Roark does not need multiple girlfriends), how she gave herself "standing orders" about style (eliminating bromides) and content (eliminating redundancy). On February 18, 1940, she criticized her work to date on the first part of the novel and set forth principles for future writing and editing.[9] She continued to monitor her progress and to articulate her principles of writing.

Her notes on her reading show that she was reading purposefully, with her novel in mind: for information about architecture in general (as art and as business), about modern architecture specifically (its practitioners and its critics). She would note, for example, that a particular critical statement was good material for Toohey, or she would ask herself what aspects of a project would depend on the architect, and which on the contractor.

Although not all of the notes are dated, the dated notes make clear that she began with the theme and the main characters and events (from December 1935 to March 1937); continued with notes on architectural books by such writers as Darcy Braddell, Lewis Mumford, and Alfred C. Bossom; and, in March 1938, returned to developing the plot. She began writing on June 26, 1938 (as noted above), but later outlined (or re-outlined) the highlights of sections as she progressed. For example, she wrote the final chapter outline for the second half of Part Two on December 17, 1941; she wrote the final chapter outline for Part Four on July 2, 1942.[10]

The notebooks are worth examining because they are Ayn Rand's first steps toward the novel; the hints of the intentions she ultimately rejected are provocative. Her procedures are also evidence of her artistic policies, which we can see by tracing passages from the notebooks to the manuscript to the novel. Her notes for the Enright House party (April 22, 1940) describe her subject and the means, i.e., what she wanted to show (second-handedness in the social setting) and how she wanted to show it (through representative remarks).[11] In the manuscript, she presents, virtually unchanged, the "what" in the form of Roark's thoughts; she presents the "how" in a sequence of brief exchanges. In the final text of the novel, she removed Roark's thoughts (and, as I will discuss later on, she was frequently to cut from the manuscript similar descriptions of his thoughts) and left only the short snatches of conversations. In *The Fountainhead*, in other words, she dispensed with the description of what she wished to show (a description she had initially transferred straight from the notes to the draft) and relied solely on the presentation of the evidence. There are many similar examples. In the final section of my essay, a section that is speculative, I will return to the notebooks to analyze them from the standpoint of a specific change in her thinking about her hero, i.e., Nietzsche-like elements.

The manuscripts of *The Fountainhead* consist of a holograph draft of approximately 2,300 pages, a typed draft that is incomplete, a third draft (complete and typed), and a set of galleys.[12] In multiple drafts, Ayn Rand considered and revised the selection of ideas, incidents, and words. She did not preserve all the evidence of her work; sometimes she discarded pages, noting only that, e.g., "161–163 cut." There are virtually no lapses in textual continuity in the holograph; nonetheless, the drafts, evidently, do not include all of the discards. But although the drafts do not constitute a full record of everything Ayn Rand did in the process of composing and editing, they reveal her intense dedication, her choices, and her command of her craft. As evidence of her purposeful choices, the drafts can serve as a guide to looking more closely at the details and character of the novel, the achieved result of those choices.

The holograph draft contains much material that will be unfamiliar to the reader of *The Fountainhead*, especially in the earlier parts of the novel. Ayn Rand deliberately wrote more than she expected to use; as she explained to her editor, Archibald Ogden (who thought that the first third of the novel was much too long), she wanted to have the entire novel completed before deciding what, in view of the whole, must be included.[13] Some of the omitted scenes are easily legible in the manuscript; others are present but crossed out; it is possible that some scenes have been removed without a trace. Among the discarded scenes and sequences are Roark's romances with Vesta Dunning and Heddy Adler; several additional scenes featuring Roark's relationship with Henry Cameron; Ralston Holcombe's job offer to Roark; Peter Keating's dishonest scheme against Tim Davis; Roark's association with Larry Dwight (a fellow draftsman at the office of John Erik Snyte); Roark's reading of the writings of Austen Heller (along with more information about Heller's crusades and friendship with Roark); additional conversations between Roark and Steven Mallory; a long, one-sided conversation between Roark and Toohey; and a meeting Roark attends of the New League of Proletarian Art.[14]

She ultimately decided, she said, to omit some scenes and sequences because they contributed nothing that was not expressed better elsewhere, or because they interfered with the overall design. One example was a sequence of scenes involving Vesta Dunning, a talented, ambitious actress romantically involved with Roark, whose desire for the approval of others was a breach in her integrity. Unable to sustain her relationship with Roark or her pursuit of her art, she was to be shown, in Part Four, as ultimately miserable and defeated.

> I cut her out before I finished the book. It was after I finished Part Three, which is the Gail Wynand part, that I realized that Vesta Dunning was a variant of the same problem, in relation to the theme . . . as a person of great talent who should have been great, but didn't quite hold out . . . it would then have taken an awful lot of psychological study and details about her, which would interfere with the major action, because she would not have been integrated to Roark's life at all. . . . Also, it would have spoiled the nature of his relationship with Dominique. The fact that Dominique was the only woman in his life stands out better without the other relationship.[15]

She comments that her overall purpose guided her and that she was happy to excise repetitive parts in order to achieve the purposeful succinctness of the whole.

Her focus on her theme, on her overall purpose, governed not only the larger-scale changes (e.g., the removal of characters and sequences) she made in the drafts, but also the line-editing of descriptions, conversations, and speeches. My examples are representative rather than exhaustive. From her earliest notes (December 4, 1935), she had identified the theme as the conflict between the first-handers, who use their own minds to know the world and to choose their values, and the second-handers, who "shift the center" of their lives from their own judgments and values to those of others.[16] The editing process shows her attempt not only to dramatize first- and second-handedness in characterizations, but also to make the reader's experience true to the theme. Roark is progressively revealed as first-handed not only in his attitude to his work, but also in his every act and utterance. The reader, too, is invited to be a first-hander. As Ayn Rand composes and edits the text, she concretizes characters to the point that the reader is able to grasp directly the characters' premises and basic values. The method of the editorial revisions coheres precisely with her theme.

In her important notes to herself of February 18, 1940, she wonders if she has given away too much of Roark too soon in the beginning of the novel.[17] Her revisions of the opening chapter, accordingly, show her shortening the description of Roark's thoughts, especially the thoughts he has while standing on the cliff, before the reader has seen him in action. She also revised, extensively, the conversation between Roark and his former Dean, to stress Roark's first-handedness; she did so in a way that encourages the reader to observe closely the action and the dialogue, and not to rely on summary. The details speak "for themselves": everything in the substance and manner of Roark's behavior serves to develop his characterization. And, by reducing narrative summary, Ayn Rand gives the reader little opportunity to escape the responsibility of paying attention to the facts presented.

In the draft, the Dean says: "My dear fellow, who will want to give you work now?" Roark, in the draft, replies: "I believe I know someone who will" (I, 51–52). The Dean insultingly implies, by his rhetorical question, that Roark is unemployable as an architect, and Roark, without challenging the implication that work is something to be "given" to him, responds that he is indeed employable, that he believes he knows someone who will give him work. Roark's reply allows the Dean to dominate the conversation; by conceding that work is to be "given," Roark, in the draft, subordinates himself both to the Dean and to the hypothetical "givers" of work.

In the final, edited text, by contrast, the Dean asks: "How do you expect to force your ideas on [clients]?" Roark replies: "I don't propose to force or be forced. Those who want me will come to me." (26) Roark does not accept the terms of his interlocutor. When insulted, he does not reply with a boast on the order of "I will force them to accept my ideas by. . . ." Roark instead changes the terms of the discussion, eliminates force from the discussion, and confidently states that clients who value his work will seek him out.

Other editorial changes show a similar pattern of highlighting Roark's independent judgment and eliminating any suggestion of his dependence on other people's judgments, on other minds. The Dean, in the draft, continues to insult Roark, saying "You are a megalomaniac," and Roark, in the draft, responds, "I have been told that before" (I, 52), as if he has been keeping track of the opinions of other people, as if he regards their views of his nature as a potentially valuable source of reliable information.

But Roark, as a first-hander, would not consider other people as authorities on such a matter as his character.

The edited text, by contrast, has a new and revealing passage. In the final text, the Dean says:

> "You know, . . . you would sound much more convincing if you spoke as if you cared whether I agreed with you or not." "That's true," said Roark. "I don't care whether you agree with me or not." He said it so simply that it did not sound offensive, it sounded like the statement of a fact which he noticed, puzzled, for the first time. (26)

The Dean's insult and Roark's response are directly focused on first-versus-second-handedness. When Roark says "That's true," he does not mean that the Dean's assertion is true, i.e., that he, Roark, would be more convincing if he sounded as if he cared about the Dean's agreement. Roark does not care to sound "more convincing" to this Dean and has no interest in hearing how to achieve a goal that is not his. But Roark, instead of taking offense at the insult, and instead of trying to learn how his attitude affects other people, takes from the Dean's statement the single feature that interests him: an observation about his own nature that his own judgment confirms. As edited and improved, Roark's response better reflects his first-handedness.

At the end of the conversation, when the Dean—in the draft and also in the final text—tells Roark, "You are a man not to be encouraged. You are dangerous," Roark, in the draft, responds: "That defines those to whom I am dangerous" (I, 52). The tone is uncharacteristically stiff and formal, indicative of a degree of care and attention: the draft's Roark is delivering a diagnosis of his opponents. Roark's response in the final, edited version of the text is different. When the Dean says, "You are dangerous," Roark replies, briefly, directly, and dismissively: "To whom?" The first version focuses on the nature of his opponents; the second version dismisses the Dean's comment as insignificant. The revised version of Roark's response emphasizes the nature of Roark himself rather than the definition of his enemies: the implied grammatical subject of Roark's sentence—"To whom [am I dangerous]?" is "I."

The revised exchange is well integrated with another small episode earlier in the conversation. The Dean asks: "My dear fellow, who will let you [build that way]?" Roark replies: "That's not the point. The point is, who will stop me?" (23). Roark's response in this earlier exchange makes explicit his dismissal of the Dean's notion that building requires permission; there as here, Roark focuses instead on his own concerns. For Roark, certain that no one can stop him, "who will stop me?" is a rhetorical question. His implicit self-confidence explains why he does not need to answer the Dean's inquiry ("who will let you?").

At the end of the scene, Ayn Rand's editing sharpens the characterization and the context with simple omissions. In the draft, Roark "bowed and left the room. 'The professor of mathematics,' thought the Dean, looking at the closed door, 'is crazy'" (I, 52). For the final text, Ayn Rand removed the Dean's thoughts. To include them is not only to feature the Dean more prominently than necessary, but to repeat what is already known.

The scene has already made abundantly clear that, for the Dean, adherence to tradition overrides any attention to engineering, which is important to the math professor. From the characterization of Roark, moreover, Ayn Rand removed the inconsistent touch of a bow. Although Roark is polite to the Dean, he is not deferential; to include the bow is to emphasize respect, which Roark does not believe the Dean deserves—not for his views on architecture, and not for his character.

An additional instance of purposeful editing appears in Roark's post-interview thoughts about the character of the Dean. In the draft: "He understood the Dean, and he had understood men such as the Dean long ago, and it had ceased to disturb him. But he still wondered, and he wondered about it often, what made those men such as they were" (I, 53). The description, in the draft, appears self-contradictory: if Roark has to wonder, often, what made men such as the Dean such as they were, how can he be said to understand them at all, much less to have understood them "long ago"? Moreover, why would a first-hander wonder, and wonder often, about other people?

The final, edited text is significantly different: "He had met many men such as the Dean; he had never understood them. He knew only that there was some important difference between his actions and theirs. It had ceased to disturb him long ago." (27) The revised text distinguishes between what Roark grasps (that these men are essentially unlike him) and what he does not grasp (what that essential difference is). The draft, with the word "often," undercuts Roark's basic imperviousness to other people—"he wondered about it often." In the final text, by contrast: "But he wondered, at times, what

made them such as they were." The "long ago" applies not to his understanding of them—because, in fact, he does not understand them even now—
but to his long-standing serenity: "it had ceased to disturb him long ago."

Within the same passage, Ayn Rand adds several sentences that, not yet
present in the first draft, figure significantly in the final text: "But he always
looked for a central theme in buildings and he looked for a central impulse
in men. He knew the source of his actions; he could not discover theirs.
. . . He had never learned the process of thinking about other people." These
new sentences may be Ayn Rand's response to her advice to herself in the
notes of February 18, 1940: "Roark looking for the 'stamp' on faces—
should be planted earlier and separately and more importantly."[18] The sentences clarify the contrast between Roark's nature and the nature of second-
handers, and also place the paragraph's emphasis more powerfully on
Roark and not on other people.

The manuscript of the early chapters of *The Fountainhead* contains numerous changes—small yet significant—in expression and emphasis. Even
after years of preparation, Ayn Rand spent many months writing and rewrit-
ing the opening chapters, to clarify and enhance the theme. But her editing
was not limited to the beginning of the book. Similarly purposeful revisions are apparent in her editing of Roark's speech at the Cortlandt trial. She
was writing rapidly, contract in hand, to meet her publication deadline. The
manuscript, nonetheless, shows her in the act of revising her text to emphasize her theme.

First-handedness is important not only in the speech itself, but in the introduction. Although Roark is speaking in public, he is not primarily concerned with his audience. Before "a hostile crowd," Roark stands "as each
man stands in the innocence of his own mind" (677). The draft also contains the following sentence: "No one ever knew that the moment preceding his speech had held the essence of human brotherhood" (IV, 568). The
sentence was intended to convey that the independence represented by
Roark is a prerequisite for any healthy human bond. But the sentence, as
originally written, calls attention to the fact that no one ever understood the
event in this way.

Ayn Rand drew a line through this sentence, probably on the spot. In editing, she removed the assertion of a conclusion not reached first-hand by
the individuals present. The account in the final text reports specifically the
actual thoughts of the audience, rather than the conclusion no one ever
knew. Roark moves his audience to emulate, to some degree, his independent stance: he inspires each of the jurors and spectators to experience
independence.

> For the flash of an instant, they grasped the manner of his consciousness. Each
> asked himself: "do I need anyone's approval?—does it matter?—am I tied?"

And for that instant, each man was free—free enough to feel benevolence for every other man in the room. It was only a moment: the moment of silence when Roark was about to speak. (677)

The description here includes a point made in the discarded sentence, i.e., that only an independent person can be benevolent toward others. The final version is superior because it limits the reader to what the characters knew first-hand and does not rely on the narrator as an expert, uninvolved witness.

Ayn Rand's revision of the aftermath of the speech is similarly purposeful, both in what it adds and what it omits. When the jury returns to deliver its verdict, and the prisoner is asked to rise and face the jury, Ayn Rand added, between the lines, the following sentence: "At the back of the room, Wynand got up and stood also" (I, 594). She edited the text to show that Wynand, Roark's tragic foil, knew that he was also on trial. A first-hander in his soul, he has acted as a second-hander in the pursuit of power. When she adds a line indicating that Wynand stands, she shows that this trial concerns not only Roark's guilt or innocence regarding a particular act, but the thematic conflict between the first-hander and the second-hander, as dramatized in the contrast between the heroic ideal and his foil. The final text of this chapter concludes with Wynand's departure: "The first movement of Roark's head was not to look at the city in the window, at the judge or at Dominique. He looked at Wynand. Wynand turned sharply and walked out. He was the first man to leave the courtroom" (686). Her edited version not only reports (as did the draft) that Wynand left first, but emphasizes the fact by having him rise when Roark rises, and by ending the chapter when Wynand walks out.

In the draft, by contrast, the chapter ends as follows: "The rest of the audience did not move to go. The commentators could not explain it afterwards: the audience was cheering" (IV, 595). In editing the chapter, Ayn Rand crossed out those sentences, which emphasize the crowd's behavior and the commentators' lack of comprehension. The revised conclusion focuses not on the crowd or the commentators, but on a single man. For Wynand, the outcome of the trial was the demonstration of the tragic futility of his self-betrayal.

Ayn Rand's editing of the trial speech itself emphasized first-handedness by removing specific historical and political references to the world outside the novel. Ayn Rand chose to omit references to Caesar, the Crusades, the Inquisition, Robespierre, Napoleon, Lenin, Stalin, and Hitler.[19] In making some of these omissions, she was following the advice of Isabel Paterson, who suggested that she cut the references to contemporary politics because "the theme of your book is wider than the politics of the moment."[20] Because the theme of *The Fountainhead* is "individualism and collectivism, not in politics, but in man's soul,"[21] the theme is wider than not only the politics of the moment, but also politics itself. Ayn Rand cut not only Stalin, but also Robespierre. By removing from Roark's speech the political references, therefore, Ayn Rand was editing her book to be more focused on its theme.

She also chose to omit several other specific historical references. The manuscript supplies names for the heroes described in the paragraph beginning "Throughout the centuries there were men who took first steps down new roads armed with nothing but their own vision" and ending "They fought, they suffered—and they paid. But they won" (678). In both draft and text, Roark refers to creators and to their achievements (the airplane, the power loom, anesthesia, etc.). But the manuscript had listed additional such heroes.

Ayn Rand originally intended to take the reader farther away from the events of the novel itself. On a hard-to-read page, with many cross-outs, Ayn Rand originally had Roark provide a list of creators and an inventory of their suffering:

> Socrates, poisoned by order of the democracy of Athens. Jesus Christ against the majority of [indecipherable] crucified. Joan D'Arc, who was burned at the stake. Galileo, made to renounce his soul. Spinoza, excommunicated. Luther, hounded. Victor Hugo, exiled for twenty years. Richard Wagner, writing musical comedies for a living, denounced by the musicians of his time, hissed, opposed, pronounced unmusical. Tchaikovsky, struggling through years of loneliness without recognition. Nietzsche, dying in an insane asylum, friendless and unheard. Ibsen [indecipherable] his own country. Dostoevsky, facing an execution squad and pardoned to a Siberian prison. The list is endless. (IV, 570)

Ayn Rand edited out the endless list. Suffering, to begin with, is less important, in this speech, than achievement; for this reason, Ayn Rand also removed the sentence stating that the "history of mankind['s] benefactors is the history of martyrs." Although Roark does not minimize the price paid by the creators, he would not wish to claim their pain as a value. To describe their specific suffering without also acclaiming their specific achievements would not suit his purpose; to explain, at his trial, the contributions made by Socrates, Galileo, Hugo, and the others would turn the speech into a history lesson. To make his point at his trial, Roark does not need such a list. To grasp his point, the reader does not need such a list. Roark himself is Ayn Rand's dramatic example of the struggle and achievement of the first-hander, the individual of unborrowed vision.

Roark is not merely one in a long line of creators. The others, to be sure, are analogous to Roark in some respects; their lives, however, are not heroic in all respects. By removing the references, Ayn Rand leads the reader to focus not on such flawed individuals as Luther or Wagner, but on the character of Roark, who exemplifies first-handedness more purely and powerfully than any of the actual historical figures.

In two instances, Ayn Rand's omission of references within Roark's trial speech appears to stem from a policy, evident in other contexts within the novel, of curtailing allusions to religion and to Nietzsche, two forms of pseudo-first-handedness. The final text of the speech contains the following sentence: "Men have come close to the truth, but it was destroyed each time . . ." (683). When Ayn Rand composed this passage, she initially made Roark much more explicit about what "coming close" might mean.

> Christ proclaimed the untouchable integrity of Man's spirit, stating[?] the first rights of the Ego. He placed the salvation of one's own soul above all other concerns. But men distorted it into altruism. Nietzsche, who loved Man, fought against altruism—and destroyed his own case by preaching the Will to Power, a second-hander's pursuit. (IV, 588a)

In her "Introduction to the Twenty-fifth Anniversary Edition" of *The Fountainhead*, Ayn Rand discusses both religion and Nietzsche. She explains that, when she had Roark speak of "the highest religious abstraction," she meant not "religion as such," but "man's code of good and evil, with the emotional connotations of height, uplift, nobility, reverence, grandeur, which pertain to the realm of man's values, but which religion has arrogated to itself" (viii). She did not, of course, intend the phrase "the highest religious abstraction" as an endorsement of religion, but she did not explain, within the novel, her purpose in using the phrase. In the introduction, she takes the opportunity of clarifying her position instead of leaving it "to implications." Ayn Rand also quotes a passage from Section 287 of Part 9 ("What Is Noble") of Nietzsche's *Beyond Good and Evil*:

> It is not the works, but the *belief* which is here decisive and determines the order of rank—to employ once more an old religious formula with a new and deeper meaning—it is some fundamental certainty which a noble soul has about itself, something which is not to be sought, is not to be found, and perhaps, also, is not to be lost.—*The noble soul has reverence for itself.*—[22]

She states that Nietzsche, in spite of his mysticism and irrationalism, "as a poet, . . . projects at times (not consistently) a magnificent feeling for man's greatness. . . ." Although Ayn Rand removed the quotation, which she had placed at the head of her manuscript, from the published book, she loved the exalted sense of life it expresses. "With this opportunity to explain it, I am glad to bring it back" (x).

Ayn Rand recognized that religious language can have the noble emotional connotations of "man's dedication to a moral ideal"(ix) and that Nietzsche's language "sums up the emotional consequences for which *The*

Fountainhead provides the rational, philosophical base" (x). It is not surprising that her drafts for *The Fountainhead* included references, implicit and explicit, to religion and to Nietzsche. But Ayn Rand was fundamentally opposed to religion and to Nietzsche's philosophy, and did not wish to endorse either of them. In editing *The Fountainhead*, therefore, Ayn Rand reduced or removed references to both.

First-handedness, the novel's moral ideal, is associated through language with religion's ideal, or God. The night after Wynand betrays Roark is one example. Realizing that he has continually betrayed his own soul, Wynand walks through the city and—in both the draft and the final text—speaks the words of confession: "*Mea culpa—mea culpa—mea maxima culpa*" (662).[23] The drafts, however, had a long additional passage in which the human creative act is described in divine terms. Wynand says:

> I had the only sacred attribute among the endowments of man. The touch of God. The quality of Roark's nature, which he recognized in me as I recognized it in him. The faculty of being a source and a beginning. Whatever the goal, I had the means of creation. Whatever the achievement, I was one of those who can achieve. I built the Banner. I fought for it, and there was fire in the fight, and courage, and gallantry. I loved the Banner. Because I had made it. May God now damn me for it. That was the sin for which there is no forgiveness. That I took genius and placed it in the service of the unspeakable. (IV, 521)

The final text, which drops the references to the "touch of God" and the unforgivable "sin," loses nothing. The episode ends, poignantly, with the words: "I was not born to be a second-hander." The term "second-hander" is specific to the novel; Wynand has learned from Roark the concept and the term.

The manuscript version, moreover, had an additional paragraph, a quotation from the Bible: Matthew 12:31–32:

> All manner of sin and blasphemy shall be forgiven unto men: but the blasphemy against the Holy Ghost shall not be forgiven unto men. And whosoever speaketh against the Son of man, it shall be forgiven him: but whosoever speaketh against the Holy Ghost, it shall not be forgiven him, neither in this world, neither in the world to come.

The quotation contrasts blasphemy against the Son of man, which is forgivable, with blasphemy against the Holy Ghost, which is not. Wynand has betrayed not only Roark, his friend, at this moment, but his own soul, his spirit, throughout his life. Roark's forgiveness, then, even though it is freely offered, is not sufficient, and Wynand does not accept it because it does not solve his problem.

The Biblical quotation adds nothing but a distracting association with religion. Removing the paragraph gives Wynand, not the Bible, the last word—

as he pronounces his spiritual death sentence. In editing the manuscript, Ayn Rand removes many such religious references, including Mallory's thought that "In the beginning was the Word" (IV, 15) and Roark's proclamation, in his speech to the jury, of loyalty to his "faith," "whose purpose, in the words of my own religious catechism, is: to praise man and glorify him forever" (IV, 593). The Roark we know does not make a point of invoking religion, even if he accepts Hopton Stoddard's statement (ghostwritten by Ellsworth Toohey) that Roark is a religious man in his own way (319).

She pursued a similar policy in removing not only the passage from Nietzsche that had stood at the head of her manuscript, but all explicit references to Nietzsche. Not only had Ayn Rand selected a Nietzsche quotation for the novel as a whole, she had also selected one for each of the novel's four sections.[24] The epigraph for "Peter Keating" was excerpted from Section 261 of *Beyond Good and Evil*.

> Vanity is one of the things which are perhaps most difficult for the noble man to understand: he will be tempted to deny it, where another kind of man thinks he sees it self-evidently. The problem for him is to represent to his mind beings who seek to arouse a good opinion of themselves which they do not possess—and consequently also do not "deserve"—and who yet believe in this good opinion afterwards.[25]

Nietzsche's passage suggests the first-hander's difficulty in understanding the second-hander.

The epigraph to "Ellsworth Toohey" was drawn from Part II of *Thus Spake Zarathustra* ("The Tarantulas"): "Ye preachers of equality, the tyrant-frenzy of impotence crieth thus in you for 'equality'; your most secret tyrant-longings disguise themselves thus in virtue-words!"[26] Nietzsche's sentences (and those that immediately follow) suggest that professional egalitarians are motivated by envy and power-lust.

The epigraph to "Gail Wynand" is taken from Part I of *Thus Spake Zarathustra* ("The Tree on the Hill"): "But by my love and hope I conjure thee: cast not away the hero in thy soul: Maintain holy thy highest hope!"[27] Gail Wynand, not born to be a second-hander, has cast away the hero in his soul.[28] The paragraphs preceding the sentence Ayn Rand quoted are also pertinent here:

> Ah! I have known noble ones who lost their highest hope. And then they disparaged all high hopes.
>
> Then lived they shamelessly in temporary pleasures, and beyond the day had hardly an aim.
>
> "Spirit is also voluptuousness,"—said they. Then broke the wings of their spirit; and now it creepeth about, and defileth where it gnaweth.
>
> Once they thought of becoming heroes; but sensualists are they now. A trouble and a terror is the hero to them.

The epigraph to "Howard Roark" is excerpted from Section 12 of the essay "'Good and Evil,' 'Good and Bad,'" in *On the Genealogy of Morals.*

> But from time to time do ye grant me—one glimpse, grant me but one glimpse only, of something perfect, fully realized, happy, mighty, triumphant, of something that still gives cause for fear! A glimpse of man that justifies the existence of man, a glimpse of an incarnate human happiness that realizes and redeems, for the sake of which one may hold fast to the belief in man![29]

The victory of Howard Roark is indeed a "glimpse of man that justifies the existence of man."

One can see the appeal of Nietzsche's poetry and the significance of the passages Ayn Rand selected. But she could hardly quote the passages without naming him, and to do so might have been taken as an endorsement. To feature another writer prominently in her own art, moreover, is to place herself, as a writer, in his shadow. She decided to do otherwise.

Ayn Rand also removed an explicit reference to Nietzsche within the text of the novel. Speaking with Steven Mallory after the Stoddard Temple trial, Roark, in the draft, starts by quoting from Part I ("Voluntary Death") of *Thus Spake Zarathustra.* "That your dying may not be a reproach to man and the earth, my friend: that do I solicit for the honey of your soul."[30] Roark continues:

> Your dying—or your suffering. Oh, can't you understand it? To love the earth . . . so much that your sense of the world cannot include suffering as a basic factor. To suffer, if necessary, but never completely, never losing the vision, never letting your suffering deny it, so that you never become a solid screaming pain and twist the world into a mere bandage. To keep that sense of the world within you alive because that is what man's life was meant to be, and is. That, Steve, is the way I want to suffer and the way I want to die some day. (II, 563)

Nietzsche says that one must die in a spirit befitting the glory of life; Roark says that neither suffering nor death can be allowed to destroy one's love for life. Although Roark's attitude regarding pain is an important element of Roark's character, this particular quotation, with its emphasis on death, is not the best match for his spirit.

After the revisions, what was left in the text of Nietzsche's language? First, Ayn Rand included an indirect allusion in Ellsworth Toohey's column on the Stoddard Temple: "It is not our function—paraphrasing a philosopher whom we do not like—to be a fly swatter, but when a fly acquires delusions of grandeur, the best of us must stoop to do a little job of extermination" (338). The philosopher he does not like is Nietzsche; the passage he paraphrases appears in Part I of *Thus Spake Zarathustra* ("The Flies of the Marketplace").[31]

This subtle allusion was acceptable in the context of the novel. The endorsement issue, to begin with, does not arise. That Toohey dislikes Nietzsche does not necessarily mean that Ayn Rand admires him. It is entirely characteristic of Toohey, moreover, to minimize the significance of philosophy by treating it as a matter of likes and dislikes. And the passage itself is an ironic choice for Toohey, who is himself the fly with delusions of grandeur, a creature whom Roark and Wynand deem unworthy of swatting.

Toohey alludes again to Nietzsche by printing in the *Banner* a photograph of Roark "at the opening of the Enright House, the photograph of a man's face in a moment of exaltation," with the caption: "Are you happy, Mr. Superman?" (342). Toohey's offensive rhetorical question implies that Nietzsche's "Overman," his image of the noble hero, is ludicrous to contemplate (as for him, perhaps, it was ludicrous to attempt to achieve it).

The final allusion to Nietzsche appears in Roark's letter to Wynand after Wynand's act of self-betrayal. Roark writes: "What you think you've lost can neither be lost nor found" (664). Ayn Rand here has Roark come close to quoting the passage she had originally placed at the head of her manuscript: "some fundamental certainty which a noble soul has about itself, something which is not to be sought, is not to be found, and, perhaps, also is not to be lost." She removed the quotation, but retained the echo.

One more echo is found within her introduction to the twenty-fifth anniversary edition of *The Fountainhead*, the very place where she took the opportunity to clarify her position regarding Nietzsche. She wrote: "This is one of the cardinal reasons of *The Fountainhead*'s lasting appeal: it is a confirmation of the spirit of youth, proclaiming man's glory, showing how much is possible." The expression "how much is possible" had earlier been featured in the thoughts of Kira Argounova in *We the Living*. Kira had thought about the "streets of a big city where so much is possible"; she had sent Leo off to the south to be cured of his illness, saying "I love you. So much is still possible!" When she died, she "smiled, her last smile, to so much that had been possible."[32] This sentiment, as we shall see, is proclaimed, repeatedly, in *Thus Spake Zarathustra*: "How many things are still possible!"[33]

Two additional special sorts of omissions are evident in Ayn Rand's editing of the characterization of Roark: she limited, severely, his thoughts and comments about his relationship with Dominique, and she removed many passages tracing his progress toward discovering the principle of first-handedness.

First, the romance with Dominique, which, in Ayn Rand's view, was the "ideal romance," and which, at first, she intended to narrate, in large part, from the viewpoint of her ideal man. In the final text of the novel, the relationship is presented overwhelmingly (though not exclusively) from Dominique's point of view. In the first draft, Roark has more much to say and to think about their romance as seen in their first meeting. The novel describes Dominique's thoughts about her first sight of Roark. And what does Roark think? The novel is silent on that point—except for what one can infer from Dominique's observations and from Roark's subsequent behavior. In the first draft, by contrast:

> Roark looked at her. His first glance at her had been a perception not of sight, but of touch; it was the consciousness not of a visual presence, but of a slap in the face. He grasped nothing save a challenge like an explosion, like a scream. Then he saw it was a woman standing on the rocks above, a woman with an invisible stamp, his own stamp, upon a white face that presented to him the final, the complete reality of what he had sought, of what he had found but a hint of in others. That face was freedom—a freedom proud enough to warrant enchainment [?]; it was strength—sure enough of itself to deserve to be fought; it was will—great enough for the honor of being broken. He stood very still looking at her as at a mirror, to reflect his power, and knew that he wanted to break this woman. But he did not state what form the act of breaking her was to assume, because he knew it, because there was but one way to it, and more—because she knew, because she was held by that knowledge. [*crossed out*: He felt his tongue press against his teeth, shut tight together. His fingers closed about the handle of the drill as if about her wrist; had it been her wrist, the bones would have broken.]
>
> Were they to speak of it for the rest of their lives, they could have added nothing; everything was said as they looked silently at each other. There were many things in that glance, but above all there was a pledge, cold and quiet in its finality, like an ultimatum declaring a war. (II, 15–15a)

In the draft, when Dominique sees Roark enter her home, she whispers: "What do you want?" He answers: "You know what I want" (II, 65). In the final text, they say nothing; at this dramatic moment, they understand each other without words, and the novel stresses that silent understanding. Ayn Rand originally planned to echo this exchange later in the novel. After learning that the man from the quarry is the architect of the Enright House, Dominique goes to Roark's apartment. He asks: "What do you want?" She replies: "You know what I want"(272). Although removing the exchange from the first scene resulted in removing the piquant contrast with the second scene, Ayn Rand decided to do so anyway, to avoid interfering with the drama of the wordless romantic encounter.

She shortened, too, the identification of Dominique's emotions during that first encounter: "She fought because she could not bear the pleasure. She fought because she hated herself for that pleasure. She fought him because she wanted him too much" (II, 68). In editing this passage, Ayn Rand removed the over-explicit description of Dominique's consciousness. Roark, of course, understands without words everything Dominique does not say.

The two of them have always understood each other without words. "They could always speak like this to each other, continuing a conversation they had not begun" (344). "They stood silently before each other for a moment, and she thought that the most beautiful words were those which were not needed" (374). "We never need to say anything to each other when we're together" (376).

In the draft, Dominique admits, later on, that she knew he could read her soul: "I lied when I fought against you. I wanted it then—I wanted what you did to me—you knew it" (II, 240). In the final text, Ayn Rand makes clear Dominique's willing embrace of Roark not only through the entire context of the Connecticut episode, but also through a phrase added for the final text: "the kind of rapture she had wanted" (217). No part of "she had wanted" is hard to understand; that some readers have missed the point does not mean Ayn Rand did not make it.

Here is a similarly over-explicit passage. At a time when Roark is trying to build his career and Dominique is trying to destroy it, they spend evenings together at a country inn. The nights are mentioned in the final text (310), but without any of the following dialogue, which appears in the first draft. Dominique asks:

"You're very busy at the office these days, aren't you?"
"Yes."
"I wonder why you take time to think of me or to come here with me."
He answered: "Don't you know that designing a building is overcoming a terrible resistance? I don't mean from clients and people. I mean, in the act of designing itself. It's facing a raw chaos where anything is possible and making it take on a single possibility, yours, making it take your rules, your shape, your meaning. It's an act of conquest. Every good building, like any living thing, has the coherence of a single, organized purpose. The giving of a purpose is the giving of life. Look at any organism. And it's the great, dead, formless, purposeless mass of the undifferentiated that fights the thing being torn out of it and the man who tears it out. Haven't you ever laughed at the damn fools who think of an artist as gentle—and give him birds, flowers or clouds for a symbol? The artist has only one symbol—the sword. All art is an act of conquest. Every single thing worth doing is an act of conquest. Being alive is an act of conquest." He smiled and leaned closer to her. "Well, do you think I'm being inconsistent when I come here? A man who loves his work can't seek rest in its opposite or in forgetting it completely. That would be the most exhausting kind of torture possible. He can seek pleasure only in another form of the same struggle. In another resistance. In another conquest."
He threw the blanket off her naked body, but he did not touch her; he sat looking at her. Then he added: "Do you want it said clearer? I like to come here because I know what you went through before you came here. That you fought against coming because you wanted it too much. That you lie here, wishing me not to touch you—because you want it too much. That every time I kiss you,

it's an act of violation—but that you welcome the violation, and the agony, and the struggle, because you want all of it as I want it, because you want nothing except as I want it. Because I . . . ."

But he did not say the word. His mouth was on hers. She whispered only: "Yes, Roark . . . .Yes. . . ." (II, 351–53)

Why did Ayn Rand edit out these and similar passages (including, for example, his waiting for her, in Part Two, to come to his apartment after she has learned who he is, or his explaining to her, in Part Three, why he does not want her to spend the night with him in Ohio)? Because, I believe, she considered this sort of explanation highly inappropriate for Roark's style as we see it and him for most of the novel. For him to speak at length—as he does, finally, with Wynand on the yacht, or as he does at his second trial— is what we have been waiting for, and the waiting, perhaps, is itself a point. The explanations offered in the unpublished passages are, in essentials, consistent with Roark's characterization, but the act of explaining at length (to himself or to anyone else) is not. In Ayn Rand's esthetic, moreover, the artist's job is to develop character through action—and a good description of action does not require separate commentary. Concretizing the human ideal, projecting the ideal man, means showing him in action—not telling about him or letting him tell about himself. In editing *The Fountainhead*, she acted on the premise that certain insights should be inferred by the reader, rather than supplied by the writer.

This point—that Ayn Rand's esthetic encourages active reading—is relevant to my second group of passages, all of which concern some degree of uncertainty or lack of clarity on Roark's part, whether explicit (not knowing the explanation for what other people are, what he is, and what the difference is) or implicit (believing that he should act differently, or experiencing some degree of hesitation, or actually approaching some degree of second-handedness). Some of these passages delineate Roark's thinking as he wonders about the principle behind the Dean, and the eureka moment when he reaches an answer.

Consider the following scene, in which Roark looks at his name on the door of his first office:

He stood in the hall for a long time, looking at that inscription. Then he thought suddenly that his eyes were not looking at it, but that he was trying to give his eyes the glances of other people who would pass down the hall and read it. He felt astonished and ashamed without reason. He went in, and slammed his door; he picked up a T-square from his desk and flung it down again carelessly, noisily, as if throwing an anchor. (I, 441)

It is difficult to imagine the Roark we know as being "ashamed without reason," or as second-handed in any way.

Here is an example of Roark telling himself that he ought to worry more than he does about the world of other people, the commissions he is not receiving:

> Those things happening to him, in those offices of strangers, were only details, unsubstantial incidents in the path of a substance they could not reach or touch. Nothing was happening to him, it was happening only in that secondary reality, in that sub-reality called himself-among-other-men. And he had no time to think of that too much: no time and no room in those boundaries within him, which were too full. He shrugged and went on, thinking that he should experience more anxiety about it, telling himself dutifully that he was anxious, that he was afraid, wondering why he could not feel it, not as a close, driving pain, not as a wrench upon his senses, the senses that remained stubbornly untouched, open, serene. (I, 342)

Compare this passage with the equivalent in the novel (101–2). It is difficult to imagine Roark wondering why he does not feel more afraid or anxious than he does.

There are a large number of passages in which Roark considers, but does not resolve, the issue of the difference between himself and others. Here, for example, is a longer version of the conversation with Austen Heller that appears in the text (159–60). In the first draft, Roark says, among other things:

> I'd beg, if I could. Only I can't. I don't know how. I'm not unwilling. I'm merely a cripple, in some respect. . . . There's something missing in me. I know it, I've always known it. But I don't know what it is. Something I have, that stops me, or something I've never had and should? I don't know. And I guess I'm calloused. I know that thing about myself and I wonder about it sometimes, but I can't make myself worry, and perhaps I should. (I, 526)

He goes on to talk, as he does in the final text, about the principle behind his "kind of people." He considers the matter, but does so, at this point, without the continual worrying.

Here are Roark's thoughts, in the first draft, about the commissions he refuses (e.g., the request for an English Tudor cottage):

> It seemed to him that each time he refused a commission, he was not losing one client: he was losing many. . . [In] corners unknown to him, some man with a building to be erected would pause for a moment of consideration before his name and would be stopped by a friend, some friend who had never seen Roark and who would say: "Roark? Oh no, not Roark! I hear he's impossible to get along with!" He knew this was happening, he wondered about it, but it did not disturb him, even though he told himself that it should. . . . (I, 574–75)

In the final text, he is aware of the rumors, but does not tell himself that he should be disturbed (174–75).

In the first draft of the Enright House party, Roark is described as "willing to learn anything, even this":

> Then Roark was introduced to many people and many people spoke to him. He listened, he looked about him, without resentment, in helpless bewilderment. He had decided not to be bored, he had decided to understand, [*crossed out*: Heller and Keating were right,] he had to learn and he was willing to learn anything, even this, if this was what people wanted of him, if this was what he had to give while they would give him buildings and let him build as he pleased, in exchange for seeing him in a drawing-room. . . . (II, 210)
>
> They did not seek to see him; they sought to be seen by him. . . . It was an immense concern with one's brothers, leading to the hatred of one's brothers.
>
> Roark saw this without understanding. He thought helplessly: that's what it is, but why? Why? He found no answer, and no one could have given him an answer; none could see the answer, because no one saw even the fact itself. Why, thought Roark. (II, 213–14)

You can see the pattern: Roark asks a question, the asking suggests the answer, he does not reach the answer, he moves on. Among the similar passages is a crossed-out remark he makes to Wynand, in the first draft, in which he says, "There's something involved that I've never been able to state. And I've always wanted to. Perhaps I will, some day" (IV, 102; 548 in the novel).

For Roark, in the first draft, there is a eureka moment on Wynand's yacht (IV, 300–305 in the first draft; 603–4 in the novel). "Roark was looking at that which he had worked to discover all his life." The moment comes when Wynand is talking about altruism and altruists, and he names Stalin and Hitler. Roark says: "There's another name for altruism," and then he says: "Oh God, Gail! . . . God help you!" Also on the page, we see that he says— as he does in the final text—"Yes, Gail," with what Wynand hears as "a reluctance that sounds almost like sadness." He continues: "It's just something I thought . . . I've been thinking of this for a long time. And particularly all these days when you've made me lie on deck and loaf." When Wynand asks him what he's been thinking about, Roark says: "Something I've known all my life, but couldn't understand. This is the first time I was able to stop and bring it all into order. Now I have. Now I know. The principle behind the Dean who fired me from Stanton." The final text of the novel includes the scene in which Ayn Rand originally planned to include this eureka moment. Roark indeed refers, during the yacht trip, to grasping the principle behind the Dean. But the moment is not presented as a dramatic, emphatic event. We need to infer its equivalent.

The first draft presents the eureka moment as Roark's discovery of the principle, as if he had not grasped it until that instant. The final version, to be sure, makes clear that Roark at one time did not grasp the principle explicitly, and that going on vacation has allowed him to reflect and to grasp it—but the drama of the moment is in Roark's thoughts about what will happen to Wynand. Ayn Rand removes from the final text the implication that we have witnessed the moment in which Roark grasps the principle—as she has removed several passages in which he grapples with the principle.

Although the passages that I have grouped together are not the same in all respects, all of them, esthetically, emphasize something in Roark that Ayn Rand deemed nonessential: the moments when Roark was not entirely Roark, or the moments when, from the standpoint of an explicit grasp of a principle, Roark was not yet Roark.

Why did Ayn Rand remove instances in which Roark was less than himself? Because, as she envisioned her ideal man, he was always essentially himself, never less than himself—that is what being an ideal man means—and she decided to focus the characterization on essentials. And why did she remove instances of Roark's thinking about the issue of second-handedness? Because his explicit thoughts on this matter were not central to the novel.

Roark as a character is what he is, essentially, always. As Steven Mallory says, Roark is immortal, and "one can imagine him existing forever "(452). Granted, he is not infallible. He admits to the mistakes of staying too long in school, of "seeing hope where [he] shouldn't" with Vesta (in the first draft), of helping Peter Keating. But *The Fountainhead* is a plot story—unlike, for example, *Anthem*, which was much more about the process of discovery. The plot involves him in conflict with the world, not with himself. He is at peace with himself. He is not deeply concerned about the people he does not understand.

The reader, by contrast, is likely to need to learn—not by narration, but through following the plot—the nature of first-handedness and second-handedness, and the consequences of choosing one rather than the other. For the novel to portray the ideal man in the act of discovery would not necessarily be a bad thing—depending on a novel's theme—but in this case it would do for the reader what the reader should be doing independently.

And so, although Ayn Rand uses the principle behind the Dean as a point of reference, she does not portray her ideal man in the act of grasping that principle. At the Dean's office, Roark has a question in his mind. When he speaks on the yacht's deck with Wynand, he has an answer, and, indeed, he says—in the novel—that he has arrived at an answer to a long-standing question. That he is changeless in his fundamentals is more important than that he undergoes some change in his understanding. The explicit grasp of a morality that has always been his implicit morality cannot figure in this novel as a climax, and hence Ayn Rand chose not to feature Roark's progress toward that explicit grasp as a major network of events in the novel. She chose instead—in the climax and throughout the novel—to show Roark in active conflict. She resolves that conflict in the Cortlandt trial and offers, as a summation and an epilogue, the final image of her ideal man, in triumphant action, as seen through the eyes of the woman he loves—and has won—who is rising to join him.

I turn now to a speculation about one important aspect of the characterization: the progressive removal from the novel, and from its hero, of philosophically bad Nietzsche-like elements that Ayn Rand found more and more objectionable and unnecessary in the course of the years she worked on this book. By eliminating from Roark these elements, she refined her characterization of her ideal man. By telling the story of Roark's triumph—and by living it, as the very writing of the novel constituted a triumph of her own—she eliminated from her own work the last shreds of the Nietzscheanism she rejected. In a sense, Ayn Rand saved Roark from the Nietzsche in him—and Roark may have done the same for her.

Ayn Rand's ultimate view of Nietzsche, as noted earlier, consisted of an appreciation of his poetic projection of a "magnificent feeling for man's greatness"—accompanied by negative judgment of his philosophical errors. After being introduced to his writing during her first year of college (by a cousin who said "He has anticipated you. He has said all the things you're saying"), she read *Thus Spake Zarathustra*, and went on to read most of the rest of Nietzsche's work, "everything that was translated in Russian." Although her reaction to his ideas was mixed (and her admiration was seriously undercut by her disagreement with his commentary, in *The Birth of Tragedy from the Spirit of Music*, on Apollo and Dionysus), the first books she bought in the United States were English translations of *Beyond Good and Evil*, *Thus Spake Zarathustra*, and *Anti-Christ*. She marked up her new copies to indicate her favorite passages.[34]

Reading her markings of *Zarathustra* and *Beyond Good and Evil* in the light of *The Fountainhead*, one notices what seem to be descriptions of the novel's characters. Here, for example, is Roark: "But at the bottom of our souls, quite 'down below,' there is certainly something unteachable, a granite of spiritual fate, of predetermined decision and answer to predetermined, chosen questions. In each cardinal problem there speaks an unchangeable 'I am this.'"[35] Here is Toohey: "For to-day have the petty people become master: they all preach submission and humility and policy and diligence and consideration and the long *et cetera* of petty virtues."[36] Here is Keating: "a soft, inflated, delicate, movable potter's form, that must wait for some kind of content and form to 'shape' itself thereto—for the most part a man without frame or content, a 'selfless' man."[37] Here is Wynand: "There are few pains so grievous as to have seen, divined, or experienced how an exceptional man has missed his way and deteriorated."[38] Here is Dominique: "Not to cleave to any person, be it even the dearest—every person is a prison and also a recess. . . . One must know how to conserve oneself—the best test of independence. . . . 'Good' is no longer good when one's neighbour takes it into his mouth. And how could there be a 'common good'! The expression contradicts itself; that which can be common is always of small value."[39] And again:

> Life is a well of delight; but where the rabble also drink, there all fountains are poisoned.
>   And many a one who hath turned away from life, hath only turned away from the rabble: he hated to share with them fountain, flame, and fruit.[40]

A reader steeped in Nietzsche might well guess, even without Nietzschean epigraphs, that the author of *The Fountainhead* was familiar with Nietzsche.

Earlier in the present essay, I quoted the passages Ayn Rand had intended to place at the beginning of each part of *The Fountainhead*, as well as the passage that stood at the head of her manuscript; she removed them all. My subject now is not the explicit citations of Nietzsche, but the hints of his language and ideas, hints that are relevant to one of the most intriguing aspects of the novel's composition: the differences between her first and final visions of Roark. I will deal, selectively, with several of these differences.

The first major area pertains to the relationship of the hero to the world outside himself: a noble soul, born to lead, superior to all others, spiritually isolated from a world entirely different from him and entirely hostile to him. Ayn Rand marked the following passage in her copy of *Beyond Good and Evil*:

> I submit that egoism belongs to the essence of a noble soul, I mean the unalterable belief that to a being such as "we," other beings must naturally be in subjection, and have to sacrifice themselves. The noble soul accepts the fact of his egoism without question, and also without consciousness of harshness, constraint, or arbitrariness therein, but rather as something that may have its basis in the primary law of things:—if he sought a designation for it he would say: "It is justice itself."[41]

She marked, additionally, a passage stating that a society of "a good and healthy aristocracy" must serve as "a foundation and scaffolding, by means of which a select class of beings may be able to elevate themselves to their higher duties, and in general to a higher existence," while the others are "reduced to imperfect men, to slaves and instruments."[42] She marked a passage in *Zarathustra* pointing to the invulnerable, changeless will: "Yea, something invulnerable, unburiable is with me, something that would rend rocks asunder: it is called *my Will*. Silently doth it proceed, and unchanged throughout the years."[43] The noble soul is resented by all others:

> Even when thou art gentle toward them, they still feel themselves despised by thee; and they repay thy beneficence with secret maleficence.
>
> Thy silent pride is always counter to their taste; they rejoice if once thou be humble enough to be frivolous.[44]
>
> And when I lived with them, then did I live above them. Therefore did they take a dislike to me. For men are *not* equal: so speaketh justice.[45]

The noble soul, therefore, is eternally separate:

> —at present it belongs to the conception of "greatness" to be noble, to wish to be apart, to be capable of being different, to stand alone, to have to live by personal initiative; and the philosopher will betray something of his own ideal when he asserts: "He shall be the greatest who can be the most solitary, the most concealed, the most divergent, the man beyond good and evil, the master of his virtues, and of superabundance of will; precisely this shall be called greatness; as diversified as can be entire, as ample as can be full."[46]

She marked passages in *Beyond Good and Evil* concerning the "will to power," and she underlined the following in *Zarathustra*: "and a right which thou canst seize upon, shalt thou not allow to be given thee!"[47]

Her initial image of Roark, in the notebook, has strong parallels with the marked passages in Nietzsche. From her notes of February 9, 1936:

> He has learned long ago, with his first consciousness, two things which dominate his entire attitude toward life: his own superiority and the utter worthlessness of the world. . . . Being thoroughly a 'reason unto himself,' he does not long for others of his kind, for companionship and understanding. . . . And being a warrior above all, he does not even consider himself a warrior. . . . The world becomes merely a place to act in. But not to feel in. The feeling—all the field of emotions—is in his hand alone . . . born without the ability to consider others. . . . He has a tremendous, unshatterable conviction that he can and will *force* men to accept him, not beg and cheat them into it. He will *take* the place he wants, not receive it from others. . . . Other people do not interest him. He recognizes only the right of exceptions (and by that he means and knows only himself) to create, and order, and command. The others are to bow.[48]

Note that this man deals with other men by "force," that he "will take the place he wants." Although it is unlikely that she has in mind physical force, she does not appear to have in mind any sort of rational persuasion, either. To act without considering others, as he is described as doing, amounts to refusing to seek any personal values from others. The distinction between himself and all others is absolute—and its basis is innate.

Ayn Rand's earlier writing had contained similar statements. Kira's Viking, dedicated to "a life that is a reason unto itself," is a benevolent expression of the will to power.[49] In an entry in her first philosophical notebook (May 16, 1934), she commented that liberal democracies are at fault for "giving full rights to quantity (majorities), they forget the rights of quality, which are much higher rights. Prove that differences of quality not only do exist inexorably, but also should exist. The next step—democracy of superiors only."[50] The clearest indication of Nietzsche-like elements in writing published during her lifetime was Bjorn Faulkner of *Night of January 16th*: "young, tall, with an arrogant smile, with kingdoms and nations in the palm of one hand—and a whip in the other."[51] Siegurd Jungquist, Faulkner's devoted bookkeeper, acknowledges his role as "instrument" of a higher man: "Herr Lawyer, when little people like you and me meet a man like Bjorn Faulkner, we take our hats off and we bow, and sometimes we take orders; but we don't ask questions."[52]

Even in the final text of the novel, there are some traces of this view of the hero. Consider the description of Roark's isolation in Stanton. The world resents the noble man: "People turned to look at Howard Roark as he passed. Some remained staring after him with sudden resentment. They could give no reason for it: it was an instinct his presence awakened in most people" (16–17).[53] He is alone: "He had not made or sought a single friend on the campus" (25). He is isolated not only in Stanton, but in general: "He was usually disliked, from the first sight of his face, anywhere he went. His face was closed like the door of a safety vault; things locked in safety vaults are valuable; men did not care to feel that" (61–62). Henry Cameron explains the resentment for the noble soul as hatred for "any man who loves his work." Cameron to Roark: "Do you ever look at the people in the street? Aren't you afraid of them? I am. They move past you and they wear hats and they carry bundles. But that's not the substance of them. The substance of them is hatred for any man who loves his work. That's the only kind they fear. I don't know why" (63–64). Roark himself, at one point, thinks of the world—writ large or writ small—as his enemy: "It was a race he was running now, a race between his rent money and . . . he did not know the name of the other contestant. Perhaps it was every man whom he passed on the street" (175). In his pain, he considers (then rejects) the possibility that he has no chance:

> He passed by buildings under construction. He stopped to look at the steel cages. He felt at times as if the beams and girders were shaping themselves not into a house, but into a barricade to stop him; and the few steps on the sidewalk that separated him from the wooden fence enclosing the construction were the steps he would never be able to take. It was pain, but it was a blunted, unpenetrating pain. It's true, he would tell himself; it's not, his body would answer, the strange, untouchable healthiness of his body. (175–76)

The manuscript has even more about his awareness that others resent and fear him for what he is, for what they see in his face (I, 333).

Dominique, in the final text, expresses a similar belief that the exceptional is feared, hated, imperiled.

> She had always hated the streets of a city. She saw the faces streaming past her, the faces made alike by fear—fear as a common denominator, fear of themselves, fear of all and of one another, fear making them ready to pounce upon whatever was held sacred by any single one they met. . . . She had liked facing them in the streets, she had liked the impotence of their hatred, because she offered them nothing to be hurt. (242)

Hence, she deplores the exposure of the Enright House to a world unworthy of it.

> A man who can conceive a thing as beautiful as this should never allow it to be erected. He should not want it to exist. But he will let it be built, so that women will hang out diapers on his terraces, so that men will spit on his stairways and draw dirty pictures on his walls. He's given it to them and he's made it part of them, part of everything. He shouldn't have offered it for men like you [Toohey] to look at. For men like you to talk about. He's defiled his own work by the first word you'll utter about it. . . . A man who knows what he must have known to produce this should not have been able to remain alive. (244)

She is, of course, similarly afraid of the exposure of Roark himself to a world unworthy of him.

As readers of the novel, we know that the full story proves Dominique mistaken: the Nietzsche in her, so to speak, was wrong. But an examination of the notebook and the early chapters of the novel shows that, at some stage of composition, the Nietzsche-elements were present in Ayn Rand and in Roark.

But even in the passages I have quoted, there is a significant difference: the noble soul is the man who loves his work—an identification Nietzsche does not make. Roark, moreover, is progressively described as less Nietzsche-like regarding isolation. Whereas Nietzsche believed that the noble soul did not seek others of his kind, Roark is described as actively seeking his kind of face, his kind of person. Hence he is capable of friendship with Mike Donnigan, described as follows in the final text:

> He worshipped expertness of any kind. He loved his work passionately and had no tolerance for anything save for other single-track devotions. He was a master in his own field and he felt no sympathy except for mastery. His view of the world was simple: there were the able and there were the incompetent; he was not concerned with the latter. (93)

The characterization of Roark in the later chapters of the novel soundly repudiates the Nietzsche-elements cited above. The view of the world as enemy is ascribed not to Roark, but to other characters—Cameron, Mallory, Dominique, Wynand—all of whom learn from Roark's example and his triumph. The image of the leader to whom others bow, the exponent and practitioner of the will to power, is matched with Wynand—and his life demonstrates the hollowness of that image. Hence Roark is not the enemy of the world. He is not the Nietzschean noble soul, entirely separated from the lesser people, who are mere instruments. His purpose is not to inspire others, but he does so, from the staff who "loved him" as an act of loyalty not "to him, but to the best within themselves" (309) to the Monadnock draftsmen, for whom the work was "the highest experience in the life of every man who took part in it" (508). At his trial, his face and his words evoke a response from the people in the courtroom—whose "faces stood out, separate, lonely, no two alike" (674), each of whom has "known a different sense of living" (675), each of whom, seeing Roark, grasps "the manner of his consciousness" and is thus "free enough to feel benevolence for every other man in the room" (677). He is, as always, independent, but he is not universally hated, or feared, or alone.

I turn now to a particular aspect of the hero's relationship to the world: his romantic encounters. In the passages marked by Ayn Rand, Nietzsche emphasizes man's domination of woman. For example:

> The happiness of man is, "I will." The happiness of woman is, "He will."
> "Thou goest to women? Do not forget thy whip!"[54]

Nietzsche does not, in any of the passages she marked, treat sexual love as an expression of love: it is entirely an expression of power.

The Roark of the notebook is described, in the entry of February 9, 1936, in terms that recall this Nietzschean treatment of male-female relations:

> Until his meeting with Dominique, he has had affairs with women, perfectly cold, emotionless affairs, without the slightest pretense at love. Merely satisfying a physical need and recognized by his mistresses as such.

Moreover:

> Even his great and only love—Dominique Wynand—is . . . merely the pride of a possessor. . . . It is primarily a feeling of wanting her and getting her, without great concern for the question of whether she wants it. Were it necessary, he could rape her and feel perfectly justified. . . .

Ayn Rand's earlier writing has passages reminiscent of Nietzsche's language. The "whip" appears in the first edition of *We the Living*.[55] In *Night of January*

16th, Karen Andre describes her first meeting with Bjorn Faulkner: "He seemed to take a delight in giving me orders. He acted as if he were cracking a whip over an animal he wanted to break."[56] The whip he implicitly cracks over this woman is analogous to his "whip over the world." Her description of Faulkner's attitude to morality, and her attitude to Faulkner, also recalls Nietzsche:

> FLINT: Now, tell us, didn't Mr. Faulkner have a clear conception of the difference between right and wrong?
>
> KAREN: Bjorn never thought of things as right or wrong. To him, it was only: you can or you can't. He always could.
>
> FLINT: And yourself? Didn't you object to helping him in all those crimes?
>
> KAREN: To me it was only: he wants or he doesn't.[57]

In these texts, to be sure, the whip is accompanied by love (as is not the case in Nietzsche). The notebook, however, appears to disavow love (in Roark's "cold, emotionless affairs") and to emphasize power and the possibility of rape (in the case of Dominique).

This view, however, begins to disappear even in the manuscript, and is repeatedly contradicted by the final form of the novel. His affairs with Vesta and Heddy, while not described as love, are not cold or emotionless. Nor is Roark indifferent to Dominique's desire, to "whether she wants it." It is true that, in the manuscript, he is described as wishing to "break" Dominique, and he is surprised by his emotions after his first sexual encounter with her: "It had carried no significance in his mind last night; it had been nothing but the released violence of his body; he knew now that it had been a high point of his spirit" (II, 72). He is portrayed as more "unfinished" in this aspect of his development, as a spiritual work in progress.

But the novel—especially in the later chapters—emphasizes not only the union of body and spirit, but also the spiritual union of these two people, rather than his power over her. In fact, the text subtly suggests that his power over her includes her power over him: "He defeated her by admitting her power; she could not have the satisfaction of enforcing it" (310). His refusal to have power over her in the sense in which she offers it to him— after her marriage to Peter Keating—is a significant milestone in their relationship. He refers to it later, in a conversation with Gail Wynand:

> "Howard, have you ever held power over a single human being?"
>
> "No. And I wouldn't take it if it were offered to me."
>
> "I can't believe that."
>
> "It was offered to me once, Gail. I refused it."

Wynand looked at him with curiosity; it was the first time that he heard effort in Roark's voice.

"Why?"

"I had to."

"Out of respect for the man?"

"It was a woman."

"Oh, you damn fool! Out of respect for a woman?'

"Out of respect for myself." (548)

Wynand will eventually learn exactly who is the damn fool regarding the issue of power. Roark already knows exactly what kind of power he has, and what kind of power he refuses—over a woman or anyone else.

I close this analysis of the hero's relationship to the outside world with a powerful image characteristic of Nietzsche and relevant to the novel—but differently relevant to different stages of composition. In her copy of *Zarathustra*, Ayn Rand marked the following passage:

> How many things are still possible! So learn to laugh beyond yourselves! Lift up your hearts, ye good dancers, high! Higher! And do not forget the good laughter!
>
> This crown of the laugher, this rose-garland crown: to you my brethren do I cast this crown! Laughing have I consecrated: ye higher men, learn, I pray you—to laugh![58]

The phrase "still possible," of course, was echoed not only in Ayn Rand's description of the spirit of youth in her "Introduction to the Twenty-fifth Anniversary Edition of *The Fountainhead*," but, as noted earlier, as a repeated theme for Kira Argounova. Hence, to the extent that Roark's laughter at the beginning of the novel is related to the Nietzschean laughter, he is, in effect, taking over where Kira left off. But Nietzsche—and Ayn Rand—had more to say about the laughter of the higher men. She wrote on June 25, 1938: "His laughter as the meaning of the earth around him, as its song, as the release of its tension. Triumphant, the complete ecstasy. (See Nietzsche about laughter.)"[59] She had copied in her *Fountainhead* notebook the following passage from *Zarathustra*:

> O my brethren, I heard a laughter which was no human laughter—and now gnaweth a thirst at me, a longing which is never allayed. My longing for that laughter gnaweth at me: oh, how can I still endure to live! And how could I endure to die at present![60]

The suggestion of the alien—"no human laughter"—is developed in the notebook through the description of Roark in relation to the world: "The alien. What had been joy in him is now arrogance, what had been strength is now a challenge, what had been freedom is a nameless threat." The man who laughs on the cliff is the man who is hated on the street.

Laughter in Nietzsche contains elements that pertain to the image of the isolated noble soul, to whom the world is hostile. As we have seen, these elements can be found in the early stages of the characterization of Roark, i.e., in the notebooks and in the early chapters. But in the later parts of the novel, the laughter changes as well. Roark's laughter is not "no human laughter." In Mallory's shack on the site of the Stoddard Temple, in "the ease of complete relaxation," the "four people who liked being there together" enjoy "the right to their lightness": "Roark laughed as Dominique had never seen him laugh anywhere else, his mouth loose and young" (336). When Roark "threw back his head and laughed" at the discovery that the Monadnock commission was given to him in an attempt to assure failure, his laughter is dismissive, not defiant—because he does not share Mallory's shock or his rage (511). Monadnock Valley itself represents laughter triumphant (505). There is no longer need or place for the Nietzsche-like laughter—in the hero's relation to the outside world.

The second major area in which there are significant differences between the first and final images of the hero pertains to the relationship of her hero to reason, or the mind. The presentation of egoism, in the notebooks, does not initially specify *rational* egoism. The beginning of the *Fountainhead* notebooks (December 4, 1935) emphasize the concept of "egoism as a new faith," loyalty to one's own distinct values "for certain definite reasons." A true egoist is "the man who puts his own 'I,' his standard of values, above all things, and conquers to live as he pleases, as he chooses, and as he believes."[61] Note that she does not specify the basis for the standard of values, and notice also that she refers to the egoist's achievement as conquest. She explains that the choices, values, and standards are individual (as opposed to concessions to faith or authority), but does not specify reason.

She herself, to be sure, had always identified reason as a high value. But she did not begin her characterization of Roark by describing him as a thinker. Although reason is implicit in independence—because the independent self is the sovereign consciousness—she did not initially present Roark as pursuing a systematic course of thought. The notebooks do not emphasize his thinking, and the early parts of the novel indicate a Nietzsche-like separation of mind from body—with the mind deemed inferior to the body. For example, from Roark's memory of months at Snyte's office:

> Some unconscious device of self-preservation had shut off within him the faculty of memory. [*crossed out*: he was clear and precise during any one moment of these days; but the moment past, nothing was left to recall it.] Whatever happened, he had decided without knowing the moment or seconds of deci-

sion, as if his body, not his thought, had resolved it for him; whatever happened was not his nor of him and his mind refused it existence in refusing it the eternity [?] of memory.[62]

From the same period of his life:

> There was no mind. There was only a body walking, joyous, in the sheer urgency of motion. He was conscious only of the swing of his thighs, of the muscles of his stomach pulled tight, of his chest and shoulders relaxed, flung forward, being carried tightly, easily, in a long, smooth flight. He wanted to move. He did not care whether or why or that he did not care. (I, 440)

From the period in which he is waiting for commissions (a period discussed earlier, as a race between his rent money and every man he passed on the street, 175–76), the manuscript has the following:

> He looked at the steel cages and his sharpest, his clearest perception was only that he could have done them better. That was real. That alone was real. There were moments, as he stood there, when he wanted to move forward, to stop the first worker in sight, to laugh, to ask him what in hell was the fool nonsense he was doing, to tell him what had to be done. For one instant, this impulse was clear and simple and natural, because he had forgotten everything else, he had forgotten the sidewalk on which he stood, the street, the men on the street and everything all these implied. He remembered, almost in the same instant, and he moved, but not toward the workers; he walked on, leaving the structure behind. He was not angry. Only he wondered why the things which stopped him were clear in his mind, but not to something quiet and secret in him, some hidden thing that had closed itself against them; why they were real to his [*crossed out:* mind] brain, but not to that thing; why he had accepted them calmly, but the thing would not accept them. And he wondered whether the calm of his acceptance had not come, perhaps, precisely from that one refusal in him, precisely because of that one closed door. (I, 576–77)

At this point in the composition of Roark, Ayn Rand describes a conflict between his mind or brain and the "hidden thing." In the final text, already quoted, the conflict is expressed as follows: "It was pain, but it was a blunted, unpenetrating pain. It's true, he would tell himself; it's not, his body would answer, the strange, untouchable healthiness of his body" (176). Her actual point here, as she would have expressed it in full maturity, is almost certainly the conflict between the explicit and the implicit. But present in the language not only of the manuscript but also the final text, is the implication that the "secret thing" or the "body" is wiser than the mind or than what a man consciously "tells himself." Nietzsche would have endorsed that implication. But as Ayn Rand moved ahead with her novel and her hero, she rejected any such implication, and instead identified the self, the ego, the "I," explicitly with the mind—and identified selflessness as the mind's enemy.

Here are a few examples, all from the parts of the novel written in or after December 1941. Kent Lansing tells Roark: "Integrity is the ability to stand by an idea. That presupposes the ability to think. Thinking is something one doesn't borrow or pawn" (313). Roark tells Mallory: "Tell me about the things you *think*" (330). Toohey attacks the mind of his niece, Catherine Halsey, and thus destroys her sense of morality and even her capacity to use language: "Don't think. Believe. Trust your heart, not your brain. Don't think. Feel. Believe." Catherine responds: "I didn't think of it that way. I mean I always thought that I must think. . . But you're right, that is, if right is the word I mean, if there is a word" (365). The *Banner*, at its worst, succeeds by bypassing the mind: "Its enormous headlines, glaring pictures and oversimplified text hit the senses and entered men's consciousness without any necessity for an intermediary process of reason" (409).

But the most dramatic tributes to the mind—and to the mind in relation to the hero—appear in Part Four. At the beginning of this section, a boy on a bicycle, fresh out of college, "wanted to decide whether life was worth living" (503). He is ominously similar to Wynand, who confronted a similar question at the beginning of Part Three. When we meet him, he is in an environment similar to that in which we found Roark, at the beginning of Part One, and he faces that environment with thoughts similar to Roark's.

> He could not name the thing he wanted of life. He felt it here, in this wild loneliness. But he did not face nature with the joy of a healthy animal—as a proper and final setting; he faced it with the joy of a healthy man—as a challenge: as tools, means and material.

The setting, and even the language, suggests Nietzsche at his best, glorifying the creator. But the boy's attitude is also close, too close, to Nietzsche's view of the isolation of the noble soul from a hostile world: "He did not want to despise men; he wanted to love and admire them. But he dreaded the sight of the first house, poolroom and movie poster he would encounter on his way" (504).

He is, as it happens, a student of music—the very subject of the Nietzsche text that most undercut Ayn Rand's admiration for Nietzsche, the subject Nietzsche treated as an invitation to celebrate the irrational. This boy, by contrast, wants to find "joy and reason and meaning in life" (503). He seeks happiness and achievement. He discovers Monadnock Valley, which is "a symphony played by an inexhaustible imagination, and one could still hear the laughter of the force that had been let loose on them, as if that force had run, unrestrained, challenging itself to be spent, but had never reached its end" (505). But this "music" is not Nietzsche's music of the irrational: it is, instead, "the discipline of reason—music was mathematics—and architecture was music in stone." He finds the courage to face a lifetime because the valley is real, and Roark built it. Roark rescues the boy from the (potential) Nietzsche in him—and reason is the means of salvation.

Roark's mind—specifically his epistemology—protects Monadnock Valley and the crusaders who built it:

> not the content of that thought, nor the result, not the vision that had created Monadnock Valley, nor the will that had made it real—but the method of his thought, the rule of its function—the method and the rule which were not like those of the world beyond the hills. (508)

His trial speech emphasizes the mind:

> Man cannot survive except through his mind.
> But the mind is an attribute of the individual. . . .
> The code of the creator is built on the needs of the reasoning mind which allows man to survive. The code of the second-hander is built on the needs of a mind incapable of survival.
> Degrees of ability vary, but the basic principle remains the same: the degree of a man's independence, initiative and personal love for his work determines his talent as a worker and his worth as a man. . . . (679–81)

Nietzsche would never have spoken these words, and Ayn Rand, when she began this novel, did not plan to give these words to Roark. But she found, as she worked, that her subject—first-handedness versus second-handedness—required a tribute to the mind.

As she wrote on an undated page of her notes: "The worst crime of all on earth—to repeat a borrowed opinion. (We can't all be geniuses, but independence of judgment is involved in any act or comment.)"[63] We can't all be geniuses. We can't all be what Nietzsche would have called the "higher men." The moral code of *The Fountainhead*, accordingly, was not a code restricted to geniuses. It was a morality for all men. But anyone can—and should—choose to use his mind. As Ayn Rand completed her novel, she left no doubt on that score.

Her statement of the novel's theme, prepared late in the composition, emphasizes the role of the mind:

> Basically, life is consciousness; to live means to think; the fundamental process which constitutes life itself is the process of thought; thought is the creator of all values; the practical application of thought is man's work, his labor, his creative activity—and all labor is a creative activity to some degree. In these two

realms—his thought and his labor—Roark is utterly independent of all men. He faces life as if he were the first man born. Nothing stands between the evidence of his senses and the conclusions his mind draws from them. "He is the life-giving principle itself, personified in a man."[64]

Did Ayn Rand intend to leave in Roark a few subtle hints of the ideas she had rejected, or did she do so inadvertently? When she wrote the early Roark, was she herself in some sense the early Roark? Did she herself share the experience of seeing her enemy as everyone she met in the street? I hesitate to say that she left anything in the novel that was not her best intention. But the final editing of the novel was rushed: she said that, if she had had time, she would have weighed the possibility of revising to bring in Dominique earlier in Part One, once she had eliminated Vesta Dunning. The novel as we know it is, in a sense, chronologically her earliest published fiction. Although *We the Living* was originally published in 1936 and *Anthem* in 1938, she revised them both, in 1959 and 1946 respectively. With a first and final publication date of 1943, *The Fountainhead* is the oldest of the four, and the only one that she completed in haste.

This preliminary study of the novel's composition shows that the Nietzsche-like elements appear prominently in the notebooks, much less so in the manuscript, still less so in the final text, and hardly at all in the sections of the novel written after she signed her contract with Bobbs-Merrill. As she completed and revised her novel, she not only took out the Nietzsche quotations, but also endeavored to eliminate several negative Nietzsche-like elements. Nietzsche implies that there are different moralities for the noble and the others, that the will to power is an expression of strength, that the world is a hostile place for the noble man, that spiritual nobility is innate rather than self-made, that the noble soul has no commerce with reason. All that, Ayn Rand repudiated.

Before she left Russia, Ayn Rand had rejected Nietzsche's irrationality: in the United States, she did not even purchase a copy of *The Birth of Tragedy*. But until she created her first ideal man, she had not entirely repudiated the rest of his philosophical errors. When she planned and began writing *The Fountainhead*, she included and even emphasized several Nietzschean elements: the world's hostility to Roark, his lack of friends, the opposition between him and the world. But she ultimately changed all of that. The hostility vanished. The friends joined him, and as traders rather than serfs. No longer is any man in the street his enemy, because any man willing to use his own mind is an ally.

Creating the real Roark, residing in his world, she is able to remove any slivers of Nietzscheanism not only from the characterization, but from herself. She knows she can win.

Had she ever doubted it? Not often. "But," she writes,

there was one evening . . . when I felt so profound an indignation at the state
of "things as they are" that it seemed as if I would never regain the energy to
move one step farther toward "things as they ought to be." Frank talked to me
for hours, that night. He convinced me of why one cannot give up the world
to those one despises. . . . [T]hat night, I told Frank that I would dedicate *The
Fountainhead* to him because he had saved it. (vi–vii)

I surmise that the night of that conversation was on or about June 10,
1940. The dedication page in the manuscript bears that date and reads:
"To Frank O'Connor who is less guilty of second-handedness than anyone
I have ever met."

In the fourth section of her novel, which she began writing on July
4,1942, she describes a similar experience of tenacity, dedication, and joy.
Under the direction of Howard Roark, his old draftsmen are building a
summer resort at Monadnock Valley. Ayn Rand writes:

the year at Monadnock Valley remained in their minds as the strange time
when the earth stopped turning and they lived through twelve months of
spring. They did not think of the snow, the frozen clots of earth, wind whistling
through the cracks of planking, thin blankets over army cots, stiff fingers
stretched over coal stoves in the morning, before a pencil could be held
steadily. They remembered only the feeling which is the meaning of spring—
one's answer to the first blades of grass, the first buds on tree branches, the first
blue of the sky—the singing answer, not to grass, trees and sky, but to the great
sense of beginning, of triumphant progression, of certainty in an achievement
that nothing will stop. (508–9)

An achievement nothing could stop, indeed. That honor belongs to the
ideal man and to the writer who brought him into being. On the last page
of *The Fountainhead*, he stands at the top of the world, higher than any of
Nietzsche's "higher men."

But in creating her ideal man, even though she eliminated from him the
problematic Nietzsche elements, she was in fact following through on an
important insight that she had gained as a result of reading Nietzsche originally. He had saved her, she said, from a philosophical error. Before she
read Nietzsche, she had thought that she needed to "defend man as the
species," and that she needed to formulate her protest against determinism
by presenting the heroic essence of mankind. "But it's a very mistaken formulation philosophically. And what Nietzsche made me realize is that it
doesn't have to be collective. In other words, that the species can be vindicated by one man."[65] This became her task: to defend her idea of the heroic
human spirit not through "the metaphysical original virtue of mankind as
such," but specifically through the presentation of a single human being. In
her fiction, she projects the human ideal through one individual. That is

why, in *The Fountainhead*, the victory of Howard Roark is, as Henry Cameron says, a victory not just for him, "but for something that should win, that moves the world" (133). The ideal man, in himself, vindicates the species. This—whatever else she rejected and repudiated—she learned from Nietzsche.

Howard Roark built skyscrapers. Ayn Rand built Roark.

NOTES

1. *Fountainhead* notebooks, Ayn Rand Archives. These notebooks, originally in loose-leaf binders, contain dated and undated notes from 1935 through 1942. Unless otherwise indicated, all of my references to the *Fountainhead* notebooks will be drawn from these unpublished, archival materials. I will also draw on additional unpublished, archival materials, identified by name—e.g., Ayn Rand's first philosophical notebook (1934), and "Outlines for 'The Fountainhead'" and "Synopses for 'The Fountainhead,'" which were not included in the *Fountainhead* notebooks. All of these materials are in the Ayn Rand Archives. Thanks to Michael Berliner and Jeff Britting for cataloging these materials and providing indispensable guidance in my work with the papers. Some of the material from the *Fountainhead* notebooks, the "Outlines for 'The Fountainhead,'" and "Synopses for 'The Fountainhead'" has been published in David Harriman, ed., *Journals of Ayn Rand* (New York: Dutton, 1997).

2. She typically dated the first page of each chapter and often also the final page. The manuscripts are contained in eight boxes at the Madison Building of the Library of Congress, where I examined them. The manuscript of each of the four parts of the novel is separately paginated. Unless otherwise indicated, I will refer—by part and page number—to the pages of the holograph, i.e., the first draft. In the Ayn Rand Archives, there are additional loose pages, both holograph and typed, that appear to be contemporaneous with the drafts.

3. Letter from Ayn Rand to Channing Pollock, 10 December 1941, Ayn Rand Archives.

4. Letter from Archibald Ogden to Ayn Rand, n.d., Ayn Rand Archives.

5. Michael S. Berliner, ed., *Letters of Ayn Rand* (New York: Dutton, 1995), 67.

6. Biographical interviews (Ayn Rand Archives).

7. On March 18, 1936, Jennie M. Flexner, Readers' Advisor at the New York Public Library, prepared an annotated list of more than a dozen books. *Fountainhead* notebooks, Ayn Rand Archives.

8. *Fountainhead* notebooks, Ayn Rand Archives.

9. "Outlines of 'The Fountainhead,'" Ayn Rand Archives.

10. "Outlines of 'The Fountainhead,'" Ayn Rand Archives.

11. "Outlines of 'The Fountainhead,'" Ayn Rand Archives.

12. Some of the material in the present article about the manuscript is a revised version of "Artist at Work: Ayn Rand's Drafts for *The Fountainhead*," *The Intellectual Activist*, vol. 15, no. 8 (August 2001), 9–20, and no. 9 (September 2001), 23–30. The two-part article also contains additional information about the manuscripts and some different examples of Ayn Rand's editing of *The Fountainhead*.

13. Biographical interviews (Ayn Rand Archives).

14. Some of the "extra" scenes, mostly drawn from the first two parts of the novel, have been published in Leonard Peikoff, ed., *The Early Ayn Rand: A Selection from Her Unpublished Fiction* (New York: New American Library, 2005). Ayn Rand's notes to herself of February 18, 1940, account for several of the omissions in the early part of the novel. See my "Artist at Work," *The Intellectual Activist*, vol. 15, no. 9 (September 2001), 27–29, for the long conversation between Roark and Toohey, which was excised from Part Four.

15. Biographical interviews (Ayn Rand Archives).

16. *Fountainhead* notebooks, Ayn Rand Archives.

17. "Outlines of 'The Fountainhead,'" Ayn Rand Archives.

18. "Outlines of 'The Fountainhead,'" Ayn Rand Archives.

19. See IV, 587. She similarly omitted contemporary political references in her revision of Toohey's speech to Keating. Compare the novel, 639, with the draft, IV, 415–19.

20. Ayn Rand, *The Art of Fiction: A Guide for Writers and Readers*, ed. Tore Boeckmann (NY: Plume, 2000), 163.

21. "Theme of 'Second-Hand Lives,'" in "Synopses of 'The Fountainhead,'" Ayn Rand Archives.

22. She marked this passage in her copy of Friedrich Nietzsche, *Beyond Good and Evil*, translated by Helen Zimmern (New York: Modern Library, 1917), 226.

23. In the first draft, this scene appears at IV, 513–24. Ayn Rand alluded to the English translation of *"mea maxima culpa"* in "Through Your Most Grievous Fault," her column about the death of Marilyn Monroe (*Los Angeles Times*, 19 August 1962); reprinted in Peter Schwartz, ed., *The Ayn Rand Column*, revised second edition (New Milford, CT: Second Renaissance Books, 1998), 30–32.

24. The epigraphs for Parts 1, 2, and 4 were preserved with the notebooks. The epigraphs for the novel as a whole and for Part 3 were preserved with the manuscript.

25. Nietzsche, *Beyond Good and Evil*, 204–5.

26. Ayn Rand marked this passage in her copy of Friedrich Nietzsche, *Thus Spake Zarathustra*, translated by Thomas Common (New York: Modern Library, 1917), 112.

27. Nietzsche, *Thus Spake Zarathustra*, 60.

28. The phrase "the hero in your soul" appears, without explicit reference to Nietzsche, in the fourth-from-last paragraph of Galt's Speech: "Do not let the hero in your soul perish," in Ayn Rand, *Atlas Shrugged*, Thirty-fifth Anniversary Edition (New York: New American Library, 1992), 983.

29. Ayn Rand cited the edition translated by Horace B. Samuel (New York: Boni and Liveright, 1921). I have not been able to examine a hard copy of this book. For context and a different translation, see *On the Genealogy of Morals*, translated by Walter Kaufmann and R. J. Hollingdale (New York: Vintage, 1967), 44.

30. Nietzsche, *Thus Spake Zarathustra*, 87.

31. Nietzsche, *Thus Spake Zarathustra*, 69. Ayn Rand, in her last article for *The Ayn Rand Letter* ("A Final Survey," vol. IV, no. 2 [November–December, 1975], 2), quotes the same passage in reference to herself: "The state of today's culture is so low that I do not care to spend my time watching and discussing it. I am haunted by a quotation from Nietzsche: 'It is not my function to be a fly swatter.'"

32. Ayn Rand, *We the Living*, Sixtieth Anniversary Edition (New York: New American Library, 1996), 25, 235, 464.

33. Nietzsche, *Thus Spake Zarathustra*, 295.

34. Biographical interviews (Ayn Rand Archives). The Archives also contain copies of the translations she read, with markings by John Ridpath that reproduce her original markings.

35. Nietzsche, *Beyond Good and Evil*, 161.

36. Nietzsche, *Thus Spake Zarathustra*, 286.

37. Nietzsche, *Beyond Good and Evil*, 127.

38. Nietzsche, *Beyond Good and Evil*, 117.

39. Nietzsche, *Beyond Good and Evil*, 47–48.

40. Nietzsche, *Thus Spake Zarathustra*, 109.

41. Nietzsche, *Beyond Good and Evil*, 212.

42. Nietzsche, *Beyond Good and Evil*, 198–99.

43. Nietzsche, *Thus Spake Zarathustra*, 124.

44. Nietzsche, *Thus Spake Zarathustra*, 69.

45. Nietzsche, *Thus Spake Zarathustra*, 137.

46. Nietzsche, *Beyond Good and Evil*, 138.

47. Nietzsche, *Thus Spake Zarathustra*, 205.

48. *Fountainhead* notebooks, Ayn Rand Archives.

49. The story of Kira's Viking, cut from the manuscript of *We the Living*, was published in Peikoff, ed., *Early Ayn Rand*.

50. "Philosophical Notebook," Ayn Rand Archives.

51. Ayn Rand, *Night of January 16th*, definitive edition (New York: Plume, 1987), 24.

52. Rand, *Night of January 16th*, 80.

53. In her later writing, Ayn Rand would not have stated, in her own voice, that the resentment was due to an instinct.

54. Nietzsche, *Thus Spake Zarathustra*, 81.

55. See my "From *Airtight* to *We the Living*: The Drafts of Ayn Rand's First Novel," in *Essays on Ayn Rand's* We the Living, ed. Robert Mayhew (Lanham, Maryland: Lexington, 2004), 32–33, for a discussion of this scene from *We the Living* (New York: Macmillan, 1936), 398.

56. Rand, *Night of January 16th*, 82.

57. Rand, *Night of January 16th*, 99.

58. Rand, *Thus Spake Zarathustra*, 295.

59. "Outlines of 'The Fountainhead,'" Ayn Rand Archives.

60. Nietzsche, *Thus Spake Zarathustra*, 168.

61. *Fountainhead* notebooks, Ayn Rand Archives.

62. Scene cut from *The Fountainhead*, 105-23-55A, Ayn Rand Archives.

63. Fountainhead notebooks, Ayn Rand Archives.

64. "Theme of 'Second-Hand Lives,'" in "Synopses of 'The Fountainhead,'" Ayn Rand Archives.

65. Biographical interviews (Ayn Rand Archives).

2

Howard Roark and Frank Lloyd Wright

Michael S. Berliner

THE ISSUE

What is the connection between Frank Lloyd Wright and Howard Roark, the architect hero of *The Fountainhead*? Biographical writings about Wright often contain references to Ayn Rand, with special attention paid to the relationship between Wright and Roark. Opinions concerning this relationship range from Ayn Rand's, according to which the connection goes little beyond their basic approaches to architecture, to that of at least one critic who believes that Roark is virtually a copy of Wright. The intent of this chapter is to explore the relationship between Roark and Wright and to determine the facts. The answer is certainly of biographical significance for both Rand and Wright. But the answer also has import regarding Ayn Rand's originality and methodology, particularly with respect to the source of her fictional characters: as a "romantic realist" she inveighed against naturalistic copying of people from real life. So, it is relevant to what extent Frank Lloyd Wright is embodied in the character of Howard Roark.

To settle the issue of Wright's relationship to Roark, I first provide some background leading to the publication of *The Fountainhead*. I then describe the answers from critics, and from Wright and Rand. After assessing these various claims, I explore the actual relationship of Wright to Roark and the role Wright played in Ayn Rand's classic novel.

BACKGROUND

In late 1935, when Ayn Rand made her first notes[1] for *The Fountainhead* (then called "Second-Hand Lives"), the careers of Rand and Wright were at much different stages. Rand was thirty years old, not yet ten years removed from her escape from the tyranny of Soviet Russia. She had recently sold her first film scenario and her first novel, *We the Living*. In contrast, in 1935, Wright was sixty-eight years old, had two hundred and thirty works to his credit,[2] and had what for most architects was a complete career.[3] His fame had grown to the point where he had appeared on the cover of *Time* magazine. When Ayn Rand moved to New York City in December 1934, she began the research for her "architecture novel." It is not known when she selected architecture as the background, but such was clearly the case by the time she made her first notes. In 1936 she began reading books about architecture, including numerous Wright books, foremost among them his autobiography.

In December 1937, Rand wrote to Wright, requesting a meeting, but he turned her down. Although she had a brief, formal introduction to him in 1938, they had no personal meeting until after the publication of *The Fountainhead*, at a 1944 get-together at the home of Wright's son Lloyd, followed in 1945 by her visit to Taliesin East as Wright's guest. For about 20 years, there was scattered correspondence between them, principally regarding *The Fountainhead* and the house (never built) that Wright designed for her in 1946.[4]

THE COMMENTATORS

Let us now turn to the controversy over how similar Roark is to Wright. That controversy has its source primarily in Wright biographers. At the one end of the spectrum—denying any significant connection—is Brendan Gill, who wrote that "Howard Roark is widely supposed to have been based on Wright, though Rand denied it many times and so, with reason, did Wright."[5] Unfortunately, Gill does not explain his position, one which few other biographers share. Some writers, such as Finis Farr, are content to repeat the claim that there is a close connection without committing to it himself:

> Wright received another distinction that he was willing to do without when he was identified by many as the hero of a work of fiction. Whether or not Miss Rand . . . had noted the facts of Wright's career, readers saw a resemblance between certain of his tribulations and some of those endured by Miss Rand's gloriously independent architect hero.[6]

Biographer Robert C. Twombly has the same viewpoint, remarking, without references, that *The Fountainhead* is "supposedly based on Wright's life."[7] And some reviewers of the 1949 film of *The Fountainhead* took the same approach, the *New York Post*'s Archer Winsten writing that the novel "is said to be based on" the career of Frank Lloyd Wright.[8]

Biographer Ada Louise Huxtable takes a similar tack:

> [T]he architect-hero, Howard Roark, commonly believed to be modeled on Frank Lloyd Wright, had made generations of young women swoon. Roark is portrayed as a brilliantly creative, fiery genius, embattled by the establishment, who defiantly blows up his consummate work of art, a skyscraper [sic], rather than see his talent and integrity compromised.[9]

Meryle Secrest, assuming that Roark was intended to be based on Wright, wrote that early chapters Rand sent to Wright "were enough to show him that she had perceived nothing about the essential Wright. . . . Her hero ought to have been an ascetic like Le Corbusier. . . . [Rand] later stated that her hero was not Frank Lloyd Wright, but she acted as if he were. . . ."[10]

Other writers are more insistent that there is a close connection. John Sergeant, in his book about Wright's Usonian houses, mentions "*The Fountainhead*, whose architect hero was a thinly disguised life of Wright. . . ."[11] *Newsweek* magazine, in its 1949 review of the film, declared that Roark "bears an unmistakable resemblance to the great Frank Lloyd Wright."[12] Responding to a published letter in *Life* magazine in 1946 inquiring about the connection, the *Life* editor wrote that

> Miss Rand has not publicly denied any connection . . . but both are complete individualists, unallied with any group or school. Wright studied under Functionalist Louis Sullivan, who was the first to build the simple, slablike office building. Roark's master was Henry Cameron, designer of functional skyscrapers. And both Roark and Wright lead very complicated lives.[13]

The editor merely suggests that Roark and Wright are closely connected and implies that if Ayn Rand didn't publicly deny it, then it might very well be true.

The most extreme position is taken by Franklin Toker, whose *Fallingwater Rising* is a history of Fallingwater, Wright's most famous building. Toker is relentless: "Wright," he alleges, "served as the model for architect Howard Roark,"[14] "Everyone knows that Rand's architect-hero Howard Roark is a stand-in for Frank Lloyd Wright,"[15] "any reader of reasonable cultural background knew that Roark was Wright,"[16] and, apparently unable to hold back any longer, Toker finally fuses the two: "She thought it was romantic to have Roark/Wright. . . ."[17] Toker at least makes an attempt to prove his position; others seem to consider it sufficient to repeat what is "commonly believed" and let that serve as evidence. But, it must be noted, Toker's evidence—in fact, his main thesis—borders on the bizarre. Obsessed with the historical importance of Fallingwater, he interprets everything as revolving around that great building. Thus, *The Fountainhead*, in Toker's scenario, is really the story of Fallingwater in disguise, with numerous hidden allusions to the building and its owner, Pittsburgh businessman Edgar J. Kaufmann Sr. "It was," claims Toker, "after the MoMA exhibition (in 1938)[18] that she changed the title to *Fountainhead*, which echoes Fallingwater in the identical twelve-letter length, the initial F, and a parallel aqueous image."[19] In fact, Ayn Rand selected that title from her thesaurus, after her editor convinced her that the working title, "Second-Hand Lives," emphasized her villains not heroes and that her next choice, "The Prime Movers," sounded like a book about movers.[20] She then selected "Mainspring," another non-aqueous title, which was already taken. Toker then cites a further example of the "disguised" nature of the novel:

> Roark's ferocious antagonist at the fictive Stanton Institute of Technology bore the name of the New York traditional architect John B. Peterkin. Though the toponym "Pittsburgh" appears nowhere in the novel, Rand evidently wanted her readers to be subliminally aware of the Kaufmanns' city.[21]

In sum, Toker's discussion of *The Fountainhead* is a case study in a priori argument, deciding his conclusion in advance and then trying to fit the evidence (most of which is speculation) to the conclusion.

A potentially more promising source is *The Fountainheads: Wright, Rand, the FBI and Hollywood*, an entire book devoted to the relationship between Wright and Rand, by Donald Leslie Johnson, an architectural historian. Johnson's book—or at least his title—is promising because it deals directly with the relationship between Rand and Wright. Johnson openly disputes the validity of Ayn Rand's statement that the only similarities between Roark and Wright are their approach to principles and their innovativeness.[22] But doubt arises with his next sentence: their personal characters and "conviction to principle" (he probably means "commitment" to principle) are similar. This, apparently, is meant to rebut Rand's claim that being principled is one of the few things they have in common, but he has "refuted" her by agreeing with her. And, of course, they could both be honest, courageous, independent, and principled without in the least contradicting Rand's claim about their disparate personalities, philosophies, and biographies. Doubt increases with Johnson's next sentence: their professional biographies and private lives, he contends, are dissimilar. In other words, they're very similar except that they aren't. Finally, he tells us that his ensuing discussion will reveal how similar they really are. But the reader waits in vain: there is no direct discussion of the similarities between Roark and

Wright, nor are these supposed similarities implicitly revealed in any of the rest of the book.

Johnson's book-length study, in fact, provides less argumentation than does a brief analysis by Andrew Saint, in his *Image of the Architect*. Saint devotes two pages to *The Fountainhead* and Wright, and additional pages to Wright himself. Saint holds that Ayn Rand's denial of "any direct connection" rings false, and he suggests that she denied it precisely because it was true that "Wright's personality and philosophy lie so close to the heart" of the novel.[23] "Nevertheless," Saint continues, "facts speak for themselves." What are these "facts" that establish the "direct connection"? Saint first mentions that Rand bought a house by a one-time Wright admirer (Richard Neutra), that she visited Wright at Taliesin, and that she commissioned a house by Wright. Then, perhaps realizing that such evidence—given that it is all post-*Fountainhead*—is less than definitive, Saint writes that "the book's own evidence is, if anything, more compelling."[24] The "more compelling evidence" provided by the book is as follows:

1. Henry Cameron (Roark's mentor) "clearly represents" Louis Sullivan (Wright's mentor), writes Saint. In fact, Cameron's similarities to Sullivan (which Rand acknowledged) is evidence only of their *own* similarities, not those of Roark and Wright.[25]

2. Roark's employment interview with Cameron, Saint claims, "mirrors Frank Lloyd Wright's portrayal of his early days with [Louis] Sullivan." In fact, Roark's dramatic encounter with Cameron has no "mirror" in Wright's description of his first interview with Sullivan[26] or in the general portrayal of his relationship to Sullivan.

3. Roark's buildings resemble Wright's. It is true that Roark's buildings were based in part on the same general architectural approach (which Wright called "organic"), but that is far from a compelling reason to hold that Roark and Wright have a connection beyond what Rand acknowledged.

4. Wright's Unity Temple "seems to have supplied some of the philosophy behind Roark's Stoddard Temple." Both, it is true, were described as temples to the spirit of man, but Rand's atheism (inherent in Roark's character) would logically lead him to such a building—more so than Unity Temple, which reflected the liberal religiosity of Wright. Saint might have read Wright's statement that he had wanted to build "a temple to man," but Saint apparently missed the conclusion of the sentence: "in which to study man himself for his God's sake."[27] Unity Temple is perhaps non-sectarian, but it is not non-religious. Its purpose, according to Wright, was "the service of MAN for the worship of God."[28]

More important than the preceding, writes Saint, are similarities in "materials and feelings of Roark's work: modern and functional, but natural and humane." These similarities, obvious but quite general, help lead Saint to conclude that Rand and Wright were in "uncanny" philosophic agreement. The crux of this agreement can be found, says Saint, in "their admiration for individualism," their contempt for the state, for mass culture, and for compromise. Both, he stresses, admired Victor Hugo, and Wright had sympathy for the philosophy of Herbert Spencer, a philosophy that, writes Saint, influenced Gail Wynand ("Roark's alter ego")—ignoring the fact that Wynand's philosophy was at odds with Roark's (and Rand's) and led to Wynand's destruction.[29] In fact, Roark and Wright seem to Saint to be in philosophic agreement merely because both are uncompromising, self-confident, and prefer to work on their own rather than as part of a "team." Neither has the approach to life and to architecture most dear to Saint: the "social approach," in which individual achievement has little or no place. Saint's antipathy toward what he considers to be individualism is reflected in both his *The Image of the Architect* and his subsequent book, *Toward a Social Architecture*.[30] But, then, in his preface, Saint makes no bones about his own philosophic perspective and the "framework" of his book: Marxism. Saint quotes with endorsement Marx's classic disavowal of free will and individualism: "It is not the consciousness of men that determines their being, but on the contrary it is their social being that determines their consciousness."[31] One must conclude that anyone who is at all independent is a threat to the collectivism endorsed by Saint, an ideology most eloquently expressed by Ellsworth Toohey, the arch-villain of *The Fountainhead*.

It is not only writers on architecture who allege a strong connection between Roark and Wright; architects themselves also weigh in. Fay Jones, a former Wright apprentice who went on to a distinguished career until his death in 2004, commented that when he was a student, "there weren't many novels about architecture at the time, so of course I read [*The Fountainhead*]. I also knew it was about Frank Lloyd Wright, and he was a hero of mine."[32] But the most revealing comment comes from famed architectural photographer Julius Shulman:

> Don't forget that every architect in the world read that book. It was one, first, front and center in the life of every architect who was a modern architect. And invariably, many architects would say to me, "Well, you know that Ayn Rand patterned Howard Roark after me?" Raphael Soriano said that. Richard Neutra said that. Gregory Ain. There are others. Oh, many people said that![33]

Although one might approve of these architects admiring and identifying with Roark, they are, it must be said, indulging in a great deal of wishful thinking.

WRIGHT ON ROARK

Let us now look at Wright's views regarding the connection between himself and Howard Roark. Sources of information are Wright's own writings and his conversations as reported by friends and by Ayn Rand. It should be noted at the outset that no clear view emerges: Wright either had conflicting opinions or varied what he said depending upon to whom he was speaking.[34] Be that as it may, what did Wright say—or allegedly say?

Wright makes no mention of Ayn Rand in his autobiography—either the original 1932 edition or the 1943 revision. The first edition was published years before he had heard of her, before her career had started, and the revised edition was written before *The Fountainhead* was published. The early chapters she sent him in 1938 would not have seemed sufficiently significant, even had he been enthusiastic: his autography contains little discussion of friends and acquaintances, being focused almost entirely on his architectural career and philosophy. So we must gather what we can from correspondence and casual remarks.

Did Wright think that he and Roark were—in any sense—one and the same?

The first clue comes in 1938, when Wright responds negatively to Rand's written request for an interview and gives her his reaction to the first chapters of *The Fountainhead*: "No man named 'Roark' with 'flaming red hair' could be a genius that could lick the contracting contrafraternity."[35] The implication seems to be that Wright was having trouble distinguishing himself from Roark, thinking perhaps that the novel was about him but that Rand had made the mistake of giving her hero red hair—not the color of Wright's hair. Architect Ely Jacques Kahn, with whom Rand did volunteer work in 1937 as research for her novel, wrote to Rand in 1946: "[Wright] admits, modestly, that he is the hero."[36] Two other supposed comments by Wright further the view that Wright thought the book was about him: Finis Farr quotes (without citation) Wright's comment that the 1949 film was "a grossly abusive caricature of my work,"[37] and Ada Louise Huxtable writes (also without citation) that "[Wright] said that Rand failed to understand him and that she never got it right. When asked if he was the model for Roark, he replied, 'I deny the paternity and refuse to marry the mother.'"[38] A variation on this theme—Wright thinking that the book was about not just his life but also his philosophy—is indicated in a 1950 newspaper column about Hollywood and architects. The author, Aline Mosby, quotes Wright: "I agree with [*The Fountainhead*'s] thesis, the right of an artist to his work, but I think she (Author Ayn Rand) bungled it. It's a treacherous slant on my philosophy."[39] Perhaps the most telling—and oft-repeated—piece of evidence comes from Rand herself and demonstrates Wright's ambiguity. At a private evening with Rand in 1944, Wright gave her some reaction to the novel, as she later related:

> And then he began to say such things as, well, he doesn't like the fact that Howard Roark was so tall. . . . I ask him why, and he very charmingly, laughing, points to his son, who is quite tall, and [to] Frank, and he says . . . "You know, well, tall men always remind me of weeds. That is, all growth." And then, kind of catching himself, he points to the two of them and he says, "Well, I wouldn't mean everybody." Something like that, like a polite "present company exempted." But the real conviction was that they grow like weeds. Now whether that was his childhood consolation to himself or what, I don't know. And he said (this part of the conversation I remember very clearly), "I don't think an architect, the symbol of an architect, he shouldn't be tall, and he shouldn't be red-headed. You know, I would see him more as a man with a mane of white hair. . . ."[40] At which point his son said, "Oh, father, after all, Miss Rand isn't writing your biography (or wasn't writing it)." And he chuckled, he said, "Yes, that's true."[41]

Did Wright believe he was Roark? There is no unequivocal answer, but the comment to his son implies that he did at least partly believe it, but when faced with the proposition, he could not admit it, even to himself.

Ayn Rand's own interpretation:

> He apparently couldn't—or didn't want to—separate the abstraction, Ideal Architect, from himself. It had to be *himself* in the most literal sense. When he was talking about this, how he *sees* the ideal architect, it was completely sincere as far as I could judge. He was kind of looking off into the distance and projecting an abstraction. And what was interesting is that the abstraction was himself. Even such issues as appearance, you see, jarred. It had to be himself literally.[42]

AYN RAND'S ACCOUNT

Ayn Rand's own position, stated on numerous occasions, *was* unequivocal. In a 1950 letter to a fan, she summed up her position:

> There is no similarity between Roark and Mr. Wright as personal life, character and basic philosophy are concerned. The only parallel which may be drawn between them is purely architectural—that is, in regard to their stand on modern architecture.[43]

Regarding his character, she denied that it was the basis for Roark:

> Absolutely not. Some of his architectural ideas, and the pattern of his career, yes, definitely, because I admire Wright very much, as an architect. But as a per-

son, as a character, as the content of Roark's philosophy, he is almost the opposite of Frank Lloyd Wright; no connection at all.[44]

Regarding Wright's architectural approach, she said that there were similarities, but only in the most general sense, and she rejected any philosophical connection between Roark and Wright:

> *The Fountainhead* is actually *not* a novel about architecture—or rather, architecture is merely the background I use for a theme which applies to all human activities and professions. [One] may be justified in seeing some parallel between Howard Roark and Frank Lloyd Wright only in a strictly architectural sense, that is, in the fact that both are great fighters for modern architecture. But if you have read Mr. Wright's books you must know that there is no resemblance whatever between Roark's personal character and the character of Mr. Wright, between the events of their lives, and between their fundamental philosophies of life.[45]

> Frank Lloyd Wright has nothing to do with Roark. Because, by the time I had read even only the biography and long before I met him, I couldn't stand the sense of life that he projected ideologically. Only in the passages when he wrote about architecture I admired him, but even then it was not Roark speaking. So that character-wise, there is absolutely nothing in common. . . .[46]

> As architect, [Wright was a springboard for Roark] only in the theoretical way, that is, what he presented as his idea of architecture, what the issue was if you went past his terms, such as organic architecture and all the mystically undefined stuff, yes. That is what you could abstract from his books and [Louis] Sullivan's on their basic theory of modern architecture, its justification, why it's first-hand as against copying the buildings of the past. That was the abstraction taken from them, in effect. But only in the broadest sense. In other words, taken as a principle, which was in fact correct. Everything else I had to devise myself. So that I've always said there is a resemblance to Wright only in the fundamentals of modern architecture and in the sense that it's a man alone who is fighting against a whole trend for a new architecture. Outside of that, no resemblance at all.[47]

And she made her position clear to Wright himself, in letters she sent to him in 1937 and in 1944:

> My hero is not you. I do not intend to follow in the novel the events of your life and career. His life will not be yours, nor his work, perhaps not even his artistic ideals. But his spirit is yours—I think.[48]

> I have taken the principle which you represent, but not the form, and I have translated it into the form of another person. I was careful not to touch upon anything personal to you as a man. I took only the essence of what constitutes a great individualist and a great artist.[49]

In sum, Ayn Rand loved his buildings and his independence in architectural design, but she strongly denied any commonality with Roark in respect to personality or philosophy. In fact, the actual psychological model for Roark was herself, as she once pointed out.[50]

ASSESSMENT

In order to assess the conflicting claims, we must determine (a) what it was that Ayn Rand knew about Wright before and during her writing of the novel, (b) what Roark and Wright have in common, and (c) whether those common elements are significant.

What did Rand know about Wright? She had selected the philosophic theme of the novel before his autobiography had even been published: a neighbor in the apartment building in which she lived in the early 1930s had inadvertently provided the basic conflict by expressing the thinking process of the second-hander, in contrast to the man of independence.[51] And, by late 1935, when the basic theme and characters were set, she had still, according to her biographical interview, only "heard of" Wright. Although the exact chronology of her reading about Wright's life and theory is not known, in 1961 she did recall:

> I had heard his name when we first lived in Hollywood, long before I had the idea for *The Fountainhead* and before I started working on it. I had heard that there was that kind of architect, and I had seen some photographs of his work, which I liked very much. But I actually had no particular interest in architecture as such. I was not studying the subject, and beyond a certain kind of abstract admiration for a few of his buildings which I had seen, I had no particular interest really. I read his autobiography only when I began doing the research for *The Fountainhead*. . . .[52]

It is impossible to determine how much Wright could have affected the concretes of her story. As far as can be established, her major sources were his pre-1938 writings (including his autobiography); the January 17, 1938 *Time* magazine cover story about Wright; and the January 1938 *Architectural Forum* issue devoted to Wright—all of which were among her effects at the time of her death in 1982. Whatever else she might have read, by the time she saw him speak in September 1938, she was able to recall, in 1961, that "it wasn't anything particularly new as far as the ideas went, because I had read everything available by him. And what he was saying was the same things he had said before about architecture. . . ."[53] The only major book published by Wright at that point was *The Disappearing City* (1932), a work dealing with his social and architectural ideas.[54]

As sources for information about his life, little was available. Her notes on his autobiography were made on March 13, 1936, not long after her original notes for "Second-Hand Lives." In 1937 she read (and made notes on) Wright's "Modern Concepts Concerning an Organic Architecture"; the first issue of his short-lived magazine, *Taliesin*; something titled in her notes "From the Life-Work of Frank Lloyd Wright"; and his *Modern Architecture*.[55] Based on the titles and contents (where available), one can conclude that most of these writings—indeed most of Wright's writings throughout his life—deal almost exclusively with his ideas on architecture and society. Her primary (if not sole) source of information about his life would, prior to her writing the novel, be his autobiography, since the *Time* story seems to rely on that as its primary source about Wright's life. So, using that as a basis, what can be said about Roark and Wright—about their comparative careers, life stories, personalities, and philosophies?[56]

Life Stories

There is virtually nothing in common in their life stories, nor do the critics even attempt to show otherwise. To list all of the aspects *not* in common would clearly be impossible, but some basic dissimilarities are worth pointing out: Roark's family life (as indicated in the novel) is almost nonexistent (with no mention of siblings or even parents), whereas Wright came from a large and close family. Roark was a loner, whereas Wright, in contrast, had many friends and even joined a fraternity at the University of Wisconsin. Roark had one romantic attachment, whom he married relatively late in life (age 38), whereas Wright was 21 at the time of his first (of three) marriages and had a scandalous affair while married. In fact, Wright's life was full of marital, financial, and legal conflicts, whereas Roark's personal life was relatively undramatic.

Their careers evince many similarities. Early on, both worked for famous and irascible modern innovators, though Roark's mentor (Henry Cameron) was at the end of his own career and an outcast, whereas Wright's mentor (Louis Sullivan) was at his height. Both found themselves battling the establishment and challenging the view that because the great achievements in architecture have already taken place, it is the architect's job to copy the "accepted" views of the past. However, Roark struggled long for professional success, whereas Wright moved swiftly to the top, gaining important commissions when quite young (his first entry in the Storrer catalogue is at age 20, and his first independent commission came at age 26). That each was at odds with the architectural establishment is neither surprising nor significant, for that situation is inherent in being an innovator and not one peculiar to Wright or Roark or to architecture.

Personalities

A reading of Wright's 1932 autobiography reveals many personality aspects that might have appealed to Ayn Rand but also many that she would likely have found unattractive at best, some of which were more akin to Roark's foil, the second-hander Peter Keating, than to Roark himself.

What aspects of Wright might have appealed to Rand? As revealed in his 1932 autobiography, Wright demonstrated independence as a young boy, intentionally trying food that his mother said would make him sick, on the premise of finding things out for himself. From his Uncle Jenkins, he got the idea that work is an adventure—an idea he was never to relinquish, and he began reading and thinking about "exciting lives." He also noted what he called "style" in nature, i.e., the shape of things as it seemed to flow from the thing itself. Wright pronounced school to be boring and with no effect on him—he seemed to be someone who was intent on looking at the world through his own eyes. Traditional education, he thought, was a waste of time, especially when there was work to be done, actions to undertake. As he grew up and became an architect, he lived for his work, finding in it the greatest joy, almost to the point of obsession. This joy was accompanied by enduring confidence in himself. Writing of his work on Midway Gardens, an entertainment complex in Chicago he designed in 1913, Wright said: "Out of a good deal of experience in such matters with Adler and Sullivan . . . I had designed the [orchestra] shell, sure it would work out."[57] As a young man, Wright knew what he wanted, learned how to do it, and did it. In addition—and this would likely have endeared him to Rand—he was generally lacking in false humility[58] and felt throughout his life that he was doing something important, criticizing those architects who merely "got by" by being conventional and copying the past.

On the other hand, there were many un-Roark aspects of Wright. Wright grew up in a highly religious environment—his most influential male relative, an uncle, was a preacher—and the young Wright seemed to revel in it, especially the sermons and the hymns and the "surrender to religious emotion, fervent and sincere!"[59] While probably in late elementary school (Wright is rarely specific about dates), he pronounced himself permanently mortified by a failure in speech class and envious of those who were admired by girls. Even more significantly, he felt the "disgrace" of his mother's divorce, writing about himself in the third person: "A wondering resentment grew in him. . . . He never got the heavy thing straight and just accepted it as one more handicap—grew more sensitive and shy than ever. And a little distrustful."[60]

After entering the University of Wisconsin, Wright joined a fraternity, trying hard to fit in and going to concerts, fancy restaurants, and costume parties—and, in this sense, seeming much more like Peter Keating than Howard Roark. One biographer wrote of Wright in the early stage of his career:

It wasn't only that he did good work; he was also careful to cultivate the appearance of respectability in suburban Oak Park, which was full of potential clients. Wright dined at the best restaurants, joined the right clubs, began speaking to civic organizations, wrote articles about architecture and city planning for newspapers, and patronized the theater, concert halls, and museums, where he often met the right sort of people. He kept fine horses and, when they became the mark of success, bought an expensive car.[61]

Financially, he was less than self-controlled, regularly living extravagantly and beyond his means. One incident must have especially dismayed Rand. In 1895, when Wright was twenty-nine years old, Nathan Moore came to him to build a home, but not like the more radical, Prairie-style Winslow home that Wright had designed two years earlier. As Wright quotes Moore: "I don't want to go down back streets to my morning train to avoid being laughed at. I would like something like this," at which point Moore presented Wright with some pictures of an English half-timber house.[62] This recalls numerous scenes in *The Fountainhead* in which Roark is asked to produce copies of historical styles, but Wright responds quite differently than does Roark: he accepted the commission, something Rand wrote about in her notes on the book: "Compromise on a house for money's sake. Subsequent shame at hearing the house praised."[63] And, although Wright characteristically expressed and often embodied great self-confidence, he also evidenced behavior that suggests his confidence might have been a disguise for lack of confidence: La Miniatura (a 1923 concrete block house in Southern California), he writes, "takes its place in the esteem and affectionate admiration of our continental judges in architecture across the sea. . . ."[64] Such boastfulness, while mild in his autobiography, became something of a Wrightean trademark: he reportedly used to describe himself as "the world's greatest architect."[65] Greatest though he likely was, one cannot imagine such boastfulness in Howard Roark, nor can one imagine Roark having the slightest temptation to publicly evaluate himself. Nor can one imagine Roark sharing the following sentiment of Wright's regarding the attitude toward him of his young students at Taliesin: "I am fond of the flattery of young people. They indulge me, and I indulge them. It is easy for them and for me to do this."[66]

In contrast, Roark, a true individualist, cared nothing about what other people thought of him, neither his professors nor the people on the street. In every fundamental sense, he was oblivious to others.

Philosophically, Wright's autobiography is also mixed. There were certainly ideas of Wright's to which Ayn Rand would have been sympathetic. He, as did Roark, refused to enter competitions: "Any competition will be an average upon an average by averages in behalf of the average."[67] Rand noted this, copying down all of Wright's reasons.[68] And, like Roark, he faced his clients as rational men: "But the architect with the ideal of an organic architecture at stake can talk only principle and sense. His only appeal must be made to the independent thought and judgment of his client"[69]—a passage that Rand also copied in her notes on the book.[70] He endorses "freedom of choice" as the basis for a proper (he calls it "Democratic") culture, with special mention of Thomas Jefferson's principle: "The government is best Government that is least Government."[71] It was obvious even from his autobiography that Wright was a champion of architectural integrity and individuality as opposed to "fashion" and standardization, even if "modern" architecture were to become the fashion.[72] Thus he attacked eclecticism and pseudo-modernism: "I have stayed 'in line' with the principles of an ideal I believe true to my own country and worth a man's time for thirty-two years. While eclecticism ran from pillar to pseudo-classic to post-modernism— I stayed 'in line' with principle."[73]

But Rand's general assessment of his philosophic ideas, expressed in 1961, was not positive:

> I could agree with, see the logic of, and admire very much, his architectural ideas, to the extent to which I could see past his formulations. And also he sometimes expressed himself very clearly on architecture, but I violently disagreed with all the rest of his ideas, particularly political and philosophical, because he was quite loosely collectivistic in some undefined sort of way. His viewpoints seem to be somewhere between collectivism and single tax.[74] Besides which, enormous touches or implications of mysticism—that's in his writing.[75]

There is, in fact, much in Wright's autobiography to which she would have reacted negatively. Reminiscing on his youth, Wright tells us that "Man's puny mind and pusillanimous aims so affront 'Nature' continually! He never knows what happens to him in consequence or because of his philosophy, his 'wisdom' which is usually by way of abstraction—something *on* life and seldom *of* life."[76] He wonders if economic growth "is the natural evil consequence of the so-called virtues which man in self-love is making for himself?"[77]

In addition to these veiled attacks on the egoistic ethics that Rand would champion in *The Fountainhead*, Wright takes swipes at the New York City that she so revered. Having just moved back to Los Angeles from Manhattan in 1943, Ayn Rand wrote to her agent about the city that had been her ideal of America and American values since her teenage years in Soviet Russia:

> I miss New York, in a strange way, with a homesickness I've never felt before for any place on earth. I'm in love with New York, and I don't mean I love it, but I mean I'm in love with it. . . . I feel the most unbearable, wistful, romantic tenderness for it—and for everybody in it.[78]

Frank Lloyd Wright had a different evaluation of Manhattan, writing of his visit in 1928:

> We drove through the new Holland Tunnel, into scenes of indescribable confusion. The village streets of New York were in turmoil of reconstruction—new subways, taller buildings. But seen here in New York is the same architectural insignificance except bigger and better in every way than the insignificance we had seen all the way along [driving across country from Arizona].[79]

Wright's objections to New York in that period pertained not just to New York but to cities in general, which he predicted and hoped would give way to a more suburban, even agrarian culture:

> So in the streets and avenues of the great city, acceleration due to the skyscraper is similarly dangerous and to any life the city may have, even though its very own interests may fail to see it. I believe the city, as we know it today, is to die. . . . Yet our "modern" civilization may not only survive the great city but profit by it because the death of the city—it is conceivable—will be the greatest service the machine can ultimately render the human being. . . .[80]
>
> The only ideal machine seen as a city will be an entirely subordinate collateral affair until it disappears. Invaded at ten o'clock, abandoned at four, for three days of the week, it will be unused the other four days of the week, which will be devoted to the more or less joyful matter of living elsewhere under conditions natural to normal manhood.[81]

That echoes a view about Chicago that Wright expressed to newspapers in the mid-1920s. Of the smoke and crowded conditions, Wright said: "This is a horrible way to live. You are being strangled by traffic." When asked for a solution, Wright is reported to have replied: "Take a gigantic knife and sweep it over the Loop. Cut off every building at the seventh floor. . . . If you cut down these horrible buildings you'll have no more traffic jams. You'll have trees again."[82] Of the skyscrapers that were a likely inspiration for *The Fountainhead* (while living in Russia, Rand used to watch American movies just to see the Manhattan skyline), Wright said: "The pretended means of relief [from auto traffic] specified by the space makers for rent—the expedient skyscraper—now renders the human distress more acute."[83] However, "the tyranny of the skyscraper" (a chapter title in his Kahn lectures) was more an opposition to what Wright considered the dogmatic and impractical use of skyscrapers rather than to skyscrapers as such.[84]

As to Wright's social views, they are a mixture of some sort of vague individualism and agrarian collectivism, influenced as he was by Walt Whitman (whom he was fond of quoting), Nathaniel Hawthorne, and Matthew Arnold. He aligned himself with various left-wing political causes—possibly less by conviction than for social approval. In fact, had she known that

Wright had gone to Soviet Russia in 1937 as a guest of the All-Union Congress of Soviet Architects, she "never would have approached him—on principle, even though it doesn't change the man. But the mere fact of saying anything friendly about Soviet Russia at all would have stopped me, because that's an absolute with me."[85]

FROM WRIGHT TO ROARK

If the lives, careers, personalities, and philosophies of Roark and Wright have only some general characteristics in common, what explains what they do have in common, and—more trenchantly—what explains the persistent belief in a strong bond between the two? The answer can be found in the shallowness of critical thought on the subject and the failure of critics to understand how a romantic writer constructs fictional characters. It is a failure to get beyond the concrete similarities and consider fundamentals. It is a failure to distinguish between Wright as a *model* for Roark (which he wasn't) and Wright as an *inspiration* for Roark (which he was).

Ayn Rand did indeed make use of real people in the creation of some of her characters. The most direct example is *We the Living*, which, she said, is the closest she would ever come to writing an autobiography. Set in Leningrad, where she lived until coming to America, the world of *We the Living* is full of people and events taken from her life. The heroine, Kira Argounova, is Ayn Rand in her ideas, convictions, and values, though not in the concretes of her life. The same can be said of other main characters, whose values and personalities reflected friends and relatives.[86] Even here, though, this is not a naturalistic book, in which fictional characters are little more than disguised real people; on the contrary, they are characters who embody the essence of some of the characteristics Ayn Rand observed in those around her. This is the method of characterization used by a practitioner of the Romantic school of writing.

> When I create a character, I find it helpful to project him visually. This gives me a concrete focus so that the character does not float in my mind as a mere collection of abstract virtues or vices. Seeing his appearance is like having a physical body on which I can hang the abstractions.
>
> That is how Roark was created. I did not base him on any particular human being; but the start of the character in my mind was the image of a redheaded man with long legs and gaunt cheekbones. I formed as clear an image of his figure as I could, and this became the focus for all the abstract characteristics I had to give him. I have done the same for all of my heroes.[87]
>
> A number of people have told me the names of architects I never heard of, swearing that I copied Peter Keating from them. You can see why. Since I present the essence of that which creates a second-hander like Keating, they can rec-

ognize in him many men who do not have his particular appearance, manner-isms, or personal problems, but who have the same essence.[88]

The process by which she constructed the character of Ellsworth Toohey is instructive.

> In regard to villains and characters who are neither particularly good nor bad, I find it helpful to focus on some acquaintance or public figure—not on the details of this person, but only on the essence. In the case of Toohey, I had in mind four living journalists and writers. I did not think of any one of them in specific detail, nor did I study their writings or lives. But my total impression of them gave me valuable clues to the manifestations of certain basic premises. These figures were the concretes that helped me to hold it all in my mind.[89]

The four writers she had in mind were Heywood Broun, Clifton Fadiman, Lewis Mumford, and Harold Laski, and it was Laski's contribution to Toohey that she later described. At the time, Laski was a political science professor at the London School of Economics, and later he became chair-man of the British Labour Party. It was in the late 1930s that some ac-quaintances invited her to accompany them to a lecture by Laski at the New School for Social Research in New York City.

> I don't remember a word of that first lecture, but what impressed me was that it was completely the soul of Toohey in the flesh. I had the character in the general sense, but the mannerisms, the kind of sarcasm, the kind of pseudo-intellectual snideness that he projected was invaluable. That's one experience that interests me as creative imagination. . . . [T]hereafter, all I had to do is remember how that man lectured, and I would know how Toohey would act in any circumstances. . . . Toohey as I presented him is much larger scale than Laski, who was a cheap little snide Pink. But the essential qualities of Toohey [are] what he projected in an unmixed way.[90]
>
> But what I gained from his appearance and way of speaking was the light-ning-like sum of the kind of personality that certain premises would produce. Anytime I would ask myself, for instance, how Toohey would act toward his niece, or what his attitude would be toward young love, I had only to remem-ber the image of that man on the speaker's pulpit and I would know unerringly what his type would do.
>
> I was using an abstraction, not a concrete. I was not copying a real-life model; from a political lecture, I had no way of knowing what the speaker's at-titude would be toward a niece or young love. He served merely to concretize and anchor certain abstractions in my mind.[91]

Laski was not Toohey or even a "model" for Toohey, but he helped her to develop the character of Toohey. William Randolph Hearst had a similar influence on the development of the character Gail Wynand. In the case of Frank Lloyd Wright and Howard Roark, the real person was not a model, nor did he help Ayn Rand in the same way that Laski helped her. Wright was more of an ongoing inspiration—this time in the positive sense. Roark embodies the spirit of Wright, the spirit of an independent creator who refuses to conform to the establishment. As she often said, *The Fountainhead* was not a novel *about* architecture (any more than *Atlas Shrugged* was a novel *about* railroads); but she used architecture as the background, the setting to dramatize "individualism versus collectivism, not in politics but in man's soul."[92] In her 1945 promotional pamphlet, "A Letter to Readers of The Fountainhead," she wrote that "when I made my first notes for *The Fountainhead* I knew nothing whatever about architecture, had never dealt with it in any way, and had never met an architect. I chose it deliberately as the background for my thesis." And in a 1943 response to a fan letter, she wrote:

> You ask me why I chose architecture as the profession of my hero. I chose it because it is a field of work that covers both art and a basic need of men's survival. And because one cannot find a more eloquent symbol of man as creator than a man who is a builder.[93]

RAND ON WRIGHT: AFTER 1943

In her 1960–1961 biographical interviews, Ayn Rand recalled in some detail her two personal meetings with Wright. Although these are "after the fact" and do not bear on what she knew about him before and while writing *The Fountainhead*, these recollections do bear on what she expected of him. Had she reacted with surprise that Wright didn't live up to Roark, we might conclude that Roark *was* Wright in some important way. Such, however, is not the case, as a look at their first meeting demonstrates.

In 1944 Ayn Rand arranged a meeting with Wright, through his son Lloyd, who was working in Hollywood. She wanted to meet him, she said, out of "curiosity" regarding his reason for his dismissive letter of 1938. Held at Lloyd Wright's home in West Hollywood, the private meeting consisted of the O'Connors and the two Wrights. Frank Lloyd Wright, she recalled, was cordial and interested in her book and ideas. It appeared to her that he remembered his letter only vaguely, and he explained his negative response by saying he was afraid she merely wanted to use him for publicity. As to her opinion of him at the meeting:

> Now the personality I liked very much, as far as you could see past the act. . . . He had a certain kind of act, and later, people who knew him told me that it's an act which he puts on for the world, for people he despises. And removes it with people whom he trusts. And this was exactly my impression. That once in awhile something phony would come across, but predominantly I liked his

manner very much during that interview. He didn't have an act, in that whole meeting at his [son's] house.[94]

[He was very philosophical, but] in a late nineteenth-century mystical way. It would be all in very broad generalities. . . , but it was obvious even in that interview that his approach to ideas was: the Truth, with a capital T, . . . mystical romanticism would define it best. As if life, art, truth, beauty, as if those generalities named anything. In other words, not a thinker. . . .

When he was on a subject he liked, particularly like architecture, he would never be phony about it. He would be talkative, he'd express himself very well, witty, in full focus, and the phoniness, or the touches of it conversationally would come in only in any issue which pertains to his relationship to others. If it's an issue of society, public reaction, there will be something phony, defensive almost, not defensive by himself, but defensive by means of offense. You know, for which he is famous. That either he would call everybody else inept architecturally, or you know, that constant insulting people before they will insult *him*. Only, he isn't that strong about it in conversation, but some of that premise is present. A kind of a defensive bitterness.

Socially, he's very much of a social metaphysician.[95] He certainly is not in architecture. My summary to myself of his character is this kind of paradox: architecturally, he has the soul of a Roark, combined with the soul of a Keating in everything else. A high-class Keating, but a Keating nevertheless. He was very much in the swim, in effect, of the modern intellectual avant-garde. . . . I had a very clear feeling that to come out in favor of *The Fountainhead* would have caused trouble for him with all of his intellectual friends. He was not a man to do that. He couldn't fight an intellectual battle and wouldn't want to, probably. And I don't mind telling you that that aspect I really despised him for.

Nor was she surprised at what she saw of Wright at their second meeting, when, in 1947, she and her husband spent a weekend as Wright's guests at his summer home and studio in Spring Green, Wisconsin. Although she noted that, at age 78, he had more "enthusiasm for life" than did any of his twenty-year old students, she reported that he believed the world to be controlled by nine or ten mysterious men and that he believed himself to be "the vehicle" of "a higher mystical power." When she asked him why he would want to ascribe his achievement to another power, he answered in a way that could not be more antithetical to her philosophy: "But to be human, that's not enough."[96]

CONCLUSION

If my conclusion is correct—that Ayn Rand's assessment of the relationship of Roark to Wright is correct—then what accounts for her attitude toward Frank Lloyd Wright, especially regarding *The Fountainhead*? Her attitude toward Wright was clearly much different than her attitude to any other inspiration for one of her characters: she pleaded with him for an interview, bought clothes she could ill afford when first meeting him, sent him the manuscript of her novel, was hurt when he brushed her off, was overjoyed when he wrote to her about the book.

The explanation is not difficult to find. She begins her preface to *The Ominous Parallels*, a book about the philosophic foundations of Nazism by her colleague Leonard Peikoff: "It gives me great pleasure to introduce the first book by an Objectivist philosopher other than myself." And she ends her preface by paraphrasing a line from *Atlas Shrugged*: "It's so wonderful to see a great, new, crucial idea which is not mine."[97] That is the key. Among the basic virtues of Objectivism is that of productiveness, and it was a virtue she personally admired, not merely espoused. Unlike so many people, she was not jealous of the accomplishments of others; to the contrary, all her life she wanted to find people she could look up to. She expressed this view in the mid-1930s, in the character of Kay Gonda in her 1934 play *Ideal*: "One has to find an answering voice, an answering hymn, an echo."[98]

Ayn Rand was a man-worshipper, a hero-worshipper—not in any religious sense, but in the sense of having the highest admiration for her highest values. Her heroic fictional characters ranged from laborer Mike Donnigan and architect Howard Roark in *The Fountainhead* to Dagny Taggart, Hank Rearden, and other industrialists in *Atlas Shrugged*. But her hero-worship was not confined to fictionalizations. As Kay Gonda says, "I want to see, real, living, and in the hours of my own days, that glory I create as an illusion."[99] Seeing such "real" men would likely have been particularly welcome to Ayn Rand in the New York of the mid-1930s, which was so left-wing that it was known as Moscow West—something she was just coming to realize with horror, having expected that no one in America would take seriously (let alone reverentially) the ideas and political system from which she had just escaped.

Thus we see admiring letters from her to such people as H. L. Mencken ("whom I admire as the greatest representative of a philosophy to which I want to dedicate my whole life"),[100] Cecil B. DeMille ("[I can now] thank you and tell you that you have always been the person for whose sake I have wanted most to succeed"),[101] Colin Clive ("I want to thank you for a little bit of real beauty which you have given me. . . . I am speaking of your great achievement in bringing to life a completely heroic human being").[102]

Wright's architectural integrity in always doing buildings "his way" and his monumental architectural achievements placed him in a unique position as someone to admire—not his personality, not his stated philosophy, for she had no sympathy with either. His achievements made them almost insignificant. As she said of his buildings: "I felt that here one had to be a hero and lead a heroic life."[103]

NOTES

1. These notes are included in the "Fountainhead notebook," which resides in the Ayn Rand Archives, Ayn Rand Papers, Box #174.

2. For a chronological catalog of Wright's work, see William Allin Storrer, *The Architecture of Frank Lloyd Wright* (Boston: MIT Press, 1978).

3. Wright designed more than 200 more buildings before his death in 1959.

4. See chapter 3, "Letters to Frank Lloyd Wright," in Michael S. Berliner, ed., *Letters of Ayn Rand* (New York: Dutton, 1995).

5. Brendan Gill, *Many Masks* (New York: Putnam, 1987), 490.

6. Finis Farr, *Frank Lloyd Wright* (New York: Scribner, 1961), 255.

7. Robert C. Twombly, *Frank Lloyd Wright: His Life and His Architecture* (New York: John Wiley & Sons, 1979), 384.

8. Archer Winsten, *New York Post*, July 9, 1949.

9. Ada Louise Huxtable, *Frank Lloyd Wright* (New York: Lipper/Viking, 2004), 225. It was, of course, a housing project and not a skyscraper that Roark blew up. This error is indicative of the shoddy quality of Huxtable's research. She also claims that the O'Connors bought the Neutra house when they decided not to purchase the house designed for them by Wright, when in fact they bought the Neutra house two years prior to the Wright design.

10. Meryle Secrest, *Frank Lloyd Wright* (New York: Alfred A. Knopf, 1992), 496.

11. John Sergeant, *Frank Lloyd Wright's Usonian Houses* (New York: Whitney Museum of Design, 1976), 140.

12. *Newsweek*, July 25, 1949.

13. *Life*, September 2, 1946.

14. Franklin Toker, *Fallingwater Rising* (New York: Alfred A. Knopf), 14.

15. Toker, *Fallingwater Rising*, 293.

16. Toker, *Fallingwater Rising*, 297.

17. Toker, *Fallingwater Rising*, 298.

18. The show actually took place in 1940. See Peter Reed and William Kaizen, ed., *The Show to End All Shows: Frank Lloyd Wright and the Museum of Modern Art, 1940* (New York: Museum of Modern Art, 2004).

19. Toker, *Fallingwater Rising*, 293.

20. For details of how she selected the title, see Ayn Rand, *The Art of Nonfiction*, ed. Robert Mayhew (New York: Plume, 2001), 168–69.

21. Toker, *Fallingwater Rising*, 295.

22. Donald Leslie Johnson, *The Fountainheads: Wright, Rand, the FBI and Hollywood* (Jefferson, NC: McFarland, 2005), 45.

23. Andrew Saint, *The Image of the Architect* (New Haven: Yale University Press, 1983), 12.

24. Saint, *The Image of the Architect*, 12.

25. In a letter, Rand wrote to a fan that "you may see a resemblance between Henry Cameron and Louis Sullivan in the general aspect of a great professional tragedy." See Berliner, ed., *Letters of Ayn Rand*, 492.

26. Frank Lloyd Wright, *An Autobiography* (New York: Longman's Green, 1932), 89ff. Saint might very well have confused Wright's first interview at Sullivan's with

Sullivan's interview with his own first employer, Frank Furness. That latter interview does somewhat "mirror" Roark's interview with Cameron. See Louis Sullivan, *The Autobiography of An Idea* (New York: Dover, 1956), 190ff.

27. Wright, *Autobiography*, 154.

28. Wright, *Autobiography*, 156.

29. In her working notes for *The Fountainhead*, Rand describes Wynand as "a man who could have been," but was instead "a slave to the masses." In contrast, Roark was the truly independent man, "a man who is what he should be." See David Harriman, ed., *Journals of Ayn Rand* (New York: Dutton, 1997), 89, 71, 89.

30. Andrew Saint, *Toward a Social Architecture* (New Haven: Yale University Press, 1987).

31. Saint, *Toward a Social Architecture*, x, quoting Karl Marx, Preface to *A Contribution to the Critique of Political Economy*.

32. Quoted in Johnson, *The Fountainheads*, 47.

33. Unpublished oral history interview, April 20, 2000. The Ayn Rand Archives.

34. In this regard, Ayn Rand suspected the latter, deeming him afraid to antagonize his friends in the liberal establishment, to whom Ayn Rand and her novel were anathema.

35. Quoted in Berliner, *Letters of Ayn Rand*, 111. Original letter with Wright's handwritten revisions are in the Ayn Rand Archives.

36. Original letter in Ayn Rand Archives.

37. Farr, *Frank Lloyd Wright*, 256.

38. Huxtable, *Frank Lloyd Wright*, 226.

39. Aline Mosby, "Vulgar Hollywoodiana," *[Hollywood?] Citizen*, January 24, 1950. In Warner Bros. Archives, University of Southern California.

40. Wright indeed possessed a mane of white hair.

41. Biographical interviews (Ayn Rand Archives).

42. Biographical interviews (Ayn Rand Archives).

43. Letter to Vera Koski, February 21, 1950. Reprinted in Berliner, *Letters*, 468.

44. Robert Mayhew, ed, *Ayn Rand Answers: the Best of Her Q&A* (New York: Signet 2005), 190.

45. Letter to Don Helgeson, February 26, 1951. Reprinted in Berliner, *Letters of Ayn Rand*, 492.

46. Biographical interviews (Ayn Rand Archives).

47. Biographical interviews (Ayn Rand Archives).

48. Berliner, ed., *Letters of Ayn Rand*, 109.

49. Berliner, ed., *Letters of Ayn Rand*, 113.

50. See Mayhew, *Ayn Rand Answers*, 191.

51. Biographical interviews (Ayn Rand Archives), and Jeff Britting, *Ayn Rand* (New York: Overlook, 2005), 50.

52. Biographical interviews (Ayn Rand Archives).

53. Biographical interviews (Ayn Rand Archives).

54. In her notebook of architectural research, Rand comments on this book: "No notes. More of Wright's ideas. Some beautiful, a great many too many not clear. More about sociology than about architecture. Except architecture as a force shaping society. (Which it isn't.)" "Fountainhead notebook," Ayn Rand Papers, Box #174.

55. Likely *Modern Architecture: Being the Kahn Lectures for 1930*, reprinted in 1987 by Southern Illinois University Press.

56. It is difficult to place Wright in Rand's pre-*Fountainhead* context, because we don't know with certainty the state of her thinking or ideas in the 1930s; there are likely to be aspects of Wright and his ideas that would have dismayed her later in life that would not have when she was just 30 years old.

57. Wright, *Autobiography*, 180. Dankmar Adler and Louis Sullivan, for whom Wright worked for many years before opening his own practice

58. In a 1953 interview with NBC's Hugh Downs, Wright stated, "Early in life I had to choose between honest arrogance and hypocritical humility. I chose arrogance and have seen no reason to change, even now."

59. Wright, *Autobiography*, 26.

60. Wright, *Autobiography*, 50–51.

61. Wendy B. Murphy, *Frank Lloyd Wright* (Englewood Cliffs, NJ: Silver Burdett Press, 1990), 34.

62. Wright, *Autobiography*, 126.

63. "Fountainhead notebook," Ayn Rand Papers, Box #174.

64. Wright, *Autobiography*, 249.

65. A legendary anecdote from Wright's life recounts his describing himself in a court of law as "the world's greatest architect." When chastised for such lack of "humility," Wright replied that he had to describe himself that way because he was under oath.

66. Wright, *Autobiography*, 236.

67. Wright, *Autobiography*, 152.

68. "Fountainhead notebook," Ayn Rand Papers, Box #174.

69. Wright, *Autobiography*, 162.

70. Wright, *Autobiography*, 120.

71. Wright, *Autobiography*, 170.

72. Wright, *Autobiography*, 232.

73. Wright, *Autobiography*, 343.

74. "Basic to the theory [of single tax] is the belief that the land and its wealth belong to all. The most effective advocate of the single tax was Henry George, who held that economic rent tends to enrich the owner at the expense of the community and is thus the cause of poverty; he believed that by appropriating all (or nearly all) economic rent, governments could wipe out social distress and even acquire a surplus without recourse to any other taxes." (Encyclopedia.com)

75. Biographical interviews (Ayn Rand Archives).

76. Wright, *Autobiography*, 58.

77. Wright, *Autobiography*, 93.

78. Berliner, *Letters of Ayn Rand*, 106.

79. Wright, *Autobiography*, 311.

80. Wright, *Autobiography*, 313–14.

81. Wright, *Autobiography*, 321.

82. In Farr, *Frank Lloyd Wright*, 185.

83. Wright, *Autobiography*, 318.

84. For whatever reason, of the 436 Wright buildings listed by Storrer, only two are skyscrapers, both of modest height, the fourteen-story Johnson Research Tower

(1944) and the nineteen-story Price Tower (1952), and there are only about six other skyscraper designs among the hundreds of unbuilt designs, the most famous being "Illinois," i.e., the so-called "Mile High" skyscraper for Chicago.

85. Biographical interviews (Ayn Rand Archives).

86. A detailed study of these similarities can be found in Scott McConnell, "Parallel Lives," in Robert Mayhew, ed., *Essays on Ayn Rand's* We the Living (Lanham, MD: Lexington Books, 2004).

87. Ayn Rand, *The Art of Fiction: A Guide for Writers and Readers*, ed. Tore Boeckmann (New York: Plume, 2000), 86.

88. Rand, *Art of Fiction*, 76.

89. Rand, *Art of Fiction*, 86.

90. Biographical interviews (Ayn Rand Archives).

91. Rand, *Art of Fiction*, 87.

92. Rand, *For the New Intellectual* (New York: Signet, 1961), 68.

93. Berliner, *Letters of Ayn Rand*, 92.

94. This and the next three excerpts are from the Biographical interviews (Ayn Rand Archives).

95. "Social metaphysician" is the Objectivist term for someone to whom other people (rather than facts) is their basic reality. It names the essence of the "second-hander" she identifies in *The Fountainhead*.

96. Biographical interviews (Ayn Rand Archives).

97. Ayn Rand, introduction, Leonard Peikoff, *The Ominous Parallels* (New York: Stein and Day, 1982).

98. Leonard Peikoff, ed., *The Early Ayn Rand* (New York: Signet, 2005), 287.

99. Peikoff, *Early Ayn Rand*, 322.

100. Berliner, *Letters of Ayn Rand*, 13.

101. Berliner, *Letters of Ayn Rand*, 11.

102. Berliner, *Letters of Ayn Rand*, 14.

103. Letter from Rand to Wright. See Berliner, *Letters of Ayn Rand*, 113.

3

Publishing *The Fountainhead*

Richard E. Ralston

FINDING A PUBLISHER

Although Ayn Rand had one novel published in America and two in Great Britain by the late 1930s, and was the author of a successful play with an extended run on Broadway, the effort to publish what proved to be her first best seller required a relentless struggle over a period of several years. In many ways it was her most challenging struggle to reach what she often described as "my kind of readers." As with all of her works, she could not just delegate the effort to find a publisher to her agent or promotional efforts for her book to a publisher. She remained intimately involved with every detail of publishing. Although for years she had relentlessly sought an agent that could adequately represent her work to publishers, she did not hesitate to fire an agent that no longer did so and, if necessary, to serve as her own agent.

Within two years after Ayn Rand began making notes and conducting research for *The Fountainhead* in 1935, she began the active search for a publisher.[1] After *We the Living* was published by Macmillan, her editor there, Jim Putnam, asked her about her next novel over lunch. His response to her brief description was "Howard is not the right name for a hero." By that time Macmillan had, in violation of contract, allowed *We the Living* to go out of print. Macmillan agreed to reprint if they could obtain rights for the next novel with an advance of $250. Unhappy with Macmillan's lack of promotion of *We the Living*, Rand would have accepted that, but required a publicity guarantee on the new book of $1,200. "I would not allow another book to be just printed and forgotten. I demanded that they advertise it, and they wouldn't."[2]

Ayn Rand's agent at this time was Ann Watkins. Watkins represented some well-established authors, such as Sinclair Lewis, and had persisted in a lengthy struggle to find a publisher for *We the Living* that culminated in the publication by Macmillan. Watkins's response to reading the first three chapters of the new book was enthusiastic, and she told Ayn Rand that it would be easy to get an advance from a publisher. She soon promised a contract from Knopf and got one, but it provided no advance until delivery of a completed manuscript, which was required in two years.[3]

In any event, it took seven years to complete the book, with an interruption for the unsuccessful production of a dramatization of *We the Living* on Broadway. Ayn Rand showed Knopf about one quarter of what she had written of the book and asked for a partial advance, but upon reading it Knopf declined an advance.

When Ayn Rand told Watkins that she needed an advance, the agent started circulating a partial manuscript to many publishers—which resulted in cascading rejections. During an intelligent conversation at a luncheon meeting with Doubleday, Rand was told that two of their three editors wanted to publish the book and that they would try to persuade the third after lunch. Ann Watkins received a negative reply that afternoon.[4]

Ayn Rand was angry with Watkins when she heard that Simon and Schuster had rejected the book because she thought that Watkins should not have submitted it to a publisher with a reputation (from the 1930s) for being sympathetic to "Red" issues. A businessman Rand knew who was related to one of the owners (Simon) did not think the rejection was due to any "Red" sympathies and arranged for a meeting between Simon and Rand. During the meeting the owner read from a report by their editor, describing *The Fountainhead* as a bad story badly written. (After years of conspicuous anti-fascism, that editor had justified the 1939 Nazi-Soviet Pact, so he was clearly a blind follower of the Moscow party line.) The owner said that the editor might have been wrong, but that his evaluation was not political. "We really are conservative . . . we even publish Trotsky." Rand said she had to make an effort not to laugh, but was not too upset because it was clear that "this was not the publisher for me."

Although Ann Watkins was not having any success pitching the novel, she introduced Ayn Rand to Richard Mealand of Paramount in New York. He had read some of the manuscript of *The Fountainhead* at a time when Paramount was considering the purchase of both book and movie rights of books prior to publication, but he could not get his management in Hollywood to buy it. Ayn Rand was looking for work as a reader (preparing synopses of novels for possible screen adaptation) to supplement her income and soon started work for Frances Hazlitt (wife of Henry Hazlitt), who was Mealand's assistant in charge of readers, earning $25 for each synopsis of a long novel.

By this time, Ayn Rand had reached the end-of-the-line with Ann Watkins. After rejection by eight publishers, Watkins's evaluation of the novel had changed, and she began to tell Rand what was wrong with it. Watkins thought the central character (Howard Roark) was "unsympathetic." Rand obviously disagreed, and Watkins had no answer when she pointed out that unsympathetic characters did not appear to be an obstacle for Faulkner. After Rand dispensed with specific objections, Watkins explained that she could not give reasons for not liking the book; it was just her "feelings."[5] Rand never simply let a comment like that go by, and the result was the end of their business relationship with respect to *The Fountainhead*, as explained in a May 17, 1941, letter to Watkins:

> Now, as to my novel, I had no desire or intention to take that away from you. I wanted to have you continue as my agent on the novel, because it was being handled personally by you and Margot [Johnson]—and I had confidence in both of you. I did not hold against you in any way the fact that the novel had not yet been sold—because I knew you had both done your best and I realize the difficulties connected with that novel perhaps even better than you do. But when I asked you whether you wished to continue with the novel, *you* told me you did not. You said that you did not want to handle the novel further because I made it impossible for you to sell it. When I asked "Why?" you answered—here are your exact words, Ann, I remember them because they made a deep impression on me and I'll remember them all my life—"Why? Why? You always ask me why. I can't answer you. I don't go by reasons, I act upon instinct." That, Ann, was the epitaph on our relations. There was nothing I could say after that. Words are an instrument of reason and instincts are unanswerable. . . .
>
> You close your letter by saying that you regret there should be in the end these repeated misunderstandings between us. That is exactly my own feeling. If you really mean it, if you do regret misunderstandings—*please* let us clear them up. I am more than willing. But any problem can be cleared up only in person, directly and on the basis of facts. If you wish to tell me your reasons for your changed attitude toward me—I'll be more than willing to listen. But it must be a sincere conversation, Ann. Without resentment, without generalities and without "instincts." What do any of us know about instincts? What do they mean? What do they prove? Only language can be a means of communication between people and a means of understanding. Words, thoughts, reasons. If we drop them—we will have nothing but misunderstandings left. If we want to face things honestly and reasonably, we can still end up as friends, and I think we both deserve that much—after the years we have behind us.[6]

From that point Ayn Rand represented the book herself. Although she later began a long relationship with Curtis Brown Ltd. for the motion picture rights, she never again had an American agent for the book. After the break with Watkins, Richard Mealand offered to recommend it to a publisher of her choice. She selected Little, Brown, because of its reputation for publishing "serious" novels. In a meeting with the publisher's New York editor, Angus Cameron, he told her that the editors in Boston thought the book was "high grade literature" but it would not sell because it was "too intellectual and controversial." Although it was later known that Cameron was a member of the Communist Party at the time, that may not have explicitly been a factor in Little, Brown's evaluation of the book. In conversation with Ayn Rand, his comments indicated that he had wildly misunderstood her point of view and assumed she was a left-wing anarchist. That night Rand told her husband that she could understand Simon and Schuster rejecting the book if they thought it was a bad novel, but her response to the rejection by Little, Brown, because the book was too good was horror.[7]

By this point, other publishers who had rejected the book included Duell, Sloan & Pearce, Doubleday, Dutton, Dodd Mead, Lippincott, Reynal & Hitchcock, and Random House. In addition to Knopf's decision to lose the book rather than pay an advance, and Paramount's lack of interest, twelve publishers had rejected *The Fountainhead* by 1941. (Macmillan, Dutton, Simon and Schuster, and Random House all became publishers of Ayn Rand's books later in the century.)

Although Rand did not want to impose further on Mealand, he was a persistent advocate for the book and encouraged her to name another publisher to whom he would provide an introduction. She selected Bobbs-Merrill in spite of their reputation for publishing undistinguished, "homey" small-town novels.

Rand hand delivered the manuscript to Archibald Ogden, the New York editor of the Indianapolis-based Bobbs-Merrill. She was not impressed with Ogden at that first meeting and was surprised when he called a week later to praise the writing, "great" theme, and the characterization of Roark. He had decided to publish the book but needed to get authorization from Indianapolis for the advance. Rand needed what was then considered a large advance of $1,200 in order to devote herself full time to finishing the book in one year. Ogden had to go to the mat for the book. One of the readers in Indianapolis reported to the editor that *The Fountainhead* was a great book but would not sell; another that it was a bad novel but would sell. Ogden asserted himself and told the editor, "If this is not the book for you, I am not the editor for you." The editor responded, "Far be it from me to dampen such enthusiasm. Sign the contract," and approved an advance of $1,000. Richard Mealand and Frances Hazlitt agreed to continue to give Rand reading assignments for weekend work. They and all of the other struggling writers working as readers for Paramount celebrated this breakthrough with her. Just before the contract was signed, the Japanese attacked Pearl Harbor. Ogden later told her that by one week later the deal would have been cancelled due to concerns about the rationing of paper (which did prove to be a challenge). Soon all publishers were looking only for manuscripts that were light, humorous, and—most importantly—short.[8]

Rand's British publisher, Cassell and Co., was still successfully selling *We the Living* and *Anthem*, and had long expressed interest in any new title from Ayn Rand to her agent in London, Lawrence Pollinger, Ltd. At that time the war imposed even more severe restrictions on British than on American publishers, and the British edition did not make it into print until 1947. The British edition stayed in print for many years, and with later paperback editions has sold about half a million copies. In 2007 a new British edition of *The Fountainhead* is being published in London by Penguin Modern Classics.

Rand had little difficulty over editorial issues with Ogden or others at Bobbs-Merrill during the next year. She had planned to publish the book with the title *Second Hand Lives*, when Ogden pointed out that the title implied that the book featured Keating and the villains rather than Howard Roark. So she immediately knew that she had to have a title describing Roark.[9]

MARKETING AND PROMOTION

After delivering the manuscript on time at the end of 1942, Rand's concern turned to reaching the book's optimal audience. She never considered massive sales to be an end in itself but was more interested in the quality than the quantity of readers. In this regard she had no expectation that reviews would call the book to the attention of the readers whom she wanted, but considered advertising by the publisher to be critical in positioning the book correctly. Unfortunately, apart from Ogden, she did not think that anyone at Bobbs-Merrill knew what kind of book they had.

Before publication, Rand was sent the first half-page ad from Bobbs-Merrill for Sunday papers. *The Fountainhead* was presented merely as a big book about architecture that would do for architects what *Arrowsmith* did for doctors. Many years later she reported that she "raised hell" with Bobbs-Merrill about the ad, but "it was like talking to cotton." Hell was raised via a long letter to Ogden on May 6, 1943, about the general failure of Bobbs-Merrill to promote the book. About the ad in question or a similar one she wrote:

> I don't mind the fact that your advertising appropriation is limited. But precisely when an appropriation is limited one must weigh the tone and nature and every word of an ad most carefully, to get the utmost good out of it. The horrible crap you read to me over the phone wouldn't sell a book to a half-wit. It is not intellectual appeal, it is not commercial appeal, it is not even good blurb-writing. It is just simply dull and meaningless. It says nothing. It's just wasted space, wasted words, wasted money.[10]

The letter evidently had an impact. An unexpected ad in *The New York Times* resulted in another letter to Ogden on July 29, 1943:

> I don't know which way one gets more out of publishers—by being a holy Russian terror or a happy Pollyanna, but at the present moment I'm not thinking of proper diplomacy. I'm just simply happy and grateful to all of you, and I hope this idyll will last for both sides.
>
> Seriously, I think the ad was excellent, wording and all, even the nude statue. . . .[11]

Rand added a postscript to the second letter: "This letter is to remain in force up to, but not including the next time I get mad at Bobbs-Merrill."

But most of the new advertising had portrayed the book as just another steamy romance. With few exceptions, reviews were no better than she expected at calling the book to the attention of the readers she was after. Thus in 1943 sales prospects did not seem to be auspicious.

As was the case when *We the Living* was published, Rand was eager to do what she could to personally promote *The Fountainhead*—in spite of her dislike for public speaking. In 1943 she accepted an invitation from Ely Jacques Kahn to address the New York chapter of the American Institute of Architects. *The New York Times* announced the meeting in advance, as well as the fact that Rand had worked in Kahn's office when researching *The Fountainhead*.[12] After the event, *The New York Herald Tribune* reported, "Ayn Rand received an exceptional recognition for her novel *The Fountainhead*; she was invited to be the guest of honor and speaker at a luncheon of the Architectural League last week. . . . The one thing we wanted to know was, did she spot any red-headed architects among those present. She said no, though she looked for one; and we'll bet every one else did too."[13]

In a lengthy interview in the *New York World*, Rand recounted her first sight of New York skyscrapers: "There was one skyscraper that stood out . . . and it seemed to me the greatest symbol of free men. That was 17 years ago, and I made a mental note that someday I would write a novel with the skyscraper as a theme. Now after all these years I have done it, and it is my tribute to America." In the same interview she described the McGraw-Hill building at 330 W. 42nd St. as the most beautiful in New York City. (McGraw-Hill moved out many years ago, but this blue-green building by architect Raymond Hood still stands on 42nd street. Hood was also the architect of Rockefeller Center—of which Rand thought only the perspective of the RCA building from Fifth Avenue was distinctive.)[14]

In October 1943, Rand participated in a weekly newspaper debate syndicated nationally called "Wake Up, America," sponsored by the American Economic Foundation. She was identified as "author of the current best seller novel on individualism *The Fountainhead*." She continued public

speaking after moving to California, as reported by R. C. Hoiles in a remarkable article in the *Santa Ana Register* (now the *Orange County Register*)
under the heading "Meeting a Close Reasoning Russian Woman":

> I had the pleasure recently of attending a dinner meeting of eleven men and
> one Russian woman at the Ambassador Hotel in Los Angeles. The dinner meet-
> ing was given in honor of Ayn Rand, author of *The Fountainhead*.
>
> The interesting part about the meeting was that the conversation lasted four
> hours, and that the Russian woman was there defending the rights of individ-
> uals with better understanding and knowledge, it seemed to me, than some of
> the men in attendance who hold degrees of Doctor of Philosophy and who
> were economists, or had been at the various colleges. The amazing part was
> that she, speaking in English with a foreign accent, which made it a little diffi-
> cult at times to catch every word, was telling men who had received the bless-
> ing of the founding fathers how they were losing their liberty and how they
> would become impoverished and enslaved unless they about-faced and more
> nearly came to respect the rights of the individual.
>
> The one thing that made me realize the very precarious position we are in
> was the erroneous belief, it seems to me, among most of the men and doctors
> attending the dinner, that the success of some people must be detrimental to
> others. In other words, they seem to believe in the Malthus theory that the pop-
> ulation would increase to the point resulting in starvations. They did not seem
> to realize that each man produces his own wealth, and every time A produces
> something different from what B produces, it benefits B. . . .
>
> I am under obligation to the host of the meeting whom I had never met un-
> til the dinner. He sent me an invitation because I had suggested that he read
> Ayn Rand's book, *The Fountainhead*, and quoted her sentence, "Civilization is
> the process of setting man free from men." He was so impressed with the book
> and the author, whom he met after reading the book, that he gave the dinner
> inviting eleven guests that they might meet the author and see the necessity of
> putting forth every effort to get people to believe in a government that at-
> tempted only to set man free from men.[15]

A businessman from Michigan, Monroe Shakespeare, was an intelligent
fan who clearly understood the central ideas of *The Fountainhead* and attempted to raise money for an advertising campaign for the book from
conservative manufacturers. The conservatives they approached were interested only in politics, which they felt was completely divorced from
books and principles, let alone philosophy. After some effort, Rand gave
up on the attempt to get conservatives to support her books or any moral
defense of individualism.[16]

Rand continued to speak in public about the book. On May 8, 1945, she
spoke to the Los Angeles Chapter of the American Institute of Architects.
The status of architecture at the time was deeply colored by years of New
Deal controls, large public works projects, and wartime conditions. Her talk

was substantial, and as recorded in the chapter's newsletter, they got the point: "Her theme is not architecture but individualism versus collectivism, presented and argued with an unusual consistency and lack of compromise." Following are two representative paragraphs from the talk:

> Those of you who have read *The Fountainhead* will understand me when I say that it is actually not a book about architecture at all. It is not about the structure of buildings, but about the structure of man. What makes a man stand or fall. What are the girders and the supports of a man's spirit, and what are the rotted beams and the shoddy foundations. It is the story of the self-respecting, self-sufficient ego against the filthy corruption which is altruism. If there is any doubt in your mind about my attitude towards the profession of architecture, please accept—as the greatest tribute I can offer you—the fact that I consider individualism the only sacred cause on earth and that I have made the champion of that cause an architect. . . .
>
> But architects, above all men, should be the guardians of human freedom. And this is what I am most anxious to say to you, since you have so generously given me an opportunity to be heard: there is a direct connection between architecture and freedom. Observe that every step in the progress of architecture has come at a time when a new step was made in the progress of man's freedom. Man's individual freedom. There is no other. Observe that the great schools of architecture were born in the great periods of individualism. I am speaking of architecture as a structural art—not as a mere piling up of masonry.[17]

Possibly due to her respect for the importance of "word-of-mouth" advertising in reaching her audience, Rand read and responded to a lot of her fan mail. (Her experience when meeting fans was not usually edifying because she found that even many of those who expressed admiration did not understand the novel.) She especially enjoyed the many letters from men in the armed forces. Years later she recalled letters from flyers who told her that after every mission they would gather around a candle and read passages from *The Fountainhead*. One soldier said that he would have felt much better if he thought that the war was being fought for the ideals of *The Fountainhead*. She answered as many of the letters from servicemen as she could.[18] When the volume of mail became overwhelming, she wrote a pamphlet entitled "A Letter from Ayn Rand, Author of The Fountainhead," which Bobbs-Merrill printed as a reply to fan mail. The entire text of this letter is included in an appendix to *Letters of Ayn Rand*.[19] Sixty years later this letter is well worth reading, as it must have been in 1945, for any "fan" of *The Fountainhead*. Here a few sentences will have to suffice: "There is nothing of any importance to be said or known about me—except that I wrote *The Fountainhead*." "The specific events of my private life are of no importance whatever. I have never had any private life in the usual sense of the word. My writing is my life." "I decided to become a writer—not in order to save the world, nor to serve my fellow men—but for the simple, personal, selfish, egotistical happiness of creating the kind of men and events I could like, respect and admire. I can bear to look around me levelly. I cannot bear to look down. I wanted to look up."

PUBLISHING HISTORY AND SALES

The initial printing by Bobbs-Merrill was 7,500 copies against an advance (pre-publication) sale of 6,000 copies. Sales in the summer of 1943 were slow. The book was occasionally at the bottom of best-seller lists in *The Herald Tribune*, but not on the list of *The New York Times*. Ayn Rand knew that if *The Fountainhead* did not make her famous, nothing ever would. When asked by Isabel Paterson, she said that she wanted a sale of at least 100,000 copies because that would ensure the book would reach "my kind of readers, wherever they are. My whole concern with sales was to reach the right minds."

By that fall a reprint was needed. Ogden recommended a second printing of 5,000, but the business manager in New York thought that the book would never sell more than 10,000 copies and ordered a printing of only 2,500 copies. Ogden bet him a dollar that he would need to reprint again by Thanksgiving. By then the book had sold 18,000 copies, and the business manager left a dollar on Ogden's desk without comment. Although the book kept running out of print due to the small press runs required by paper rationing, the book sold almost 50,000 copies in its first year.

Wartime paper quotas were allocated to publishers based on their sales in a base year. Blakiston, a small publisher of a one-shot Red Cross manual in that year, had a much larger quota than it could use and based on their government-provided access to paper made license deals with major publishers that now sound like a scene from *Atlas Shrugged*. After years of frustration with Bobbs-Merrill's inept advertising and production problems, she thought that the company's decision to sub-license *The Fountainhead* to Blakiston was the most decent thing it had done. To Rand's delight, Blakiston ran ads that stated the theme of the book as the story of an individualist, and they sold nearly 100,000 copies by 1945—more than Bobbs-Merrill during the same period. The book began to appear on best-seller lists in various cities. Rand thought that this was an example of word-of-mouth: her "special readers" telling other special readers about the book. In 1949 the book reappeared on best-seller lists after the release of the motion picture based on the book. The hardcover edition has remained in print by Bobbs-Merrill, and through mergers and acquisitions by Macmillan, Simon and Schuster, and Scribner.

In 1945 Bobbs-Merrill received an offer of $20,000 for rights to an abridged paperback edition. Rand refused to give permission for an abridgement. In 1952 Signet was licensed to print a complete paperback edition. That and other paperback editions have always remained in print, and through mergers and acquisitions Signet, as a part of New American Library, is now a division of Penguin Group (USA). In recent years Penguin acquired all American rights and publishes hardcover (Dutton) and trade-paperback editions (Plume).

By 1967 Bobbs-Merrill reported that more than 452,500 hardcover copies had been sold, including Blakiston and Peoples Book Club editions, and that New American Library had reported paperback sales of 1,424,182.[20] Ten years after they began publishing the hardcover edition in 1985, Macmillan reported that they had sold 29,632 copies in that period—an unusually high sales volume for an expensive hardcover novel in print for fifty years.[21]

Translations of *The Fountainhead* have been published in Chinese, Czech, Dutch, French, German, Greek, Hebrew, Italian, Japanese, Korean, Norwegian, Portuguese, Russian, Spanish, Swedish, and Turkish. Most of these translations are still in print, and the novel is currently being translated into additional languages.

At this writing sales of *The Fountainhead* in English, stated conservatively, have exceeded six and one-half million copies.[22] (Many more copies are "in-print.") That is remarkable for a lengthy and serious novel of ideas and has assured that the book has achieved much of Ayn Rand's objective of "reaching the right minds." The phenomenon is not just historic but contemporary and dynamic as annual sales have continued to climb since Rand's death in 1982. *The Fountainhead* is increasingly a part of the established curriculum of American literature in secondary schools, reaching more young readers every year with what Rand described as "a confirmation of the spirit of youth, proclaiming man's glory, showing how much is possible."[23]

NOTES

1. Biographical interviews (Ayn Rand Archives).
2. Except where indicated, Ayn Rand quotes are from the Biographical interviews (Ayn Rand Archives).
3. Biographical interviews (Ayn Rand Archives).
4. Biographical interviews (Ayn Rand Archives).
5. Biographical interviews (Ayn Rand Archives).
6. Unpublished letter (Ayn Rand Archives).
7. Biographical interviews (Ayn Rand Archives).
8. Biographical interviews (Ayn Rand Archives).
9. See Ayn Rand, *The Art of Nonfiction: A Guide for Readers and Writers*, ed. Robert Mayhew (New York: Plume, 2001), 168–69.

10. Michael S. Berliner, ed., *Letters of Ayn Rand* (New York, Dutton, 1995), 69.

11. Berliner, *Letters of Ayn Rand*, 86.

12. *New York Times*, June 23, 1943.

13. *New York Herald Tribune*, July 4, 1943.

14. *New York World*, June 7, 1943.

15. *Santa Ana Register*, December 27, 1943.

16. Biographical interviews (Ayn Rand Archives).

17. Newsletter of the Los Angeles Chapter of the American Institute of Architecture, June 1945.

18. Biographical interviews (Ayn Rand Archives).

19. Berliner, *Letters of Ayn Rand*, 669.

20. Unpublished Bobbs-Merrill memorandum (Ayn Rand Archives).

21. Unpublished letter from Macmillan (Ayn Rand Archives).

22. Publishers' Reports (Estate of Ayn Rand).

23. Introduction to the Twenty-fifth Anniversary Edition, *The Fountainhead* (various editions).

4

The Fountainhead Reviews

Michael S. Berliner

Ayn Rand's first novel, *We the Living*, was published in 1936. After slowly selling its print run of 3,000 copies, it went out of print in the United States for 23 years. Her second novel, *The Fountainhead*, published in 1943, made the best-seller list twice—in 1945 and again in 1949, when the Warner Bros. film was released—and it brought her fame. Yet, *We the Living* was much more widely reviewed. In Ayn Rand's collection of reviews there are more than 100 *We the Living* reviews, some of which were reprinted via syndication. In contrast, there are fewer than 20 reviews of *The Fountainhead*.

Many factors help account for this discrepancy. *We the Living* was timely and political—a novel with the background of Soviet Russia—and likely more attractive to reviewers. *The Fountainhead*, in contrast, has a more esoteric background, that of architecture. Then, too, by 1943 consolidation had reduced the number of daily newspapers. It is also possible that the press clippings services (Luce's and Southwest) that provided *The Fountainhead* reviews were less capable than Romeike's, which provided hundreds of *We the Living* clippings.

THE BOOK

Although fewer in number, *The Fountainhead* reviews were of greater significance, both professionally and personally; in fact, her 1960–1961 biographical interviews contain comments on many of these reviews. Heading that list—in fact, heading her list of all-time favorite reviews—was that in the *New York Times Book Review* (May 16, 1943). Lorine Pruette wrote that "it was the only novel of ideas written by an American woman that I can recall." She describes villain Ellsworth Toohey as "a brilliant personification of a modern devil," "the fascist mind at its best and worst; the use of the ideal of altruism to destroy personal integrity," "the use of sacrifice to enslave." The characters, she wrote, "are amazingly literate" and "romanticized, larger-than-life as representations of good and evil." This review had a profound effect on Ayn Rand, an effect she described in a May 18, 1943, letter to Pruette:

> You have said that I am a writer of great power. Yet I feel completely helpless to express my gratitude to you for your review of my novel.
>
> You are the only reviewer who had the courage and honesty to state the theme of *The Fountainhead*. Four other reviews of it have appeared so far, in the daily papers—and not one of them mentioned the theme nor gave a single hint about the issue of the Individual against the Collective. They all spoke of the book as a novel about architecture. Such an omission could not be accidental. You have said that one cannot read the book "without thinking through some of the basic concepts of our time." You know, as I do, that the theme is actually overstated in my novel, that it's in every line. If one reviewer had missed the theme, it could be ascribed to stupidity. Four of them can be explained only by dishonesty and cowardice. And it terrified me to think our country had reached such a state of depravity that one was no longer permitted to speak in defense of the Individual, that the mere mention of such an issue was to be evaded and hushed up as too dangerous.
>
> That is why I am grateful to you in a way much beyond literary matters and for much more than the beautiful things you said about me and the book, although they did make me very happy. I am grateful for your great integrity as a person, which saved me from the horror of believing that this country is lost, that people are much more rotten than I presented them in the book and that there is no intellectual decency left anywhere.
>
> If it is not considered unethical for an author to want to meet a reviewer, I would like very much to meet you. I have met so many Ellsworth Tooheys that it would be a relief to see a person of a different order.[1]

Eighteen years later, in 1961, she commented on this review during biographical interviews:

> That [review] really saved my universe in that period. I expected nothing like that from the *Times*. And it's the only intelligent review I have really had in my whole career as far as novels are concerned. Later, we began to get some reviews on *The Fountainhead* from other cities. And there were several very good ones that were intelligent and which I appreciated. But you know that professionally nothing counts except the New York reviews. And more than that, the ones from the provinces, though intelligent, were not really intellectual, if you know the difference. They would summarize fairly, a great many of them weren't afraid to mention the issue of individualism, but it wouldn't be in the terms in which it's stated in the book. I remember one of the best one of them that

praised my theme, described Roark as a selfless architect.[2] It's that sort of thing, you see, that undercuts any possible value it could have had for me personally.

What she especially liked about the Pruette review was

the fact, above everything else, that [Pruette] named the issue of individualism and collectivism, that she praised me as a writer, and that she quoted from Roark's speech. Otherwise I would not say that it's a review that would make me particularly happy, because of her comparisons to *The Magic Mountain* and *The Master Builder*. Why, I don't know to this day, except that she wanted to suggest literature on a grand scale, apparently. So I can appreciate the intention. But this isn't the kind of review that I would consider what I *really* would have wanted to give me a thrill. But within this culture and this context, it was better than I could expect from today's people. . . . It was intelligent throughout. And that pleased me very much.[3]

Another prominent New York review was that in the *Herald-Tribune* (May 30), written by Albert Guerard, then an English professor at Harvard University. Guerard praised the novel as daring and colorful, intellectual but not "highbrow," with a style that "would satisfy the most exacting professor." However, he characterized the selfless Peter Keating as "utterly selfish," voiced the anti-Romanticism view that the characters aren't "human," and wrote that Ayn Rand is a Nietzschean who doesn't understand America, which (he opined) is based on the rights of the majority and the Jeffersonian idea of equality, not "the divine right of genius." But, he concludes, *The Fountainhead* is a "magnificent promise" and "marvelously clever." In 1961 Ayn Rand also commented on this review:

[T]he review in the *Herald Tribune* was a horrible job. They gave it a very prominent place and all, but it was by some Leftist professor, who made a very careful job of not being clear what was *his* idea and what *I* was saying. So you couldn't untangle from his review where facts ended, that is, what *I* said, what were *my* ideas, or what was the story, and [where] his commentary began. The two were completely a package deal. And he sat very carefully on every side of the fence. He was attacking and praising at the same time. And, you see, the key line was: This book is going to sell by the carload. And you could see that he was covering himself against that potentiality, that he didn't like the book at all. This is the one that I disliked most, morally, as a review.[4]

If she read Orville Prescott's May 12 review in the daily *New York Times*— she neither comments on it nor is there a copy in her collection—she must have found it as confused as that of Albert Guerard. Seemingly unaware of (or unable to understand) the novel's ideological content (he describes Roark's dedication as "selfless"), Prescott considers it nothing more than a melodrama. And he rides the fence: on the one hand, he holds, *The Fountainhead* makes no "claim to being art," is filled with "grotesquely peculiar characters," fails to make Roark "an understandable or sympathetic character," and is difficult to take seriously. On the other hand, "seldom indeed has one first novel shone with so much concentrated intellectual passion"; *The Fountainhead*, he concludes, is "a whale of a book about architecture."

Another New York review (author and date unknown) was singled out for her displeasure:

> But the worst to me was the so-called conservatives. For instance, this man on the *Sun* wrote one of those reviews which is damning with faint praises. . . . Very interesting book. Yes, very nice, about architecture, in effect. That tone. Not one mention of the philosophical issue. It was strictly a book about two architects, one idealistic and one corrupt—that is the way he summarized it. But the worst of it was his conclusion of the summary. He said: This novel will give us great food for thought and would urge us—its message, in effect, is to urge us—to do something about clearing the slums. Believe it or not. Either the fool had never read the book, or had just glanced through it, and assuming it's architectural, he just decided that necessarily had to be the message.[5]

The most outspokenly positive review came from the *New York Journal-American*'s syndicated columnist Benjamin De Casseres, who—in the second of his two columns (May 16 and August 11) on the book—wrote that "Howard Roark towers over any man in the United States," that he is more real than any living American, and that he's a real hero (not just the central character) in "the most original and daring book of fiction written in this country. . . . the 'fountainhead' is the ego—your ego, my ego—which is the dynamo of all action and thought whatsoever." Casseres's columns, which he sent to Miss Rand, led her to write to him, saying that she'd been a reader of his column for years and always thought that Roark would be a testing-stone, by which readers' reactions would measure their own natures.[6]

Another important—albeit small—review appeared in the *Nation*, part of a long column on "Fiction in Review" by Diana Trilling.[7] It was a review that Ayn Rand termed a "nasty smear":

> Ayn Rand's "The Fountainhead" is a 754-page orgy of glorification of that sternest of arts, architecture. What Ruth McKenney's Jake Home[8] is to the proletarian movement, Ayn Rand's Howard Roark is to public and domestic buildings—a giant among men, ten feet tall and with flaming hair, Genius on a scale that makes the good old Broadway version of art-in-a-beret look like Fra Angelico. And surrounding Howard Roark there is a whole galaxy of "lesser monsters": Gail Wynand, who is Power, and Peter Keating, who is Success, and Dominique, who is Woman. When Genius meets Woman, it isn't the earth that rocks, but steel girders. Surely "The Fountainhead" is the curiosity of the year, and anyone who is taken in by it deserves a stern lecture on paper-rationing.

Other major publications dealt with the book: the *Saturday Review of Literature* (May 29), in a review by N. L. Rothman, gave it a mixed assessment but had the marvelous insight that "Roark is like the sun: it is difficult enough to see him, but to see anybody else afterward is impossible." This was another review to draw a comment from Ayn Rand in 1961:

> There was one review I liked, not as content, but as showing certain integrity in the writer, and that was in *The Saturday Review of Literature*. Because he very carefully synopsized what the book was about, praised it enormously literarily, and then in the concluding paragraphs he stated which ideas he doesn't agree with, and that he would disagree with the author on issues such and such and such. Now he didn't state the whole philosophical premise; it was more narrowly about responsibility to society or personal selfishness, so a little narrower than the theme actually is. What I admired, and which is unusual to this day, is that he could differentiate the two. That being obviously liberal, he was intellectually quite honest. . . . He did not indicate the basic ideology in the way that Lorine Pruette presented it very clearly. But he did indicate it enough that at least people would know this is not a book about architects.[9]

Aside from the New York reviews, there were, as she said, some "very intelligent ones" from other cities. Of particular meaning to her was that by Bett Anderson in the *Pittsburgh Press* (May 30). "Miss Rand," offered Anderson,

> has written an allegory, pitting Good against Evil, the individual against the herd. . . . She has set up a temple of words dedicated to all that is good and noble in man. She has written a book that is magnificent and bitter and challenging. Its impact is so terrific that the reader cannot fail to be shaken by its philosophy and its realism. Long after the book is finished, the feeling remains that it was a privilege to know Howard Roark, Architect.

And—in a brilliant prediction—Anderson termed it "a book which could conceivably change the life of anyone who read it." Five years later, Anderson wrote to Bobbs-Merrill, requesting a signed copy of the novel. In response, Ayn Rand sent her a tip sheet, writing that Anderson's review was "one of the only two which I shall always remember. Thank you for giving me hope at a time when I need it badly."[10]

Marjorie Davis's review in the *Birmingham News* (May 30) was the most philosophically oriented: "The book is the story of selfishness and unselfishness. It is an argument that the world is destroying itself by its selflessness, by it collectivist trend. The premise is that true selfishness, ego, the right of one man to be what his own mind demands, to create, alone, regardless of the pressure of opinion and of usage, is the fountainhead of human progress."

Kenneth Horan, writing in the *Chicago Tribune* (May 30), called the book original and brilliantly written, noting that it was against collectivism and in praise of the individual, but Horan thought that architecture was the *subject* rather than merely the background of the novel. In the *Boston Herald* (May 19), Alice Dixon Bond called the novel "provocative, powerful and at times brilliant" and identified the main issue as individualism vs. collectivism, quoting Ayn Rand that "there is no such thing as a collective brain."

Noted writer and critic Harvey Curtis Webster began his review[11] (headlined "You'll Admire This Radical") with a lengthy quote from Howard Roark at his trial ("one of the most moving trials in literature"), lauded all of the characterization and—though he considered the book a "half-truth" (since there have been self-appointed saviors who have helped humanity)—he nevertheless branded *The Fountainhead* "one of the better novels of our time."

None of the weekly news magazines, such as *Time* and *Newsweek*, reviewed it. It was, however, reviewed (but not positively) by major trade publications, so important in sales to bookstores and libraries. Felix E. Hirsch, in the *Library Journal* (April 15), thought it too long, made no mention of any ideas, and warned that "the amorous ways of Dominique Francon may not appeal to all." In *Book Week* (June 13), August Derleth found Ayn Rand's style to be "offensively pedestrian" and opined that she "has much to learn before she can write."

Four years after the U.S. publication, *The Fountainhead* was published in England but was as sparsely reviewed as in America. The *Times Literary Supplement*, in an unsigned review on November 15, 1947, said that it was not "responsible fiction," was thickly padded with concrete, an absurdly written book about a preposterous architect, pretentious and humorless, with gargoyles rather than characters—but sincere and surprisingly readable! The less-than-perceptive reviewer failed to grasp Roark's architectural philosophy (thinking it ultrafunctional, skeletal modernism) or Ayn Rand's style, damning it as "ultra-naturalistic."

A curious review appeared June 13, 1957, in the *Jewish Post*, a Winnipeg paper, which pointed out that Jewish youths were turning away from liberals and to *The Fountainhead*, despite it having "no Jewish characters, no Jewish issues." Apparently, the individualistic message of the novel was lost on that reviewer.

In 1968, on the occasion of the twenty-fifth anniversary edition of *The Fountainhead*, the *New York Times* (May 7) published a retrospective on the novel's history and on Ayn Rand by Nora Ephron,[12] a piece so snide that Ephron was described in the author line as promising never again to read the novel. Ephron's cynical theme was a standard one for opponents of Ayn Rand: it's a novel and philosophy that she liked as a youth ("it is better read when one is young enough to miss the [philosophical] point"), but then she grew up and now realizes it's fit only for immature, unsophisticated teenagers—a sentiment that Ayn Rand had already analyzed in her preface to that particular edition.[13]

THE FILM

In 1949, six years after the publication of *The Fountainhead*, the film version opened. In her biographical interviews, Ayn Rand had little to say about the film reviews, though she did deplore some of the "conservative" reviews, such as that in the *Chicago Tribune*, whose Mae Tinee (July 26) found the script "a first-rate bore," the characters "intolerant," and the film in general "incredibly stupid." Miss Rand's collection contains only a few reviews, mostly from New York and Los Angeles. Most of the Los Angeles papers were very positive, in fact more positive than was Ayn Rand herself. The *Los Angeles Times'* Ruth Waterbury (June 24) couldn't imagine better casting than Gary Cooper as Roark, a performance praised by the other Los Angeles dailies. All reviews mention (almost in passing) that the theme is "rugged individualism." Harrison Carroll of the *Evening Herald-Express* (June 24) wrote that Cooper's "performance, like the character, has integrity," and the *Mirror*'s Jack D. Grant (June 24) wrote that "seeing such heroes and heroines on the screen, I wonder why Hollywood bothers to turn out so many biographies of real people. Most real ones are far less interesting." However, Darr Smith of the *Los Angeles Daily News* (July 24) was in the unique position of maintaining that the ideas of *The Fountainhead* were confusing, in fact "gargantuan" in their lack of clarity: "it is as if the producers were afraid to state any idea clearly—afraid that they might be called capitalistic social pariahs on [the] one hand or dangerous radicals on the other."

The trade publications were also generally positive, *Box Office Digest* (June 25) calling King Vidor's directing "masterful" and Gary Cooper's performance "powerful" and quoting *Variety*'s conclusion that it's "a blue-chip picture." In a rave review, *Daily Variety* (June 23) termed Ayn Rand's adaptation of her novel "masterful" and "a memorable achievement." *The Hollywood Reporter* (June 23) was mixed, calling the film "compelling" but the characters "weird" and Ayn Rand's dialogue "a poor imitation of Eugene O'Neill."

National magazines were less than positive. *Newsweek* (July 25) complained that the "intellectual and moral issues become so complicated that it will bewilder anyone who has been clinging to the few wisps of logic that survive an even more baffling narrative." And, rather than grant the film a review, *Life* magazine (March 6, 1950) merely listed it as one that it was "not sorry to snub," branding it "a masterpiece of inanity."

The New York media were brutal: "pretentious" (*World-Telegram*), "absurd" and "confusing" (*Daily News*); "silliest picture of the year" (*Sun*); and "half-baked philosophy" (*Daily Mirror*).[14] *Cue* magazine (July 9, 1949) found the film even more "incomprehensible" than the novel and thought Ayn Rand had turned it into a "Sunday supplement story fit for the tabloids and the trash basket." *The New Yorker* (July 17, 1949) made fun of the plot and revealed its own philosophic premises when it concluded that the "trial scene adds up to an endorsement of the notion that a talented individual owes nothing to society, a point of view that was probably popular in Cro-Magnon days."

But the most important comments came in the *New York Times*, where it was reviewed by Bosley Crowther, the dean of reviewers, and in such a way as to presage much of the treatment of Ayn Rand in the next 33 years. In his formal review (July 9, 1949), Crowther blasted the film as "twaddle" and a "long-winded preachment on the rights of the individual." But it was his July 17 column ("In a Glass House: Reckless Ideas Spouted by 'The Fountainhead'") that drew Ayn Rand's written response. Crowther twitted Warner Bros. for making the film because, he opined, it justifies writers destroying films if studios change them. Crowther said almost nothing about the film, instead focusing on the message. Without naming any of the film's ideas, he charged it with having contempt for the masses, with being pretentious, and with having illogical, absurd, empty, and half-baked ideas. And, of course, a megalomaniac hero. One week later (July 24), the *Times* printed, as a letter to the editor, Ayn Rand's 750-word response.[15] After praising Warner Bros. for its integrity and for producing "the most faithful adaptation of a novel ever to appear on the screen," she proceeded to name the things that Crowther damned by innuendo, i.e., the "dangerous ideas" and the "high-sounding but absurd and empty things." "Man," she wrote,

> has an inalienable right to his own convictions and to his own work, the right to exist for his own sake, neither sacrificing himself to others nor sacrificing others to himself; neither forcing his ideas upon others nor submitting to force, violence or breach of contract on their part; the only proper form of relationship between men is free exchange and voluntary choice. To whom can this philosophy be dangerous? Only to the advocates of man's enslavement, the Collectivists, such as Communists, Fascists, and all their lesser variations. To them, this philosophy is very dangerous indeed. . . . Am I to understand that Mr. Crowther shares [that] philosophy?[16]

With *The Fountainhead*, Ayn Rand became a presence in America culture. Her next (and final) novel, *Atlas Shrugged*, was not published for 14 years. Although she was far from pleased with reviews of *The Fountainhead*, they mark a high point: no other Ayn Rand book was reviewed positively in the *New York Times* until *Letters of Ayn Rand*, published 13 years after her death. Reviews of *Atlas Shrugged* (1957) and subsequent nonfiction books were generally so vitriolic as to make the *Fountainhead* reviews seem glowing by comparison.

NOTES

1. Michael S. Berliner, ed., *Letters of Ayn Rand* (New York: Dutton, 1995), 74–75. Ayn Rand's daily calendars note four meetings with Pruette, the first in 1947 on one of her visits to New York from California. The Ayn Rand Archives contains seven letters to her from Pruette and six letters from her to Pruette, between 1946 and 1951.

2. S. M. Sharkey Jr., in the *Philadelphia Inquirer Public Ledger*, May 23, 1943.

3. Biographical interviews (Ayn Rand Archives).

4. Biographical interviews (Ayn Rand Archives).

5. Biographical interviews (Ayn Rand Archives).

6. See Berliner, *Letters of Ayn Rand*, 75, 91.

7. The *Nation*, June 12, 1943. In her 1993 memoir, former Communist sympathizer Trilling writes that "As fiction critic of the *Nation*, I would write as an avowed anti-Communist" (*The Beginning of the Journey* [New York: Harcourt Brace, 1993], 181). However, she remained an avowed "liberal," who had become disillusioned with Stalin rather than with left-wing ideology—and thus hardly sympathetic to Ayn Rand's individualism.

8. Jake Home is a character in Ruth McKenney's 1943 novel of the same name.

9. Biographical interviews (Ayn Rand Archives).

10. In the Ayn Rand Archives.

11. The clipping in the Archives contains the date (June 6) but omits the name of the newspaper. A longtime professor at the University of Louisville, Webster reviewed books for many major publications.

12. "*The Fountainhead* Revisited" is one of twelve chapters in *Wallflower at the Orgy*, a collection of Ephron essays (Viking Press, 1970).

13. "It is not in the nature of man—nor of any living entity—to start out by giving up, by spitting in one's own face and damning existence. . . . Some give up at the first touch of pressure; some sell out; some run down by imperceptible degrees and lose their fire, never knowing when or how they lose it. Then all of these vanish in the vast swamp of their elders who tell them persistently that maturity consists of abandoning one's mind; security, of abandoning one's values; practicality, of losing self-esteem. Yet a few hold on and move on, knowing that the fire is not to be betrayed, learning how to give it shape, purpose and reality. But whatever their future, at the dawn of their lives, men seek a noble vision of man's nature and of life's potential. There are very few guideposts to find. *The Fountainhead* is one of them." (xi)

14. Alton Cook, *New York World-Telegram*, July 9, 1949; Wanda Hale, *New York Daily News*, July 9, 1949; Eileen Creelman, *New York Sun*, July 9, 1949 (Creelman also lamented that Roark "had no thought for the people who'd been counting on those homes" he blew up); Lee Mortimer, *New York Daily Mirror*, July 9, 1949.

15. For the complete letter, see *The Intellectual Activist*, March 1996.

16. The film continues to attract attention (usually unsympathetic) as a subject of cultural analyses. See, for example, Peter Biskind's *Seeing is Believing* (Pantheon, 1983) and Robert Spadoni's "Guilty by Omission: Girding *The Fountainhead* for the Cold War" (*Literature Film Quarterly*, January 1, 1999).

5

Adapting *The Fountainhead* to Film

Jeff Britting

INTRODUCTION

In 1943 Ayn Rand was hired by Warner Bros. Pictures, Inc., to write the motion picture adaptation of her novel *The Fountainhead*. The finished film, based on Rand's script, was released in 1949.[1] However, the script's development phase—one supervised by producer Henry Blanke[2]—did not involve Rand alone. Hollywood studios rarely entrusted their film adaptations to the authors of primary works; multiple writers frequently were employed. In addition, studio executives, producers, directors—and censorship boards—contributed to the shaping of final scripts. Rand's experience at Warner Bros. was no exception.

Indeed, during Rand's tenure on the project, Warner Bros. hired two other writers to create separate, competing adaptations of *The Fountainhead*. These writers were familiar with the novel and Rand's initial screenplay. Their alternative versions are revealing, not only of a process unfolding behind studio walls but of Hollywood's general attitude toward the controversial book and its ideas—an attitude against which Rand was steeled to fight.

The fact of these three competing versions posed a basic question: Would the film adaptation of *The Fountainhead* remain "*The Fountainhead*" that Rand originally conceived?[3]

AYN RAND'S FIRST DRAFTS

When Ayn Rand first considered adapting the novel, her goal was book promotion. While early sales of the novel appeared promising, she considered her publisher's marketing effort inept. Convinced that book sales of 100,000 copies would ensure that the novel reached its core readership, she imagined that a film adaptation would increase the likelihood of such sales.[4]

Story departments of Hollywood studios evaluated newly published works in order to determine their screen potential. When Warner Bros.'s own synopsis of *The Fountainhead* came to the attention of Henry Blanke, one of the studio's most distinguished producers, he was initially unimpressed. It remained for Barbara Stanwyck, a political conservative under contract to Warner Bros., to persuade Blanke to read the actual book. This transformed Blanke's opinion of the story. His enthusiasm led to its purchase by Warner Bros. and to his assignment as its producer. Rand's contract included the opportunity to write the preliminary script. However, in keeping with standard Hollywood practice, the studio reserved the right to make changes of any kind and at any time.[5]

Although pleased with her contract and the potential book promotion, Rand expressed reservations about *The Fountainhead*'s suitability as film material. In fact, she was certain that the book was *not* ideally suited, and she identified several problems with the novel. First, the biographical nature of the story encompassed an overly expansive eighteen-year period of time. Second, the novel's events were predominately psychological. The "direct climax," as she put it, did not occur until the novel's final part. Nonetheless, Rand thought that the novel could be made into a good, technically acceptable film. And toward that end, Blanke directed Rand to draft a literal adaptation that would include as much of the story as possible. He envisioned a "play form" script out of which a shorter version would be crafted.[6]

Rand began her preliminary notes in December 1943. She focused on the story's action, i.e., the *events* intended to carry the theme of her story. Her mature views on literary action and theme are presented in *The Romantic Manifesto* and are worth recalling here.[7]

In her *Manifesto* Rand writes that a fictional story about men's lives has to be presented in action, i.e., in terms of events. Events are the "building blocks of a novel." It is by exercising "selectivity in regard to events" that a literary artist manipulates and recreates reality. "The means of exercising that selectivity and of integrating the events of a story is the plot." A plot is *"a purposeful progression of logically connected events leading to the resolution of a climax."*[8] Literary events are not random. They add up to and express a central topic, or *theme.* A "cardinal principle of good fiction," she writes, one applying equally to plot-novels and their film adaptations, is: *"the theme and the plot of a novel must be integrated."*[9]

To achieve such integration, an important transition between selecting a theme and devising a plot is the work's "plot-theme." Rand defines plot-theme as "the central conflict or situation of a story—a conflict in terms of action, corresponding to the theme and complex enough to create a purposeful progression of events." And further: "The *theme* of a novel is the core of its abstract meaning—the *plot-theme* is the core of its events."[10]

Ayn Rand's effort to adapt *The Fountainhead*—i.e., to re-craft the novel's action—began with two key statements. First, she defined the "general theme" (elaborating this even further in an undated note as "Specific theme, as presented in the screenplay"). Second, she set out the screenplay's plot-theme.

She would define the theme of her novel as: "Individualism versus collectivism, not in politics but in man's soul."[11] The novel's events express this theme over the full range of human affairs: politics, creativity, love, art, a view of life and the world. Each character embodies aspects of either *individualism* or *collectivism*. The novel's 694 pages (in the original hardback edition) provide the widest possible scope for the characters and their actions. However, film adaptation requires condensing, omitting, or restating the novel's events and/or introducing new ones. From her notes we learn that what apparently governed the selection of these events was a reworking of the theme. While the theme remained essentially the same, she appeared to narrow it somewhat, creating, in effect, a new principle governing the condensing of the novel's action.

In notes dated December 13, 1943, Rand defined the restated theme of her script as: "Man's integrity."[12] Elaborating the theme "as presented in the screenplay," she writes the following:

> Independence—as against obeying the wishes of others, as against the "social" spirit, which is: Keating, who tried to live by public polls; Wynand, who tried to use the mob; Toohey, who consciously used collectivism for the purpose of gaining power and enslaving mankind.
>
> Therefore, Roark's speech must summarize the above, give it a statement— the *good* is not the *social*, but the *individual*, not the herd-instinct, but independence; to live for yourself or for others is an issue of the spirit, the choice between one's own judgment and the surrender of one's judgment, between integrity and mental prostitution. The form of a society will be the result of this basic issue.[13]

Turning to the story's plot-theme or the "core of its events," she sets out the following:

> Howard Roark, an architect, a man of genius, originality and complete spiritual independence, holds the truth of his convictions above all things in life. He fights against society for his creative freedom, he refuses to compromise in any way, he builds only as he believes, he will not submit to conventions, traditions, popular taste, money or fame. Dominique Francon, the woman he loves, thinks that his fight is hopeless. Afraid that society will hurt and corrupt him, she tries to block his career in order to save him from certain disaster. When the disaster comes and he faces public disgrace, she decides to take her revenge

on the man responsible for it, Gail Wynand, a powerful, corrupt newspaper publisher. She marries Wynand, determined to break him. But Roark rises slowly, in spite of every obstacle. When he finally meets Wynand in person, Dominique is terrified to see that the two men love and understand each other. Roark's integrity reaches Wynand's better self, Roark is the ideal that Wynand has betrayed in his ambition for power. Without intending it, Roark achieves his own revenge—by becoming Wynand's best friend. Dominique finds herself suffering in a strange triangle—jealous of her husband's devotion to the man she loves. When Roark's life and career are threatened in a final test, when he becomes the victim of public fury and has to stand trial, alone, hated, opposed and denounced by all—Wynand makes a supreme effort toward his own redemption. He stands by Roark and defends him. Wynand loses, defeated and broken by the corrupt machine he himself had created. But Roark wins without his help—wins by the power of his own truth. Roark is acquitted—and Dominique comes to him, free to find happiness with him, realizing that the battle is never hopeless, that nothing can defeat man's integrity.[14]

With theme and plot-theme firmly in mind, Rand was ready to begin writing. The first 33 script-pages were delivered on January 15, 1944. Over the course of five months, the studio logged eight additional deliveries, with the final one occurring on May 27, 1944.[15]

Blanke was impressed with the professional quality of her work.[16] In a letter to Archibald Ogden, her Bobbs-Merrill editor and great champion, Rand stated that Blanke "loves *The Fountainhead*, he admires my style of writing and he is crazy about Roark. He says there is no one in Hollywood who can write dialogue as I do. Whatever he decides to do with the story later, this much I can hold to his credit."[17] In a letter to Richard Mealand, her former boss and story editor at Paramount Pictures, she wrote, "I realize that I can't tell what will happen later, but so far everything has been wonderful for me."[18] Near the end of her work on her first draft, she wrote to Frank Lloyd Wright, whose architectural esthetics (but not his life or philosophy) was shared by Howard Roark, that given Blanke's enthusiasm, she was no longer "too afraid" of what Hollywood would do with her book. She was willing to take a chance. And though a "ruined screen version" was still a possibility, the film would still attract readers to the book, where she had stated her full case.[19]

Ayn Rand's first draft of the screenplay was 283 pages in length.[20]

Her opinion of the result was divided. Imposing the cinematic form and the screenplay style appropriate to Warner Bros. on her novel was not difficult. However, from a personal point of view, the assignment proved "boring." Although Rand enjoyed devising the script sequences, the process meant rehashing a story properly told in another medium. Yet, despite these reservations, Rand knew she "would fight to the death" to complete the adaptation herself.[21]

On the other hand, the studio's reaction was uniformly positive. In a June 1944 letter to Archibald Ogden, she describes Blanke's "complete enthusiasm and understanding of the story and no mention of changing it, ruining it or vulgarizing it. I wrote the whole script—and he made no changes whatever, except minor technical ones, which were very valuable—but no story changes at all." Although Rand was aware that the front office might impose changes at any time, that likelihood seemed improbable. "I won't repeat the compliments I got on the script—but it was really wonderful. Blanke was crazy about it."[22] In a letter to Jack Warner she wrote how glad she was to have carried out the novel's adaptation, "preserving its theme and spirit, without being asked to make bad taste concessions, such as a lesser studio would have demanded."[23]

Rand reaffirms her confidence in a second letter to Frank Lloyd Wright. "Mr. Blanke is as anxious as I am to prove to the world that an honest picture with a great message *can* come out of Hollywood."[24]

However, Rand did not realize the cost of such proof. From December 1944 to March 22, 1948, the day the studio called her to confirm that she would write the final script—less than four months before the start of filming—the studio's choice of writer remained undecided.[25] Meanwhile, two other writers at Warner Bros. had written—or actually *were* writing—separate adaptations of *The Fountainhead*, inserting their own, very different messages.

THE THAMES WILLIAMSON VERSION

By the summer of 1944, preliminary work on the film version of *The Fountainhead* came to a close. After the completion of the initial drafts, the project became one of the many studio literary properties vying for production.

The resumption of interest by Warner Bros. in *The Fountainhead* occurred nearly six months after Ayn Rand completed the initial script.[26]

Director Mervyn LeRoy—newly engaged under a long-term contract—persuaded the studio to let him direct what was now considered an important studio property.[27] He recalled: "For weeks, we had gradually whittled away at the book's 754 pages and had forged what I think was an excellent screenplay."[28] Under LeRoy's stewardship, the forging of the screenplay appears to have been assigned to writer Thames Williamson.[29] Williamson's notes, treatment, and 61-page script survive from a two-month period of work, which ended on April 3, 1945.[30] LeRoy called the project a "war casualty." Like many films at the time, its development was halted by the "War Production Board, because the sets . . . would use too many strategic materials." LeRoy recalled his failure to direct the film a "bitter disappointment."[31]

Williamson's analysis and script sample indicate the unrealized direction of this "casualty." He appears to write in direct response to Rand's own presentation of "man's integrity." Since the brunt of Williamson's suggested revisions involved Dominique, Rand's basic approach to the character is worth reviewing.

In Rand's script, the events or literary building blocks are a series of "entities" linked by their "actions." But the series comprising the story is not a random one. The underlying entities are conscious human beings, and the actions they undertake reflect their fundamental values. And because the story is fiction, not journalism, their goals are subject to increasing conflict and potential frustration at every stage of the story. The characters' personal stakes intensify, and their motives are clarified. This sequence continues until the specific issues motivating the characters in the first place reach their climax and are resolved.

For example, Dominique is a character with a passionate interest in integrity and a bitter contempt for a world she regards as incompatible with integrity. In Rand's script, Dominique is introduced criticizing Keating and her father's architecture for its lack of originality. She then flees from their world of convention by sequestering herself in her father's county home. Rather than escaping, she finds herself confronting Roark, a character who won't allow her to temporize. She chooses to engage him. Later, she discovers that his character matches his physical presence. This heightens her conflict: it is the tension between a man she wants and her belief that such a man is not possible in the world she despises. Thereafter, Dominique decides to destroy Roark before the world can wreck him. She does this by offering up her own self-destruction. Yet, when she attempts to destroy herself by marrying Wynand, her marriage brings her into closer contact with Roark and his integrity. The issue for Dominique sharpens. Ultimately, given her character (and actions), she faces a fundamental choice: losing what she really values (Roark) versus discarding her mistaken view of the world. She chooses Roark. But even this decision, made with total serenity of spirit and inner confidence, is, nevertheless, a decision made when the stakes for both Roark and her are at their highest. This is the period after Roark's arrest and before his trial, when his future imprisonment is a real possibility.

Rand draws Dominique's character in an extremely calculated, romantic literary style; nothing is accidental. This is true of all of her characters, whether they are seeking independence in order to pursue the work they value (Roark) or are seeking to instill dependence and, therefore, control over the people they fear (Toohey).

Man has free will. He has the capacity for choice, and his choices matter. And he chooses according to his values. These elements are essential to a literary school Rand called "romantic." Rand considered herself a Romantic Realist.[32]

Williamson appears drawn to the realism side, at least to the extent that he makes an effort to stay within the basic confines of the story. However, his own style is the opposite of Rand's romanticism. Instead, Williamson is a *naturalist*. Whereas Rand's script contains a plot (i.e., a logical progression of events) and a specific theme uniting these events, Williamson removes the plot entirely. Instead, his literary building blocks are not entities linked by their actions (and purpose); they are entities distinguished by their randomness. These entities are still conscious human beings, but the actions they undertake no longer reflect their fundamental values. There are no fundamental values. His story is at best a chronicle: not fiction but quasi-journalism; in effect, his *report* on *The Fountainhead*.[33]

Williamson begins with a general assessment of Rand's script. In his preliminary notes, he observes that in order to "keep the story clear, straight and absorbing" most of the dialogue should be rewritten, much of which "is now either stuffily intellectual, too obvious, out of character, out of focus, or just plain over-written." While anticipating the inevitable shortening of the script—for instance, he suggests omitting the Stoddard Temple and other "scenes not contributing to the central story line"—the bulk of his analysis concerns the "all-important attitude of Dominique towards Roark."[34]

How does Williamson recast this attitude? What is her motive? Without the conflict between Dominique's passionate devotion to integrity and her mistaken belief that the world is set against integrity—and the plot built from that conflict—what other conflicts are possible?

Williamson begins by identifying three:

First, according to Williamson's preliminary notes, Rand's script has Dominique objecting to Wynand's friendship with Roark out of "jealousy." However, this "is a trivial and confusing motive; she should object because Fate and Roark are turning Wynand into a deserving husband, and since she is Roark's woman she cannot bear the resulting implication."[35]

Second, Williamson also notes that Rand's Dominique overcomes her fear of the world and, after years of estrangement, Roark learns the news. However, Dominique still remains Wynand's wife, a fact that Rand missed turning into conflict:

> Dominique, now having morally earned Roark, must want to leave Wynand for Roark; Roark, always strong and fair, refuses her because Wynand has proven himself a man and therefore does not deserve to be sold short.[36]

Third, Williamson observes that Rand's Dominique is "deeply moved" by Wynand's effort to defend Roark after the dynamiting of Cortlandt. But Williamson asks: "What is her feeling?":

> In the script it is neither clear nor properly exploited. Wynand should be played by a very attractive actor, who in this scene appears to be winning Dominique away from Roark. *This is a vital switch.*[37]

(At this point, as added character note, Williamson writes: "About twice, in richly moving poignant scenes, Roark should employ a pet name for the girl—for instance Dommie or Neeki.")[38]

A close comparison of Rand's script and Williamson's synopsis reveals other changes with respect to Dominique.

In Rand's script, Dominique and Roark begin their love affair under antagonistic circumstances. The encounter is touched by irony. Ultimately, Dominique is attracted to more than Roark's brute physicality. The irony is dramatized by Roark's obvious intelligence as a mere quarry worker replacing the broken marble. It is also present in the sharp, knowing exchange between Dominique, on horseback, and Roark, on foot, which occurs after he has spurned her by not returning to re-set the marble himself. These dramatic exaggerations are made plausible—and the irony real—because of the extreme intelligence and sensitivity of the characters involved.[39]

Williamson's interpretation is different. The characters are totally recast: "Bored and restless," Dominique goes to her father's granite quarry, where she encounters Roark. She "entices" him to her home with a "tale" of a job. Roark comes but spurns her. Williamson notes: "Omit his lecture on marble, in order to keep him apparently a workman." Roark "sends Pasquale to do the inset job, the enraged Dominique seeks Roark out and makes a monkey of him, he follows her home and rapes her." Thames notes: "Omit the device of Dominique on horseback slashing him across the face—this is dime-novel corn."[40]

In Rand's script, Dominique encounters Roark at a party and discovers his true identity. She expresses her admiration for his Enright House design. Later, Dominique comes to Roark's apartment, confessing her love for him. She also reveals what she regards as the hopelessness of his effort to build according to his principles. She declares she will destroy Roark before the world does.[41]

Again, Williamson recasts the situation. When Dominique comes to Roark's apartment, he redefines the motives of both characters. "In this scene, Dominique's antagonism toward Roark is purely personal and sexual, arising from wounded pride when she finds she cannot twist him around her feminine finger." Wishing to leave, "she is held by her passion for him. Even as she gives in, however, she says she will break him—Roark laughs and proceeds to collect his flesh."[42]

Williamson proposes a major change for Roark as well.

In Rand's script, Roark dynamites Cortlandt—and the public's fury against Roark flows into the courtroom, where Roark goes on trial. In his own defense, Roark gives a speech presenting the philosophy of individualism, including its view of human survival and the importance of firsthand creativity. Roark derives a case for his own innocence in view of the deliberate destruction of *his* work.[43]

While Williamson writes that adhering to the final portion of Rand's book is proper, nevertheless, "the whole dynamiting business will have to be done differently. . . . As it is, it would ruin the picture." He explains:

> Roark's long and academic defense is not legal argument, does not come to grips with the indictment against him, and very possibly would not even be permitted in a court of law. The judge would certainly instruct the jury to bring in a verdict of guilty; even if an emotionally swayed jury were to vote for acquittal, the audience would refuse to accept such a verdict. The audience would probably consider Roark outrageously and criminally high-handed, and—in these days of housing shortage—they would go out of the theatre thinking him nothing short of a monster.[44]

Williamson ends his notes on *The Fountainhead* "more and more convinced that it can be a great picture—and this without sacrificing or changing of any of the fundamental values of the book."[45]

The real question is: What did Williamson regard as those "fundamental values"?

The answer is not clear. Interestingly, though, one comment does indicate a fundamental value in Williamson's approach. Noting that when Wynand agrees to reverse the position of the *Banner* on Cortlandt, thereby indicating Wynand's failure to

> live up to Roark's ideals, Roark's character requires him to now want to take Dominique away for his own, but the girl . . . is retained by her compassion for Wynand. . . . *Fate has blocked Roark and Dominique once more*, and they are freed only when Wynand kills himself.[46]

According to Rand, "fate" is an essential attribute of literary *naturalism*. Fate determines that circumstances outside a writer's control will, ultimately, shape a story and propel its characters. In such a universe, free will is absent. Williamson approaches Rand's script not as a moralist presenting a new approach to integrity, but as a journalist, reporting on the characters' psychologies (and actions) without wider significance. Rand's integrated plot structure is omitted. There are no significant goals. The characters derived from Rand's story no longer (and can no longer) embody anything beyond the moral commonplaces in life, as Williamson reports them.

As a result of Williamson's journalistic perspective, no combination of intelligence and sensitivity will make the dramatic situations in Rand's script convincing. Such situations are unseemly exaggerations or "dime-novel corn" when compared to more "realistic" explanations of human behavior, such as Dominique's "wounded pride" or Roark's impulse to "collect his flesh."

To summarize Williamson's naturalism: The reason that Roark and Dominique are fated to join each other after Wynand's suicide, or that Roark
should appear a criminal "monster" when defending himself philosophically
also explains why Williamson found Rand's original script "stuffily intellectual, too obvious, out of character, out of focus" and "plain over-written."
The reason is the empty pretense at a self-determination that human beings
simply do not possess.[47]

There is no evidence that Ayn Rand read Williamson's script.[48] However,
in a letter to Blanke composed six months after the work described above,
Rand addresses issues very similar to those raised by Williamson. Her letter
is an almost point-for-point rebuttal of Williamson's view of her script's
story structure, romanticism, and intellectual content.

Rand calls her letter to Henry Blanke a "postscript to the script of *The
Fountainhead*." After acknowledging the "truly inhuman . . . awful landslide
of contradictory opinions possible," she writes that her own letter is her

> attempt to stand by you in spirit in a battle that is mine, too, but which I will
> not be present to share. This letter is in the nature of ammunition that I'd like
> to give you. I'd like you to refer to it when you find yourself in doubt and un-
> der fire.[49]

The Fountainhead, she continues, "is in a class of its own." It is "constructed like a very delicate and complex mechanism." Any inept handling
"will make it collapse into junk." The literary mechanism or *form* that Rand
refers to is Romantic Realism. In what could be a direct reference to
Williamson's naturalism, she writes:

> The method of romantic realism is to make life more beautiful and interesting
> than it actually is, yet give it all the reality, and even a more convincing reality
> than that of our everyday existence. Life, not as it is, but as it could be and
> should be.

Noting that her approach cannot succeed without full understanding of
this method, she writes that the contemporary school of writing "aims at
cheap journalistic realism—trying to represent life 'just like the folks next
door.' Any touch of that approach would destroy *The Fountainhead*."

The characters of *The Fountainhead* "are unusual people who do unusual
things." (Williamson would probably describe such characters as being
"over-written.") And audiences will accept such characters only when they
are presented consistently. However, if these characters "are weakened and
diluted" through humanizing, journalistic touches, "they will become un-
real, false—and silly."

The whole of her script has been "stylized to a heroic scale." The script
will not survive tampering "by people who mean 'vulgar and common-

place' when they say 'human.'" Heroes on this scale do not "have toothaches, don't act like the folks next door and don't use dialogue like: 'Gee, it's swell.'" (The parallel in Williamson is Roark's use of "Dommie or Neeki.")

In an interesting (unanticipated) reference to Williamson's criticism of Rand's dialogue as "stuffily intellectual," Rand writes:

> I know that you will be subjected to a deluge of advice, suggestions, interference and criticism, all of it to the effect that "The characters aren't human—their dialogue is too literary—the whole thing is too intellectual—it won't play well—it's not a *regular* movie—etc." I know it because I have gone through all that before. *That* was precisely the kind of opposition I found when I submitted my book to publishers. Twelve publishers rejected it. They rejected it because they said it was *too intellectual to be popular*.

The "practical moral" to be drawn is that the novel "represents something totally new; what it represents is wanted and liked by the public; but since it is so new, it frightens and bewilders all the so-called experts." Rand offers a "specific rule" to follow throughout production:

> Whenever anything is suggested, just ask yourself: *is this the way it's usually done in pictures?* If it is, you can be certain that it's wrong for *The Fountainhead*. Whenever anything is criticized because *it hasn't been done before*, you can be certain that it's the right thing.

The most "pernicious" of possible tampering, she warns, would consist of trying to please those who admire *The Fountainhead* and those who dislike it. The essence of this position is: "We don't have to worry about the book's admirers—we've got them anyway. Now let's appease the dissenters and we'll get everybody." Rand writes: "*This* is the worst of all possible courses to take—the most surely fatal. It never works that way. It works exactly the other way around. You don't please everybody—you lose everybody. It's what's known as 'sitting between two chairs.'"

She also writes: "You must believe the thesis of *The Fountainhead* in regard to its production. That thesis is not just fiction and it does not apply just to architects: *man must act on his own judgment.*"

One paragraph, though, dramatizes the dangers ahead:

> You have a Stoddard Temple on your hands. Unless everyone whom you select to work with you and whom you allow a voice in the production shares the spirit of Roark—what you'll get will be a Home for Subnormal Children.

As a "war casualty," the Williamson script died before it had the opportunity to present "unusual people who do unusual things" in a journalistic manner, portraying "man as he is." A second adaptation, however, would offer a view of man as he "ought to be"—and with its writer basing that ideal on the philosophy expressed by the *villain* of the novel.

THE HARRIET FRANK JR. VERSION

From December 1945 to February 1948, work on *The Fountainhead* appears to have been placed on hold.[50] Rand would not learn about the resumption of production plans until she read the studio's own notice in the Hollywood trade press.

On February 18, 1948, Warner Bros. announced that King Vidor would direct *The Fountainhead*.[51] Several days later the studio announced that the film's scenes would be shot in New York City, Chicago, and Rio de Janeiro. On April 1, Warner Bros. announced that Rand would begin scripting the screenplay. These announcements, however, omit an eleventh-hour effort by another screenwriter to adapt *The Fountainhead*.[52]

On March 23, 1948, Harriet Frank Jr. submitted 17 pages of character and script analysis, followed on March 30 by a 33-page screenplay sample of *The Fountainhead*. These materials—partly delivered to the studio on the very day Rand herself entered the studio to begin final work on her own script—could not have been more opposite philosophically from Rand's.[53]

Unlike Williamson, Frank made Roark, not Dominique, the focus of her criticism—and this criticism would result in a major revision of the ethical and political content of the script.

In Frank's view, Roark as presented in the book is "completely divorced from his human relationships." He "is not concerned with public opinion, the opinions of the people for whom he builds, the attitudes of his critics, or even the solicitude of his friends." Rather than jelling into a character of "heroic proportions," Roark "becomes a sort of automaton, rarely moved to compassion, and even less frequently to love." This affects his relationship with Dominique "in almost a pathological way. He is happiest when she is threatening to destroy him, which indicates a sort of masochism." As a corrective, Frank suggests that in presenting "a man who has great integrity, who believes in the freedom of the artist . . . . [i]t should be apparent that he must also be a man of great human warmth." She recommends including "a sense of humor" and evidence of being "subject to disappointment and anger, the same as any other man." Such character attributes will not "impinge on his creative drive or his convictions. . . ," rather, they will "lessen somewhat the absurdity of a man who at every turn delivers his opinions as though he were handing down the Ten Commandments."[54]

On the other hand, Dominique is "as pure a case history as one might find in any textbook on psychology." Her goal to destroy Roark is "a thin cover-up for a passion for self punishment." This "censurable and pathological" behavior, even if allowed on screen, exhibits a "degree of abnormality" that would be "incomprehensible to most audiences." Frank, however, offers an explanation. Dominique's background could include a relative, such as her mother, who "had tried desperately to rise above the limitations of her social background and had tried to express herself artistically and had died trying." This would explain Dominique's conviction that "it is not worth the struggle to be an honest human being." When Dominique falls in love with Roark, she realizes that he is a man "who 'will die trying.'" Frank explains that because Dominique "has been reared and educated in a parasite background among phonies, she knows how quickly they can reduce Roark to financial and artistic disaster." Convinced that Roark's struggle is futile, Dominique "would rather see him unrecognized and unsung . . . than be forced against the wall. She cannot endure a repetition of what she has seen once in her lifetime." Thus, "It is only when she becomes convinced that Roark's enormous strength will carry him though that she returns to him."[55]

Wynand's character, she writes, "is drawn as a man whose chief amusement in life is a destruction of honest human beings." Upon meeting Roark, "a man whom he cannot destroy," Wynand, "[c]ontrary to any basic psychology," becomes Roark's "devoted admirer, and through this admiration he becomes regenerated." Frank concludes that this progression is "sheer nonsense and completely out of character." Though Wynand lacks "scruples," his character is not entirely evil. His "lack of a moral code" is the result of his "arduous climb from the slums of New York City," which has determined "the only methods that he knows." A man of "consuming vanity and a kind of self-possessed arrogance. . . ," Wynand regards himself as "invulnerable, until he meets a woman with whom he falls in love." After realizing that Dominique "belongs to another man, the veneer of civilization drops away from him and he reverts to type." Wynand's "contempt for humanity makes him Roark's natural enemy."[56]

Peter Keating and Catherine Halsey are subjected to comments of narrower scope. She recommends that Keating be depicted with "greater viciousness and greater pathos." Catherine, who appears "almost feebleminded" in the novel, should "become one of those unattractive women whose great tenderness of heart and courage make her attractive. It is her struggle to preserve a weakling [Keating], to lend him her own strength, that makes their love story interesting and moving."[57]

About collectivist critic Ellsworth Toohey, Frank writes the following, which I present in its entirety:

> Miss Rand's boogy-man, is much too much involved politically. Unless you wish to embark upon delicate political matters, it would appear to be a wiser course to transform him into a slightly feminine, witty "yes" man to Gail Wynand.[58]

Curiously, in seeking to avoid "delicate political matters," it appears that Frank kept such "matters" flowing rather delicately beneath the surface of her scenario, by indirection rather than open statement. Like Williamson, Frank constructed her story on "social realism." But unlike Williamson, who stayed away from morality altogether, Frank embraced whole-heartedly the very philosophy of collectivism attacked in the novel.

The first sign of the politicization of Frank's analysis is her note that Dominique "has been reared and educated in a parasite background."[59] Other examples follow.

In Rand's script, the story opens with Roark, an architect in private practice, seeking a new commission. Roark is portrayed as an entrepreneur trading his services in exchange for money. This portrayal is a corollary of Roark's independence. He is both able and willing to exchange value for value and to earn profits in a free market. The commercial nature of his work is no barrier to the practice of his art; it actually facilitates it.[60]

In Frank's scenario, the story opens as Roark's six-month effort to win the Frink National Bank commission is foundering. Roark refuses to compromise his plans. "He is unable to do so, because of his basic integrity and a fierce desire to do his creative work as he sees fit without the encumbrance of convention or *the compromise of commercialism.*"[61]

In Rand's script, Dominique, a columnist for the *Banner*, criticizes Keating and her father's firm for its lack of originality. Rebuffing Keating's personal interest, Dominique explains that she neither wants nor expects anything of value from the hypocritical and conventional world around her.[62]

In Frank's scenario, Dominique, a "cold blooded, intelligent, dissatisfied young *aristocrat,*" is introduced driving with Peter Keating to her Connecticut estate. She is "running away from her *oppressive social background* and her pending marriage to Gail Wynand," urgently seeking to "escape *the artificiality of her life.*" Although Keating is interested in Dominique, she dismisses him.[63]

In Rand's script, Dominique protests the destruction of the Stoddard Temple's physical and spiritual integrity. By marrying Wynand, who was responsible for the temple's destruction, she hopes to destroy him as well as herself. When Dominique meets Wynand, they compare basic motives: Dominique seeks to preempt integrity because the world will not permit it to exist; Wynand seeks to destroy man's pretense at integrity in a world he presumes to control. But their meeting reveals an underlying similarity: they both observe a suppressed respect for integrity and a desperate need to see it in others. This unexpected compatibility creates a certain mutual respect. Thereafter, they agree to marry.[64]

In Frank's scenario, the aspiring, albeit twisted respect for integrity (and each other) exhibited by both Dominique and Wynand is removed. Now, Dominique goes to Wynand, telling him "that they are cats out of the same alley and that they might as well be married. [Wynand] is amused at her lack of romanticism, quite willing to accept her on any basis whatsoever."[65]

In Rand's script, Peter Keating is a minor character, one introduced and developed only as required by the screenplay. Keating is Roark's professional foil. He is not important enough to expand into a major role. As a complete parasite, he is a spiritual and productive dead-end.

In Frank's scenario, Keating is not only accorded prominence in the story—"with greater viciousness and greater pathos"—he is also the means through which a minor character in the novel (who does not appear in Rand's version of the screenplay) is given a new and significant role in the screenplay. Roark returns to his New York office. A young woman waits to see him. It is Catherine Halsey, Keating's secretary, who is also in love with Keating. Catherine explains that she understands Keating for what he is, "a social climber." Further,

> she knows that his attentions to her in the past have been born of propinquity, but she doesn't care. She has come to Roark because Peter is in trouble. There is a possibility that he could be the designing architect of the huge Cortlandt project. She bets he could get the commission, except for one thing: he has been drunk and on the town for weeks and is afraid that like a surgeon with shaky hands, his designs will carry no authority. She tells Roark that she knows about his relationship to Peter and that Peter is not worth saving, except that if he recovers she feels he might marry her. She faces Roark calmly and tells him with touching honesty that some women learn that they cannot afford the luxury of being loved for themselves. She is one, but she doesn't care.
>
> Roark is profoundly moved by her innate integrity.[66]

In Rand's script, Keating attempts to build Cortlandt Homes, a housing project advanced by the collectivist Toohey and stymied by a major design problem. When Keating discovers that he cannot solve the problem, he asks Roark to design Cortlandt and to allow Keating to place his own name on the project. Roark knows that he would never be able to get past Toohey. Nevertheless, Roark is intensely interested in the design challenge. Roark agrees to Keating's request provided that Cortlandt is built as Roark designs it. However, Roark is not finished until Keating understands Roark's primary motive fully: Roark's goal is his work done his way, and does *not* involve any possible beneficiary of the housing project.[67]

In Frank's version, Roark's motive is changed radically:

> by some fluke, Keating has a chance to do what [Roark] has always wanted to do. [Roark then] explains . . . with great intensity what this housing project can mean. How he can complete it cheaply; how he will *introduce beauty to people who don't know the meaning of the word. They can live in it and with it,* etc., etc.[68]

And further:

> The plans are altered. The costs of the building soar. The whole intent of the
> project is now distorted, and with it *Roark's idealistic dream of a new way of life
> for a great many people.*[69]

Roark looks for Keating and finds him at the housing project. "They
fight—an accident results from a kerosene lantern. The Cortlandt project
burns."[70]

In Rand's script, on the day of Roark's defense, "a mob of feet are rising
up broad marble steps. . . . The people who speak are loose-faced, nasty,
sensation seeking-types." Some remark that they hope to see Roark in "jail
for life" or working "in a jute mill." Inside the courtroom, Toohey states: "I
want to see Roark in jail. You understand? In jail. Behind bars. Locked,
stopped, strapped—and alive." After being sworn in, Roark delivers a five-
and-a-half-page speech defending his actions according to the philosophy
of individualism. He is acquitted. Wynand commissions Roark to build the
Wynand building and then commits suicide.

The final scene begins with a long shot of the building under construction. The unfinished "top part of the steel skeleton is still naked. . . . It is a
long white streak slashed through space, the tallest structure in the world, a
thing of magnificent power and beauty." Dominique enters a lift that moves
up the side of the building on top of which stands "A tall, gaunt, proud figure, the heroic figure of man's creative genius."[71]

In Frank's script, Roark's trial is "preceded by small vignette scenes in
which *we see the people Roark's work has reached, those who were to live in the
housing project.*" His admirers boycott "the *Banner.*" ("Wynand still has contempt for the *small people.* They will bend to his will.") The trial proceeds
and "the accusers give their testimony. . . . Roark has no defense, except his
own final speech. Couched in very simple terms, he tells them that he never
could have set fire to the project, and why. In his own defense he makes an
eloquent plea." Roark is found not guilty.[72]

It is now spring, and Dominique enters a lift on the side of Cortlandt
Homes, "a la the Peter Cooper Village" in New York City, where she rises
into space and up to the figure of Howard Roark standing atop a public
housing project.[73]

To summarize Frank's adaptation of *The Fountainhead*'s moral plot-
theme: the creator is a man of "great integrity" and "human warmth" who
defends the "freedom of the artist," the nature of which is defined by his
moral obligation: while open to "disappointment and anger, the same as
any other man," the artist pursues his vision in the face of great obstacles,
overcoming "the compromise of commercialism" in order to serve the welfare of others.

A moral obligation based on self-sacrificial service to others, where the primary moral beneficiary is not one's self, but others, is an altruistic obligation. In the West, the primary intellectual source of the ethics of altruism is Christianity. While Frank's script does not adapt *The Fountainhead* into *The Passion of the Christ*,[74] it does incorporate ideas from the catechism of Christianity's secular equivalent: Marxism. Among these ideas are: the wealthy as "parasites"; the fascist domination of "small people"; the attack on "commercialism," i.e., capitalism; one's "social background" as the source of one's morality—and in a rich integration, the introduction of the explicitly self-less Catherine Halsey as a significant moral ideal and the idealization of the public-housing project as humane habitat.[75]

Ultimately, Warner Bros. did not choose the Frank adaptation.

However, decades after her stillborn effort, Frank would successfully complete a more congenial adaptation. In 1979 Frank received an Academy Award nomination for best-adapted screenplay from another medium for *Norma Rae*. This pro-union-themed motion picture is described in *Film and the American Left: A Research Guide* as "one of the most prominent films about organized labor in the history of American cinema, probably exceeded only in this sense by the anti-union *On the Waterfront*."[76]

There is no record of Ayn Rand having read or commented on Frank's script for *The Fountainhead*, and of course there is no possibility of it having exerted any influence on Rand's screenplay.[77] In any case, Rand's final script preserved the philosophical conflict between individualism and collectivism: Roark builds Cortlandt for his own selfish reasons, not out of altruistic concern for its future occupants, and Toohey retains his communist political sympathies.

AYN RAND'S FINAL DRAFT

Ayn Rand's return to the project was, in her view, the result of the studio's basic uncertainty over the book and its audience. The studio "did not know what to make of the book"; therefore, they "didn't know what would ruin it and what would or would not antagonize my readers. That was my great protection."[78]

Rand's first task was to review her early script, which she had not read in four years. After doing so, she discovered that the script was too literal in its approach. Without the book's context, the "same scenes, without all the rest of the complicated structure, lost their power. It showed my writing was much more integrated than I expected. To achieve an equivalent effect," the scenes had to be rewritten.[79]

For the next several weeks, Rand worked closely with Blanke and Vidor. At Blanke's request, the beginning of the script was revised to simulate the opening of the book. Also, the Stoddard Trial sequence was eliminated. Keating (now engaged to Dominique) was moved earlier in the story. Wynand was moved earlier as well, becoming the catalyst for the breaking of Keating's engagement to Dominique.[80]

A lengthy note by Rand analyzes Dominique's psychology during her scene at Roark's apartment following the Enright House opening. It suggests that character psychology remained a major concern. She viewed the scene as dramatizing "the entire progression of Roark's and Dominique's love affair in the book. Dominique's part in the scene gives her a chance to show every aspect of her character." "Dominique's basic conflict," writes Rand,

> is the violent conflict between her passion for Roark and her despair. The more she admires him, the more certain she is that he will be destroyed. She is so hurt herself that she is driven to hurt him, but her cruelty to him is only an extreme expression of her love. We must be certain that there is never a touch of feminine cattiness, vanity or malice in Dominique's performance. She defies Roark because she worships him. She defies him for the pleasure of seeing him master her. Her real desire is always to see him win.

Roark's reaction to Dominique's cruelty and despair is

> to sweep all her objections away simply by showing her the greatness of their love for each other. To him, the world can never be a threat and can never stand in the way of his own happiness.
>
> It is only when Dominique falls down on her knees and starts pleading with him that he realizes completely the extent of her despair. Then he understands that he cannot force her into his own attitude toward life, which she will have to learn herself. He acts toward her on the same principle as he acts in his professional career. He wants a voluntary acceptance, he will not force his ideas on anyone.[81]

Work on the script progressed rapidly. Rand revised it without great difficulty.[82]

In an April 1948 letter to Isabel Paterson, Rand mentions the possibility that the studio might retain her to make further script changes throughout the actual filming: "I'll tell you in person how many things have happened to justify your prediction that the studio will not be able to ruin the story. You said that the idea of the story would protect itself—and so far it has done just that."[83] The prospects for preserving the intellectual integrity of her story looked promising. She wrote to DeWitt Emery that her screenplay would result in the work of the "the first truly pro-American picture ever produced. . . . If all goes well, as I hope, you will see a real 'Manifesto of Individualism' on the American screen. I don't have to tell you how much the country needs it at present."[84] Then to Archibald Ogden, she wrote that her script "has been completed in a blaze of glory. Everyone is very happy about it, both the studio and myself. If all goes well, as it has so far, the picture will be great. The actual shooting is scheduled to start on July 8th."[85]

Rand recalled that she was willing to compromise with Blanke and Vidor on a scene if their recommendations were merely "artistically dubious" (but not ideologically wrong). She reserved all her "intellectual thunder" for the philosophic issues. She recalled that in that arena "they were really scared of me."[86]

One final writing task remained: the resolution of the dynamiting of the Cortlandt Housing Project and its defense at the trial in Roark's speech.

On June 12, 1948, less than three weeks from the commencement of filming, the "revised Temporary Script" was completed. Work on the "Final script" began. The process consisted of Rand, Blanke, and Vidor "reading the script aloud and discussing every possible cut or change for the final editing." At this point, the major critical issue became the content of Roark's speech. Rand wrote that "[t]his is the most difficult thing to write in condensed form, and the most dangerous politically and philosophically, if written carelessly."[87]

In the novel, Roark's courtroom speech is the abstract explanation of the climax of the novel, the dynamiting of the Cortlandt public housing project, a project altered without his consent. The destruction of Cortlandt links all the major characters and their themes, from Toohey to Wynand.[88] The speech defends Roark's actions according to a specific philosophy—the philosophy of individualism, which defends a man's right to his own life and work. This defense, however, proved a greater bone of contention in the creation of the screenplay than the explosive beginnings of Roark and Dominique's love affair.[89]

Without Roark's explanation, the dynamiting becomes a purely criminal act. A major studio could not permit itself to defend dynamiters. Therefore, a proper explanation was necessary. However, the only reasonable explanation was one according to Rand's philosophy. Yet, in the eyes of Hollywood authorities, such an explanation was even more fearsome.

The speech, writes Rand,

> had to be written as carefully as a legal document. I had to weigh every word, every thought—in order not to leave any loopholes which would permit anyone to accuse us of some improper ideology. I had to make every idea crystal clear, cover every possible implication, guard against any chance misunderstanding, avoid any possibility of confusion. I did it—and preserved the dramatic and literary qualities of the speech at the same time.[90]

Explaining Roark's actions meant breaking with the altruistic moral precepts of Judeo-Christianity, and thus with both the liberal left and the conservative right. Only on a basis of rational egoism can individuals successfully defend their inalienable right to life and property.[91]

In 1943, during the early phase of the script's development process, Rand wrote that "Blanke has given me no objections and no restrictions, except on the sex side—we'll have to be careful of the Hays office and treat such scenes as my famous rape scene through tactful fade-outs."[92] Rand recalled that the Production Code Administration (a.k.a. the Hays Office) had greater reservations over the philosophical content of Roark's speech than over the sexual interaction between Roark and Dominique.[93] Both producer and director were supportive but remained silent. They turned to Rand for a defense.[94]

The speech was revised a total of six times. From June 14 to September 8, eight conferences were convened in order to discuss the speech. Participants included representatives from the Warner Bros. front office, the Production Code Administration, the producer, the director, Gary Cooper's attorney, and Rand's attorney.[95]

The gist of the objections was Rand's doctrine of individualism and her rejection of self-sacrifice as a moral ideal. A letter from the Production Code Administration official, former judge Stephen S. Jackson, to Jack Warner captures this concern:

> The basic objection to the philosophic concepts of this story seems to stem from what appears to be a confusion in the conflict of two ideas. On the one hand, there is the condemnation of the subordination of the dignity, idealism, and intellectual freedom of the individual by what is characterized as "collectivism." Such a control and regimentation of individuals by force of an authoritarian state or regime is obviously repugnant to the American concept and to sound principles which recognize the dignity of the individual. The antithesis to this ideology as set forth in the story is absolute individualism, which, according to the ratiocinations set forth in the script, is absolute and supreme. The confusion seems to arise in characterizing the voluntary submission of one's intellectual attainments to the welfare of others as being the same as involuntary subjugation of individual rights and prerogatives. Self-sacrifice is regarded as the same as enforced subordination to collectivistic control.
>
> The error in such a thesis would not be of such importance in this script were it not for the fact that *this doctrine of the absolute supremacy of individualism—even to the point where it is in derogation of the rights of others and a crime against the laws of society, is formally condoned and approved by the court in the acquittal of Roark.*
>
> This unequivocal and unconditional approbation of Roark's serious violation of the law and transgression of the rights of others *is too flagrant an instance of presenting something which is wrong as being right to warrant approval under the express provisions of the Production Code.*
>
> It is suggested, therefore, in an attempt to preserve, as far as it is possible to do so consistent with the Production Code, the theme and structure of the story, that the correct position with respect to Roark's actions be set forth in the script. Whatever means the writer wishes to employ to effect this change

is, of course, not the concern or prerogative of the Production Code in any way to dictate.[96]

The waiver of the prerogative to dictate philosophical content was ambiguous. As an organization, the Production Code Administration was an offspring of private persuasion and government force. In point of fact, the administration maintained *de facto* dictatorial control over the content of motion picture scripts. At the time of *The Fountainhead*'s production and eventual release, motion pictures were not considered a constitutionally protected form of free speech. (The Supreme Court reversed its position on this matter in 1952.)[97] Thus, without Production Code approval, a completed motion picture faced arbitrary re-cutting by state and local censorship boards, or even outright prohibition.[98]

Rand's initial meeting with Production Code Administration officials, which, according to Rand, included a Catholic scholar, illustrates the administration's prerogative.[99] While supposedly non-sectarian in their moral viewpoint, the officials raised objections of a decidedly religious nature against Roark's speech. Rand recalls:

> [T]he Catholic expert, apparently, did not quite know how to phrase his objections. In other words, it was very clear to me he objected to the philosophical content but had no right to state it that way. And so he began talking about such things as, "Well, the speech is really materialistic." So, I ask him, "How can you say that?" And I point to Wynand's speech [the editorial on behalf of Roark that states man's self is his spirit]. . . . And here is this man saying, "Oh, that was a wonderful speech. We have no objection to *that* speech. But, you see, Roark's speech sounds materialistic."

The PCA official did not object to Wynand's speech because it contained the word "spirit." Ironically, Rand recalled Wynand's speech as being "much more philosophically objectionable to their viewpoint than the whole of Roark's speech."

As a result of this meeting, Blanke told Rand: "Take all the time you want, and include . . . any of the things he thinks he was confused about. . . . You explained them so well, now include all those explanations." Rand continues her narrative:

> They came a second time with the new version. And here we got into a discussion with this man, and I was telling him, "Well look, the speech advocates reason." And he began to say . . . "Well, it might be offensive to many religious people, to their religion." And I said, "How can it be? Thomas Aquinas, the great champion of reason?" That knocked the props from under him. He obviously knew nothing about Aquinas, besides knowing that that is an official Catholic saint. And anytime I told him, "Now here is what Aquinas said . . .

here is the Aristotelian line"—I gave him a few explanations—he had to agree to everything.

But the crucial point came when he . . . said, "Well, this isn't the Catholic viewpoint," something like that. I said, "Are you saying that you are going to censor or judge this speech from the point of view of whether anything agrees or disagrees with the Catholic Doctrine?" He retreated, but so fast, Blanke was about to jump in. And the man knew he had put his foot in [his mouth].[100]

By clarifying its philosophic content, Rand expanded the length of the speech. At approximately six and a half minutes, it is one of the longest in Hollywood history. Rand recalled that the Production Code Administration actually "did me a favor."[101]

Eventually, the objections from all parties were satisfied, including, for the moment, the studio front office. The filming was completed in September 1948. Warner Bros. received Production Code approval on November 24, 1948.[102] Rand's adaptation of *The Fountainhead* was shot intact.[103]

In a letter to John Chamberlain, Rand recounts her personal reaction to these events:

My experience with the movie has been perhaps even more miraculous than with the book. I wrote the screenplay myself, preserving my theme and philosophy intact. For the first time in Hollywood history, the script was shot verbatim, word for word as written. . . . [Such a picture] will be—not some weak, compromising, middle-of-the-road script—but the most uncompromising, most extreme and "dangerous" screenplay they ever had. I think this is an illustration of the power of an honest idea to reach people and to accomplish things which no amount of force or collective pressure could accomplish.[104]

CONCLUSION

A modern skyscraper of "sculptural simplicity" stands alone against what appears to be empty sky. The camera tilts upward "stressing the impression of immeasurable height and triumphant soaring." Suddenly a hand comes into the frame, "a beautiful hand with strong, masculine fingers," which closes "possessively over one of the building's set-backs."

Thus begins Rand's original 1944 screen adaptation.

The camera pulls back and reveals Roark as he is described in the novel, with a "hint of suppressed elation in his face" while he looks at the model of his building. A voice comes over the shot: "Well, Mr. Roark, the commission is yours."

The camera pulls back further, revealing the Manhattan Bank Company and three bankers seated at a table. On the table are the model and a pile of "architectural plans and drawings." The men congratulate Roark on his "beautiful job." They note his tremendous struggle and the fame-establishing opportunity the commission represents. Roark acknowledges their remarks "calmly and solemnly."

Then one of the bankers reaffirms their offer, "on one minor condition."

The building's exterior is of no known style. It is "too original." And on this account "the public won't like it." Not wishing to alter the plans in any way—the plan's ingenuity being the selling point of Roark's project—they offer, instead, a "softening" adjustment to the building's exterior. A cardboard form is slipped over the model, replacing the "beautiful modern simplicity" with what becomes a "grotesque, offensive parody" in the Classical style. "We must always," says the chairman soothingly, "compromise with the general taste, Mr. Roark. You understand, I'm sure."

In the scene, Howard Roark does *not* understand. And, as the historical record shows, neither did Ayn Rand.

Speaking for Rand, Roark throws off the Classical cardboard form and explains that honesty in men or in architecture requires that each be of "one piece and one faith." Roark says: "A man doesn't borrow pieces of his soul. A building doesn't borrow hunks of its form." He also states:

> No two materials are alike. No two sites on earth are alike. No two buildings have the same purpose. The purpose, the site, the material determine the shape. Not borrowing, copying and stealing.

This same principle applies to Hollywood adaptations. Three screenwriters adapted *The Fountainhead*. Their approaches differed, sometimes radically. Yet, for each writer, the assignment contained the issues depicted in Roark's confrontation with the committee of the Manhattan Bank. And the historical record shows what happened when two of these writers did not share the original writer's esthetic philosophy or general philosophy. They ended up "copying" the story naturalistically (Williamson) or "stealing" an opposite philosophy (Frank).

"Of course, we wouldn't alter your plans in any way," states the chairman of the bank. "It's the beautiful ingenuity of the plans that sold us on the building." So too with Warner Bros. It was the enormous success of the novel—and its continuing and growing popularity throughout the 1940s—that kept the project a possibility. And the screenwriters hired by Warner Bros. to adapt the work faced that possibility where their own integrity mattered most. Paraphrasing Roark, the purpose of the job was to erect a building called *The Fountainhead*, from one site to another, from literature to film, using the materials and concepts proper to its final shape, according to the story's original purpose or theme.[105]

The writers had to judge—and enact—the theme for themselves, subjecting their finished pages to the question posed by the chairman: "You see? It doesn't spoil anything. *Does it?*"

Fortunately, the writer who answered correctly also became the screenwriter of record—thereby insuring that *The Fountainhead* would remain "*The Fountainhead.*"[106]

NOTES

1. Production Company: Warner Bros.—First National Pictures Inc.; producer: Henry Blanke; director: King Vidor; screenplay: Ayn Rand, from her novel *The Fountainhead*; principal cast: Gary Cooper as Howard Roark; Patricia Neal as Dominique Francon; Raymond Massey as Gail Wynand; Robert Douglas as Ellsworth Toohey; Kent Smith as Peter Keating.

2. Henry Blanke was born in Berlin, Germany, December 30, 1901. He joined Universum-Film AG (UFA) in Berlin and became personal assistant to Ernst Lubitsch. His career at Warner Bros. spanned more than 30 years, during which time he worked as a producer on such significant films as *The Adventures of Robin Hood, Juarez, The Maltese Falcon*, and *The Treasure of the Sierra Madre*. "With the coming of sound Warner's became a major studio. Quickly Blanke moved into third position of power at the studio, behind only the founding brother Jack and Warner's ace assistant Hal Wallis. When Wallis left for Paramount in the mid-1940s, Blanke had no rival other than the brothers Warner themselves. He would leave the company only when it was sold to outsiders in the 1950s." Tom Pendergast and Sara Pendergast, eds., *The International Dictionary of Films & Filmmakers: Volume 4—Writers & Production Artists*, 4th ed. (Detroit: St. James Press, 2000), 100.

3. Omitted from this essay is a discussion of the overall filmmaking process, including other aspects of preproduction, as well as production and postproduction. Also omitted is an examination of the promotion and release of the film, including a look at the commercial and critical reaction, plus the re-make history. These and other topics will be addressed in my book, currently in preparation, on Ayn Rand, Hollywood and *The Fountainhead*.

4. Jeff Britting, *Ayn Rand* (New York: Overlook Press, 2004), 68.

5. Biographical Interviews (Ayn Rand Archives). The contract between the Bobbs-Merrill Company and Warner Bros. Pictures, Inc., November 3, 1943, includes the following wording: "Without in any way limiting any of the other provisions hereof, the Purchaser shall have the absolute and unlimited right for the purpose of any photoplays produced or distributed hereunder to make such changes, variations, modifications, alterations, adaptations, arrangements, additions in and/or eliminations and omission from said Writings and/or the characters, plot, dialogue, scenes, incidents, situations, actions, language and theme, therefore, . . . as Purchaser, in its uncontrolled discretion may deem advisable. . . ." (Section 17); File No. 2872—"The Fountainhead" Story File [Part 2] (Warner Bros. Archives, USC).

6. Biographical interviews (Ayn Rand Archives). By contrast, Rand thought that her novels *We the Living* and *Atlas Shrugged* would make excellent films.

7. Ayn Rand, *The Romantic Manifesto: A Philosophy of Literature*, revised edition (New York: Signet, 1975).

8. Rand, *Romantic Manifesto*, 82.

9. Rand, *Romantic Manifesto*, 85 (emphasis in the original).

10. Rand, *Romantic Manifesto*, 85. She defines art as a selective recreation of reality that expresses an artist's view of himself and his relation to the world. See *Romantic Manifesto*, 19.

11. Ayn Rand, *For the New Intellectual* (New York: Signet, 1963), 62.

12. David Harriman ed., *Journals of Ayn Rand* (New York: Plume, 1999), 234.

13. Harriman, *Journals of Ayn Rand*, 235.

14. Harriman, *Journals of Ayn Rand*, 234–35.

15. File No. 1904, "The Fountainhead" Story; Misc. (Warner Bros. Archives, USC).

16. Biographical interviews (Ayn Rand Archives).

17. Michael S. Berliner, ed., *Letters of Ayn Rand* (New York: Dutton, 1995), 105.

18. Berliner, *Letters of Ayn Rand*, 123.

19. Berliner, *Letters of Ayn Rand*, 112.

20. Ayn Rand, first draft: "The Fountainhead," *Special Collections*: 9-A,W,F,F,M-5a (Ayn Rand Archives); at least four drafts exist, but these do not include partial revisions, including some alteration made on the set during actual filming. See Rand to Collins, September 18, 1948, *Ayn Rand Papers*: 123-26-15-G (Ayn Rand Archives), 8.

21. Biographical interviews (Ayn Rand Archives).

22. Berliner, *Letters of Ayn Rand*, 152.

23. Berliner, *Letters of Ayn Rand*, 147.

24. Berliner, *Letters of Ayn Rand*, 114.

25. Rand to Alan Collins, September 18, 1948, *Ayn Rand Papers* (Ayn Rand Archives), 1.

26. A blurb written by Louella O. Parsons mentions director Mervyn LeRoy and Warner Bros.: "'The Fountainhead,' by Ayn Rand is the attractive bait that brings him there to direct it before he starts "The Robe" next August for Frank Ross. That's big news, my friends. The Rand novel is a hot property." January 22, 1945, Louella O. Parsons, Motion Picture Editor, International News Service, *Ayn Rand Papers*: 100-23-35 (Ayn Rand Archives).

27. Meryvn LeRoy was born in San Francisco in October 1900. His first effort as director was *No Place to Go* (1927), earning him the nickname "The Boy Wonder" of Warner Bros. LeRoy produced MGM's classic *The Wizard of Oz* in 1939 and *The Bad Seed* in 1956. Over his career LeRoy would direct 13 different actors in Oscar-nominated performances. LeRoy died in September 1987. Source: John Wakeman, ed., *World Film Directors, Volume One, 1890–1945* (New York: The H.W. Wilson Company, 1987), 651–57.

28. Mervyn LeRoy and Dick Kleiner, *Mervyn LeRoy: Take One* (New York: Hawthorn Books, 1974), 153.

29. Thames Williamson, described by *The New York Times* as a screenwriter/short-story author, wrote such works as "Next Time I Marry," 1938 (short story); *Cheyenne*, 1947 (screenplay); *Escape Me Never*, 1947 (screenplay); *The Last Bandit*, 1949 (screenplay); *Brimstone*, 1949 (screenplay); "The Savage Horde," 1950 (short story); *A Bullet Is Waiting*, 1954 (screenplay); *Taming Sutton's Gal*, 1957 (screenplay).

30. "The Fountainhead" production files (Warner Bros. Archives, USC).

31. LeRoy and Kleiner, *Mervyn Le Roy: Take One*, 153.

32. Rand, *Romantic Manifesto*, 167.

33. See Rand, *Romantic Manifesto*, 23.

34. Thames Williamson, "Analytical Memo on the Subject of *The Fountainhead*," January 31, 1945 (Warner Bros. Archives, USC), 1.

35. Williamson, "Analytical Memo," 1.

36. Williamson, "Analytical Memo," 1. For Rand's view of the conflict between romantic competitors and its proper resolution, see Ayn Rand, *Atlas Shrugged*, Thirty-fifth Anniversary paperback edition (New York: Signet, 1992), 741.

37. Williamson, "Analytical Memo," 2 (emphasis added).

38. Williamson, "Analytical Memo," 2.

39. Ayn Rand, first draft, 44–53.

40. Thames Williamson, "The Fountainhead" Story—Outline of Treatment, March 3, 1945, Warner Bros. Archives (USC), 4.

41. Rand, first draft, 69–87.

42. Williamson, "The Fountainhead," 5.

43. Rand, first draft, 226–29, 264–69.

44. Williamson, "The Fountainhead," 14.

45. Williamson, "The Fountainhead," 15.

46. Williamson, "Analytical Memo," 2 (emphasis added).

47. For Rand's views on volition and determinism in literature, see Rand, *Romantic Manifesto*, 100–102.

48. Various clippings mention LeRoy (*Ayn Rand Papers*: 100-23-35 [Ayn Rand Archives]) and a copy of Rand's script, dated January 20, 1945, is inscribed with LeRoy's name (*Ayn Rand Papers*: 102-23-27 [Ayn Rand Archives]).

49. Berliner, *Letters of Ayn Rand*, 242–48. Unless otherwise indicated, quotes in this section come from this letter.

50. For an overview of Rand's life and professional activities during this period, see Britting, *Ayn Rand*, 68–77.

51. King Vidor was born in 1894 in Galveston, Texas, and is regarded as one of the great directors of the silent cinema. "Vidor succeeded during most of his long career in working within the context of the commercial studio establishment without ever compromising either the artistic quality or the strong social awareness of his films." After making his name with such critically acclaimed silent films as *The Big Parade* (1925) and *The Crowd* (1928), thereafter "Vidor was principally recognized as a highly successful director of ambitious prestige subjects alternating with bizarre melodramas. . . . *The Citadel* (1938), *Northwest Passage* (1940), *Duel in the Sun* (1946), *Ruby Gentry* (1952), *War and Peace* (1956), *Solomon and Sheba* (1959)." Dr. Roger Manvell, ed., *The International Encyclopedia of Film* (New York: Crown Publishers, Inc., 1972), 494.

52. Miscellaneous media material, possibly all from "Spot News Daily Wire Service" from Warner Bros. Pictures, Inc., NYC, File 12734, "The Fountainhead" Legal (Warner Bros. Archives, USC).

53. An accomplished writer, Frank, along with her writing partner and husband, Irving Ravetch, wrote a string of well-known films, including *Hud, Stanley and Iris*, and *Murphy's Romance*. The writing team was described by *Architectural Digest* in the

April 1990 "Academy Awards Collectors edition!" as having come of age "during the depression . . . their customary escape from the grim scenery around them was, as for so many people in America in the thirties, the picture palace." Her professional efforts began at Warner Bros. in the 1940s, when she was employed to "'masculinize' the dialogue for a Dane Clark boxing picture, and she wrote *Silver Bullet*, an Errol Flynn western directed by Raoul Walsh." In an interview prepared for the release of *Murphy's Romance*, Frank stated that as far as their selection of subjects, "[w]e're committed to do what we do, and we pick our projects carefully because we want to do work we have convictions about" (Columbia Pictures, *Murphy's Romance*, 1985, media kit bio). See Harriet Frank Jr., Biography File (The Margaret Herrick Library, Academy of Motion Picture Arts and Sciences).

54. Harriet Frank Jr., "The Fountainhead, Character Analysis and Scene Outline," March 25, 1948, The Fountainhead production file: F-85/1904 (Warner Bros. Archives, USC), 1.

55. Frank, "The Fountainhead, Character Analysis," 2–3.

56. Frank, "The Fountainhead, Character Analysis," 3–4.

57. Frank, "The Fountainhead, Character Analysis," 4.

58. Frank, "The Fountainhead, Character Analysis," 4.

59. Frank, "The Fountainhead, Character Analysis," 3.

60. Rand, first draft, 4–10.

61. Frank, "The Fountainhead, Character Analysis," 5 (emphasis added).

62. Rand, first draft, 25–33.

63. Frank, "The Fountainhead, Character Analysis," 7 (emphasis added).

64. Rand, first draft, 155–67.

65. Frank, "The Fountainhead, Character Analysis," 10.

66. Frank, "The Fountainhead, Character Analysis," 11–12.

67. Rand, first draft, 204–9.

68. Frank, "The Fountainhead, Character Analysis," 13 (emphasis added).

69. Frank, "The Fountainhead, Character Analysis," 15 (emphasis added).

70. Frank, "The Fountainhead, Character Analysis," 16.

71. Ayn Rand, first draft, 260–83.

72. Frank, "The Fountainhead, Character Analysis," 17 (emphasis added).

73. Frank, "The Fountainhead, Character Analysis," 17.

74. Distributor: Newmarket Films; director: Mel Gibson (2004).

75. In Rand's view, such collectivists as Marxists merely substitute society for God as the object of worship and the collector of sacrifices. See Leonard Peikoff, ed., *The Voice of Reason: Essays in Objectivist Thought* (New York: New American Library, 1989), 114.

76. M. Keith Booker, *Film and the American Left: A Research Guide* (Westport, Connecticut: Greenwood Press, 1999), 293.

77. A "Notice of Tentative Writing Credit," listing Rand, Williamson, and Frank Jr. as writers, is among Rand's papers. The form is a notification that gives the various parties an opportunity to "protest" proposed credits. Rand's "on screen" as of August 10, 1948, is: "Novel and Screenplay by Ayn Rand" and suggests that she was at least aware of the other writers. *Ayn Rand Papers*: 105-23-54 (Ayn Rand Archives).

78. Biographical interviews (Ayn Rand Archives).

79. Berliner, *Letters of Ayn Rand*, 403.

80. Biographical interviews (Ayn Rand Archives).

81. Harriman, *Journals of Ayn Rand*, 234–39.

82. Biographical interviews (Ayn Rand Archives).

83. Berliner, *Letters of Ayn Rand*, 216.

84. Berliner, *Letters of Ayn Rand*, 396.

85. Berliner, *Letters of Ayn Rand*, 400.

86. Biographical interviews (Ayn Rand Archives).

87. Rand to Collins, September 18, 1948, *Ayn Rand Papers*, 8–9.

88. This is also true in the novel. For insightful commentary, see Leonard Peikoff, *Objectivism: The Philosophy of Ayn Rand* (New York: Dutton, 1991), 430–32.

89. The Production Code's concern with *The Fountainhead* script addressed such sexual/moral matters as female modesty, illicit relationships, and lustful thoughts. See Production Code Administration Files: The Fountainhead (W.B., 1948), Special Collections (Margaret Herrick Library).

90. Rand to Collins, September 18, 1948, *Ayn Rand Papers*, 10.

91. See Ayn Rand, *The Virtue of Selfishness: A New Concept of Egoism* (New York: New American Library, 1964), and Ayn Rand, *Capitalism: The Unknown Ideal* (New York: New American Library, 1966).

92. Berliner, *Letters of Ayn Rand*, 105.

93. "The Motion Picture Producers and Distributors of American (MPPDA) was formed in 1922 primarily to defend the film industry against censorship. Will Hays was appointed and remained president of the organization until his retirement in the mid-1940s." Thereafter, the organization was renamed the Motion Picture Association of America. The actual Production Code was created in 1930. Its administrator was Joseph I. Breen. Quote from "Motion Picture Association of America/Production Code Administration—Records" Finding Aid, Inventory by Barbara Hall and Val Almendarez, 1985; Special Collections (Margaret Herrick Library).

94. Biographical interviews (Ayn Rand Archives).

95. Rand to Collins, September 18, 1948, *Ayn Rand Papers*, 9. The final speech and the evolution of its language and arguments are outside the scope of this present study.

96. Stephen S. Jackson, "Memorandum for the Files, June 30, 1948, Re: The Fountainhead, Production Code Administration Files: The Fountainhead (W.B., 1948), Special Collections (Margaret Herrick Library, Academy of Motion Picture Arts and Sciences) (emphasis added).

97. *Joseph Burstyn, Inc. vs. Wilson, Commissioner of Education, et al.*, 343 U.S. 495 (1952).

98. This situation potentially jeopardized a studio's financial investment. The alternative was to comply or fight the code—the latter alternative, according to Rand, was too frightening a prospect for "timid" Hollywood executives. See Biographical interviews (Ayn Rand Archives).

99. This was likely Joseph I. Breen.

100. Biographical interviews (Ayn Rand Archives).

101. The examination of these revisions is outside the scope of this essay. However, the resolution of Roark's defense also involved the issue of intent, a point clarified by the judge in his charge to the jury. Under the administration's guidance, Rand prepared a lengthy statement, excerpts from which are quoted here: "The de-

fendant has admitted his act. The question which you must now decide is whether a criminal intention was involved. Did the defendant consider his act as wrong and did he intend a deliberate violation of the law? . . . If Howard Roark had an opportunity to seek redress through lawful channels, but resorted to violence, instead— then he is guilty of a deliberate crime. If the chance of a recourse to law was denied to him—then he acted in protest against the violation of his rights. . . . If you find that an essential factor in establishing this crime, namely that of intent, is lacking, you may recommend acquittal providing that the property rights of those who may have invested their funds innocently, are protected by adequate compensation." This charge was shortened considerably in the final script. Production Code Administration Files: The Fountainhead (W.B., 1948), Special Collections (Margaret Herrick Library).

102. PCA Approval, Certificate: 13358, November 24, 1948, Production Code Administration Files: The Fountainhead (W.B., 1948), Special Collections (Margaret Herrick Library).

103. Except for her script, Rand disliked the finished film. And while the film was shot as written, the studio unexpectedly deleted a line from Roark's speech in the final cut of the film: "I came here to say that I am a man who does not exist for others."

104. Berliner, *Letters of Ayn Rand*, 415. As to Rand's reaction to the finished film, which was not favorable, see Britting, *Ayn Rand*, 71–72.

105. Rand, first draft, 2–4.

106. I would like to thank Michael S. Berliner and Robert Mayhew for helpful editorial comments, Adam Piergallini for efficient editorial assistance, and Donna Montrezza for copyediting services. I would also like to thank Haden Guest, Curator, USC Warner Bros. Archives, for information concerning the Warner Bros. studio organization; Damien Bosco for legal insights; Chris Patrouch and Sharyn Blumenthal for additional editorial comments. In addition, the staff of the Margaret Herrick Library is to be thanked for assistance with Special Collections and clipping-file materials. Materials from *The Fountainhead* production files, courtesy Warner Bros. Entertainment Inc.

II

THE FOUNTAINHEAD
AS LITERATURE AND
AS PHILOSOPHY

6

The Fountainhead
as a Romantic Novel

Tore Boeckmann

This is the Heller House:

> The house on the sketches had been designed not by Roark, but by the cliff on which it stood. It was as if the cliff had grown and completed itself and proclaimed the purpose for which it had been waiting. The house was broken into many levels, following the ledges of the rock, rising as it rose, in gradual masses, in planes flowing together up into one consummate harmony. The walls, of the same granite as the rock, continued its vertical lines upward; the wide, projecting terraces of concrete, silver as the sea, followed the line of the waves, of the straight horizon. (124)

The Heller House, Howard Roark's first commission in *The Fountainhead*, is designed according to the architectural principles he has proclaimed in the novel's opening chapter:

> Here are my rules: what can be done with one substance must never be done with another. No two materials are alike. No two sites on earth are alike. No two buildings have the same purpose. The purpose, the site, the material determine the shape. Nothing can be reasonable or beautiful unless it's made by one central idea, and the idea sets every detail. A building is alive, like a man. Its integrity is to follow its own truth, its one single theme, and to serve its own single purpose. . . . Its maker gives it the soul and every wall, window and stairway to express it. (24)

What is the "one central idea" of the Heller House? We cannot be certain, since the house exists only as a brief description in a novel. But one feature of that description is striking: the combination of walls, which continue the vertical lines of the rock, and projecting terraces, which follow the lines of the sea and the horizon.

119

Not only the site, but the materials used are integrated with this idea: the granite of the walls is the same as the rock, the concrete of the terraces is "silver as the sea." And as for the building's purpose, when Austen Heller tells Roark, "You were very considerate of me," Roark answers, "You know, I haven't thought of you at all. I thought of the house. Perhaps that's why I knew how to be considerate of you" (136–37). The implication is not that Roark was indifferent to his client's needs, but that these were so well integrated into the central design idea that Roark could just go ahead and let the building "follow its own truth."[1]

A central idea, in Roark's sense, determines everything else about an art work. It "sets every detail." It is the artist's standard of selection, governing all his choices. And if the Heller House's central idea is indeed found in the description given of the house,[2] then, qua standard of selection, this idea has several interrelated characteristics worth noting.

First, the idea is an original creation of Roark's.

Second, the idea is unique to the Heller House. "The purpose, the site, the material determine the shape"—and these are different for every building. The site of the Heller House is particularly unusual, as is the client (and thus the purpose). So Roark has not simply copied the central idea of some other building; and he will design no more Heller Houses.

Third, the Heller House's central idea is *internal* to the building and its site, a part of their *substance*. The idea is not an abstraction like "the abode of a crusading columnist," but an imagined combination of the actual granite, concrete, sea, and horizon that will constitute the house, site, and wider setting.

These characteristics of Roark's central idea point to a distinctive method of artistic creation. "Creation," in Ayn Rand's words, "means the power to bring into existence an arrangement (or combination or integration) of natural elements that had not existed before."[3] In a superficial sense, any building is a creative achievement. But the Heller House is much more profoundly creative than most buildings, since Roark has originated not only the combination of natural elements which constitutes the completed house, but also the *standard of selection* governing his design of this totality. That standard, Roark's "one central idea," is *itself* an original combination of natural elements, unique to the Heller House, internal to it, a part—the core part—of its substance.

Creation by means of such *core combinations* is, I submit, the method of artists like Howard Roark—and of the romantic school of art.[4]

THE CLASSICIST STANDARD

In *The Fountainhead*, Roark confronts the influence of architectural classicism. For instance, it is demanded of him that he give his design for the

Manhattan Bank Company building a classical façade, which means adding columns and an entablature designed by the rules of one of the five classical orders. (The bank's board suggests Doric.) Such a façade bears no relation to Roark's central idea for the building, and so he turns down the commission.

The combination of Roark's modern design and a classical façade would be a bastard abomination to a true classicist no less than to Roark. But consider how Roark's method of creation differs from that of the classicist who sets out to design, by his own standards, a *good* classical building. This architect knows from the start that his façade must have columns and an entablature—regardless of the building's purpose, site, or material. Further, the columns must have a shaft, a capital, and (except in the Doric order) a base, and the entablature an architrave, a frieze, and a cornice. The radius of the columns is the module that decides the relative sizes of the other elements; for instance, if the order is Doric, the columns are fourteen modules high, the architrave one module high, the capitals two and one-sixth modules wide (according to Vitruvius in *De Architectura*). In the Doric order, the shafts must have flutes. Whatever the order, the building must be horizontally symmetrical.

This is just a brief indication of the mind-numbingly complex set of rules that governs not merely the façade, but every part of a classical building's design. Indeed, it has been said (with some exaggeration) that from the tiniest fragment of a classical building, the whole can always be reconstructed. Given a few optional parameters like the size of the building and the order, the rules set every detail. They are a classicist architect's standard of selection.

This standard is obviously not an original creation of the individual architect, or unique to his building, but derives from ancient models and authorities. Nor is the standard internal to the substance of a building. Rather, the rules are imposed from outside, from the textbooks, on the building's material, purpose, and site.

We can see why Howard Roark, in the first chapter of *The Fountainhead*, tells the dean of his school, "I see no purpose in doing Renaissance villas" (22). The classicist method of creation is the exact opposite of his own. The Dean, a champion of classicism, tells Roark:

> You must learn to understand—and it has been proved by all authorities—that everything beautiful in architecture has been done already. There is a treasure mine in every style of the past. We can only choose from the great masters. Who are we to improve upon them? We can only attempt, respectfully, to repeat. (23)

According to the Dean, "all the proper forms of expression have been discovered long ago" (24). Roark replies, "Expression—of what? The Parthenon did not serve the same purpose as its wooden ancestor. An airline terminal does not serve the same purpose as the Parthenon" (24). And yet, as Roark comments, "here we are, making copies in steel and concrete of copies in plaster of copies in marble of copies in wood" (24).

Roark's meeting with the Dean takes place in 1922, almost a century after Victor Hugo published his play *Cromwell* (1827), with its famous "Preface" that became the manifesto of the romantic movement in literature. In words that closely foreshadow Roark's confrontation with the Dean, Hugo attacks the classicist literary establishment of his time. "We were told that everything was done, and God was forbidden to create more Molières or Corneilles. Memory was put in place of imagination."[5] Hugo rejects the classicist "unities" of time and place, according to which the action of a play must unfold in one day and in a single location; and to the anticipated objection that "this rule that you discard is borrowed from the Greek drama," he answers, "Wherein, pray, do the Greek stage and drama resemble our stage and drama?"[6]

He asks:

> And whom are we to copy, I pray to know? The ancients? We have just shown that their stage has nothing in common with ours. . . .
> Whom shall we copy, then? The moderns? What! copy copies![7]

Just as Roark tells the Dean that "what can be done with one substance must never be done with another," Hugo says:

> Every plot has its proper duration as well as its appropriate place. Think of administering the same dose of time to all events! of applying the same measure to everything! You would laugh at a cobbler who should attempt to put the same shoe on every foot.[8]

Like the rules of architectural classicism, the unities of time and place are not the original creation of the individual artist, or unique to his work. They derive from ancient models and, supposedly, from the authority of Aristotle (who does not in fact prescribe them). As standards of selection, they are not internal to the subject matter of any given play but are imposed from outside, from the textbooks, on whatever plot idea an author starts with.

The unities of time and place govern primarily the organization of a classical play's events, but the standard that governs the nature of the events themselves is just as external to the playwright's subject matter. As one scholar puts it:

> The work of the classical artist is to give individual expression, the beauty of form, to a body of common sentiments and thoughts which he shares with

his audience, thoughts and views which have for his generation the validity of universal truths.[9]

In literature, this attitude led the classicists to make conventional ideas of *propriety* a standard of selection. For instance, they objected when, in *Hernani*, Victor Hugo has a noblewoman fall in love with a bandit. For a woman to love beneath her station was improper by common sentiment and thought. Two centuries earlier, in the heyday of classicism, Corneille was attacked for having the hero of *Le Cid* appear before the heroine after he has killed her father—a similar breach of etiquette.

In the classicist view, the inclusion of such behavior in a story is as incongruous as a Doric column without flutes. Literary characters must conform to social conventions—and this is a literary convention to which an author must conform.

THE PLOT-THEME AS A LITERARY CORE COMBINATION

Rejecting the unities of time and place, Hugo champions the "unity of plot":

> This one is as essential as the other two are useless. It is the one which fixes the view-point of the drama; now, by that very fact, it excludes the other two. There can no more be three unities in the drama than three horizons in a picture.[10]

Like unity of time and place, plot is a kind of formal organization. Ayn Rand defines it as "a purposeful progression of logically connected events leading to the resolution of a climax."[11] However, in contrast to unity of time and place, unity of plot is not imposed from outside on a story's subject matter but springs from within, from the core of that subject matter itself.

Plot is based on conflict and presupposes what Ayn Rand calls a "plot-theme." The plot-theme is "the central conflict or 'situation' of a story—a conflict in terms of action, corresponding to the theme and complex enough to create a purposeful progression of events."[12] How does the central conflict "create" a plot progression? By virtue of its inner logic, which makes it unfold in a series of logically connected events.

In a plot story, the *plot-theme* is the standard of selection, the central idea that determines everything else and sets every detail. For instance, as Hugo puts it, subplots are allowable only on the condition that "these parts, being skillfully subordinated to the general plan, shall tend constantly toward the central plot."[13] Similarly, since the plot-theme determines the plot, it also determines (to repeat Hugo's phrase) the plot's "proper duration as well as its appropriate place."

The plot-theme is an original creation of the writer's, a new combination of natural elements, unique to the given story. A plot-theme is a different kind of combination than the central idea for the Heller House: a writer works not with granite and concrete and the line of the horizon, but with human action and motivation, and the elements of these are what he re-arranges. But in a deeper sense, a plot-theme is exactly like Roark's central architectural idea: both constitute a standard of selection internal to an art work—a standard at the core of the work's substance.

Both are *core combinations.*

THE CORE COMBINATION OF *THE FOUNTAINHEAD*

The relationship between Howard Roark and Dominique Francon is only a part, although an important part, of the central conflict situation in *The Fountainhead*—yet even on its own, this relationship is a core combination in miniature.

Prior to meeting Roark, Dominique has "kept herself clean and free in a single passion—to touch nothing" (242). The world, she believes, recognizes no true ideals and thus is poised to crush them.

> You want a thing and it's precious to you. Do you know who is standing ready to tear it out of your hands? You can't know, it may be so involved and so far away, but someone is ready, and you're afraid of them all. And you cringe and you crawl and you beg and you accept them—just so they'll let you keep it. (143)

Dominique's answer is to pursue no serious values. "If I found a job, a project, an idea or a person I wanted—I'd have to depend on the whole world" (143). This she refuses to do—not out of indifference to values as such, but out of a strong desire to protect them from an inimical world. When asked, "What if you found something you wanted?" she answers, "I won't find it. I won't choose to see it" (144).

Then she goes to her father's granite quarry, stands at "the edge of the great stone bowl," and she "looked down."

> She knew it was the most beautiful face she would ever see, because it was the abstraction of strength made visible. She felt a convulsion of anger, of protest, of resistance—and of pleasure. (204–5)

Dominique "had lost the freedom she loved" (209). She has found a great value that ties her to the world. She tries to stay away from the quarry, but she comes back again and again. Recognizing Roark as a true hero, she cannot resist the desire to see him. Nor can she resist him when he comes to her at night. She does not give him "the one answer that would have saved her: an answer of simple revulsion—she had found joy in her revulsion, in her terror and in his strength" (219).

The relationship of Roark and Dominique, and Dominique's inner conflict, is an original creation of Ayn Rand's—a new combination of natural elements. That some men are heroes; that some women are hero-worshipers; that some think the good is doomed to defeat; that some act to avoid whatever threatens their freedom or purity of soul; that men and women fall in love; that lovers seek the sight of their beloved, and have sex—all of this can be observed in the world. But the combination of these elements into the conflict of a woman torn between an idealistic withdrawal from values and her passionate love for a hero—that is unique to *The Fountainhead*.

This situation functions as a standard of selection for the rest of the novel. For instance, the situation dictates the violence of Roark and Dominique's first sexual encounter, where she resists him with every means possible *except* those that would actually stop him (calling for help or showing revulsion). Given her love for Roark, Dominique does not stop him; given her struggle against that love, she resists him. Any other kind of sex scene, featuring, say, a sultrily seductive or sensuously eager Dominique, would be incongruous in the context of the central conflict.

The same conflict determines Dominique's later actions. When she is told that the man "with very bright orange hair" has left the quarry for New York, she makes an unusual decision. "She would not ask for his name. It was her last chance of freedom" (220). But she returns to New York and goes for long walks through the streets. "Each step through the streets hurt her now. She was tied to him—as he was tied to every part of the city. . . . She came home, after these walks, shaking with fever. She went out again the next day" (242–43). These actions express both Dominique's love for Roark and her resistance to that love.

Dominique's campaign to sabotage Roark's career also flows from the central conflict.

Seeing a drawing of Roark's Enright House, she judges it "the most beautiful building in New York" (273). She learns that its architect is the man she loves. When her acquaintance Joel Sutton plans to give Roark a big commission, Dominique skillfully manipulates him to give the commission to Peter Keating instead. That night she comes to Roark and tells him, "I'm going to fight you—and I'm going to destroy you. . . . I will fight to block every step you take. I will fight to tear every chance you want away from you" (272).

Dominique thinks that Roark's dedication to his career makes him vulnerable to the world, which will not merely destroy him, but given his genius, destroy him through a process of slow torture. She wants to spare him this torture—by hastening his defeat. As she says, "when I go swimming I don't like to torture myself getting into cold water by degrees. I dive right in and it's a nasty shock, but after that the rest is not so hard to take" (248). Dominique in effect wants to push Roark into the cold water, to make the rest not so hard to take.

Dominique first meets Roark when he works in the quarry; and she starts her campaign against his career a few hours after Ellsworth Toohey tells her about the terrible struggle with society that led Roark to such a position. These facts are important for understanding her actions: they make her motives concretely real. Since Roark was once reduced to a workman after making a promising start, Dominique can realistically fear that it will happen again (as indeed it almost does, after the Stoddard trial). Dominique *could* have sabotaged Roark's career simply on the basis of her general premises. As she tells him, "Roark, everything I've done all my life is because it's the kind of world that made you work in a quarry last summer" (284). But this is a very abstract statement of Dominique's unusual motives. Her motives appear much more forceful and pressing when, with reference to the *actual* quarry incident, she says, "Roark, you worked in that quarry when you had the Enright House in you, and many other Enright Houses, and you were drilling granite" (273).

Dominique is here reacting to the conflict of Roark versus society—an element of the plot-theme of *The Fountainhead* different from the Roark-Dominique conflict. The *combination* of these two plot-theme conflict strands is what leads inevitably to Dominique's campaign.

A third strand is constituted by the relationship between Roark and Gail Wynand.

Like Dominique, Wynand has concluded that idealism has no chance against society. The difference is that Wynand—who has "the will of life, the prime power" (483)—does not retreat from the world. He wants to act, to live for his own sake, and so he pursues the only means to that end he thinks possible: power. "I wanted power over a collective soul and I got it" (604). His tool is the *New York Banner*—a popular newspaper he has built by expressing "the opinions, the desires, the tastes of the majority" (603).

"I've never justified myself to anyone" (493), Wynand tells Dominique in a line that is telling but untrue. For Wynand to "justify himself" would contradict his entire philosophy: it is precisely in order to act without justifying himself to anyone that he has sought power, believing that reason and justice are impotent among men. Yet no man can give up his integrity and not feel unclean—or, if he has Wynand's soul, a sense of treason. Thus, without understanding his own motive, Wynand is driven to justify himself *to himself*.

He does so by breaking men of integrity, like Dwight Carson, a talented young champion of individualism whom he drives to write a column extolling the masses. This "proves" to Wynand that integrity is a sham. "The man I couldn't break would destroy me. But I've spent years finding out how safe I am," Wynand tells Dominique. "The thing I've missed"—or, in another words, betrayed—"it doesn't exist" (497).

And then he meets Roark.

It is love at first sight. Each man responds to "the prime power" in the other—and Wynand responds to Roark's integrity. Yet given Roark's professional success (at this point of the story), his integrity is a threat to Wynand. "According to my judgment and experience," Wynand says, "you should have remained in the gutter" (548). Roark's existence disproves Wynand's philosophy, so Wynand decides to break him. He has commissioned a residence from Roark, and he tells him that the house will be the last Howard Roark design. Thereafter, Roark will build in historical styles—"within forms chosen by the taste of the people" (532)—or Wynand will drive him to bankruptcy and make sure even the granite quarries are closed to him.

Roark gaily adapts the elevation of the Wynand house on the back of an envelope. Confronted with this demonstration of what his demand would mean in practice, Wynand gives in.

Wynand is not destroyed by this defeat. He has another way of justifying himself. "I've sold my life," he tells Roark, "but I got a good price. Power. I've never used it. I couldn't afford a personal desire. But now I'm free. Now I can use it for what I want. For what I believe. For Dominique. For you" (604).

His opportunity comes with the Cortlandt Homes affair. When Roark's design of this housing project is disfigured by politically connected second-handers, Roark blows up the project. In the frenzy of public hysteria against Roark, Wynand steps forward to defend him. "We've always made public opinion," he tells his staff. "Let's make it. Sell Roark" (624).

They are powerless to do so. The support of the *Banner* hurts Roark instead of helping him. As for the *Banner*, Wynand's lawyer says: "An unpopular cause is a dangerous business for anyone. For a popular newspaper— it's suicide" (628). The *Banner* is almost destroyed, and Wynand gives in to popular pressure, abandoning Roark's cause. He realizes that in catering to the mob, he has turned himself into its slave. "Here I am, my masters," he says, addressing in his mind the faceless masses. "I am coming to salute you and acknowledge, wherever you want me, I shall go as I'm told. I'm the man who wanted power" (659).

Roark's acquittal at his trial is his final triumph and the seal of Wynand's defeat.

The central conflict situation of *The Fountainhead* is the standard that governs the choice of these events. Given the characters of Roark and Wynand, it is logical that they would love each other, that Wynand would try to break Roark, and that Roark—the ultimately stronger personality—would prevail in this encounter. It is logical that defending Roark against the collectivist society would be the cause in which Wynand decides to test his power over the mob—and that he will find his power illusory.

In the climax, the separate plot-theme strands again work as a unity. Wynand at first sides with Roark in his conflict against society. And for Dominique, Wynand's defeat is the ultimate confirmation that the men she thought owned the world "don't own it. They own nothing. They've never won. I have seen the life of Gail Wynand, and now I know" (665). She does not have to fear that the world will crush Roark.

Ayn Rand once said that *We the Living* has the best plot of all her novels, "because it's a simple story" that has "almost a classic progression of one event leading to another." *The Fountainhead* and *Atlas Shrugged* have plots, she continued, "but on so grand a scale, and with so many involvements, that they are not as perfect one-line plots as in *We the Living*."[14]

In making this comparative literary judgment, Ayn Rand is applying unity of plot as an external standard. But she did not do so in plotting *The Fountainhead*. Instead of imposing some kind of "perfect unity" on the novel, she let the plot-theme govern the choice of events. Observe that the superior unity of *We the Living* springs from the simplicity of its central situation.[15] *The Fountainhead* has a much more complex plot-theme, encompassing the three conflict strands we have discussed, and also the characters of Peter Keating and Ellsworth Toohey. The development of this complexity cannot form a textbook example. But since the plot-theme strands do constitute a unity, they create a coherent novel—of monumental scope.

In *The Fountainhead*, Dominique sabotages the career of a hero of independence and integrity. Wynand tries to coerce this same hero to abandon his principles and cater to the mob. Ayn Rand regarded both of these characters as moral, although profoundly mistaken. In making this judgment, she was applying her moral philosophy as an external standard. But she did not do so in choosing the events of the novel. She did not ask herself, What would a moral person do in this or that situation? A moral person, holding Ayn Rand's philosophy, would not act like Dominique or Wynand. Rather, Ayn Rand asked herself, What would *Dominique* do, in the context of this particular plot development, given her particular premises? What would *Wynand* do? (I am not here presumptuously putting thoughts in Ayn Rand's brain, but describing the *method* of romantic plot construction.)

Ayn Rand is not a classicist and does not use morality (let alone propriety) as an external standard of artistic selection.[16] She selects by the standard of her core combination, the plot-theme, which is of her own creation, unique to her novel, and part of its subject matter.

NATURALISM IN *THE FOUNTAINHEAD*

The action of *The Fountainhead* spans eighteen years and locations from New York City to the South Pacific. Yet the literati of Ayn Rand's time were not outraged by her violation of the unities of time and place. They were outraged by something else. People like Howard Roark, Dominique Francon, and Gail Wynand, they fumed—as their heirs are fuming still—do not exist. The events of *The Fountainhead* mirror nothing observable in the world around us.

Victor Hugo had won the battle against literary classicism. After the "Preface to *Cromwell*," romanticism flourished briefly as the dominant school. Then it was supplanted by naturalism—the portrayal of "things as they are." It was against naturalism that Ayn Rand would be fighting *her* esthetic battle.

What is the naturalist standard of selection?

Consider the following touches from *Elmer Gantry*, Sinclair Lewis's portrayal of a smarmy American evangelist.

At the beginning, Elmer is a boorish young lout. His views on religion are characteristic of his type: "after giving minutes and minutes to theological profundities Elmer had concluded that 'there must be something to all this religious guff if all these wise old birds believe it, and some time a fellow had ought to settle down and cut out the hell-raising.'"[17]

Much later in the novel, at a low point in his career as a preacher, Elmer makes a brief excursion into the New Age (or "New Thought") movement of his time. What is his attitude?

> In some ways he preferred New Thought to standard Protestantism. It was safer to play with. He had never been sure but that there might be something to the doctrines he had preached as an evangelist. Perhaps God really had dictated every word of the Bible. Perhaps there really was a hell of burning sulphur. Perhaps the Holy Ghost really was hovering around watching him and reporting. But he knew with serenity that all of his New Thoughts, his theosophical utterances, were pure and uncontaminated bunk.[18]

The reader chuckles at this, recognizing the acuity of Lewis's observation: this *would* be Elmer's attitude. Why? Because the dogmas of traditional religion have been inculcated in him from a very young age by men of graver moral authority than the peddlers of New Thought—as indicated in the first quote from the novel.

Every aspect of Elmer's childhood, college years, religious awakening, life at a theological seminary, and preaching career is on the same order: it contributes to a pattern that is taken from real life. Lewis has observed that certain traits—emotions, thoughts, actions—commonly occur together to constitute a type of man. His observations govern his creative process: he selects the most telling of the relevant traits and unites them in his novel, drawing a portrait the reader can recognize as accurate from his own perception of reality.[19]

The naturalist standard of selection is *an observed characteristic pattern*.

This standard is more first-handed than that of classicism. It takes perceptiveness and a complex process of abstraction to identify a (significant) characteristic pattern and then select its essential features, discarding accidental details. This is why Lewis's portrait of Elmer Gantry can be simultaneously recognizable by and a revelation to the reader, who has encountered this type of man in real life but has not done the same mental work.

A naturalist's standard of selection is (or should be) his own original *identification*, and unique to his work. But as in classicism, the naturalist standard is not the individual artist's *creation* and is not internal to his work. It is found in the outside world. The artist combines certain elements in his art because he has seen them go together like that in reality.

At the time when she started planning *The Fountainhead*, Ayn Rand listed Sinclair Lewis as her favorite author.[20] This evaluation was presumably caused not by Lewis's naturalist method, but by his brilliant satire of aspects of American society that Ayn Rand too despised. Nevertheless, a definite methodological influence of Lewis *is* apparent in *The Fountainhead*. (And Ayn Rand would not have named him her favorite in any other period of her life.)[21]

A typical Lewis novel features some broad sociological field of early twentieth-century America—medicine in *Arrowsmith*, religion in *Elmer Gantry*. In charting the career of his protagonist from college onward, Lewis presents not merely a certain type of man, but a satirical survey of an entire profession. This is what Ayn Rand does for architecture in the first part of *The Fountainhead*.

Lewis's systematic studies of his subject matter have been compared to "anthropological field research."[22] For *Elmer Gantry*, he not only read widely on religion and interviewed countless clergymen (sometimes, as he put it, "getting them drunk enough to tell the truth"), but he also spoke from the pulpit in Kansas City churches, "to give me a real feeling of the church from the inside."[23] Similarly, Ayn Rand read widely on architecture—and worked for six months as a file clerk for a prominent New York architect.

The fruits of her research are found manly in Part One of *The Fountainhead*, which tells the story of two architects and the first six years of their careers. At the beginning, Howard Roark, a creator of intransigent integrity, and Peter Keating, an opportunistic parasite, leave the same school. At the end, Keating is made partner in a leading architectural firm. Roark goes to work in a granite quarry.

How is this story told?

Consider the key steps of Roark's career. He is expelled from architectural school for refusing to copy the Greeks. He works as a draftsman for the one architect he admires, Henry Cameron. When Cameron retires, his health broken by his struggle with society, Keating gets Roark a job with Guy Francon. Roark again refuses to copy the Greeks, and Francon fires him. Making the rounds of architects, Roark is turned down everywhere until John Erik Snyte hires him. Roark starts his own practice when he secures a commission from Snyte's client Austen Heller, who wants the Heller House as originally designed by Roark, not as conventionalized by Snyte. Roark turns down Snyte's offer of a reconciliatory bribe. The Heller commission leads to a few more, but Roark loses many prospective clients by refusing to copy established styles. In the end, he runs out of money, closes his office, and sets out for the quarry.

In broad terms, there is nothing unusual about most of these events. Aspiring architects work as draftsmen for established architects. They often seek the mentorship of someone they admire; but if they have no choice, they work for anyone who will hire them. They sometimes get jobs through acquaintances. As in many professions, they often establish their own practices by taking with them one or more clients of their last employer's.

Those aspects of Roark's (and Cameron's) career that involve an unusual integrity are also based on real life. In researching *The Fountainhead*, Ayn Rand read biographies of Louis Sullivan and Frank Lloyd Wright, the pioneers of modern architecture. She noted about Sullivan: "Ousted by inability to conform to the prevailing mode, the majority" and "Lack of social ability to get jobs. Arrogance with customers. Refusal to comply with their tastes." And about Wright: "Apprenticeship in architects' offices. Originality and insubordination" and "Attempt to bribe [him] into submission to prevailing styles and commercial success—on the very basis of the originality of his talent."[24]

Roark's struggle in Part One of *The Fountainhead* is the story of Louis Sullivan, of Frank Lloyd Wright, and of all the other great independent creators in history. Such men have been expelled, fired, denied jobs and commissions, offered bribes to conform, and been reduced to poverty—for the same reason that all these things happen to Roark.

Now consider Keating. On the day that Roark is expelled from school, Keating graduates at the head of his class—and is offered a job in Guy Francon's firm. Thereafter, Keating works to secure Francon's patronage, while enacting little schemes in order to advance. He schemes to have the favored draftsman fired, so that he can take over his position, and then to make the chief designer resign, so that he can take over *his*. He tries to establish a romantic relationship with Francon's daughter. And he attempts to blackmail Francon's partner into retirement—which causes the man to die of a stroke.

Keating's course is even less unusual than Roark's. Untold numbers of real-life opportunists reach early success through patronage rather than professional excellence and innovation. This type of man will scheme to outmaneuver his rivals. And the strategy works because many successful men of a certain age desire a protégé.

In characterization and style, Part One of *The Fountainhead* is anything but naturalistic.[25] But in regard strictly to the broad selection of events, *this part* of the novel follows a predominantly naturalistic method. The events are chosen by reference not to a central conflict, but to observed characteristic patterns relating to architectural careers, innovators, and opportunists.

Observe that there is little sustained existential conflict in this part. Roark's conflicts with Cameron and Keating are psychological and do not impact his career. The conflicts which do—those with the Dean, Francon, Snyte, and various actual or prospective clients—involve people with walk-on parts in Roark's life and are generally confined to some particular episode. Similarly, Keating is not in conflict with Francon, who knows what kind of man Keating is: a cruder variant of himself, and thus safe and comfortable.

Given the absence of a central conflict, the career steps of Roark and Keating do not constitute the logically connected events of a plot. For instance, Roark does not take a job with Cameron *because* he has been expelled from Stanton; he would have sought that job had he graduated with honors (though it might have occurred a year later). Roark simply takes the cleanest jobs and commissions he can get, and Keating looks out for the next chance to advance his career. In the case of neither man does one step follow inevitably from another.

When Roark goes to work for Francon, he tells Keating, "I'm selling myself, and I'll play the game that way—for the time being" (88). He does not mean that taking the job is a breach of his integrity, merely that he is acting conventionally: he is a draftsman accepting a job offer from a prominent architect.

But when Roark goes to the quarry, he does *not* act conventionally.

The great innovators of history have struggled as Roark struggles—but they have not taken workmen's jobs. They have preferred a more genteel, middle-class form of poverty. Roark does not. When a friend tells him, "You can get a nice clean job," he answers, "I would have to think on a nice clean job. I don't want to think. Not their way" (198). So he takes the larger-than-life action of seeking the lowest job society can offer him. (And the complete believability of his action is a testament to the fact that, as a *character*, Roark has never been a naturalistic portrait.)

In going to the quarry, Roark ends the "naturalistic" part of *The Fountainhead* and sets the stage for the romantic plot drama that is to follow. As Dominique tells him later in the novel, "Anyone else would have taken a job in an architect's office." Roark answers, "And then you'd have no desire at all to destroy me" (273).

The "naturalism" of Part One of *The Fountainhead* is not a breach of artistic integration but serves the full development of the novel's plot-theme. Observe that both Dominique and Wynand, Roark's key antago-

nists, have very unusual characterizations. They are particularly far removed from "people as they are." Yet their special premises have been
formed precisely in confrontation with things as they are—with the conventional and mediocre. In the context of the full novel, the nature of
Roark's initial struggle grounds the psychologies of Dominique and
Wynand. It provides a realism that prevents the rest of the novel from becoming a fantasy semi-detached from reality. Having seen Roark's struggle
against things as they are, we can see *why* Dominique and Wynand would
think that idealism has no chance.

Ayn Rand is not a naturalist. When she uses the naturalistic method, she
does so ultimately by reference to her own kind of standard: her plot-
theme, or core combination.

Yet Ayn Rand recognizes that a method other than her own is possible,
unlike the critics who complain that *The Fountainhead* does not present
things as they are. Never having been taught any method but the naturalist
one, they do not identify Ayn Rand's own method, or criticize her applica-
tion of it. They simply complain that she is not a good naturalist.

The irony is that, when she wanted to be, she was.

THE FOUNTAINHEAD AND AYN RAND'S VALUES

Ayn Rand identified the theme of *The Fountainhead* as "individualism versus
collectivism, not in politics, but in man's soul; the psychological motiva-
tions and the basic premises that produce the character of an individualist
or a collectivist."[26]

The theme of a novel, Ayn Rand writes, "sets the writer's standard of selection, directing the innumerable choices he has to make and serving as
the integrator of the novel."[27] The plot-theme, she says, is "the link between
the theme and the events"—"the first step of the translation of an abstract
theme into a story, without which the construction of a plot would be impossible."[28] A plot requires a central conflict situation, and once this has
been decided, *it* becomes the operative standard of selection.[29] But insofar
as the plot-theme *corresponds* to the theme, and thus is an appropriate
means of translating it into a story, the theme remains the ultimate, abstract
integrator of the totality.

The conflict strands in the central situation of *The Fountainhead* do correspond to the theme. An innovative, independent architect fights a (psychologically) collectivist society; an idealistic heroine is torn between her
passionate love for the hero and her withdrawal from values, which she
considers doomed by the forces of collectivism; a brilliant man with the
soul of an individualist, who seeks to rule the collective, loves and is loved
by the hero. The actions that follow by logic from this plot-theme will

necessarily dramatize the theme of "individualism versus collectivism, not in politics, but in man's soul."

Early in her career, Ayn Rand wrote in a letter, "That one word—individualism—is to be the theme song, the goal, the only aim of all my writing."[30] The issue of individualism versus collectivism is central to all of her novels. So the theme of *The Fountainhead* is without doubt expressive of Ayn Rand's values.[31] However, the novel's plot-theme, and thus the actions that follow from it, *is more richly expressive of Ayn Rand's values than is the theme.*

Take the conflict strand "an innovative, independent architect fights a (psychologically) collectivist society." Here, the single word "architect" represents Ayn Rand's choice of the hero's profession, a choice which has enormous consequences for the novel. Everything from the main events to the smallest details involves the practice of architecture.

From all the possibilities, Ayn Rand chose architecture for two reasons, she once said. First, since her youth she had wanted to write a story glorifying the American skyscraper "as a symbol of achievement." Second, no profession better shows "the creative element in man" than one which combines "art, science in the sense of engineering, and business."[32]

The ideas that skyscrapers symbolize human achievement, and that engineering and business best show man's creative element, are distinctive of Ayn Rand. They spring from her rejection of the conventional mind-body dichotomy, the belief in an opposition between man's higher, spiritual aspirations and his low, material existence. Ayn Rand champions mind-body union. This is why she makes her innovative, independent hero an architect, rather than (as a conventional writer would have done) a starving poet.

Similarly, she made the heroes of *Anthem* and *Atlas Shrugged* scientist-inventors. These heroes also are individualists who fight a "thematic" battle against a collectivist society. But as in *The Fountainhead*, their specific professions express important values of Ayn Rand's *beyond* the thematic advocacy of individualism.

The next plot-theme strand is "an idealistic heroine is torn between her passionate love for the hero and her withdrawal from values, which she considers doomed by the forces of collectivism." Besides corresponding to the theme, this strand sets up a conflict between the hero and the heroine. In Ayn Rand's words, the Roark-Dominique romance is "sex through antagonism," which "of all forms of romance . . . is the most powerful."[33] This value-judgment of Ayn Rand's is not directly relevant to the theme, but it is contained in the plot-theme and, therefore, expressed in the novel's events.

Ayn Rand holds that "the essence of femininity is hero worship—the desire to look up to man." This does not mean that a woman will worship any man; on the contrary, "the higher her view of masculinity, the more severely demanding her standards." Also, hero worship places demands on the woman: she "has to be worthy of it and of the hero she worships."[34]

As a test of strength, a conflict between the hero and heroine of a story dramatizes the essence of sex. The hero proves himself worthy of the heroine's worship because he bests her; she proves herself worthy of worshiping him because she makes his feat difficult. This is the sexual—and extra-thematic—meaning of the Roark-Dominique romance, and of the John Galt-Dagny Taggart romance in *Atlas Shrugged*. The issue is captured in the way Dagny smiles at Galt: "it was the dangerous smile of an adversary, but her eyes were coldly brilliant and veiled at once, like the eyes of an adversary who fully intends to fight, but hopes to lose."[35] Similarly, Dominique is speaking as a woman when she tells Roark both that "I'm going to fight you—and I'm going to destroy you" and "I'm going to pray that you can't be destroyed" (272).

Ayn Rand's favorite character in Fritz Lang's movie *Siegfried* was Brunhild, the Valkyrie who challenges her suitors to physical tests of strength. Brunhild, Ayn Rand commented, should have been the story's heroine, instead of the "little clinging vine" (Kriemhild), whom the hero loves. As it is, she said, the story is "anti-sex."[36] But in her own stories, Ayn Rand does not make the test of strength between hero and heroine physical—except in actual sex scenes.[37] The conflicts are primarily intellectual. In both the Roark-Dominique and Galt-Dagny romances, the heroine is honestly mistaken on an issue of philosophy, whereas the hero wins in the end because he holds the correct view. Her way of casting these conflicts reflects Ayn Rand's view of heroism as fundamentally intellectual and not primarily an issue of performing physical feats. And this in turn reflects her view of reason as the essence of human nature.

Dominique meets Roark when he is a worker in a granite quarry. Galt is a track worker in the tunnels of the railroad of which Dagny is vice-president. The hero of *Anthem* is a street sweeper. All these men belong at the pinnacle of any rational social hierarchy, yet they are thrown (at least temporarily) to the very bottom. This device is thematic: the hero is an outcast in a collectivist society *because* he is a brilliant individualist. However, casting the hero down to the lowest echelon of society adds drama not merely to the thematic conflict, but also to the hero's conflict with the heroine—who (except in *Anthem*) comes from the highest echelon.

When Dominique meets Roark in the quarry, she is for the first time glad of her position as the chatelaine of the countryside. "She thought suddenly that the man below was only a common worker, owned by the owner of this place, and she was almost the owner of this place" (205). Yet Dominique knows that this man is more than a common worker, and that it is he who "stood looking up at her; it was not a glance, but an act of ownership" (205). Her thrill comes from knowing that, in the test of strength that is inevitable between them, he can best her—even though, in social position, he starts with the severest handicap.

In itself, the theme of individualism versus collectivism has nothing to do with the issue of "sex through antagonism." But the plot-theme *combination* of a hero-versus-society conflict and an antagonistic romance offers Ayn Rand unique opportunities to express her sexual values.

The third plot-theme strand of *The Fountainhead* is "a brilliant man with the soul of an individualist, who seeks to rule the collective, loves and is loved by the hero." The implied conflict between Roark and Wynand corresponds to the theme; the bond of love between them expresses extrathematic values. Ayn Rand defined romantic love as the love felt for someone who is irreplaceable in one's own life: the loved one is a unique individual who, if lost, would leave a permanent void in the lover's soul.[38] In Ayn Rand's view, love of this nature does not necessarily involve a sexual component; it can exist between members of the same sex, without any implication of homosexuality. Ayn Rand was attracted to the idea of such an emotional bond—in effect, romantic love without the aspect of sex—between two men. She depicts such relationships, in *Atlas Shrugged*, between Hank Rearden and Francisco d'Anconia, and between Francisco and Galt. And the love between Roark and Wynand is on the same order. As Roark tells Wynand, "You have been the one encounter in my life that can never be repeated" (654).

Leonard Peikoff has pointed to the love between the Marquis of Posa and King Phillip II of Spain in Schiller's *Don Carlos* as a parallel to the Roark-Wynand relationship.[39] The parallel is real, but as one would expect, Ayn Rand's *use* of love between two men is distinctive. Unlike Schiller, she makes it an element of a romantic triangle that involves the heroine. In *The Fountainhead*, Wynand is married to Dominique when he meets Roark. The main heroes of *Atlas Shrugged* all love Dagny and at some stage have a sexual relationship with her.

Further, in the typical Ayn Rand triangle, there is at least an indication that the two men feel more strongly for each other than for the heroine. And just as Dagny fears that Galt will sacrifice himself and let Francisco have her,[40] so Dominique fears that Roark will sacrifice himself and leave her to Wynand (620). But neither man does in the end make this sacrifice.

While these triangles are not specified in the plot-themes of the two novels, the plot-theme conflict strands hint strongly at their possibility and thus facilitate a richer expression of Ayn Rand's values than does the theme as such.

The plot-theme of *The Fountainhead*, and consequently the events, expresses not only a broad range of the author's values, but also their metaphysical presuppositions. Ayn Rand's admiration for the profession of architecture presupposes her view of mind-body union. The intellectuality of her protagonists and their conflicts presupposes her view of man as a rational being. And to touch on an aspect we have not yet mentioned, the fact that the *main* personal conflicts of the novel are between good characters, not good and evil, presupposes Ayn Rand's view that evil is ultimately impotent.

These extra-thematic values and metaphysical views are what really matter in the novel.

"Fundamentally," Ayn Rand says, "what is important is not the message a writer projects *explicitly*, but the values and view of life he projects *implicitly*."[41]

Art is the means of presenting not a didactic theme, but a concretization of metaphysics by means of "a selective re-creation of reality."

> By a selective re-creation, art isolates and integrates those aspects of reality which represent man's fundamental view of himself and of existence. Out of the countless number of concretes—of single, disorganized and (seemingly) contradictory attributes, actions and entities—an artist isolates the things which he regards as metaphysically essential and integrates them into a single new concrete that represents an embodied abstraction.[42]

But observe that an artist cannot first select a bunch of disconnected concretes and then glue them together somehow. If he is to create a single new concrete (an embodied abstraction) from the multiplicity of concretes he regards as metaphysically essential, he cannot treat selection and integration as distinct processes. He needs a standard of selection that is simultaneously his concrete *integrator*. For instance, the naturalist selects on the basis of an observed characteristic pattern, and that same pattern constitutes his unity. The classicist selects on the basis of established conventions about which things go together and form a proper whole.

In and of themselves, the methods of naturalism and classicism carry a profound metaphysical message. The motto of both schools is: What other men have joined together, let no artist put asunder. By the nature of his standard of selection, the naturalist or classicist can present the values he observes in other men, or those of stale convention, but no values that are distinctly his own. This implies the passive acceptance of human values as givens beyond individual choice or judgment—i.e., determinism.

In practice, a classicist or naturalist cannot remain fully true to his method, i.e., completely detached from his own personal values.[43] One can tell Racine from Corneille or Sinclair Lewis from Tolstoy. As one small example, Lewis's portrayal of Elmer Gantry's career is tinged with a moral indignation that would be foreign to Tolstoy. But the point is that Lewis's moralism is extraneous to his basic method of creation (in fact, it contradicts his method). The same goes for all his other individualizing touches: they are incidental to the essence of his work.

In a romantic art work, the artist's own values are *not* incidental. The essential attribute of romanticism, in Ayn Rand's words, is "the independent, creative projection of an individual writer's values."[44] (This applies not only to writers, but to romantic artists in all the arts.[45])

Before we look more closely at the *method* of romanticism, observe that the projection of an individual artist's values carries a profound metaphysical message in and of itself. It implies that the individual is capable of choosing his own values—and that this fact is essential to his nature. Thus Ayn Rand defined romanticism as "a category of art based on the recognition of the principle that man possesses the faculty of volition."[46]

Romanticism has an objective basis: man does in fact possess volition, and his choice of values is the central issue of his life. It is sometimes asked: what is the value of a school of art which projects *individual* values, when most of those values are based on philosophical error? After all, the range of values projected by romantic artists is enormous. The values of Ayn Rand and Joseph Conrad, of Victor Hugo and Terence Rattigan, of Edmond Rostand and Dostoevsky and Ibsen and Schiller and Oscar Wilde—these values are not only wildly different, but often incompatible. They cannot all be objectively valid. But neither are the values of men in real life. Men's actual values differ wildly, and are often incompatible. What they do have in common is that they are chosen by each individual—who is defined by his choice. "Man," in Ayn Rand's formulation, "is a being of self-made soul."[47]

In this sense, romanticism is the school of art that really does present things as they are.

We have said that a romantic artist's values are not incidental to his work. Let us now be more precise: a romantic art work is *stylized*.

To "stylize" is to condense an object to essential characteristics, relative to a specific value-perspective.[48] The object, and the value-perspective, involved may be simple or complex: a single reed depicted in a delicate drawing, or the story of *The Fountainhead*; an appreciation of a certain kind of graceful elegance, or all of Ayn Rand's important values and their metaphysical presuppositions. But regardless of complexity, *every* feature or quality of the stylized object exhibits the essence of the stylizing value-perspective.

This perspective is an *abstraction* (or a set of abstractions) drawn from observed concretes. For instance, an abstraction of graceful elegance might be drawn from the curve of a swan's neck, the leap of a ballerina, the posture of an English gentleman, the swaying of a reed in the wind. In abstracting, only the essential characteristic(s) uniting these concretes is retained, while their concrete differences are disregarded. Some of the concrete matter being disregarded will be closely related to the quality of "graceful elegance," such as the height of the gentleman or the slenderness of the reed, but most of the disregarded matter is irrelevant to the abstraction being drawn: the texture of the swan's feathers, the length of the ballerina's nose, the color of the gentleman's coat. These concretes are wholly accidental.

Now suppose an artist wants to paint a painting with no such accidental concretes: every feature or quality of his subject matter is to exhibit the essence of "graceful elegance." He cannot succeed by making this abstraction his direct standard of selection. If he tried, what would come to his mind is: a swan's neck, a leaping ballerina, an English gentleman—with all their concrete features and differences. Even if he focused only on the features most intimately connected with the abstract characteristic of "graceful elegance," he would be left with an assortment of rather disembodied concrete characteristics like a certain male-figure height or a certain reed thickness. And in order to combine (some of) these in an intelligible artwork—say, in a painting of a gentleman duck-hunter hiding in reeds—the artist would have to fill in a lot of accidental concretes (e.g., a shotgun).

To achieve a stylized object—one purged of the accidental—an artist cannot first select the concretes of his work and *then* combine them. Like the naturalist and classicist, the stylizing romanticist needs a standard of selection that is also his (concrete) integrator. He needs a core combination.[49]

Suppose Ayn Rand had tried to write *The Fountainhead* without a plot-theme, guided only by her theme. The central value-perspective would be unchanged: pro-individualism and anti-collectivism. But without the core-combination idea of an architect's struggle, it is unlikely that Ayn Rand would have thought of any feature of the actual novel. Instead, she might have thought of the communists she met in Soviet Russia; a brave young student who stood up to them and was sent to Siberia; her own struggle in Hollywood to sell her unconventional story ideas; some Broadway social climber she met when her first play was produced. These concretes might be perfectly good concretizations of the theme—but they range all over the map and would not integrate into a stylized object. The theme of *The Fountainhead* is too abstract a standard of selection to yield the elements of a concrete unity.

The plot-theme changes the situation. Take the main strand: "an innovative, independent architect fights a (psychologically) collectivist society." This standard of selection expresses the same value-perspective as does the novel's abstract theme—yet it is *concrete*. As a consequence, further concretes selected by this standard simultaneously exhibit the essence of "pro-individualism and anti-collectivism" *and* relate to a single architect's career struggle. The result is an object—Roark's struggle—condensed to essential characteristics.

Not all themes are too abstract to yield a (kind of) concrete unity. In fact, a naturalistic theme, like "a typical smarmy American evangelist," *is* a particular unity of concretes: an observed characteristic pattern. Or take "the impact of the Civil War on Southern society." This theme immediately suggests essential character types—former slave owners, black sharecroppers, carpetbaggers, Ku Klux Klanners—who interrelate in characteristic patterns.

In other words, "the impact of the Civil War on Southern society" could easily be a naturalistic theme, yielding a concrete unity of the naturalistic kind. But the characteristics of such a unity would be essential only relative to the purely cognitive abstraction of the given patterns, not to a value-perspective.

However, suppose we supplied this theme with a plot-theme: "the romantic conflict of a woman who loves a man representing the old order, and is loved by another man, representing the new."[50] This standard of selection is also concrete—yet it provides a specific authorial *value-perspective*: the view that the ideals of the old South were noble but are now obsolete, and that acting on them is heroic but ultimately foolish. Further concretes selected by the standard of this plot-theme will relate to a single woman's romantic conflict *and* will be essential relative to the governing value-perspective. The result is an object—the story of Scarlett O'Hara in *Gone With the Wind*—condensed to essential characteristics.

The core combination is *the means of stylization*. It is an engine for selecting concretes that exhibit the essence of a certain value-perspective *and* combine into a self-sufficient concrete unity, making it unnecessary to flesh out the selection with accidental material.

The value-perspective of a stylized work is always richer than that of the theme alone. As an abstract integrator, a theme cannot be a set of disparate abstractions, like "individualism versus collectivism, architecture as a heroic profession, mind-body union, sex through antagonism, and man as a rational being." But these values and metaphysical views can all be carried by the *concrete* integrator—as they are by the plot-theme of *The Fountainhead*—since a single concrete (of some complexity) may express a wide variety of abstractions. And the principle here is the same as for the thematic value-perspective: on their own, these abstractions would not yield a concrete unity. As expressed in the core combination, they do.

The abstractions expressed in the core combination should integrate into a coherent viewpoint; a romantic art work should project the values and view of life of an intelligible *personality*. In the broadest sense of the word, this total ethical-metaphysical viewpoint can be considered a romantic art work's "theme." But this kind of theme cannot be condensed into a retainable statement (which is an essential reason why it needs to be concretized in a work of art[51]) and thus cannot function as a *conscious* standard of selection or integrator.[52]

The core-combination device an artist uses must be appropriate to the art form he works in. As we have seen, an architectural core combination differs in nature from a plot-theme.[53] But to be the means of stylization, any core combination must be a *structural* device.

The central idea for the Heller House is the standard for selecting the features that translate that idea into a functioning structure of habitation. A plot-theme is the standard for selecting the events that logically proceed from that central conflict and constitute a plot *structure*.

Each element of a plot serves a structural function mandated, directly or indirectly, by the plot-theme. In *The Fountainhead*, Roark's dynamiting Cortlandt is the lead-in to the climactic resolution of the plot-theme conflict strands. At the very end, Dominique's rising to meet Roark on top of the Wynand Building rounds out the totality of the novel by briefly concretizing the most important consequences of the climax.[54]

Note that the structural function of these elements is not just to provide a generic "resolution" or "triumphant conclusion," but to resolve the *particular* conflicts of the plot-theme and round out the novel's *particular* climax. And it is their highly particular function that determines the *form* of these elements. In Louis Sullivan's famous words, "form follows function."[55]

For instance, the crux of Roark's conflicts with society, Dominique, Wynand, and Toohey is the unbreached integrity of his architectural designs. It is therefore appropriate that the climax turns on his ultimate act of upholding this integrity, in regard to some specific building. In other words, the Cortlandt explosion represents form following function. But suppose Ayn Rand had resolved her conflict strands by having Roark's antagonists die in a flu epidemic. Here form would *not* follow function—not the function of resolving *these* particular conflicts.

The form of such a climax would be not only *functionally* accidental, but also *abstractly* inessential relative to the novel's governing value-perspective. A flu epidemic as such has nothing to do with individualism versus collectivism, the nobility of architecture as an expression of man's creativity, mind-body union, or any of the other abstractions carried by the plot-theme of *The Fountainhead*. By contrast, the Cortlandt explosion has been cut from the same cloth as the conflicts it resolves—a cloth impregnated with the right kind of abstract essentiality—and so naturally exhibits the essence of "individualism versus collectivism," "architecture as expressing man's creativity," "mind-body union."

Or suppose Ayn Rand had decided to round out her novel by having Roark and Dominique climb a mountain in Peru. *Something* about the form of this ending would fit its function: Roark and Dominique would be shown united as a couple; and reaching a mountaintop can be an ecstatic experience, sweeping aside any emotional residue from past conflict. But most of the form in this example would be completely accidental to the function. This ending would *not* be cut from the same cloth as the plot-theme and its other developments, nor exhibit the essence of any relevant abstractions.

In the actual ending, Roark stands on top of the Wynand Building, the greatest structure in New York, which he has been commissioned to build "as a monument to that spirit which is yours" (692). This is form following function—the function of concretizing Roark's total victory in the particular battle he fights throughout the novel: the battle to erect his own kind of buildings against the opposition of a collectivist society. Consequently, this rounding out of Roark's battle exhibits the same essence as does the battle itself: "pro-individualism," "the nobility of architecture," "mind-body union."

As Dominique rises toward Roark, she "saw him standing above her, on the top platform" (694). This, too, is form following function—the function of rounding out the Roark-Dominique relationship, which began in the stone quarry when Dominique "looked down" and Roark "stood looking up at her." He has won their test of strength; and when she is now looking up at him, and rising to him, this final note exhibits the same essence as does their whole relationship: "femininity as hero worship—the desire to look up to man."

In stylized art, there is an inherent harmony between functionality and abstract essentiality. Within a structure created by a core combination, the form of each element will naturally exhibit the essence of the core combination's value-perspective—*if* the form is determined by the given element's function within that particular structure. And this is the key to the creative process of stylization, which involves a tricky dual purpose: concrete unity and abstract essentiality. The harmony of functionality and abstract essentiality allows the artist to focus on the former, with the latter following as a matter of course. If a romantic artist were asked how he achieved his seemingly impossible goal—a single concrete whose every feature exhibits the essence of his values—he might answer with Louis Sullivan that "the function *created* or organized its form."[56]

Now, if an artist is to create a stylized object, there can be no *external* limits to his freedom of selection. If the function is to "organize its form," the allowable forms of an artist's values cannot be prescribed prior to the creative process. This is why a classicist cannot stylize.

Classicism deals, ostensibly, with grand value-abstractions—"harmony," "nobility," "statesmanship"—but its field of selection is limited to conventional exemplars of these abstractions. If a classicist chooses the theme "the martyrdom of integrity," he will think of: Socrates, Jesus, Galileo. What about an architect who is put on trial for protecting the integrity of his work? The classicist would politely ask which obscure Greek myth is being alluded to.

His limited repertoire of conventional concretes does not allow the classicist to create a unity of essentials. For instance, in *The Death of Socrates*, Jacques Louis David combines the concretes of Socrates and Jesus under the theme "the martyrdom of integrity": he paints Socrates about to drink hemlock—surrounded by twelve disciples. But while the presence of twelve disciples is evocative of the Last Supper and the Passion, it is completely inessential to the abstraction of "martyred integrity." Yet what is David to do, except create on some such pattern? He cannot work with a core combination whose functional requirements determine the forms of his concretes, since all the allowable forms of his values are given to him by convention. (A classicist who tried to stay true to a core combination would be forced to cheat on his classicist standards, as happened to Corneille with *Le Cid*.)

By the nature of his method, the stylizing romanticist rejects any external limits to his selectivity other than the nature of the elements of reality. He follows Victor Hugo's advice:

> We must draw our inspiration from the original sources [nature]. It is the same sap, distributed through the soil, that produces all the trees of the forest, so different in bearing power, in fruit, in foliage. It is the same nature that fertilizes and nourishes the most diverse geniuses.[57]

To which the classicist will answer (in Hugo's summation): "But the graces; but good taste! Don't you know that art should correct nature? that we must *ennoble* art? that we must *select?*"[58]

We can see here the essence of two vastly different mind-sets. The romanticist draws his normative abstractions—and, as needed, the concretes which illustrate them—from reality. But for the classicist, there are no normative abstractions beyond those of convention, and these in turn subsume only conventional concretes. Consequently, the classicist cannot even grasp that what the romanticist does is precisely *select*—and "correct nature" and "ennoble art"—on a level he himself could never dream of equaling.

That a naturalist does not think abstractly about human values is obvious. The interesting point is that, appearances to the contrary notwithstanding, neither does a classicist.

Only the romanticist holds his values as true abstractions—romanticism, Ayn Rand says, is "the *conceptual* school of art" ("Introduction to the Twenty-fifth Anniversary Edition," v)—and then, with the help of his core combination, he presents them in a stylized object.

Ayn Rand writes:

> I see the novelist as a combination of prospector and jeweler. The novelist must discover the potential, the gold mine, of man's soul, must extract the gold and then fashion as magnificent a crown as his ability and vision permit.
>
> Just as men of ambition for material values do not rummage through city dumps, but venture out into lonely mountains in search of gold—so men of ambition for intellectual values do not sit in their backyards, but venture out in quest of the noblest, the purest, the costliest elements.[59]

Ayn Rand found the gold mine of man's soul. *The Fountainhead* is the crown she fashioned.

THE FOUNTAINHEAD AND *CHANTECLER*

Like Howard Roark, the hero of Edmond Rostand's play *Chantecler* dedicates himself above all to the integrity of his work, battles social forces hostile to any individual quest for the ideal, and loves a female who wants him to give up his calling.

Unlike Roark, Chantecler is a barnyard cock.

Rostand's dramatic fable takes place on a farm and in the surrounding countryside. Chantecler is the ruler of the barnyard. But his exalted calling is his crowing, which heralds—and, he secretly believes, *causes*—the sunrise.

Like most of Rostand's heroes, Chantecler is essentially a poet. The mere fact that his profession has nothing to do with science, engineering, or business does not imply a mind-body dichotomy. But such a dichotomy *is* reflected in the clash between Chantecler's ideal calling and material reality: he does not in fact cause the sunrise.

The mind-body dichotomy is as central a concern to Rostand as individualism is to Ayn Rand. The dichotomy runs through all of his plays and poetry and was expressed even in his ideas for interior decoration. During the writing of *Chantecler*, Rostand was building his dream house in the French countryside—and wanted to face his library doors with false book covers representing the planned but unwritten works of other authors (i.e., noble but unfulfilled aspirations).[60]

Rostand views the mind-body dichotomy as a tragic fact of human existence, and he values above all else man's unbending integrity in pursuing spiritual values regardless of their clash with material reality. There is always such a clash in Rostand's plays; an ideal *in harmony* with the material world would have been regarded by him as insufficiently spiritual to be of dramatic interest.[61] This is why he would not make one of his heroes an architect like Howard Roark.

The theme of *Chantecler* is a simple statement of Rostand's central value: "An individual must stay loyal to his ideal calling in defiance of all inimical forces—even if his ideal clashes with material reality." The two strands of the plot-theme correspond to the theme: "An idealistic barnyard cock, who secretly thinks his crowing makes the sun rise, confronts the forces of self-doubt, ridicule and envy," and: "The hero's beloved, a pheasant hen, is jealous of his dedication to the dawn and schemes to become his only love."

This plot-theme is more richly expressive of Rostand's values than is the theme.

First of all, the hero is a cock, which fact expresses Rostand's patriotism: the cock is a symbol of France. Also, the cockiness appropriate to a cock—the bold, brash, swashbuckling self-confidence—is both characteristically

French and distinctive of a Rostand hero. (Ayn Rand's protagonists are less self-consciously heroic.)

Next, observe the *non*intellectual nature of Chantecler's conflict with his beloved. The Pheasant Hen is not a passionate idealist like Dominique, but is conventionally feminine, even frivolous. She wants Chantecler to abandon his ideal calling because she craves his undivided affection, an attitude that is meant to be typical of her sex. As Chantecler puts it, the Pheasant Hen is "A woman,—ever jealous of the Dream!"[62]

Ayn Rand, who knew just as well as Rostand did that most women are contemptuous of ideas (as are most men), would not have made such a woman a heroine. By choosing the Pheasant Hen as an appropriate love interest for his hero, Rostand expresses a lower regard than does Ayn Rand for the importance of reason and the intellect in love affairs—and, therefore, in human life. In other words, he expresses extra-thematic sexual values and their metaphysical presuppositions.

The main plot-theme strand of *Chantecler* specifies three forces inimical to the hero's ideal calling: self-doubt, ridicule, and envy.

Chantecler's *self-doubt* manifests itself on occasion throughout the play: he sometimes feels unworthy of his glorious mission; he fears the loss of an inspiration whose nature he does not understand; too much introspection of his technique makes him unable to perform. Probably autobiographical on the author's part, these self-doubts are logical consequences of the belief in a mind-body split. A man will not feel worthy of his ideals if he thinks they are unreachable, or in control of his inspiration if he thinks it comes from a realm opposed to the material world he can grasp by sense perception and reason. Thus, Chantecler's self-doubts reflect concerns derivative of the author's broader metaphysical outlook. (By contrast, when Roark sees that he has "been wasting too much paper lately and doing awful stuff" [601], he feels no self-doubt about his inspiration, but simply concludes that he is overworked and needs a rest.)

The force of *ridicule* is represented in *Chantecler* above all by the Blackbird—"the professional cynic," as Ayn Rand once described the type, "whose sole motive is to sneer at everything; specifically, at *any kind of values*."[63] Chantecler, who worships the ideal, is the main object of the Blackbird's scorn.

The dog Patou warns of the effects of the Blackbird's mocking. The black-dressed Blackbird is like "An undertaker's man, who buries Faith."[64] Because of him, "Whoever speaks of stars today must lower his voice."[65] Patou is proven right when Chantecler attends the Guinea Hen's fashionable salon and learns that he is widely resented in the barnyard. Chantecler defiantly reveals his secret belief that he raises the sun, and he is met with gales of laughter and scorn.

Underlying such ridicule is *envy*—a motive clearly stated by the animals who join in a conspiracy to murder Chantecler. "I hate the Cock because I am so plain," says a Chicken. "I hate him," says the Duck, "he has no web between his toes, / And so he traces stars where'er he goes." And the Capon (a castrated cockerel) gives the dry remark, "I do not like the Cock."[66]

The Blackbird of *The Fountainhead* is Ellsworth Toohey, who is driven by envy and hatred of all values, and who uses ridicule in order to destroy. Toohey says:

> Laughter is an instrument of human joy. Learn to use it as a weapon of destruction. Turn it into a sneer. It's simple. Tell them to laugh at everything. Tell them that a sense of humor is an unlimited virtue. Don't let anything remain sacred in a man's soul—and his soul won't be sacred to him. Kill reverence and you've killed the hero in man. (636)

Like Chantecler, Roark is resented not just by a single public commentator, but by a broad segment of society. One of the first things we learn about him is that "People turned to look at Howard Roark as he passed. Some remained staring after him with sudden resentment. They could give no reason for it: it was an instinct his presence awakened in most people" (16–17).

Rostand and Ayn Rand present this kind of feeling not as an end in itself, but in order to stress, by contrast, an issue which in Ayn Rand's words "is involved in every line of *The Fountainhead*": "*man-worship*."

> The man-worshipers, in my sense of the term, are those who see man's highest potential and strive to actualize it. The man-haters are those who regard man as a helpless, depraved, contemptible creature—and struggle never to let him discover otherwise. (viii–x)

Rostand and Ayn Rand are the only writers who understand this issue and have made it a central motif of a work of fiction. Both *The Fountainhead* and *Chantecler* are stressed portraits of a hero who *does* actualize the highest human potential.

This extra-thematic value-projection is prepared for in the plot-themes of the two works.

The main strand of each plot-theme pits an individual pursuing his ideal calling against a general opposition—"a (psychologically) collectivist society" or "the forces of ridicule and envy"—to be concretized along the way. The individualized conflicts are relegated to adjunct strands. This is not an ideal way to construct a plot-theme, and it is another reason, in addition to sheer complexity, why *The Fountainhead* technically has a less than ideal plot. *Chantecler*, a much simpler story, has a similarly loose progression of events.

However, these technical deficiencies are *virtues*, given the purpose of the two authors.

Observe that Roark and Chantecler are so focused on their work that they barely notice their opposition. Roark does blow up Cortlandt Homes (Ayn

Rand always gives her hero the plot's central action), but otherwise he ig-
nores his enemies and goes on with his career. Chantecler fights a duel with
a vicious gamecock (it would not be a Rostand play without a duel), but
otherwise he goes on with his crowing. Even in their conflicts with the good
characters—Dominique, Wynand, and the Pheasant Hen—Roark and
Chantecler assume a curiously passive role. It is the other characters who
take most of the dramatic actions—in response not so much to particular
acts of the heroes, as to their very *existence*. The heroes, on their part, simply go on being what they are.

Their detachment from interpersonal conflicts does not make for the best
plot progression. But it is necessary for the projection of man-worship. In a
stressed portrait of someone who actualizes the highest human potential,
the hero cannot be too concerned with other men but must be fully occupied with his ideal calling. There lies his true exaltation.

Ayn Rand and Edmond Rostand share crucial values and have some op-
posing ones, but their artistic *method* is identical. Both project their values
partly through the theme of their works, but much more richly through the
plot-theme; and thus they stamp their own, uniquely individual personality all over their artistic creation.

The "local colour" of a drama—says Hugo, speaking of an individual
writer's values—

> should not be on the surface of the drama, but in its substance, in the very
> heart of the work, whence it spreads of itself, naturally, evenly, and, so to speak,
> into every corner of the drama, as the sap ascends from the root to the tree's
> topmost leaf.[67]

So it is in *The Fountainhead*—and in *Chantecler*.

FALSE ROMANTICISM

In the "Preface to *Cromwell*," Victor Hugo warns against "false romanticism,
which has the presumption to show itself at the feet of the true."

> For modern genius [romanticism] already has its shadow, its copy, its parasite,
> its *classic*, which forms itself upon it, smears itself with its colours, assumes its
> livery, picks up its crumbs, and, like the sorcerer's pupil, puts in play, with
> words retained by the memory, elements of theatrical action of which it has
> not the secret.[68]

It is the fate of all great romantic art to be copied. In her research journals for *The Fountainhead*, Ayn Rand notes about Frank Lloyd Wright,
"He fought against the cheap imitators of his work, who copied his forms

without understanding his principle, who made a new 'style' and formula out of his forms."[69] In *The Fountainhead*, Ayn Rand mentions "the men who had been safe in copying the Parthenon," but who now chose "to walk Cameron's path and make it lead them to a new Parthenon, an easier Parthenon in the shape of a packing crate of glass and concrete" (474).

Similarly, Ayn Rand has been copied by artists who paint naked men on cliffs, hair waving against the sky (after the opening scene of *The Fountainhead*), or write novels where the rebellious young hero confronts the dean of his school.

Unable to create and work from original core combinations that reflect *their own* values, such false romanticists can only copy concretes. Most of them represent nothing more than individual amateurishness and have no significance. But sometimes their efforts come to dominate an artistic field. Hollywood thrillers now consist exclusively of old, endlessly rearranged inventions from an earlier tradition of romantic popular literature.[70] As Ayn Rand notes in her journals, much of modern architecture is "modernism in set mass-forms, a modernism as stiff and frozen and unoriginal as the old traditions."[71] The phenomenon of modernism as a new Parthenon is also evident in the second-handed mannerisms of modern painting, like those of cubism (although here there are no romantic leftovers).

This is the opposite of the romantic method—and of the method of Howard Roark. As Cameron tells Roark,

> What you're doing—it's yours, not mine, I can only teach you to do it better. I can give you the means, but the aim—the aim's your own. You won't be a little disciple putting up anemic little things in early Jacobean or late Cameron. (76)

He won't be, because there is nothing in his art that is not selected by a standard of his own creation.

CONCLUSION

In the climactic speech of *The Fountainhead*, Howard Roark states the essence of the novel's theme when he says that man

> can survive in only one of two ways—by the independent work of his own mind or as a parasite fed by the minds of others. The creator originates. The parasite borrows. The creator faces nature alone. The parasite faces nature through an intermediary. (679)

In the novel, Roark represents the creator, who faces nature alone. And he does so primarily by virtue of his method of artistic creation—the *same method* by which *The Fountainhead* has been conceived and written. Thus, on a level deeper than its specific content, *The Fountainhead* itself is the demonstration of its own thesis.

In the "Preface to *Cromwell*," Hugo warns artists to "beware especially of copying anything whatsoever."

> It were better to be a bramble or a thistle, fed by the same earth as the cedar and the palm, than the fungus or the lichen of those noble trees. The bramble lives, the fungus vegetates. Moreover, however great the cedar and the palm may be, it is not with the sap one sucks from them that one can become great one's self. A giant's parasite will be at best a dwarf. The oak, colossus that it is, can produce and sustain nothing more than the mistletoe.[72]

For a brief period, a school of art flourished that heeded Hugo's admonition. Then romanticism was killed as a leading movement by the rise of naturalism and the plague of false romanticism.[73]

To use a metaphor from *The Fountainhead* (which Ayn Rand apparently adapted from the "Preface to *Cromwell*"), "The palm tree had broken through; the fungus came to feed on it, to deform it, to hide it, to pull it back into the common jungle" (474).

As a young woman recently arrived in America from Russia, Ayn Rand one day asked an elderly lady librarian if she had a novel with a good plot and a serious idea. The lady looked at her kindly and said, "I know exactly what you mean. They don't write them anymore." Ayn Rand thought, "I will."[74]

In 1943, she published *The Fountainhead*.

The palm tree had broken through once again.[75]

NOTES

1. Later in the novel, Roark says, "I'm never concerned with my clients, only with their architectural requirements. I consider these as part of my building's theme and problem, as my building's material—just as I consider bricks and steel." (578)

2. To be precise, the description would be the verbal summation of a somewhat more specific visual-structural idea.

3. Ayn Rand, "The Metaphysical Versus the Man-Made," *Philosophy: Who Needs It* (New York: Signet, 1984), 25.

4. The kind of modern architecture created by Howard Roark, and in real life by Frank Lloyd Wright, can legitimately be called romantic. The first designs of this school date from the beginning of the romantic era in the late eighteenth century, when some French architects "rejected any imitation of the past" and, as in the case of Claude-Nicholas Ledoux, "wanted the creative mind to depend upon its own thinking, and exhorted the artist to dare in order to overcome the past." (Emil Kaufmann,

Three Revolutionary Architects, Boulée, Ledoux, and Lequeu [Philadelphia: Transactions of the American Philosophical Society, New Series 42.3, 1952], 434, 479.) A few of these architects' designs are eerily proto-Roarkian, like Ledoux's House of the Surveyors of the Loue or Etienne-Louis Boulée's Entrance to a Cemetery.

5. Victor Hugo, "Preface to *Cromwell*," in Charles W. Eliot, ed., *Prefaces and Prologues to Famous Books* (New York: P F Collier & Son Company, 1910), 385.

6. Hugo, "Preface to *Cromwell*," 377.

7. Hugo, "Preface to *Cromwell*," 382–83.

8. Hugo, "Preface to *Cromwell*," 378.

9. Herbert Grierson, quoted in Mario Praz, *The Romantic Agony* (Oxford: Oxford University Press, 1970), 7.

10. Hugo, "Preface to *Cromwell*," 379.

11. Ayn Rand, "Basic Principles of Literature," *The Romantic Manifesto: A Philosophy of Literature*, revised edition (New York: Signet, 1975), 82. This sentence is italicized in the original.

12. Rand, "Basic Principles of Literature," 85.

13. Hugo, "Preface to *Cromwell*," 379.

14. Robert Mayhew, ed., *Ayn Rand Answers: The Best of Her Q & A* (New York: New American Library, 2005), 189.

15. Ayn Rand discusses the plot-theme of *We the Living* in Ayn Rand, *The Art of Fiction: A Guide for Writers and Readers*, ed. Tore Boeckmann (New York: Plume, 2000), 38.

16. In *The Art of Fiction*, 58, Ayn Rand cautions young writers not to "check yourself against your moral code" when imagining events. Such checking, she implies, properly comes later.

17. Sinclair Lewis, *Elmer Gantry* (New York: Signet, 1967), 17.

18. Lewis, *Elmer Gantry*, 224.

19. See Ayn Rand's remarks on the method behind another of Lewis's character portraits, Babbitt, in "The Psycho-Epistemology of Art," *Romantic Manifesto*, 21.

20. See Jeff Britting, *Ayn Rand* (New York: Overlook Duckworth, 2004), 48.

21. Ayn Rand notes the presence of naturalistic elements in *The Fountainhead* but does not mention any influence from Sinclair Lewis, in Mayhew, *Ayn Rand Answers*, 200. Robert Mayhew discusses the similar styles of satire in *The Fountainhead* and *Elmer Gantry* in "Humor in *The Fountainhead*," in the present collection, 209.

22. Mark Schorer, "Afterword," in Lewis, *Elmer Gantry*, 419.

23. Schorer, "Afterword," 422.

24. David Harriman, ed., *Journals of Ayn Rand* (New York: Dutton, 1997), 118.

25. In her lecture course on literature, Ayn Rand used this part of *The Fountainhead* to illustrate romantic characterization and style, as opposed to the naturalism exemplified by Sinclair Lewis's *Arrowsmith*. See *Art of Fiction*, 59–83, 112–14, 127–28.

26. Ayn Rand, *For the New Intellectual* (New York: Signet, 1963), 68. The word "versus" is italicized in the original.

27. Rand, "Basic Principles of Literature," 81.

28. Rand, "Basic Principles of Literature," 85.

29. Ayn Rand makes this point in *Art of Fiction*, 31.

30. Michael S. Berliner, ed., *Letters of Ayn Rand* (New York: Dutton, 1995), 33.

31. As formulated by Ayn Rand, the theme of *The Fountainhead* could technically express a pro-collectivist, anti-individualist value-perspective. But a collectivist using this theme would probably choose slightly different wording, e.g., he might speak of "atomistic individualism." This kind of issue is mentioned in *Art of Fiction*, 17.

32. Biographical interviews (Ayn Rand Archives).

33. Berliner, *Letters of Ayn Rand*, 430.

34. Ayn Rand, "About a Woman President," *The Voice of Reason: Essays in Objectivist Thought*, ed. Leonard Peikoff (New York: New American Library, 1988), 268.

35. Ayn Rand, *Atlas Shrugged* (New York: Random House, 1957), 760.

36. Unpublished note headlined "Siegfried" and dated March 31, 1967, in the Ayn Rand Archives.

37. The first sexual encounter of Roark and Dominique is the obvious example. But see also the sex scene between Hank Rearden and Dagny Taggart: she knows that "her defiance was submission, that the purpose of all of her violent strength was only to make his victory the greater." Rand, *Atlas Shrugged*, 251.

38. Leonard Peikoff, "Eight Great Plays as Literature and as Philosophy," 1993, lecture 4, "Don Carlos," question period.

39. Peikoff, "Eight Great Plays," lecture 4, "Don Carlos," question period. I base my treatment of the larger issue of love between men on Peikoff's discussion of this literary parallel.

40. Rand, *Atlas Shrugged*, 796–98.

41. Rand, *Art of Fiction*, 15.

42. Rand, "Psycho-Epistemology of Art," 19–20.

43. See Mayhew, *Ayn Rand Answers*, 200.

44. Ayn Rand, "What is Romanticism?" *Romantic Manifesto*, 111.

45. I discuss romantic painting in my unpublished essay "Caspar David Friedrich and Visual Romanticism."

46. Rand, "What is Romanticism?" 99.

47. Rand, *Atlas Shrugged*, 1020.

48. See Ayn Rand, "Art and Cognition," *Romantic Manifesto*, particularly pages 67, 72. She comments on the stylized aspect of romantic art in Mayhew, *Ayn Rand Answers*, 224–25.

49. While a core combination is a necessary means to the stylized, creative projection of an individual artist's values, it is not a *sufficient* means if considered as a purely formal esthetic feature. There are mixed cases where a core combination does not engage with and carry the artist's personal values, but instead is used for a fundamentally classicist or naturalistic end. For instance, certain dramas of the classical tradition, like *Oedipus Rex* and *Le Cid*, have brilliant plot-themes—which engage with and carry *conventional* values. And in some very artistic naturalist short stories, like Guy de Maupassant's "The Necklace," the core-combination device of an O. Henry–like "twist" ending gives poignancy to what is in essence an observed characteristic pattern. By contrast, the twist-at-the-end ideas of O. Henry himself *do* engage with the author's values, and his stories are romantic.

50. These formulations of the theme and plot-theme of *Gone With the Wind* are from Rand, "Basic Principles of Literature," 86.

51. See Leonard Peikoff, *Objectivism: The Philosophy of Ayn Rand* (New York: Dutton, 1991), 414–19.

52. It does function as a *sub*conscious standard. See Ayn Rand, "Art and Sense of Life," *Romantic Manifesto*, 34–44.

53. I discuss how plot constitutes a value-expressive structure in "What Might Be and Ought to Be: Aristotle's *Poetics* and *The Fountainhead*," in the present collection, 155. Plot-theme is not the only form of core combination possible in fiction, although it is by far the most important. I mention twist endings in a preceding endnote. For an indication of yet another device, see my discussions of Ayn Rand's *Anthem* and Ibsen's *Peer Gynt* in Tore Boeckmann, "*Anthem* as a Psychological Fantasy," in Robert Mayhew, ed., *Essays on Ayn Rand's* Anthem (Lanham, MD: Lexington Books, 2005). I discuss visual core combinations in my unpublished essay "Caspar David Friedrich and Visual Romanticism." But much more needs to be said (and discovered) about the nature of the different core-combination devices in the various arts.

54. By contrast, the events of a naturalistic story are selected because they fit the reality-based pattern being presented, not in order to serve any structural need of the story as such. A classical column and its features serve no structural purpose (in a modern building). While a classical building can stand, and a naturalistic novel can have a loosely coherent story, structural concerns are not essential to selecting the concretes of such works.

55. Louis H. Sullivan, *The Autobiography of an Idea* (New York: Dover Publications, Inc., 1956), 258.

56. Sullivan, *Autobiography*, 290. This process is not automatic but requires creative genius at every step. Ayn Rand once described the challenge of finding the right climax for *The Fountainhead* as "a real mind-breaker." Harriman, *Journals of Ayn Rand*, 165.

57. Hugo, "Preface to *Cromwell*," 384.

58. Hugo, "Preface to *Cromwell*," 363–64.

59. Ayn Rand, "The Goal of My Writing," *Romantic Manifesto*, 165–66.

60. Sue Lloyd, *The Man Who Was Cyrano* (Bloomington, Indiana: Unlimited Publishing, 2002), 235.

61. Unique among Rostand's heroes is Jesus, who appears in *The Woman of Samaria*. Rostand being a Christian, his Jesus suffers from no mind-body dichotomy, and interestingly, the play is completely plotless.

62. Edmond Rostand, *Plays of Edmond Rostand, Volume Two*, translated by Henderson Daingerfield Norman (New York: The Macmillan Company, 1921), 351.

63. Harriman, *Journals of Ayn Rand*, 707.

64. Rostand, *Plays*, 236.

65. Rostand, *Plays*, 237.

66. Rostand, *Plays*, 259–60.

67. Hugo, "Preface to *Cromwell*," 387.

68. Hugo, "Preface to *Cromwell*," 405, some emphases removed.

69. Harriman, *Journals of Ayn Rand*, 148.

70. In order to impose some structure on such hashes, Hollywood has developed its own set of pseudo-classicist rules about "character arcs" and "second-act turning points."

71. Harriman, *Journals of Ayn Rand*, 108.

72. Hugo, "Preface to *Cromwell*," 384–85.

73. See Rand, "What is Romanticism?" especially 118–19.

74. Biographical interviews (Ayn Rand Archives).

75. I am grateful to the Ayn Rand Institute for a grant that supported the writing of this essay, to Michael Berliner of the Ayn Rand Archives for providing helpful information, and to Robert Mayhew and Gregory Salmieri for making astute comments on various drafts.

7

What Might Be and Ought to Be

Aristotle's *Poetics* and *The Fountainhead*

Tore Boeckmann

In her 1945 letter "To the Readers of *The Fountainhead*," Ayn Rand writes:

> I decided to be a writer at the age of nine—it was a specific, conscious decision—
> I remember the day and the hour. I did not start by trying to describe the folks
> next door—but by inventing people who did things the folks next door would
> never do. I could summon no interest or enthusiasm for "people as they are"—
> when I had in my mind a blinding picture of people as they could be. . . .
>
> This attitude has never changed. But I went for years thinking that it was a
> strictly personal attitude toward fiction writing, never to be discussed and of no
> interest to anyone but me. Later I discovered I had accepted as the rule of my
> life work a principle stated by Aristotle. Aristotle said that fiction is of greater
> philosophical importance than history, because history represents things only
> as they are, while fiction represents them "as they might be and ought to be."
> If you wish a key to the literary method of *The Fountainhead*, this is it.[1]

The historian, writes Aristotle in the *Poetics*, "speaks of events which
have occurred," the poet (fiction writer) "of the sort of events which could
occur."[2]

In going from "could occur" to "might be and ought to be," did Ayn
Rand misquote Aristotle? Perhaps in the most literalistic sense.[3] But she is
exactly right on the *implications* of Aristotle's "could occur"—and of his
central argument in the *Poetics*. It is to this argument that we must turn in
order to see fully how the *Poetics* holds the key to the literary method of
The Fountainhead.

THE PRINCIPLE OF NECESSITY OR PROBABILITY

When he says that the poet speaks of events that "could occur," Aristotle does not mean simply that fictional events are possible, since this is equally true of historical events. As he himself puts it, "actual events are evidently possible, otherwise they would not have occurred."[4] Rather, "events which *could* occur" are events which "are possible by the standards of probability or necessity."[5]

What Aristotle calls "the principle of necessity or probability" applies to both characterization and plot. "In characterization," he says, "one should always seek [this principle], so that a necessary or probable reason exists for a particular character's speech or action."[6] And at the same time, the events "should arise from the intrinsic structure of the plot, so that what results follows by either necessity or probability from the preceding events."[7]

These two points are inextricable aspects of one whole, for the following reasons.

First, Aristotle's view of characterization is ethics-centered. His word for "character" is "*êthos*," from which we get the English "ethics." Stephen Halliwell notes, in *Aristotle's Poetics*, that Aristotle

> defines *êthos* (which is both "character," an attribute of persons, and "characterisation," a property of the work of art) twice in the course of the treatise . . . both times in very similar language. The first of these passages reads: "character (characterisation) is that which shows the nature of deliberate moral choice . . . consequently there is no character in those speeches in which there is nothing at all that the speaker chooses or rejects" (50b 8–10). The word which Aristotle uses here for choice, *prohairesis*, is not a casual ingredient in anything that people do or say, but a carefully delimited matter of conscious desire and intention, based on dispositions which are those of virtue and vice.[8]

As for the choice between presenting virtue or vice, Aristotle is clear: the "first and foremost" aim of characterization is "that the characters be good."[9]

Second—although this is a point Aristotle does not make explicitly—no particular action follows with necessity from moral character, apart from context. For instance, productiveness is a virtue (at least in Ayn Rand's moral philosophy, if not in Aristotle's), and planting potatoes is a productive act, but it does not follow that if a man is virtuous, he will plant potatoes. "Productiveness" is an abstraction that subsumes an open-ended number of concretes. A virtuous man will take *some* productive action, but *what* action depends on his context—on the values, knowledge, and circumstances that are particular to him.

To show that a particular action follows from a man's moral character, one must show that it follows from his character *in his context*. And the context for a fictional event is the preceding events of the story. Thus, a fiction writer can show an event as necessitated by moral character only by simultaneously showing it as necessitated by the preceding events.

The result is an event that, in Aristotle's phrase, "could occur"—and also one which *should* occur, if the moral character in question is good.

For instance, the central event in *The Fountainhead* is Howard Roark's dynamiting Cortlandt Homes. The foremost aspects of Roark's moral character are his independence and integrity. In his own words, "The only thing that matters, my goal, my reward, my beginning, my end is the work itself. My work done my way" (579). But a man who is independent and has integrity will not necessarily blow up government housing projects. While Roark's action does follow from his character, it does so only in the context of the novel's preceding events.

First, Roark *designed* Cortlandt and made sure that the government agreed to build it exactly as designed. Then Gordon Prescott and Gus Webb, two second-hander architects with bureaucratic pull, disfigured Roark's design. The disfigured design is now under construction; if Roark does nothing, it will stand forever. His achievement will have been desecrated, which is intolerable to a man of his character. It is made clear that he cannot sue the government. His only recourse is to blow up the project, so he dynamites the whole monstrosity.

Had the preceding events been different, e.g., had there been no breach of contract, Roark would have acted differently. (Earlier in the novel, he does not dynamite the disfigured Stoddard Temple.) And had Roark's character been different, e.g., had he been Peter Keating, he would have acted differently. Just as no particular action follows from character apart from context, so none follows from context apart from character. But given his character *and* his context, Roark necessarily acts as he does.

Note that Roark acts by *logical*, not deterministic, necessity. There is no implication of determinism in Aristotle's use of the word "necessity," and none in Ayn Rand's portrayal of Howard Roark.[10] The point is that *if* Roark remains true to his premises, he will blow up Cortlandt. This action is not "what necessarily had to be," but what *could* be—and should be.

THE ROLE OF CONFLICT IN LITERATURE

Although a fictional event can follow from character only in the context of the preceding events, not all "preceding events" constitute a necessitating context. For instance, designing Cortlandt is difficult and exhausting for Roark (585). When the work is completed, he takes a vacation lasting several months. This is plausible: even before Cortlandt, Roark has been very busy for years, and he might well need a rest. But his vacation hardly follows by necessity from his character and the preceding events. Had no mention of a vacation been made in the novel, the reader would have sensed nothing amiss.

Nor is this an atypical case. On the contrary, it represents the ordinary pattern of human actions, which are motivated not by a few antecedent events in isolation, but by the full context of a man's values, knowledge, and circumstances. And this full context is too vast to be specified in a story, which can include only the partial context of the preceding events, plus some adjunct exposition. For instance, Ayn Rand writes the following to explain Roark's vacation: "The work in the office did not require Roark's presence for the next few months. His current jobs were being completed. Two new commissions were not to be started until spring" (601). This provides part of the relevant context, but not nearly enough to make Roark's vacation a logically necessitated action. All we are told is that Roark has some free time—which he might just as plausibly have used to take golf lessons.

This leads us to the following principle: to show an action as following logically from moral character, a writer must turn the *partial* context of the preceding events into the action's only *relevant* context.

The primary (but not exclusive) means to this end is the introduction of a *threat* to someone's important value.

Suppose a man is climbing toward the rim of an inactive volcano. Why does he do so, rather than any of the million other things one can do on earth? We cannot tell from the context. But now suppose the volcano erupts and molten lava streams down toward the man, who turns and runs. Why does he run? Because of the threat to his life.

This threat makes any other aspects of the man's *full* context irrelevant to his action. It doesn't matter whether he is married or single, carefree or troubled, interested in or indifferent to volcanic geology or Etrurian pottery; of all the actions possible to him, running from the lava moves right to the top of the list—if he values his life. In the *partial* context given, his action follows by necessity from the moral premise of self-preservation.

The same principle holds for Roark's dynamiting Cortlandt. The prospect of his achievement's permanent disfigurement is an intolerable threat to an important value of his. There is only one action Roark can take to counter the threat: blow up Cortlandt. This action thus follows logically from his character—in the partial context of the preceding events, and irrespective of any further particularities of Roark's full context. (A necessary condition is that Roark's action is morally legitimate. For instance, he would not have dynamited Cortlandt if this had entailed a breach of contract, let alone the killing of innocent people.)

The heroine of *The Fountainhead*, Dominique Francon, also faces a threat to her values. She is a passionate idealist who believes that the overwhelming majority of men are corrupt and debased, and that the good has no chance among them. It follows from this viewpoint that *any* genuine value is a threat to the valuer: it makes him vulnerable to the onslaughts of an in-imical world. In her own life, Dominique has countered this threat in the only way she thinks possible: by pursuing no serious existential values. In this manner, she has shielded herself and maintained her peace of mind.

Then she meets and falls in love with Roark.

Recognizing his genius, she thinks he is doomed, as true genius always is. The world will inevitably destroy him. In other words, another important value of hers is under threat. This time the threat comes not only from the world, but also from Roark himself, who disagrees with her viewpoint and refuses to give up his career, as she has given up pursuing serious values. Dominique thus faces the prospect of standing back and watching Roark rise—knowing that the higher he rises, the harder and more painfully he will be brought down.

But there is one way that she can counteract this threat: she can seize every opportunity to impede Roark's career and thus soften the blow she thinks is coming.

Dominique's campaign against Roark's career follows logically from her premises and her love for Roark. Given her character, no further particular-ities of her context could possibly be relevant to her—not so long as Roark is about to be crushed and she can act to protect him.

The examples given of necessitated action all involve *conflict*. Dominique is in conflict with the world and with Roark; Roark is in conflict with Prescott, Webb, and the government; and at least in a metaphorical sense, the volcano climber is in conflict with the streaming lava. Indeed, it is a com-monplace observation that conflict is the essence of drama and storytelling.

Yet conflict is undesirable in life. A threat to one's values must be squarely confronted—but it would be better if no threat existed in the first place.

Why does one want to contemplate in fiction what one rationally hopes to avoid in life? We have indicated the answer. Conflict in literature posits a threat to someone's important value, a threat he can counteract only by some specific action. This action then follows by necessity from his moral premises, since the specified context neutralizes the potential relevance of any further particularities of his full (unspecified) context.

Paradoxically, conflict makes possible the literary presentation of that which might be and ought to be.

ETHICS-CENTERED CHARACTERIZATION
VERSUS "PEOPLE AS THEY ARE"

An ethics-centered view of literary characterization rests on an ethics-centered view of human *character*. It is incompatible with the assumption, widespread in the modern world, that *emotions* are irreducible motivational primaries. On the modern view, abstract moral deliberation is more likely a mere rationalization of emotional impulses than the true arbiter of human action. Such an emotion-centered view of character in turn leads to a literary approach to characterization very different from Aristotle's.

Stephen Halliwell perceptively describes the difference:

> A significant element in the divergence between Aristotelian and modern ideas of character lies in the contrast of the relative narrowness and determinacy of the former with the fluidity and uncertainty of the latter. . . . Psychological inwardness is a major assumption in modern convictions about character, and this in turn leads to typical emphases on the uniqueness of the individual personality and on the potential complexities of access to the character of others. If character is thought of in strongly psychological terms, then the possibility readily arises that it may remain concealed in the inner life of the mind, or be only partially and perhaps deceptively revealed to the outer world; but, equally, that it may be glimpsed or intimated in various unintended or unconscious ways. Such ideas and possibilities . . . are by their very intricacy and indefiniteness the antithesis of the theory of dramatic character presented in the *Poetics*.[11]

Consistent with their basic view of human character, modern writers present people who act, not on abstract moral premises, but strictly on emotion (or "psychology"). And in the absence of an abstract premise and a necessitating context, no amount of emotion-centered characterization can make an action follow with logical necessity. No matter how perceptively the emotional life of a "modern" literary character is delineated, the possibility always remains that crucial aspects of his psychology "remain concealed in the inner life of the mind" or are "only partially and perhaps deceptively revealed to the outer world." Ultimately, one has to take as a *given* that the character simply felt like doing what he did.

By contrast, it is not a given that a character on the ethics-centered pattern acts as he does. He acts with *logical* necessity, given some premise, but he has to hold and apply his premises by choice. (I discuss ethics-centered, volitional characterization versus emotion-centered, deterministic characterization in "Conscious vs. Subconscious Motivation in Literature."[12])

Proponents of modern characterization say that it reflects "people as they are." In real life, they say, people's actions are normally determined by all kinds of factors of which onlookers lack knowledge. There *are* significant "complexities of access to the character of others." Their motives may be "glimpsed or intimated" in various ways, but we rarely see logical necessity.

Proponents of ethics-centered characterization will answer that this is precisely the problem overcome by establishing a necessitating context. Such a context provides what is elusive in real life—transparent access to human motivation—by making specific actions follow by logical necessity from moral universals.[13]

Which side of this divide one falls down on ultimately depends on one's view of the role of morality and emotion in human motivation. For instance, Halliwell shares all the modern presuppositions. Thus, after intelligently identifying Aristotle's view of characterization, he describes it as "narrow" and implies that it is simplistic, as opposed to the "intricacy" of the modern approach.

I would reply that ethics-centered characterization may be highly complex, as in the case of Dominique. And as Halliwell himself notes, Aristotle's "*êthos* is a matter of generic qualities (virtues and vices)."[14] In other words, the ethics-centered approach deals with broad abstractions. It is the opposite of narrow.

THE UNION OF THE UNIVERSAL AND THE PARTICULAR

In the key passage of the *Poetics*, Aristotle writes:

> It is [because the poet speaks not of events which have occurred but of events which could occur] that poetry is both more philosophical and more serious than history, since poetry speaks more of universals, history of particulars. A universal comprises the *kind* of speech or action which belongs by probability or necessity to a certain *kind* of character.[15]

How can poetry (fiction) speak more of universals than does history? The events of fiction are no less particular than those of history. Roark's blowing up Cortlandt is a *particular* action. It does concretize abstractions—independence and integrity—but so do historical events. A good historian does not merely list facts, but shows, say, how George Washington's courage, integrity, and loyalty to republican values made him a great general and statesman. (In this sense, good history writing does not show people "as they are" in the primacy-of-emotion way of modern literary characterization.)

However, the particulars of fiction do more than simply concretize abstractions.

To see the difference, take again the example of a man planting potatoes. This is a concretization of the virtue of productiveness; but as we have said, the fact that a man is virtuous does not mean that he will plant potatoes. A modern man has an almost limitless range of productive options, and his choice of any one of them depends on an enormously complex context. Conversely, the fact that a man plants potatoes does not mean that he is virtuous. Maybe he is a stagnant family traditionalist who works the farm he happens to have inherited—"because that's what my father and grandfather did." In other words, since the man has countless productive options, his specific choice might be governed by immoral premises.

But now suppose that a man is stranded on a desert island where potatoes are the only edible vegetation. In his context, planting potatoes is not one of a range of productive options, but the *only* such option. (Or nearly so, if we assume that the man can also fish and build a hut.) If this man holds productiveness as a virtue, he will plant potatoes.

Desert-island stories like *Robinson Crusoe* turn man's productiveness—the long-range material sustenance of his life—into necessitated particulars. The castaway's full context of knowledge and values is made irrelevant to his actions, not this time by a threat to his values, but by the radical constriction of his existential circumstances. However, the result is the same: just as the man running from lava has one option if he is to live, and Roark has one option if he is to protect the integrity of his work, so the castaway has one option if he is to produce (and survive long-range).

The castaway's planting potatoes, the volcano climber's running, and Roark's blowing up Cortlandt are more than simple concretizations of abstractions: in the context in which these actions occur, they *become one* with the normative premises that necessitate them.

We can now see why "poetry speaks more of universals, history of particulars." This is not because fiction discusses universals as such and history is unconcerned with them, but because the particulars of fiction represent, in their context, the unique *union* of the universal and the particular.

Moral abstractions like productiveness, self-preservation, and integrity prescribe what men should do, but not what they should do concretely. But in a necessitating context, a moral abstraction *does* prescribe a concrete. The castaway *should* plant potatoes. The volcano climber *should* run. Roark *should* blow up Cortlandt.

Ethics-centered characterization (and plotting) puts the *should* into concretizations of moral abstractions. This is an enormous literary virtue. A work of fiction is not a lecture on ethics. A reader or theatergoer does not primarily seek illumination about what a man should do abstractly, but wants to see him do it concretely. As Ayn Rand explains:

> Although the representation of things "as they might be and ought to be" helps man to achieve these things in real life, this is only a secondary value. The *primary* value is that it gives him the experience of living in a world where things are *as they ought to be*. This experience is of crucial importance to him: it is his psychological life line.
>
> Since man's ambition is unlimited, since his pursuit and achievement of values is a lifelong process—and the higher the values, the harder the struggle—man needs a moment, an hour or some period of time in which he can experience the sense of his completed task, the sense of living in a universe where his values have been successfully achieved. It is like a moment of rest, a moment to gain fuel to move farther. Art gives him that fuel. Art gives him the experience of seeing the full, immediate, concrete reality of his distant goals.[16]

It does so by presenting the perfect union of the abstract and the concrete in the realm of human values.

WHAT OUGHT AND OUGHT NOT TO BE

The values concretized in fiction may be material or social, as in science fiction or utopias. Primarily, however, fiction is concerned with values of character. (This is a point missed by those who object that *The Fountainhead* and *Atlas Shrugged* do not present "what ought to be," since the heroes confront an inimical society.)

The character values presented in a story may be basic, as with the man running from lava, who is preserving his life but whose character is not further delineated. Or the values may be advanced ethical abstractions, as with Howard Roark's pursuit of integrity and independence.

They may also be dubious.

For instance, Dominique Francon is wrong about the world—as she discovers by the novel's end. The good is *not* doomed to defeat; a Howard Roark can succeed, triumphing over the worst of obstacles.

Insofar as Dominique's actions to sabotage Roark's career are based on a mistaken premise about the world, they are not "what ought to be." But those same actions *are* what ought to be—insofar as they are based on Dominique's passionate desire to protect the human ideal. And this last trait is Dominique's real essence. In other words, a character's actions are not always necessitated by a single, isolated premise but may be based on a *set* of premises. If these premises are inconsistent, it is by identifying what is morally essential that one decides whether the character is good, and to what extent his actions are admirable.

The best example is the famous scene in *Les Misérables* where the Bishop of Digne gives his silver candelabra to the thief Jean Valjean. In one respect, the Bishop's gesture is the ultimate act of altruism. Yet this scene was greatly admired by Ayn Rand, the foremost philosophical opponent of altruism, who saw the essence of the Bishop's gesture in the self-assertive grandeur with which he acts on his convictions.[17] (The author himself, Victor Hugo, would have agreed with Ayn Rand in regard to the grandeur, but would in addition have admired the element of altruism.)

When Dominique's actions against Roark's career fail to stop him, she realizes that to remain his mistress means being forever torn between her love for him and her fear of his destruction. Lacking the strength for this torture, she decides to leave him. But she concludes that to allow herself any measure of happiness thereafter would be a compromise with a world she despises. In effect, the possibility of such happiness constitutes a threat to her purity of soul—a threat she counters by the most effective means at hand. She marries Peter Keating.

Dominique's campaign against Roark constitutes a solid contradiction: an idealistic pursuit based on the premise that ideals are doomed. In marrying Keating, she resolves the contradiction by acting more consistently with the *mistaken* part of her mixed premises. Her marriage therefore does not represent "what ought to be" in the assertive, colorful way that her actions to protect Roark do—not if what ought to be is Dominique's essential idealism. From the viewpoint of that idealism, her marriage to Keating is a heartbreaking defeat (like a tragic ending, only in this case a temporary one).

On Keating's part, the marriage represents unqualified immorality.

Note first that Keating does not marry Dominique for love.[18] He loves Katie Halsey. He is goaded into marrying Dominique by Ellsworth Toohey, who tells him:

> "[L]ooking at you tonight, I couldn't help thinking of the woman who would have made such a perfect picture by your side."
>
> "Who?"
>
> "Oh, don't pay attention to me. It's only an esthetic fancy. Life is never as perfect as that. People have too much to envy you for. You couldn't add *that* to your other achievements."
>
> "Who?"
>
> "Drop it Peter. You can't get her. Nobody can get her. You're good, but you're not good enough for that."
>
> "Who?"
>
> "Dominique Francon, of course." (321)

Keating's marrying Dominique will impress others, Toohey tells him. (In the novel, he adds that a marriage to the socially awkward Katie will impress no one.) And Keating is a second-hander, a man who attempts to achieve self-esteem from the opinion of others. He himself states his primary motivating premise: "always be what people want you to be. Then you've got them where you want them" (261). Given this premise, and the context of the novel, Keating *necessarily* says yes when Dominique proposes.

Note that Keating faces no threat to his values that makes irrelevant his full context (which includes his love for Katie). His action is logically necessitated for two other reasons. First, his motivating premise enjoins him precisely to disregard the full context and heed only the partial context of fashionable opinion—which in this case has been expressed by the authoritative voice of Toohey. Second, Dominique is not just one rich and beautiful society girl among others. She is (as Toohey correctly implies) in a class by herself, and marrying her is a *unique* opportunity for Keating to achieve his central goal of impressing others. So we need no more wonder why he says yes than why a man who values money abstains from tearing up a winning lottery ticket. In either case, it is hard to see what particularities of the full context could motivate a different choice.

As necessitated by a normative premise and the story context, Keating's decision to marry Dominique is an example of ethics-centered characterization and story construction. Yet his premise is immoral, and his action is that which ought *not* to be. Should we then speak in general of "what might be and ought *or ought not* to be"? No, for the same reason that Thomas Jefferson did not speak, in the Declaration of Independence, of the rights to "Life or Death, Liberty and the pursuit of Happiness or Misery." The statement of a principle must focus on fundamentals, not derivative issues. And evil is a side issue in literature. What matters is the good; not Peter Keating, but Howard Roark.

Take Roark's reaction to Dominique's marriage:

Dominique, if I told you now to have that marriage annulled at once—to forget the world and my struggle—to feel no anger, no concern, no hope—just to exist for me, for my need of you—as my wife—as my property . . . ?

She answers, "I'd obey you." But Roark tells her:

If you married me now, I would become your whole existence. But I would not want you then. You would not want yourself—and so you would not love me long. To say "I love you" one must know first how to say the "I." The kind of surrender I could have from you now would give me nothing but an empty hulk. If I demanded it, I'd destroy you. That's why I won't stop you. I'll let you go to your husband. (376)

Dominique's marriage to Keating is obviously a threat to Roark's values. But the one thing he could do to make her reconsider would pose an even greater threat: it would turn Dominique into an unthinking appendage. So Roark necessarily *foregoes* the action.

This is what might be and ought to be—without qualification.

Aristotle, who says that the first aim of characterization is "that the characters be good," does allow for some portrayal of moral baseness if the poet "makes use" of it.[19] And in *The Fountainhead*, Ayn Rand makes use of Keating's immorality. She makes it part of the necessitating context for the actions of the ideal man: Howard Roark.

ADVERSITY, CONFLICT, AND PLOT STRUCTURE

A work of fiction, Aristotle says, should be a whole.

> By "whole" I mean possessing a beginning, middle and end. By "beginning" I
> mean that which does not have a necessary connection with a preceding event,
> but which can itself give rise naturally to some further fact or occurrence. An
> "end," by contrast, is something which naturally occurs after a preceding event,
> whether by necessity or as a general rule, but need not be followed by anything
> else. The "middle" involves causal connections with both what precedes and
> what ensues. Consequently, well designed plot-structures ought not to begin or
> finish at arbitrary points, but to follow the principles indicated.[20]

Plot is the principle of necessitated action applied to the *structure* of a
story. An example is the progression in *The Fountainhead* from Dominique's
meeting Roark—to her campaign against his career—to her leaving him—
to Keating's accepting her proposal—to Roark's letting her go—to the climax of the novel, where Dominique sees that the world can never beat
Roark, and she marries him. Their conflict is resolved and "need not be followed by anything else."

In a plot, the events are connected by the principle of necessity or probability in that one action establishes the context which necessitates the next
one. Such a structure presupposes a unifying element of *adversity*, which
generates a series of linked value-threats across time, as does the conflict between Roark and Dominique.

Some stories present necessitated action without adversity, for instance,
Robinson Crusoe. (Having to work to survive, even under primitive, desert-
island conditions, does not constitute dramatic adversity, since no value-
threats are involved.) But observe that Crusoe's necessitated productive actions are not linked in a *structure* of necessity. The novel has no plot.

Aristotle stresses the importance of adversity in literature. A tragedy, he
says, presents "a probable or necessary succession of events which produce
a transformation either from affliction to prosperity, or the reverse."[21] At
one point, he says that a fine plot should "involve a change from prosperity to affliction (rather than the reverse)."[22] Here he probably has in mind
the main dramatic situation,[23] not the final resolution, since he later implies a preference for happy endings.[24] In any case, Aristotle is clear on the
larger issue: a tragic hero must confront adversity. (The word translated
above as "affliction" [*dustuchia*] also means "adversity."[25])

Adversity is a somewhat wider term than conflict (which is one form of
adversity). The literary role of both phenomena is to pose threats to values.
But while the threats in a novel like *The Fountainhead* proceed from conflicts
of values, adversity is the better term for the source of value-threats in the
Greek tragedies Aristotle analyzed.

Consider one of his favorites: Sophocles's *Oedipus Rex*.

The play opens as the citizens of the Greek city Thebes approach their king, Oedipus, in supplication. Oedipus greets them with these words:

> What is the matter? Some fear? Something you desire?
> I would willingly do anything to help you;
> Indeed I should be heartless, were I to stop my ears
> To a general petition such as this.[26]

His subjects tell Oedipus that the city is stricken with famine and pestilence. Oedipus, who came to Thebes as a young man and became its king after he defeated a terrible monster, the Sphinx, is now asked to save the city again. He replies that he is aware of the current affliction and has already done something—"The only thing that promised hope." He has sent his brother-in-law Creon to an oracle of Apollo, "to learn what act / Or word of mine could help you."[27]

Oedipus is a pious man faced with a mysterious disaster that implies the loss of divine favor. It is logical that an appeal to the oracle would seem to him "the only thing that promised hope." Further, Oedipus is not "heartless" but, as he claims, a benevolent ruler who cares about the welfare of his subjects. Therefore, faced by the threat of the city's continuing affliction, he would necessarily *do* "the only thing" that can save the city.

By contrast, the emperor Nero, who fiddled while Rome burned, was not a benevolent ruler. Admittedly, Rome's burning was merely part of his context (and one aspect of his full context might well have been a keen interest in music). But if Nero had been a benevolent ruler, the threat to his values posed by the city's affliction would have made any lesser factors motivationally insignificant, and he would have been helping his subjects cope with the fire.

In *Oedipus Rex*, Creon returns with Apollo's answer: the unavenged killing of the city's previous king, Laius, is polluting Thebes. Oedipus is told that Laius was killed while traveling outside the city. Blood must be paid for his blood, but so far no one has found or punished the murderer. Oedipus swears to do so.

This is a necessary action for several reasons. First, the capture of Laius's killer is the only action that can save Thebes from affliction. Second, as a prudent man, Oedipus must catch the regicide, who (he says) might come for *him* next. Third, as a pious man, Oedipus *would* obey Apollo and the duty of blood revenge. (This "pious necessity" is not occasioned by a value-threat but is a matter of simple obedience to a supernatural authority.)

In fact, Oedipus is himself the killer, and the son, of Laius. He has also married Laius's widow, Jocasta—his own mother. When he starts to investigate Laius's killing, Oedipus does not know the truth. But clues soon surface, and others beseech him to let a sleeping dog lie. (They regard the truth as disastrous for Oedipus, since the blood duties he has transgressed, however unwittingly, are out-of-context, supernaturally ordained absolutes.) Jocasta tells him: "No! In God's name—if you want to live, this quest / Must not go on." Yet Oedipus is adamant. "I must pursue this trail to the end," he says. "I cannot leave the truth unknown."[28]

Oedipus's investigative persistence follows from a trait of character: his absolute refusal to evade the truth about himself. As he puts it: "I ask to be no other man / Than that I am, and *will know who I am.*"[29] This premise necessitates his actions—in the implied context of *a threat to his pride*. Oedipus can abandon his quest but not erase from his mind the preliminary evidence and his suspicion about the facts. These would remind him constantly that he is guilty of evasion. And Oedipus is first and foremost a proud man—so he chooses the only course that can possibly save his pride: to press on and take his chances with the truth.

The plot of *Oedipus Rex* is a structure of necessitated action depending on a unifying element of adversity: divine disfavor. It is Apollo who causes the famine and pestilence, who demands blood revenge for Laius's death, and ultimately, who has engineered Oedipus's strange fate.

But observe that Apollo does not do any of these things because his moral premises differ from Oedipus's. And Oedipus, who bears no fault for having killed his father and married his mother, does not challenge the premise that his actions, as violations of blood taboos, place him outside the realm of moral values. The acts and decrees of the gods are treated as givens, to be accepted without evaluation; they simply strike Oedipus as disease or accident might strike another man. When Oedipus finally learns the truth and is asked what power has driven him to his tragic end, he answers, "Apollo, friends, Apollo / Has laid this agony upon me."[30]

In *The Fountainhead*, Roark battles a different kind of adversity. The threats to his values are caused by the differences between his own values and those of his adversaries. He struggles in his romantic life because Dominique thinks that a man of integrity and independence is doomed. He struggles in his career because most men lack his dedication to integrity and independence. In other words, Roark faces *conflicts of values*.

Ayn Rand's reliance on such conflicts reveals her as a thoroughgoing *romantic*.

The distinguishing characteristic of the romantic era was its emphasis on the particular values of *individuals*, and thus on the importance of the differences among men's values. This emphasis represented a radical break with tradition, best illustrated by the rise in the nineteenth century of the ideal of romantic *love*. For the Greeks, in the words of Morton M. Hunt, love was "an amusing pastime and distraction, or sometimes a god-sent affliction."[31] The same view dominated Western culture as late as the eighteenth century: love was a pleasant game or, in Jonathan Swift's words, a "ridiculous passion which hath no being but in play-books and romances."[32] Romanticism swept aside this tradition, holding that a profound value-affinity between two individuals, as contrasted with all others, is not a form of madness, but the proper basis for love (and marriage).

The same break with tradition occurred in literature. While there is conflict in pre-romantic fiction, the idea of literary adversity as based primarily on differences of abstract values is the great romantic literary innovation.

We will examine the further significance of the difference between Greek adversity and romantic value-conflicts in the next section. Here we need only note that, while Aristotle does not discuss conflict in the *Poetics*, Ayn Rand, the romanticist, stresses its importance. In "Basic Principles of Literature," she writes:

> Since a plot is the dramatization of goal-directed action, it has to be based on *conflict*; it may be one character's inner conflict or a conflict of goals and values between two or more characters. Since goals are not achieved automatically, the dramatization of a purposeful pursuit has to include obstacles; it has to involve a clash, a struggle—an action struggle, but not a purely physical one.[33]

Here Ayn Rand offers a metaphysical justification for adversity and conflict in literature ("goals are not achieved automatically"). But elsewhere, in a more extensive but extemporaneous discussion (addressed to writers), she says:

> To illustrate the achievement of a purpose, you have to show men overcoming obstacles. This statement pertains strictly to writers. Metaphysically—in reality—one does not need obstacles in order to achieve a purpose. But you as a writer need to *dramatize* purpose, i.e., you have to isolate the particular meaning that you want your events to illustrate—by presenting it in a *stressed* action form.[34]

It is possible, she goes on, that in real life an architect like Howard Roark would

> achieve great success without any opposition. But that would be completely wrong artistically. Since my purpose [in *The Fountainhead*] is to show that a man of creative independence will achieve his goal regardless of any opposition, a story in which there *is* no opposition would not dramatize my message. I have to show the hero in a difficult struggle—and the worse I can make it, the better dramatically.[35]

The essence of plot structure, she sums up, is "struggle—therefore, conflict—therefore, climax."[36]

Here Ayn Rand offers an *esthetic* justification for adversity and conflict in literature: these are needed in order to isolate some particular meaning of the events, and thus to dramatize a message.

Or as I would argue: adversity and conflict, qua central generators of value-threats, create a structure of actions which embody specific (isolated) moral abstractions and dramatize moral values.

ADVERSITY, CONFLICT, AND THE ETHICS-CENTERED APPROACH

Discussing the difference between romantic and pre-romantic plots, Ayn Rand observes that

> in Greek tragedies, although the events follow from each other once they start, both the start of a chain of events and particularly the ending are not determined by the characters of the drama. The actions of the characters follow from some event, some issue, over which they really have no control—an issue not of their choice. And the resolution ultimately comes from the gods, from fate, from an issue not of their choice. In other words, the characters are not motivated and concluded on the ground of *their* choices, *their* values. They are not started nor finished by their own hand.[37]

Ayn Rand's point is demonstrated by *Oedipus Rex*, where the hero battles and is defeated by the disfavor of Apollo.

Stephen Halliwell makes a very similar point when he writes that

> the universe portrayed in all the Greek tragedies we know—including those which Aristotle himself cites most frequently—is one in which significant human action is never regarded as wholly autonomous or independent of larger, non-human powers. By contrast with this, Aristotle's own understanding of dramatic action posits, it seems to me, nothing other than intrinsic and purely human criteria of plausibility and causal intelligibility.[38]

This does not mean that Aristotle is unaware of the fatalistic aspects of Greek tragedy. But he cautions the poet against them. In regard to endings, he writes: "It is evident that the dénouements of plot-structures should arise from the plot itself, and not, as in *Medea*, from a *deus ex machina*." More broadly, he states that "No irrational element should have a part in the events, unless outside the tragedy (as, for example, in Sophocles' *Oedipus*)."[39] ("Outside the tragedy," I take it, refers to that which gives rise to the necessitated chain of events, but is not itself part of the chain.)

It is with this in mind that we should read an odd passage in the *Poetics*. Aristotle says that "good men should not be shown passing from prosperity to affliction, for this is . . . repulsive." The proper hero of a tragedy, he concludes, is a man "who is not preeminent in virtue and justice, and one who falls into affliction not because of evil and wickedness, but because of a certain fallibility (*hamartia*)."[40]

Here Aristotle seems to be contradicting himself. The foremost aim of characterization, he has said, is "that the characters be good." He has also said that a plot should "involve a change from prosperity to affliction." Yet now he finds it repulsive if good men are shown passing from prosperity to affliction, and he concludes that tragedy should not present morally perfect men.

Aristotle's ambivalence toward the portrayal of adversity in fiction is best understood by comparing it to a somewhat similar attitude of Ayn Rand's. "I have to show the hero in a difficult struggle," she said, "and the worse I can make it, the better dramatically"; but this does not mean that she approved of all kinds of adversity. At age twelve, she was angered by the ending of Walter Scott's *The Bride of Lammermoor*, where the hero accidentally rides into quicksand and perishes. As an adult, she loathed Hemingway's *A Farewell to Arms*, where the heroine dies in childbirth.[41]

In fiction, Ayn Rand held, *accidental* adversity and tragedy implies a profoundly malevolent metaphysical outlook: it conveys the message that moral values are irrelevant to human success or failure, and thus to human life. In an ethics-centered work, such an element obviously contradicts and wipes out the message of the rest of the story. Accidental adversity is less incongruous in an emotion-centered work like *A Farewell to Arms*. But in either case, a reader on the ethics-centered premise would justly regard such adversity as metaphysically repulsive.

By contrast, in Ayn Rand's own novel *We the Living*, the heroine dies at the end—but not accidentally. Kira Argounova is killed by an agent of the same communist state that she has been battling throughout the story. Similarly, the tuberculosis of her lover (a key part of the adversity governing her necessitated plot actions) is not an accidental affliction, but a consequence of the living conditions imposed under communism. Here, the adversity comes from moral premises and can be morally evaluated. The evaluation should be negative: the actions and premises of the communists in the novel are *morally* repulsive. But this kind of adversity does not contradict the ethics-centered approach of the rest of the story; on the contrary, it underscores the importance of moral values in human life. It is not *metaphysically* repulsive.

In Ayn Rand's view, "both adversaries [of a proper plot conflict] must have free will; two choices, two sets of values, must be involved."[42] This, we can now see, is a requirement of a *consistently* ethics-centered approach to literature.

It is also a thoroughly *romantic* conception of literary adversity, resting on philosophical presuppositions not available in Ancient Greece and certainly not reflected in its literature.

Thus Aristotle's dilemma: given the limitations of the literature familiar to him, he is left with divine affliction as the price for ethics-centered characterization. But he finds such affliction as repulsive as Ayn Rand found accidental tragedy, and for the same reason: it contradicts the ethics-centered approach on the deepest metaphysical level. Aristotle tries to solve this dilemma by requiring some kind of minor moral flaw or error in the hero that provides an *ethical* explanation for his falling into misfortune.[43] But I believe it is an indication of his commitment to this solution that he provides little concrete discussion of what exactly he has in mind.

Aristotle's dilemma was only solved with the advent of romanticism. And there is no greater testament to his genius than the fact that he identified the might-be-and-ought-to-be principle (i.e., the ethics-centered approach) from studying Greek tragedies, more than two thousand years before the rise of the literary school that consistently practices his principle.

CONCLUSION

Writes Aristotle in the *Poetics*:

> Since the poet, like the painter or any other image-maker, is a mimetic [representational] artist, he must in any particular instance use mimesis to portray one of three objects: the sort of things which were or are the case; the sort of things men say and think to be the case; the sort of things that should be the case.[44]

Aristotle gives an example of the latter method from the field of painting: "it may be impossible that there are people such as Zeuxis painted them, but it is better so, for the artist should improve on his model."[45] Lack of literal verisimilitude, he says, is not a failure of poetic art "if the poet *intends* to portray something which is erroneous, such as a horse with its two right legs simultaneously forward."[46] In such a case, "if the charge is one of falsehood, a possible defence is that things are being portrayed as they *should* be."[47]

Ayn Rand held similar views. "There is a story told about Michelangelo," she writes in a 1944 letter to a fan of *The Fountainhead*,

> on one of his statues (that of David, I believe) he made a muscle which never existed on a real human body; when he was told that nature never created such a muscle, he answered that nature should have. *That* is the true artist.

Ayn Rand went on:

You said that some people told you that much of *The Fountainhead* couldn't happen. Tell them for me that it happened in *The Fountainhead*.[48]

NOTES

1. Michael S. Berliner, ed., *Letters of Ayn Rand* (New York: Dutton, 1995), 669–70.

2. Stephen Halliwell, *The* Poetics *of Aristotle* (London: Duckworth, 1987), 41 (*Poetics* ch. 9).

3. And even this is not clear. Robert Mayhew comments that the "could occur" is "a translation of *an genoito*, a potential optative. The potential optative expresses possibility, but may also carry a normative flavor. As Herbert Smyth writes (§ 1824): 'The potential optative with *an* states a future possibility, propriety, or likelihood, as an *opinion* of the speaker; and may be translated by *may, might, can* (especially with a negative), *must, would, should* . . .' (*Greek Grammar*, rev. ed. [Cambridge: Harvard University Press, 1956], 407). This combination of possibility and propriety is no doubt what [is aimed for] in translating the Greek 'might be and ought to be.'" Robert Mayhew, "Ayn Rand as Aristotelian: Literary Esthetics," paper presented before the Ayn Rand Society, at the December 2005 Eastern Division Meeting of the American Philosophical Association. Mayhew notes that Ayn Rand probably borrowed her English version of Aristotle's phrase from Albert Jay Nock's *The Memoirs of A Superfluous Man* (New York: Harper and Brothers, 1943), 191. But her familiarity with and admiration for the *Poetics* was certainly not limited to what she might have gotten from Nock. In a 1960s lecture on "The Esthetics of Literature" she said that "the only work of *major* value" in the field of esthetics "is Aristotle's" (typescript in the Ayn Rand Archives). See also Robert Mayhew, ed., *Ayn Rand Answers: The Best of Her Q&A* (New York: New American Library, 2005), 218, 224.

4. Halliwell, *The* Poetics *of Aristotle*, 41 (*Poetics* ch. 9).

5. Halliwell, *The* Poetics *of Aristotle*, 40 (*Poetics* ch. 9).

6. Halliwell, *The* Poetics *of Aristotle*, 48 (*Poetics* ch. 15).

7. Halliwell, *The* Poetics *of Aristotle*, 42 (*Poetics* ch. 10).

8. Stephen Halliwell, *Aristotle's Poetics* (Chicago: University of Chicago Press, 1998), 150–51. See also Halliwell, *The* Poetics *of Aristotle*, 75–76.

9. Halliwell, *The* Poetics *of Aristotle*, 47 (*Poetics* ch. 15).

10. See Halliwell, *The* Poetics *of Aristotle*, 99–100. Ayn Rand, discussing *Les Misérables*, says approvingly that "each event is necessitated by the preceding one—necessitated not deterministically, but *logically*. 'If A, then B logically had to follow.'" Ayn Rand, *The Art of Fiction: A Guide for Writers and Readers*, ed. Tore Boeckmann (New York: Plume, 2000), 25. She is here speaking extemporaneously. In her published writings she makes the same point exclusively in terms of "logical connections" and not "necessity," probably because the latter word now has connotations of determinism that it would not have had for Aristotle. (I owe this point to Harry Binswanger.)

11. Halliwell, *Aristotle's Poetics*, 150.

12. Tore Boeckmann, "Conscious vs. Subconscious Motivation in Literature," *The Intellectual Activist* 7.4–5 (July and September 1993).

13. See Ayn Rand, "Basic Principles of Literature," *The Romantic Manifesto: A Philosophy of Literature*, revised edition (New York: Signet, 1975), 83–84.

14. Halliwell, *Aristotle's Poetics*, 151.

15. Halliwell, *The* Poetics *of Aristotle*, 41 (*Poetics* ch. 9).

16. Ayn Rand, "The Goal of My Writing," *Romantic Manifesto*, 170.

17. I base this interpretation of Ayn Rand's views on comments she made in the question period to lecture 16 of her 1969 nonfiction-writing course. These comments are somewhat garbled in the existing tape recording, which is at the Ayn Rand Archives.

18. Actions flowing *directly* from love cannot be presented in fiction as necessary, since love always depends on one's *full* context. This is why stories dealing only with love as such are boring.

19. Halliwell, *The* Poetics *of Aristotle*, 63 (*Poetics* ch. 25).

20. Halliwell, *The* Poetics *of Aristotle*, 39 (*Poetics* ch. 7).

21. Halliwell, *The* Poetics *of Aristotle*, 40 (*Poetics* ch. 7).

22. Halliwell, *The* Poetics *of Aristotle*, 45 (*Poetics* ch. 13).

23. In chapter 18, he implies that the main transformation to prosperity or affliction occurs early in a play.

24. See Halliwell, *The* Poetics *of Aristotle*, 47 (*Poetics* ch. 14). A "tragedy," for Aristotle, is a serious drama, as opposed to a comedy, and can have a happy ending—as does one of his favorites, Euripides' *Iphigenia in Tauris*.

25. See Halliwell, *Aristotle's Poetics*, 204.

26. Sophocles, *The Theban Plays*, translated by E.F. Watling (London: Penguin Books, 1947), 25–26.

27. Sophocles, *Theban Plays*, 27.

28. Sophocles, *Theban Plays*, 55.

29. Sophocles, *Theban Plays*, 55. The emphasis is Watling's.

30. Sophocles, *Theban Plays*, 62.

31. Morton M. Hunt, *The Natural History of Love* (New York: Alfred A. Knopf, 1959), 16.

32. Quoted in Hunt, *Natural History*, 255.

33. Ayn Rand, "Basic Principles of Literature," 86.

34. Ayn Rand, *Art of Fiction*, 22. She makes the same points in "Cyrano de Bergerac," taped radio interview, Ayn Rand Archives.

35. Ayn Rand, *Art of Fiction*, 22.

36. Ayn Rand, *Art of Fiction*, 23.

37. "Our Esthetic Vacuum: Questions and Answers with Ayn Rand," taped radio interview, the Ayn Rand Bookstore.

38. Halliwell, *The* Poetics *of Aristotle*, 13.

39. Halliwell, *The* Poetics *of Aristotle*, 48 (*Poetics* ch. 15).

40. Halliwell, *The* Poetics *of Aristotle*, 44 (*Poetics* ch. 13).

41. See Biographical interviews (Ayn Rand Archives) and Mayhew, *Ayn Rand Answers*, 202–3.

42. Ayn Rand, *Art of Fiction*, 23.

43. Halliwell provides a very similar interpretation in chapter 7 of *Aristotle's Poetics*, 202–37.

44. Halliwell, *The* Poetics *of Aristotle*, 61 (*Poetics* ch. 25). Turned into consistent creative *methods*, these three approaches lead to the three foremost schools of art in modern history: naturalism, classicism, and romanticism. See my "*The Fountainhead* as a Romantic Novel," in the present collection, 119.

45. Halliwell, *The* Poetics *of Aristotle*, 63 (*Poetics* ch. 25), revised following Richard Janko, *Aristotle: Poetics* (Indianapolis: Hackett, 1987), 40.

46. Halliwell, *The* Poetics *of Aristotle*, 61 (*Poetics* ch. 25).

47. Halliwell, *The* Poetics *of Aristotle*, 62 (*Poetics* ch. 25).

48. Berliner, *Letters of Ayn Rand*, 141. I am grateful to the Ayn Rand Institute for a grant that supported the writing of this essay, to Robert Mayhew for answering my questions on points of Aristotelian scholarship, and above all to Harry Binswanger for many enlightening conversations over the years on the topics treated here.

8

Three Inspirations for the Ideal Man

Cyrus Paltons, Enjolras, and Cyrano de Bergerac

Shoshana Milgram

"The motive and purpose of my writing is the projection of an ideal man."[1] With Howard Roark of *The Fountainhead*, Ayn Rand achieved that goal, for the first time. Roark marked a milestone in her pursuit of an ambition that had begun nearly thirty years earlier. When she was nine, she had found her first hero in a French magazine; a few months later, she decided to become a writer. My purpose here is to examine the first heroes she discovered—in the light of her memories of her reading, and in relation to the first hero she created through her writing.

CYRUS PALTONS OF *LA VALLÉE MYSTÉRIEUSE* (1914) BY MAURICE CHAMPAGNE

Cyrus Paltons, a British captain serving in India, was the hero of an adventure novel published in a French magazine for boys. For several months of 1914, Alisa Rozenbaum (Ayn Rand) devoured the serial installments of *La Vallée Mystérieuse* [*The Mysterious Valley*], written by Maurice Champagne (1868–1951) and illustrated by René Giffey (1884–1965). It was later published in book form, with 35 chapters, 19 in Part 1 and 16 in Part 2.[2] In recalling her appreciation of the novel, Ayn Rand pointed to her interest in the events (e.g., the kidnapping of British officers by trained tigers, the officers' crossing a pool of crocodiles by attaching a rope to a tree trunk, and their climbing a ladder up a cliff), which she preferred to the sort of everyday events that had bored her in other publications intended for children. She liked the color and excitement of the genre: a lively adventure of physical danger in an exotic setting. She liked the ingenuity of the positive characters, one of whom takes advantage of the Indians' superstition and ignorance of technology to stage a "miracle" by means of flashlights. But far more than she liked the story or the background or the atmosphere, she loved the novel's hero: "that kind of feeling I have for him, it still exists. . . . There's nothing I can add in quality to any serious love later on that wasn't contained in that."[3]

Cyrus Paltons is introduced in the novel's early chapters as one already dead, who in life had been "joyeux et vaillant" [cheerful and valiant] (Part 1, chapter 1).[4] Cyrus was "cet homme intrépide, brave jusqu'à la témérité, cet être tout de sang-froid et d'adresse" [that intrepid man, brave to the point of temerity, so skillful and self-possessed] (Part 1, chapter 1).[5] His comrades mourn him bitterly and painfully, and have no doubt that he is gone forever. The illustration at the beginning of the second chapter shows him evidently helpless, in the clutches of a tiger; the chapter is entitled "Le Mort de Paltons" ["Paltons' Death"]. For most of the first half of the novel, the other characters believe him to be lost in a brave yet futile attempt to rescue four brother officers who had been carried off by tigers. Then, in chapter 19 (the final chapter of the first part of the novel), he enters the novel in the flesh. In a striking illustration (the first in which we glimpse his face), we cannot see sharply the features or form of Cyrus—but we see his proud stance, as he holds the bars of a cage that is being wheeled on a cart, and looks out, while four other men, almost indistinguishable, are huddled on the floor of the cage. He is described in the text as being in direct contrast to his companion captives:

> Quatre sont étendus sur une sorte de litière de paille et semblent accablés. Le cinquième, grand, large d'épaules, se tient fièrement debout, se retenant des deux mains aux barreaux de sa prison.

> [Four were stretched out on a litter of straw, and seemed to be overwhelmed by their captivity. The fifth man, tall and broad-shouldered, stood arrogantly, his two hands clutching the bars of the prison.][6]

We thus learn that he, and the men he had attempted to rescue, are alive in a mysterious valley, in the hands of a villainous old rajah, who intends to torture them as part of a generalized hatred of Britain. And once Cyrus joins the course of the novel's events, he takes over, spiritually and existentially.

He speaks, more eloquently than any of his companions, of his confidence that the villains will not be victorious. Several chapters later, while he is still in captivity, we hear, for the first time, his voice, defying his enemies and their leader, taunting them:

> Tu nous tiens, chien! . . . oui, tu nous tiens; mais que sommes-nous en raison du nombre d'Anglais qui restent derrière nous et qui, quoi que tu fasses, sauront te dominer, t'écraser le jour où cela leur plaira? Tu n'es pas un lion, tu es un chacal, et tu te cacherais si nos armées pénétraient dans cette vallée qui

n'est pas un royaume, mais un repaire de bandits. Va, va, tu peux torturer nos corps, mais tu ne pourras pas nous abaisser, tu entends, chien! fils de chien!

[You have us, dog! . . . yes, you have us, but what about all the Englishmen who will come after us and who, no matter what you do, will know how to beat you and wipe you out any time they choose? You aren't a lion, you're a jackal, and you'll hide yourself if our armies penetrate into this valley which isn't a king-dom, but a bandit's hide-out. Go, begone with you! You may torture our bod-ies but you cannot abase us, do you hear me, you dog? You son of a dog?] (Part 2, chapter 4)[7]

In later episodes, Cyrus shows an ability to develop and execute daring plans. The bravest of the brave, he brings out the bravery in his companions. But his virtues go beyond courage, competence, and cleverness. Champagne makes a special point, in two episodes, of showing that Cyrus is not merely capable, but principled.

In the first of these episodes, Cyrus and his companions are following a Hindu guide, who intends to lead them to their death: the guide tells them that the water ahead is safe for them, that there is no danger of crocodiles. But is the guide telling the truth? Théodore Bardin, one of the more intelli-gent in the group, throws the Hindu into the water, just to make sure. As the crocodiles gather, several of the companions, moved by pity, look for a stick or a pole so that the treacherous guide can be saved. But Cyrus will have none of that.

Pas un pas de plus, amis; . . . cet homme est condamné. Ce misérable va payer sa trahison de sa vie, et c'est juste. Pour étouffer le mouvement de pitié qui fait bondir votre coeur, vous n'avez qu'à vous souvenir que l'un de nous, sans la présence d'esprit de M. Bardin, serait peut-être, à cette minute même, à la place de ce bandit.

[Not another step, my friends; . . . that man is doomed. The wretch is going to pay for his treachery with his life, and justly so. To stifle the pity that's swelling in your hearts, you have only to remember that if it weren't for Monsieur Bardin's presence of mind, perhaps one of us would be in that ruffian's place even at this very moment.] (Part 2, chapter 7)[8]

Some of the men still want to save the traitor's life, but, we are told, "Pal-tons demeure inébranlable" [Paltons stood firm]. After the traitor is at-tacked by sixty crocodiles, "se battant, se bousculant, se hissant les uns par-dessus les autres, à qui sera le premier à prendre sa part du festin" [jostling, climbing on top of each other, fighting over which would be first to take part in the feast], as "une violente odeur de musc et de pourriture emplit l'air" [a strong odor of musk and decay filled the air], the men finally un-derstand the issue: "Eux aussi, à présent, ont, comme Paltons, la vision nette et effroyable du sort qui les eût attendus" [Now they too, like Paltons, could see clearly and horribly the fate that would have been theirs].[9] Whereas the other men require a perceptual demonstration in order to grasp the point, Cyrus understands what the traitor is, what he meant to do, and what should be done to him; he prevails against their desire to extend mercy, he insists on justice, and in the end, they see it his way. He was right to be ruthless, and they ultimately acknowledge that fact.

The other episode involves the rescue of an Englishwoman, Ellen Wood, who has also been kidnapped and who is still in the hands of the beings Cyrus deems to be monsters. When he recognizes that there is an innocent victim to be rescued, his course is clear.

> Il ne lui vient pas une seconde à l'esprit qu'il est à l'air, libre, presque sauvé, et qu'en repénétrant dans ce temple redoutable il va peut-être se rejeter béné-volement dans les griffes de ses bourreaux. Il ne se dit pas que la chance inouïe qui les servit juqu'alors ne sera pas toujours pour lui; non, dans son cerveau, une seule idée s'est installée en maîtresse souveraine.
>
> Il veut découvrir et sauver la prisonnière inconnue, et pas autre chose.
>
> Ce qu'il entreprend lui semble très naturel. . . .

> [He didn't spend even a moment thinking that he was out in the open air, at liberty, almost saved, and that in re-entering this perilous temple he was per-haps throwing himself right back into the hands of his executioners. He didn't remind himself that the extraordinary luck they had enjoyed so far couldn't last forever; no, one sole idea dominated his mind.
>
> He wanted to discover and save the unknown prisoner—that, and nothing else.
>
> What he was undertaking seemed quite natural to him. . . .] (Part 2, chapter 10)[10]

Cyrus, who could have walked away to safety, has returned to rescue the captive woman and has done so without hesitation: "Il n'entre pas dans son caractère de discuter longuement avec ses sentiments" [It wasn't part of his character to waste time debating what to do].[11] His act is not an instance of self-sacrifice—even though the woman is unknown to him and does not represent a personal value. His motivation, as presented by Champagne, is admirable: he is, in effect, defending civilization. Not only is he saving him-self and his companions from the savages, but he is telling the enemy, in ac-tion, what he told them in words: you will never win. Never. Only over my dead body will you claim a single victim.

The illustration accompanying this passage was singled out by Ayn Rand:

> And he was a perfect drawing of my present hero. Tall, long-legged, with . . . trousers and leggings, the way soldiers wear, but no jacket, just an open-collared shirt, torn in front, . . . opened very low, sleeves rolled at the elbows and hair falling down over one eye.[12]

She also points to the illustration, described above, to Part 1, chapter 19, the image that introduces him as a living character.

> The first illustration, he is standing, holding onto the bars of the cage, while everybody else is on the bottom, sitting down or cringing at the bottom of the cage. And while they were all afraid, he was hurling insults at the rajah and he was saying, "You can do what you wish, England will beat you. We'll get even." And he was threatened with torture . . . and he was completely defiant about it. He was going to be whipped to pieces. And he was laughing at them and being insulting.[13]

Remembering the picture more than forty years after she had last seen it, Ayn Rand is not entirely accurate, as far as the publication facts of the story. This illustration is not the first illustration of Cyrus to appear in the text; as noted above, he is initially depicted in the illustration at the beginning of the second chapter. The caged Cyrus is, however, the first image that dramatizes the special qualities of Cyrus. It would have been more effective for this image to be in fact the first illustration of Cyrus, for him to be introduced dramatically, the way Ayn Rand remembered it. Her memory has changed, and improved, the timing of the presentation of the image.

Her memory, similarly, has changed, and improved, the content of the scene itself. In her memory, Cyrus delivers his defiant speech as he stands, holding the bars of the cage, above his companions. But in fact Champagne separates the speech from the cage scene. He does not tell us what, if anything, Cyrus says in the cage. In Ayn Rand's memory, though, the defiant posture and the defiant speech were integrated, for dramatic effect.

In memory, she made an imaginative inference about Cyrus's demeanor in his speech. She remembers Cyrus as laughing. He is, indeed, portrayed as mocking his enemies. "Debout en une attitude hardie et combative, il promène autour de lui son regard bleu narquois et provoquant" [As he stood in an impudent, combative attitude, his blue eyes gazed around with a bantering and provocative look] (Part 2, chapter 4).[14] Laughter itself, however, is nowhere indicated in the text. As the scene progresses, in fact, Cyrus's manner is described as angry. He responds to the lowering of the cage bars with "un veritable sursaut de rage" [a veritable fit of rage] and stares, with a "regard devenu féroce" [ferocious gaze] at the vicious rajah who presides over the mysterious valley. For Ayn Rand, though, defiant laughter was appropriate as a response to enemies one does not take seriously or respect, and, in her personal image of Cyrus, he was laughing.

The image of Cyrus, she said, "was everything that I wanted."[15] What we see in examining that image is not only its visual qualities (tall, long-legged, open collar, hair falling over one eye) and not only the qualities of character that she named (strong, resolute, unstoppable), but also the fact that, in working through the image and the narrative in her mind, she made it better, and she made it hers—even before she set out to create her own ideal man.

Ayn Rand said that she was in love with Cyrus "in a metaphysical sense," and "the intensity was almost something unbearable." She paid tribute to him, in a private allusion, when she wrote her first novel, giving the heroine the name Kira, the feminine of Cyrus. And when she created her first ideal man, she portrayed his admirable qualities on a grander scale.

She commented on these qualities, comparing him to the heroes of her novels:

> [Cyrus] was very much a cross between Rearden and Roark . . . grim, but not repressed. It would be Francisco in his active moment . . . the man of action who is totally self-confident, enormously defiant, and nothing could stand in his way, no matter what the circumstances. And he'd always find a way out. From the moment he entered the story, he was the absolute leader of everything.[16]

The positive qualities of Cyrus—self-confidence, resourcefulness, leadership, strength, defiance, and invincible resolution—typify not only Cyrus, but also her own heroes. In creating Roark and her other heroes, however, Ayn Rand, in effect, sees Champagne and raises him. She heightens the stakes.

The scope of Cyrus's heroism is physical action in an emergency; Ayn Rand's ideal men have heroism in both physical and intellectual action over a lifetime. The entire course of *The Fountainhead* is the supporting evidence for Roark's heroic nature. The significance of Roark's actions and victory—Ayn Rand's version of Cyrus's encounters with enemies and other obstacles—is the subject of the other articles in this volume. What Ayn Rand admired in Cyrus—self-confident and defiant, ruthless and resourceful—is what she shows in Roark, in his policies and choices throughout every aspect of his life, from his class assignments at Stanton through his romance with Dominique to his final courtroom speech. As Mike Donnigan tells Steven Mallory, nothing can defeat Roark: "He can't lose, quarries or no quarries, trials or no trials. They can't beat him, Steve, they just can't, not the whole goddamn world" (508). And for Mallory, among others, he serves Cyrus's function of inspiration (a subject I will address more fully later, in discussing the parallels between Roark and Victor Hugo's Enjolras).

Reading Champagne's novel after reading Ayn Rand's novels, the reader is reminded of several resourceful, self-confident, and defiant heroes. She herself mentions Rearden and Francisco. John Galt, for another example, is like Cyrus in being introduced late in the narrative[17]—in a mysterious valley, no less, with comrades who have been supposed to have disappeared permanently. Like Cyrus, Galt faces torture.[18] Like Cyrus, he turns his back on safety to return to danger to rescue the woman who becomes his mate.

But it is worth remembering that Cyrus was the first hero she read, and Roark was the first ideal hero she wrote. In creating Roark, she gave him the qualities she had treasured in Cyrus: his self-confidence, his leadership, his competence, his imperturbable serenity in the face of obstacles. When she introduces Roark to the reader in the novel's first paragraph by means of a dramatic action—laughter in defiance of his expulsion and the ideas behind it—she gives him the demeanor she herself had added to her memory of her first image of her first literary hero.

ENJOLRAS OF *LES MISÉRABLES* (1862) BY VICTOR HUGO

The opening scene of *The Fountainhead* contains a description that suggests the image of a different literary hero, her love for whom was part of a more wide-reaching literary admiration. Although Ayn Rand loved Cyrus and *La Vallée Mystérieuse*, she did not, to my knowledge, seek out other works by Champagne.[19] Victor Hugo, by contrast, was the novelist Ayn Rand ranked first, and Enjolras of *Les Misérables* had a special place in her reverence for Hugo's writing.[20]

In the opening pages of *The Fountainhead*, Ayn Rand introduces her hero's face, with "a contemptuous mouth, shut tight, the mouth of an executioner or a saint" (6). He stands on a rock, on stone that "glowed, wet with sun-rays," as the "wind waved his hair against the sky" (5). Enjolras, a second-ary character in Hugo's *Les Misérables*, is "ce grave jeune homme, bourreau et prêtre, de lumière comme le crystal, et de roche aussi" [this severe young man, executioner and priest, luminous like the crystal and rock also] (Part 4, book 12, chapter 8).[21] He is described as having a "lèvre inférieure . . . facilement dédaigneuse" [underlip, readily disdainful]—as well as "cette chevelure tumultueuse au vent" [that hair flying in the wind] (Part 3, book 4, chapter 1).[22] Observe the common features: Roark, like Enjolras, is de-scribed as a combination of executioner and religious figure; he is associ-ated with rock and light; his mouth is contemptuous, and his hair blows in the wind.[23] Both men, when we first encounter them, are 22.

When Alisa Rozenbaum discovered Victor Hugo in her early teens, she loved his "magnificent" drama and the grandeur of his vision of man and life—but Enjolras, the leader of the young revolutionaries, had been the only character in *Les Misérables* who "had a personal sense of life meaning" for her. As with Cyrus, her response to whom she had described as a seri-ous, metaphysical love, she responded to Enjolras with passionate intensity: "I fell in love with Enjolras."[24]

Enjolras, as a character, is less central to the narrative than is Cyrus to *La Vallée Mystérieuse*. He appears only in the third and fourth of the five parts of the novel, and—by contrast with Fantine, Cosette, Marius, and Jean

Valjean—is not a title character for any of the sections. He is characterized through extensive descriptive passages, through a long speech, and through two sequences of action: his ruthlessness in battle at the barricades and his death. Although he does not occupy a large number of pages, his impact on Ayn Rand outweighed that of any other character in the novel. In tracing the function of Enjolras as an inspiration for Roark, I will consider primarily the descriptive passages and the scene of his death ("my highlight," according to Ayn Rand), along with the speech he makes to his comrades.[25]

The extended description that introduces Enjolras features an element Ayn Rand identified as crucial to her admiration: "a man of exclusive, devoted purpose," "heroically dedicated to a one-track mind purpose."[26] Hugo describes him as follows: "Il n'avait qu'une passion, le droit, qu'une pensée, renverser l'obstacle" [He had one passion only, justice: one thought only, to remove all obstacles] (Part 3, book 4, chapter 1).[27] Enjolras is a man for whom will and action are one: "qui avait cette qualité d'un chef, de toujours faire ce qu'il disait" [who had this quality of a leader, always to do as he said] (Part 5, book 1, chapter 2).[28] Regarding Roark, perhaps the simplest description of an Enjolras-like dedication is spoken, in envy, by Peter Keating, in a conversation with Ellsworth Toohey.

[Toohey:] "Did he always want to be an architect?"

[Keating:] "He . . ."

"What's the matter, Peter?"

"Nothing. It just occurred to me how strange it is that I've never asked myself that about him before. Here's what's strange: you can't ask that about him. He's a maniac on the subject of architecture. It seems to mean so damn much to him that he's lost all human perspective. . . . You don't ask what he'd do if he didn't want to be an architect."

"No. . . . You ask what he'd do if he couldn't be an architect."

"He'd walk over corpses. Any and all of them. All of us. But he'd be an architect." (238)

The purposeful dedication of Enjolras is accompanied by austerity. "Il voyait à peine les roses; il ignorait le printemps, il n'entendait pas chanter les oiseaux; . . . pour lui, . . . les fleurs n'étaient pas bonnes qu'à cacher l'épée. Il était sévère dans ses joies" [He hardly saw a rose, he ignored the spring, he did not hear the birds sing. . . . to him, . . . flowers were good only for hiding the sword. He was severe in his pleasures] (Part 3, book 4, chapter 1).[29] Roark too is described at one point as "austere in cruelty, ascetic in passion" (216), and his general demeanor is such that Peter Keating asks him, reproachfully:

Do you always have to have a purpose? Do you always have to be so damn serious? Can't you ever do things without reason, just like everybody else? You're so serious, so old. Everything's important with you, everything's great, significant in some way, every minute, even when you keep still. Can't you ever be comfortable—and unimportant? (89)

What troubles Keating, of course, is precisely the quality that inspires Roark's friends—and the quality that makes Enjolras the leader of the A.B.C. revolutionaries.

The stern austerity of Enjolras is described in terms of marble: "C'était l'amoureux de marbre de la Liberté" [He was the marble lover of liberty] (Part 3, book 4, chapter 1).[30] He has the "immobilité de marbre" [marble immobility] (Part 4, book 12, chapter 8).[31] Roark, too, is associated with marble—in his strength and purity, and as a material with which he creates. In the first draft of the first chapter, Ayn Rand describes him in terms of marble: "The sun, hitting him through the water, made a dancing marble of his skin, with green veins and white snakes of fire twinkling over his back."[32]

The most striking similarity between Enjolras and Roark, however, is that Hugo presents his hero as the specifically intellectual leader of the insurrectionists, the members of the A.B.C. He is "la logique de la révolution" [the logic of the Revolution] (Part 3, book 4, chapter 1).[33] Hugo portrays the members of the A.B.C. as relying on Enjolras for their image of the meaning behind their actions, the actions of their best selves. Not only does he give orders about eating, sleeping, fighting, and killing, but he speaks to them about their purpose and exemplifies purposefulness. Progress, he says, is a romantic adventure. Enjolras tells his comrades:

Citoyens, vous représentez-vous l'avenir? Les rues des villes inondées de lumières, des branches vertes sur les seuils. . . . Refléchissez à ce qu'a déjà fait le progrès. Jadis les premières races humaines voyaient avec terreur passer devant leurs yeux l'hydre qui soufflait sur les eaux, le dragon qui vomissait du feu, le griffon qui était le monstre de l'air et qui volait avec les ailes d'un aigle et les griffes d'un tigre; bêtes effrayantes qui étaient au-dessus de l'homme. L'homme cependant a tendu ses pièges sacrés de l'intelligence, et il a fini par y prendre les monstres.

Nous avons dompté l'hydre, et elle s'appelle le steamer; nous avons dompté le dragon, et il s'appelle la locomotive; nous sommes sur le point de dompter le griffon, nous le tenons déjà, et il s'appelle le ballon. Le jour où cette oeuvre prométhéenne sera terminée et où l'homme aura définitivement attelé à sa volonté la triple Chimère antique, l'hydre, le dragon et le griffon, il sera maître de l'eau, du feu et de l'air, et il sera pour le reste de la création animée ce que les anciens dieux étaient jadis pour lui. Courage, et en avant!

[Citizens, do you imagine the future? The streets of the cities flooded with light, green branches on the thresholds. . . . Reflect on what progress has already done. Once the early human races looked with terror on the hydra, which blew on the waters, the dragon, which vomited fire, the griffin, monster of the air, which flew with the wings of an eagle and the claws of a tiger; fearful animals that were above man. Man, however, has laid his snares, the sacred snares of intelligence, and has at last caught the monsters.

We have tamed the hydra, and he is called the steamship; we have tamed the dragon, and he is called the locomotive; we are on the point of taming the griffin, we already have him, and he is called the balloon. The day when this promethean work will be finished, and man will have definitely harnessed to his will the triple chimera of the ancients, the hydra, the dragon, and the griffin, he will be the master of water, fire, and air, and he will be to the rest of living creation what the ancient gods formerly were to him. Courage, and forward!] (Part 5, book 1, chapter 5) [34]

He tells them that they are the representatives of progress, that they are Promethean, that their ultimate role is to make men themselves into what the gods once were to men.

Citoyens, le dix-neuvième siècle est grand, mais le vingtième siècle sera heureux. . . . Amis, l'heure où nous sommes et où je vous parle est une heure sombre; mais ce sont là les achats terribles de l'avenir. Une révolution est un péage. Oh! Le genre humain sera délivré, relevé et consolé. Nous le lui affirmons sur cette barricade.

[Citizens, the nineteenth century is great, but the twentieth century will be happy. . . . Friends, this hour we are living in, and in which I am speaking to you is a somber one, but such is the terrible price of the future. A revolution is a tollgate. Oh! The human race will be delivered, uplifted, and consoled! We are affirming it on this barricade.] (Part 5, book 1, chapter 5)[35]

He tells them that their efforts will make possible a glorious future. Enjolras is leading his comrades by explaining the principle and the large-scale context of their action. He is not primarily a tactician, but a moralist. He links action with values. He makes of these men—the diverse nature of whom we see in the chapter in which Hugo introduces the members of the A.B.C.—not a mass or a unit, but individuals unified by purpose. The struggle they share ennobles them. They are not surrendering themselves to the cause; the cause gives a value to them.

Enjolras is their chief. They look up to him as the purest essence of what they aspire to be.

In *The Fountainhead*, similarly, Roark has a life-giving effect on others, including Steven Mallory, Austen Heller, and, for a year, a small band of draftsmen during the construction of Monadnock Valley. As Steven Mallory sees it, their protection was the architect who walked among them . . . the man who had made this possible—the thought in the mind of that man—and not the content of that thought, nor the result, not the vision that had made Monadnock Valley, nor the will that had made it real—but the method of that thought, the rule of its function—the method and the rule which were not like those of the world beyond the hills. That stood on guard over the valley and over the *crusaders* within it. [emphasis added] (508)

Roark, like Enjolras, is the logic of a revolution.

Early in *The Fountainhead*, the significance of Roark's ultimate victory is stated by his mentor, Henry Cameron, a brilliantly original and embittered architect, when he looks at a snapshot of the entrance door to Roark's first office:

It doesn't say much. Only "Howard Roark, Architect." But it's like those mottoes men carved over the entrance of a castle and died for. It's a challenge in the face of something so vast and so dark, that all the pain on earth—and do you know how much suffering there is on earth?—all the pain comes from that thing you are going to face. I don't know what it is, I don't know why it should be unleashed against you. I know only that it will be. And I know that if you carry these words through to the end, it will be a victory, Howard, not just for you, but for something that should win, that moves the world—and never wins acknowledgment. (133)

And like Enjolras, Roark serves as personal inspiration by virtue of what he himself is. As Steven Mallory says to Roark the day he meets him: "Roark, I wish I'd met you before you had a job to give me. . . . So there would be no other reason mixed in. Because, you see, I'm very grateful to you. Not for giving me a job. Not for coming here. Not for anything that you'll ever do for me. Just for what you are" (329).

John Galt, in Ayn Rand's next novel, has parallels with Enjolras in this respect. The personal commitment of the strikers to Galt is intimately integrated with their dedication to the cause, as was true for the members of the A.B.C. For example, the description of Francisco d'Anconia's "greatest achievement"—refraining from retaliation against Hank Rearden's physical and verbal blows, on the evening Francisco learns about the relationship between Dagny and Rearden—stresses "enraptured dedication," his strength, his pride, his willingness to endure:

He looked as if he were facing another presence in the room and as if his glance were saying: If this is what you demand of me, then even this is yours, yours to accept and mine to endure, there is no more than this in me to offer you, but let me be proud to know that I can offer so much.[36]

Galt's speech, later in *Atlas Shrugged*, contains an image that is found in the speech of Enjolras. The prospect of meeting one's death in an environment of spiritual dawn appears also in Galt's speech: "should you die without reaching full sunlight, you will die on a level touched by its rays."[37] In the words of Enjolras: "Frères, qui meurt ici meurt dans le rayonnement de l'avenir, et nous entrons dans une tombe toute pénétrée d'aurore" [Brothers, whoever dies here dies in the radiance of the future, and we are entering a grave illuminated by the dawn] (Part 5, book 1, chapter 6).[38]

It would be tempting to see Galt, more than Roark, as the direct heir of the fighter Enjolras—were it not for one striking element of the characterization of Enjolras: his friendship with Grantaire, which very much impressed Ayn Rand, and which has no parallel in *Atlas Shrugged*. Hugo introduces Grantaire as an unlikely friend for the idealistic Enjolras. "Le scepticisme, cette carie sèche de l'intelligence, ne lui avait pas laissé une idée entière dans l'esprit" [Skepticism, that dry rot of the intellect, had not left one entire idea in his mind] (Part 3, book 4, chapter 1).[39] Nonetheless:

> Grantaire admirait, aimait et vénérait Enjolras. . . Sans qu'il se rendît clairement compte et sans qu'il songeât à se l'expliquer à lui-même, cette nature chaste, saine, ferme, droite, dure, candide, le charmait. . . . Ses idées molles, fléchissantes, disloquées, malades, difformes, se rattachaient à Enjolras comme à une épine dorsale. Son rachis moral s'appuyait à cette fermeté. Grantaire, près d'Enjolras, redevenait quelqu'un.

> [Grantaire admired, loved, and venerated Enjolras. . . . Without understanding it clearly, and without trying to explain it to himself, that chaste, healthy, firm, direct, hard, honest nature charmed him. . . . His soft, wavering, disjointed, diseased, deformed ideas hitched onto Enjolras as to a backbone. His moral spine leaned on that firmness. Beside Enjolras, Grantaire became somebody again.]
> (Part 3, book 4, chapter 1)[40]

Grantaire's admiration for Enjolras has parallels with Wynand's admiration for Roark. Wynand believes that his friendship with Roark enables him to discover, or regain, his best self. When he meets him, he feels "a sense of being carried back intact, as one is now, back to the beginning" (535). Roark becomes the person who means most to him on earth, and in having Roark build the Wynand Building, he feels: "It's a kind of reward. It's as if I had been forgiven" (593).

Ayn Rand commented that one scene with Enjolras was "actually the Wynand-Roark in spirit."[41] She was referring, I believe, to his death scene (her personal highlight in the novel, as noted above) and specifically to the fact that Grantaire, after sleeping through most of the action on the barricades, awakens to see Enjolras on the point of being shot—and promptly asks permission to be shot along with him.

He rises from his drunken stupor to see Enjolras facing the firing squad as if "rien que par l'autorité de son regard tranquille, ce jeune homme . . . contraignît cette cohue sinistre à le tuer avec respect" [merely by the authority of his tranquil eye, this young man . . . compelled that sinister mob to kill him respectfully] (Part 5, book 1, chapter 23).[42] Grantaire wants to share that authority and that respect. He wants to be literally beside Enjolras, even in the direst extremity. Recognizing that to die with Enjolras would be an honor and a privilege, he asks permission, which Enjolras graciously grants. Smiling, Enjolras extends his hand. The shots ring out.

The "Wynand-Roark in spirit" is the transfusion of values from a great man to one who has not lived up to his own potential for greatness. The love the lesser man feels for the greater one carries with it the hope that it is not too late for the two to join hands and minds.

In *The Fountainhead*, Roark does not face a literal firing squad, but when he sees what has become of Cortlandt, while he was away on Wynand's yacht: "He stood straight, the muscles of his throat pulled, his wrists held down and away from his body, as he would have stood before a firing squad" (609). He later arranges to face a metaphorical firing squad. And when he does, Wynand chooses—for a time—to join him. Hugo's Grantaire and Enjolras die together, as heroes, hands outstretched to each other. Ayn Rand does not let her Enjolras die with Grantaire; she does not let her Enjolras die at all. But her Grantaire, i.e. Wynand, releases the hand he is clasping and dies, spiritually, alone. From what Ayn Rand said, it appears that she had in mind Enjolras and Grantaire as she contemplated the relationship of Roark and Wynand: its beginning, its course, and its end. Although her own hero triumphs instead of dying at the barricades, she has remembered, and transformed, her favorite scene of her childhood literary hero.

CYRANO OF *CYRANO DE BERGERAC* (1897) BY EDMOND ROSTAND

Another literary hero—and another whose tragic death Ayn Rand transformed into triumph both spiritual and existential—is the protagonist of *Cyrano de Bergerac*, which she read when she was thirteen. She "liked it enormously"[43] and ultimately judged it to be "the greatest play in world literature."[44] Before she went to college, she had read all of Rostand, in French.[45] She owned an early French edition, as well as the classic 1923 translation by Brian Hooker.[46] In a radio interview about the play, her remarks made it clear that she knew the play by heart.[47] In a column for the *Los Angeles Times*, she praises the play and condemns a contemporary television performance of it, with particular reference to Cyrano's "No, thank you" speech in Act 2, Scene 8, which she called "Rostand's triumphantly proud celebration of integrity."[48] A full analysis of the character and the play is beyond my scope here. I will consider—as inspirations for Roark— primarily the "No, thank you" speech and Cyrano's final scene.

Cyrano, poet and playwright, has refused an opportunity to have his play produced by a powerful cardinal because the price is too high: the risk of re- visions. When he is advised by his friend Le Bret to avoid ruining his every chance by antagonizing people, he replies:

> What would you have me do?
> Seek for the patronage of some great man,
> And like a creeping vine on a tall tree
> Crawl upward, where I cannot stand alone?
> No thank you! Dedicate, as others do,
> Poems to pawnbrokers? Be a buffoon
> In the vile hope of teasing out a smile
> On some cold face? No thank you! Eat a toad
> For breakfast every morning? Make my knees
> Callous, and cultivate a supple spine,—
> Wear out my belly grovelling in the dust?
> No thank you! Scratch the back of any swine
> That roots up gold for me? Tickle the horns
> Of Mammon with my left hand, while my right
> Too proud to know his partner's business,
> Takes in the fee? No thank you! Use the fire
> God gave me to burn incense all day long
> Under the nose of wood and stone? No thank you!
> Shall I go leaping into ladies' laps
> And licking fingers?—or—to change the form—
> Navigating with madrigals for oars,
> My sails full of the sighs of dowagers?
> No thank you! Publish verses at my own
> Expense? No thank you! Be the patron saint
> Of a small group of literary souls
> Who dine together every Tuesday? No
> I thank you! Shall I labor night and day
> To build a reputation on one song,
> And never write another? Shall I find
> True genius only among Geniuses,
> Palpitate over little paragraphs,
> And struggle to insinuate my name
> In the columns of the *Mercury*?
> No thank you! Calculate, scheme, be afraid,
> Love more to make a visit than a poem,
> Seek introductions, favors, influences?—
> No thank you! No, I thank you! And again I thank you!—But . . .
> To sing, to laugh, to dream,

To walk in my own way and be alone,
Free, with an eye to see things as they are,
A voice that means manhood—to cock my hat
Where I choose—At a word, a *Yes*, a *No*,
To fight—or write. To travel any road
Under the sun, under the stars, nor doubt
If fame or fortune lie beyond the bourne—
Never to make a line I have not heard
In my own heart; yet, with all modesty
To say: "My soul, be satisfied with flowers,
With fruit, with weeds even; but gather them
In the one garden you may call your own."
So, when I win some triumph, by some chance,
Render no share to Caesar—in a word,
I am too proud to be a parasite.
And if my nature wants the germ that grows
Towering to heaven like the mountain pine,
Or like the oak, sheltering multitudes—
I stand, not high it may be—but alone![49]

As Leonard Peikoff pointed out in his lecture on *Cyrano de Bergerac* in his course on *Eight Great Plays*, Cyrano defends his artistic integrity here in a speech that could have been written by Ayn Rand.[50] Cyrano, "too proud to be a parasite," repudiates the spurious "success" that comes at the price of compromise. In *The Fountainhead*, Roark hears, in various forms, the equivalent of Le Bret's advice. Peter Keating, for example, assumes that Roark will join the A.G.A. and is shocked to learn that Roark has no such intention:

"What do you mean, you're not joining? You're eligible now."

"Possibly."

"You'll be invited to join."

"Tell them not to bother."

"What!"

"You know, Peter, we had a conversation just like this seven years ago, when you tried to talk me into joining your fraternity at Stanton. Don't start it again."

"You won't join the A.G.A. when you have a chance to?"

"I won't join anything, Peter, at any time."

"But don't you realize how it helps?"

"In what?"

"In being an architect."

"I don't like to be helped in being an architect."

"You're just making things harder for yourself."

"I am."

"And it will be plenty hard, you know."

"I know."

"You'll make enemies of them if you refuse such an invitation."

"I'll make enemies of them anyway." (131)

Keating returns to the theme repeatedly:

> Why don't you come down to earth? Why don't you start working like every-
> body else? . . . Just drop that fool delusion that you're better than everybody
> else—and go to work. In a year, you'll have an office that'll make you blush to
> think of this dump. You'll have people running after you, you'll have clients,
> you'll have friends, you'll have an army of draftsmen to order around! . . .
> You'll be rich, you'll be famous, you'll be respected, you'll be praised, you'll be
> admired—you'll be one of us! (191–92)

Austen Heller, who is free of Keating's second-handedness, envy, and corruption, nonetheless tells Roark that he "must learn how to handle people"
(159) and must seek commissions. When Heller asks him to "stand a few
hours of boredom for the sake of future possibilities," Roark replies, "Only
I don't believe that this sort of thing ever leads to any possibilities" (253).
    The essence of Roark's answer to the advice of Le Bret is the equivalent of
Cyrano's "Non merci."
    Cyrano's swaggering, flamboyant style, to be sure, is not Roark's. To the
Dean, for example, Roark speaks firmly yet quietly: "I've chosen the work I
want to do. If I find no joy in it, then I'm only condemning myself to sixty
years of torture. And I can find that joy only if I do my work in the best way
possible to me. But the best is a matter of standards—and I set my own
standards" (24). But Cyrano's famous speech, with all of its implications,
adds to the qualities of Cyrus and Enjolras the crucial element of the hero
of *The Fountainhead*, an element that is implicit but not stressed in Cyrus
and Enjolras: the specific virtue of integrity.[51]
    Integrity, as Ayn Rand noted, is the play's theme, and its events dramatize
it powerfully:

> The play is about the issue of human integrity, and it presents the figure of a
> man of perfect integrity who preserves that integrity to the end in spite of the
> most dreadful challenges to his spirit. . . . If the hero never had any difficulties,
> or obstacles, in real life he would still be a man of integrity; obstacles are not
> what create integrity. . . . But on the stage in the form of a play, you could not
> possibly present a man of integrity if there were no temptations, if there were
> no tests, if there were no events which tested his integrity. Therefore, in order

to isolate the abstraction which represents the theme, Rostand as a dramatist necessarily had to present his hero in the worst situation possible, he had to present every kind of defeat, existentially, in order to show that his hero preserves his integrity in spite of the worst combination of circumstances that Rostand could invent for him.[52]

Cyrano's dying speech sums up "the worst circumstances possible":

Pendant que je restais en bas, dans l'ombre noire, | D'autres montaient cueillir le baiser de la gloire! . . . | Oui, vous m'arrachez tout, le laurier et la rose! | Arrachez! Il y a malgré vous quelque chose | Que j'emporte, et ce soir, quand j'entrerai chez Dieu, | Mon salut balaiera largement le seuil bleu, | Quelque chose que sans un pli, sans une tache, | J'emporte malgré vous, et c'est . . . . Mon panache.

[While I stood in the darkness underneath, | Others climbed up to win the applause—the kiss! . . . | Yes, all my laurels you have riven away | And all my roses; yet in spite of you, | There is one crown I bear away with me, | And tonight, when I enter before God, | My salute shall sweep all the stars away | From the blue threshold! One thing without stain, | Unspotted from the world, in spite of doom | Mine own!—And that is . . . My white plume.] (Act 5, Scene 6)[53]

Ayn Rand views this speech as the epitome of the hero:

Cyrano . . . declares that in spite of the fact that his enemies in life robbed him of all rewards, both professionally and personally—as he states, they robbed him of fame and they robbed him of love—but there is something which he dies carrying to heaven untouched, unsullied . . . "mon panache," which means: "plume of honor belonging to knights." What is it a symbol of? Integrity. What Cyrano is saying: In spite of the worst that life could do to me, I have preserved—untouched, unbreached—my integrity, and he dies with his full pride and self-esteem. That is the theme of Cyrano. Therefore, for a dramatization of human integrity, I would challenge anyone to imagine, let alone to execute, that theme better.[54]

I can say what she did not: that she herself did not fall short of that challenge. While it is true that presenting integrity in art requires challenges to that integrity, Cyrano's final existential defeat is not a requirement. In *The Fountainhead*, Roark suffers the worst life can do to him.[55] He is—for a time—robbed of rewards, fame, and love. The woman he loves is not in his possession; she is married to his enemies. Roark's designs are signed by Keating, who takes the credit (as Cyrano's letters to Roxane were signed by Christian, and as Cyrano's scenes were stolen by Molière). But *The Fountainhead* does not conclude at the end of Part 2—with the destruction of the Stoddard Temple, Keating's second-hand victory in the Cosmo-Slotnick competition, and Keating's marriage to Dominique. *The Fountainhead*, by contrast, allows Roark eventual victory on all levels. Roark is willing, as was Cyrano, to dispense with existential rewards. He tells Keating:

> You'll get everything society can give a man. You'll keep all the money. You'll take any fame or honor anyone might want to grant. You'll accept such gratitude as the tenants might feel. And I—I'll take what no one can give a man except himself. I will have built Cortlandt. (581)

The novel concludes with Roark's receiving in full measure what he had been robbed of—rewards, fame, and love—without ever sacrificing his irreplaceable "panache."

The Cyrano-like element (ghostwritten letters to another man's sweetheart) is a likely source of Ayn Rand's interest in Chris Massie's *Pity My Simplicity* (filmed as *Love Letters*).[56] Of several possible projects, she chose this story as the basis for the first screenplay she wrote for Hal Wallis.[57]

And—as was the case with Cyrus and Enjolras—Cyrano has a parallel not only with Roark, but with Galt. Apart from the general Cyrano-like virtues of integrity and independence, Galt is in a situation that recalls—and revises—the Cyrano-Roxane-Christian love triangle. In the valley, Galt has the chance to step aside and to relinquish the woman he loves to his friend Francisco. When he does not do so, Dagny sees, "with the sudden, immediate vividness of sensory perception, an exact picture of what the code of self-sacrifice would have meant, if enacted by the three of them": the "waste of the unreached and unfulfilled" for Galt, "self-deceit" and "hopeless longing" for her, and, for Francisco, "his life a fraud staged by the two who were dearest to him and most trusted, . . . struggling down the brittle scaffold of a lie over the abyss of the discovery that he was not the man she loved."[58] The circumstances, to be sure, are not identical—but the key point, which emerges in spite of the differences of detail, is that Galt's choice here, while the opposite of Cyrano's renunciation, is the epitome of nobility by the standards of his moral code (as was Cyrano's by the standards of his code). Dagny "knew, only after it was over, what had hung for her on his decision; she knew that had his answer been different, it would have destroyed the valley in her eyes" (734). But Ayn Rand does not destroy valleys—or heroes.

To point to three French literary heroes as literary influences on Ayn Rand is not to accuse her of the artistic second-handedness that *The Fountainhead* condemns. Ayn Rand acknowledged happily and gratefully the joy and inspiration she received from a few other writers; at the same time, she knew—from a first-person perspective—how she wrote her books and she knew that imitation was not her method.[59] It is nonetheless true that Cyrus, Enjolras, and Cyrano, all of whom Ayn Rand came to know in her youth, were inspirations for Roark, far more so than Frank Lloyd Wright, who was the model for the architectural career but not for the character.[60]

Roark was, to be sure, also inspired by Ayn Rand's husband, who was, she said, the inspiration for all her heroes. The dedication page of the manuscript, dated June 10, 1940, reads: "To Frank O'Connor who is less guilty of second-handedness than anyone I have ever met."[61] The wording reflects the fact that, at that point, the title of the novel was to be "Second-Hand Lives." In the final text, the dedication reads simply, "To Frank O'Connor."

A fundamental inspiration for her own ideal man, finally, was none other than herself. "My research material for the psychology of Roark," she said, "was myself, and how I feel about my profession."[62] She too was one-track, as was Roark. She had in common with Roark the experience of having her work rejected, as was his work, for reasons other than lack of quality, while mediocre art was acclaimed. And she had her own Stoddard Temple, at the same age (30) at which Roark had his, when her play *Penthouse Legend*, renamed *Night of January 16th*, was altered against her wishes.[63]

She had in common with Roark the experience of arduous labor that was also ecstasy. In December 1941, she signed a contract to deliver the novel—two-thirds of which remained to be written—within a year. Of that year, she wrote: "I spent the last and final year writing steadily, literally day and night; once I wrote for thirty hours at a stretch, without sleep, stopping only to get some food. It was the most enjoyable year of my life."[64]

On the last page of *The Fountainhead*, on the manuscript she submitted on December 31, 1942, stands Roark, triumphant: Ayn Rand's first ideal man—with Cyrus's defiant courage and resourcefulness, with Enjolras's austere dedication to a cause, with Cyrano's proud integrity, and also something greater: the epitome and incarnation of first-handedness. Man at his best, presented for our contemplation by the first-handed genius of his creator.

NOTES

1. Ayn Rand, *The Romantic Manifesto: A Philosophy of Literature*, revised edition (New York: Signet, 1975), 162.

2. The French firm of Delagrave first serialized the novel in two magazines: *St. Nicolas: journal illustré pour garçons et filles*, starting in April 1914, and its lower-priced magazine, *L'Écolier illustré*, one month later. Delagrave then published the entire story in book form (Paris, 1915). A photocopy of the French text was provided by Bill Bucko, who also translated it as *The Mysterious Valley* (Lafayette, Colorado: Atlantean Press, 1994), with an introduction by Harry Binswanger and the original illustrations by René Giffey. Quotations from the novel will appear first in French, the language in which Ayn Rand read it, and then in Bill Bucko's translation. References in the text will identify the part and chapter of the novel; references in the

notes will identify the relevant page numbers, first in French and then in English. I am grateful to Bill Bucko for discovering the magazines that originally published *La Vallée Mystérieuse* and for donating them to the Ayn Rand Archives. Thanks also to Arthur Evans, Maria Le Guen, Anita Haney, and especially John J. Pierce for helping me look for them.

3. Biographical interviews (Ayn Rand Archives).

4. Champagne, 4; Bucko, 4.

5. Champagne, 6; Bucko, 5.

6. Champagne, 129; Bucko, 119.

7. Champagne, 150; Bucko, 141.

8. Champagne, 170; Bucko, 160–61.

9. Champagne, 170; Bucko, 161.

10. Champagne, 192; Bucko, 181–82.

11. Champagne, 192; Bucko, 182.

12. Biographical interviews (Ayn Rand Archives).

13. Biographical interviews (Ayn Rand Archives).

14. Champagne, 149; Bucko, 140.

15. Biographical interviews (Ayn Rand Archives).

16. Biographical interviews (Ayn Rand Archives).

17. This fact was noted by Bill Bucko in his "Heroes, Tigers and Cobras: Adventures in Translating *The Mysterious Valley*," *Atlantean Press Review*, vol. 2, no. 4 (summer 1995), 5. He notes additional parallels. The full article is 3–24.

18. Ayn Rand comments: "I think my concern with torture is somewhat from that story" (Biographical interviews, Ayn Rand Archives). Harry Binswanger, in his introduction to the English translation of the novel (Bucko, xii–xiii), refers in this context to the lashing of the hero of *Anthem* and the torture of Galt in *Atlas Shrugged*.

19. It is possible that she read additional works by Champagne in one of the French magazines of which her mother had ordered subscriptions. For more information about Champagne, including an extensive list of his publications, see Jean-Marc Lofficier and Randy Lofficier, *French Science Fiction, Fantasy, Horror and Pulp Fiction* (Jefferson, NC: McFarland, 2000), 346, 367, 529–30. Jacques Sadoul discusses Champagne, as a writer in the tradition of Jules Verne, in *Histoire de la Science-Fiction Moderne (1911–1984)*, revised and completed edition (Paris: Robert Laffon, 1984), 394–95.

20. See Shoshana Milgram, *"We the Living* and Victor Hugo: Ayn Rand's First Novel and the Novelist She Ranked First," in Robert Mayhew, ed., *Essays on Ayn Rand's* We the Living (Lanham, MD: Lexington Books, 2004), 223–56.

21. *Les Misérables*, ed. Marius-François Guyard, 2 vols. (Paris: Garnier, 1966), II, 348; *Les Misérables*, translated by Lee Fahnestock and Norman MacAfee, based on the translation by C. E. Wilbour (New York: Signet, 1987), 1116. Quotations from the novel will appear first in French, the language in which Ayn Rand read it, and then in English. References in the text will identify the part and chapter of the novel; references in the notes will identify the relevant page numbers, first in French and then in English.

22. Guyard I, 773–74; Fahnestock, MacAfee, Wilbour, 648–49.

23. The manuscript of *The Fountainhead* suggests additional similarities. The lower lip of Enjolras is specifically described not only as disdainful, but as thick: "la lèvre inférieure épaisse" [thick underlip] (Part 3, book 4, chapter 1); Guyard I, 773;

Fahnestock, MacAfee, Wilbour, 648. The holograph draft of *The Fountainhead* contains that detail as well. Roark's lower lip is, like that of Enjolras, thicker than his upper lip (*The Fountainhead*, first draft, Part 1, 8). The word "executioner," as applied to Roark, occurs not only in the introductory description, but also, in the first draft, to describe Roark's face at the time of the first sexual encounter between Roark and Dominique (*The Fountainhead*, first draft, Part 2, 65).

24. Biographical interviews (Ayn Rand Archives).

25. In Milgram, "*We the Living* and Victor Hugo," I discuss his impact on the characterizations of Leo, Kira, and Andrei; his ruthless actions at the barricades are part of that discussion.

26. Biographical interviews (Ayn Rand Archives).

27. Guyard I, 773; Fahnestock, MacAfee, Wilbour, 648.

28. Guyard II, 417; Fahnestock, MacAfee, Wilbour, 1178.

29. Guyard I, 773; Fahnestock, MacAfee, Wilbour, 648.

30. Guyard I, 773; Fahnestock, MacAfee, Wilbour, 649.

31. Guyard II, 347; Fahnestock, MacAfee, Wilbour, 1116.

32. *The Fountainhead* [Second Hand Lives], first draft, Part 1, 11. The drafts of *The Fountainhead* are located at the Library of Congress, where I consulted them.

33. Guyard I, 774; Fahnestock, MacAfee, Wilbour, 649.

34. Guyard II, 430; Fahnestock, MacAfee, Wilbour, 1189.

35. Guyard II, 432; Fahnestock, MacAfee, Wilbour, 1191.

36. Ayn Rand, *Atlas Shrugged* (New York: Random House, 1957; Signet thirty-fifth anniversary paperback edition, 1992), 591–92.

37. Rand, *Atlas Shrugged*, 983.

38. Guyard II, 433; Fahnestock, MacAfee, Wilbour, 1191.

39. Guyard I, 784; Fahnestock, MacAfree, Wilbour, 657.

40. Guyard I, 784; Fahnestock, MacAfee, Wilbour, 658.

41. Biographical interviews (Ayn Rand Archives).

42. Guyard II, 499; Fahnestock, MacAfee, Wilbour, 1250–51.

43. Biographical interviews (Ayn Rand Archives).

44. Question period of *Objective Communication*, lecture course by Leonard Peikoff, 1980, quoted in *Ayn Rand Answers*, Robert Mayhew, ed. (New York: New American Library, 2005), 196.

45. Biographical interviews (Ayn Rand Archives).

46. List of books in Ayn Rand's library (Ayn Rand Archives).

47. "Ayn Rand on Campus," WKCR radio series at Columbia University, second series, program 3 (October 16, 1962).

48. "Vandalism," *Los Angeles Times*, 16 December 1962 [review of 6 December 1962 NBC television production of *Cyrano de Bergerac*], reprinted in Peter Schwartz, ed., *The Ayn Rand Column*, revised second edition (New Milford, CT: Second Renaissance, 1998), 76. Review is 75–77.

49. Edmond Rostand, *Cyrano de Bergerac*, translated by Brian Hooker (New York: Holt, 1923; rpt. New York: Bantam, 1950), 75–76. The French original, which I am including here (rather than in the text) for reasons of space, is as follows:

. . . Et que faudrait-il faire? | Chercher un protecteur puissant, prendre un patron, | Et comme un lierre obscur qui circonvient un tronc | Et s'en fait un tuteur en lui léchant

l'écorce, | Grimper par ruse au lieu de s'élever par force? | Non, merci. Dédier, comme
tous ils le font, | Des vers aux financiers? se changer en bouffon | Dans l'espoir vil de voir,
aux lèvres d'un ministre, | Naître un sourire, enfin, qui ne soit pas sinistre? | Non, merci.
Déjeuner, chaque jour, d'un crapaud? | Avoir un ventre usé par la marche? une peau | Qui
plus vite, à l'endroit des genoux, devient sale? | Exécuter des tours de souplesse dorsale?
. . . | Non, merci. D'une main flatter la chèvre au cou | Cependant que, de l'autre, on ar-
rose le chou, | Et, donneur de séné par désir de rhubarbe, | Avoir son encensoir, toujours,
dans quelque barbe? | Non, merci! Se pousser de giron en giron, | Devenir un petit grand
homme dans un rond, | Et naviguer, avec des madrigaux pour rames, | Et dans ses voiles
de soupirs de vieilles dames? | Non, merci! Chez le bon éditeur de Sercy | Faire éditer ses
vers en payant? Non, merci! | S'aller faire nommer pape par les conciles | Que dans des
cabarets tiennent des imbéciles? | Non, merci! Travailler à se construire un nom | Sur un
sonnet, au lieu d'en faire d'autres? Non, | Merci! Ne découvrir du talent qu'aux mazettes?
| Etre terrorisé par de vagues gazettes, | Et se dire sans cesse: "Oh! pourvu que je sois |
Dans les petits papiers du *Mercure françois?*" . . . | Non, merci! Calculer, avoir peur, être
blême, | Aimer mieux faire une visite qu'un poème, | Rédiger des placets, se faire présen-
ter? | Non, merci! non, merci! non, merci! Mais . . . chanter | Rêver, rire, passer, être seul,
être libre, | Avoir l'oeil qui regarde bien, la voix qui vibre, | Mettre, quand il vous plaît,
son feutre de travers, | Pour un oui, pour un non, se battre, ou—faire un vers! | Travailler
sans souci de gloire ou de fortune, | A tel voyage, auquel on pense, dans la lune! | N'écrire
jamais rien qui de soi ne sortît, | Et modeste d'ailleurs, se dire: mon petit, | Sois satisfait
des fleurs, des fruits, même des feuilles, | Si c'est dans ton jardin à toi que tu les cueilles!
| Puis, s'il advient d'un peu triumpher, par hasard, | Ne pas être obligé d'en rien rendre à
César, | Vis-à-vis de soi-même en garder le mérite, | Bref, dédaignant d'être le lierre para-
site, | Lors même qu'on n'est pas le chêne ou le tilleul, | Ne pas monter bien haut, peut-
être, mais tout seul!

Edmond Rostand, *Cyrano de Bergerac* (Paris: Hachette, 1951), 73–74.

50. Leonard Peikoff, "Cyrano de Bergerac," *Eight Great Plays* (New Milford, CT:
Second Renaissance, 1995), Lecture 9.

51. It is possible that Maurice Champagne, creator of Cyrus, knew Rostand's
Cyrano de Bergerac; the two writers were contemporaries, born in the same year.
Champagne was a rival playwright; the WorldCat database credits him with author-
ship of *Mademoiselle Aurore, Comédie-vaudeville en trois actes* (Paris: P. V. Stock, 1905).
The name "Cyrus" seems to suggest "Cyrano."

52. "Ayn Rand on Campus," WKCR.

53. Rostand, 183, 187–88; Hooker, 192, 195–96.

54. "Ayn Rand on Campus," WKCR.

55. For her comments on devising the worst possible obstacles in order to dramatize creative independence in Roark, see Ayn Rand, *The Art of Fiction: A Guide for
Writers and Readers*, ed. Tore Boeckmann (New York: Plume, 2000), 22.

56. Chris Massie, *Pity My Simplicity* (London: Faber and Faber, 1944), retitled
The Love Letters for American publication (New York: Random, 1944). *Love Letters*,
dir. William Dieterle, perf. Joseph Cotton and Jennifer Jones, Hal Wallis Productions, 1945.

57. Biographical interviews (Ayn Rand Archives).

58. Rand, *Atlas Shrugged*, 735.

59. See Ayn Rand, *Fiction Writing: A Thirteen-Lecture Course* (1958), Lecture 8,
quoted in Milgram, "*We the Living* and Victor Hugo," 252–53.

60. Among the many sources for her position, see Michael S. Berliner, ed., *Letters of Ayn Rand* (New York: Dutton, 1995), 468, 492, and Michael S. Berliner, "Howard Roark and Frank Lloyd Wright," in this volume.

61. *The Fountainhead,* first draft, dedication page.

62. Mayhew, *Ayn Rand Answers,* 191.

63. Ayn Rand, "Introduction," *Night of January 16th,* definitive edition (New York: Plume, 1987), 6–16.

64. Berliner, *Letters of Ayn Rand,* 672.

9

Understanding the "Rape" Scene in *The Fountainhead*

Andrew Bernstein

No scene in *The Fountainhead* engenders more confusion than its controversial "rape" scene.[1] In two decades of lecturing on Ayn Rand's novels at American universities, I have been asked repeatedly: If Dominique does not explicitly consent to having sex with Roark, then isn't his action abhorrent? The question is understandable given these students' indoctrination with "politically correct" dating codes. But even longtime admirers of Ayn Rand's novels and philosophy ask: Why does Howard Roark rape Dominique? Given the monstrous nature of rape, isn't that a monumental breach of morality?

Ayn Rand was asked, and answered, just this question. In answer to a 1965 fan letter, she wrote:

> You say you were asked whether "the rape of Dominique Francon by Howard Roark was a violation of Dominique's freedom, an act of force that was contrary to the Objectivist Ethics?" The answer is: of course not. It was not an actual rape, but a symbolic action which Dominique all but invited. This was the action she wanted and Howard Roark knew it.[2]

Roark does not rape Dominique. Many readers sense this but cannot explain why Dominique resists if she wants to make love to Roark. To understand this scene, it is necessary to understand more about her character.

Rape, the forcing of unwanted sex on an unwilling victim, represents a terrible violation of a woman's rights. Is Dominique unwilling to sleep with Roark? The events of the novel provide the evidence to answer this question.

Dominique goes to the quarry one hot morning and observes the laborers. Her eyes stop on the orange hair of a man who looks at her with scorn.

She thinks that his "was the most beautiful face she would ever see, because it was the abstraction of strength made visible" (205). She stares at his body, at the "wet shirt clinging to his ribs, the lines of his long legs" (205). Later, she thinks of him, of his hands that break granite, and feels "weak with pleasure" (206) at the thought of being broken. Speaking with him for the first time, she experiences "a desire to let her skin touch his; to let the length of her bare arm press against the length of his" (208). She realizes from his words that he does not "belong here," that he does not "talk like a worker" (208). But he remains silent regarding his actual profession.

After their first conversation, Dominique is filled with a single desire: to return to the granite quarry. She resists it by visiting wealthy neighbors, taking a "vicious" thrill in the contrast between the "fastidious elegance" (209) of her surroundings and the smoldering intensity of her thoughts about the worker's body. Back in the safety of her house, she permits herself to realize that the worker wants her. It makes her happy, because she knows the suffering she can now inflict on him. But the house is too safe, so she challenges it. She pounds the marble of her bedroom fireplace with a hammer, seeking to smash it. She succeeds in scratching it, then tells the worker that it needs to be replaced. He agrees to do it.

She asks the elderly caretaker and his wife to remain in the house that evening. The worker looks at the fireplace and realizes the truth. He splits the slab with a blow of his hammer and orders the new piece of marble. When he takes his payment from her, he sees "the edge of her long black sleeve trembling over her closed fingers" (213).

Dominique waits for the marble with the "feverish intensity of a sudden mania" (214). When the stone finally arrives, she sends immediately for the worker. But that evening, another worker comes instead. Dominique "had to get out of the room. She had to run, not to be seen by anyone, not to be seen by herself if she could escape it" (214). Days later, when she feels that "she could not live through another night" (215), she rides on horseback to the quarry. In the woods she catches up to the worker and asks why he did not come to set the marble. He responds, "I didn't think it would make any difference to you who came. Or did it, Miss Francon?" (215). Dominique raises the branch she holds in her hand and slashes him across the face.

The evidence is conclusive: Dominique feels an overwhelming attraction to Roark. She is the aggressor throughout the scene—flaunting her name and her beauty, scratching the marble, pursuing Roark after work, striking him with the branch. The sexual tension Dominique feels explodes in her act of violence. Through this action, she makes explicit to Roark what had been implicit—that she wants him in the strongest way, and that the frustration of not having him is unendurable.

She has to endure it for three more days, for despite her confession, he still does not come to her. He makes her wait. On the night of the third day, she has the French doors open to her bedroom, and she does not ask the caretaker and his wife to stay in the house. She thinks she will "try to sleep" (215). She feels "relief in the cold contracting bite of [perfume] on her skin" (215–16). Finally, he enters her bedroom. When he embraces her, she is not certain whether she at first twists to escape or lies still in his arms. This is the "rapture she had wanted" (217), this is the "thing she had thought about, had expected, had never known to be like this, could not have known, because this was not part of living, but a thing one could not bear longer than a second" (216).

She struggles against him—"but she makes no sound"; the caretaker and his wife live close by, and because of this she does "not call for help" (216). Later, after he departs, Dominique refuses to take a bath, wanting "to keep the feeling of his body, the traces of his body on hers, knowing also what such a desire implied" (217–18).

Based on the evidence, it is clear that Dominique desires desperately to sleep with Roark. Why, then, does she resist? Why does she struggle violently, pick up a lamp with the evident intention of hitting him, and fight against the satisfaction of her most fervent desire? This question is intimately tied to other questions about her: Why does she destroy the priceless Greek statuette she cherishes? Why, despite her brilliance and her independence, does she seek no career? Why does she ally herself with Toohey—the evil figure she loathes—seeking to end the career of the man she loves and admires? The answers all involve the same error. As Ayn Rand describes it:

> Dominique's error is one from which many good people suffer, only not in so extreme a form. She was devoted to values, was an individualist, had a clear view of what she considered ideal, only she didn't think the ideal was possible. Her error is *the malevolent universe premise*: the belief that the good has no chance on earth, that it is doomed to lose and that evil is metaphysically powerful.[3]

Dominique's character is an amalgam of idealism and pessimism. An idealist is one who understands man's capacity for greatness and expects him to live up to it. Dominique holds a vision of man's proper stature and will accept nothing less.

But she is also a philosophical pessimist, who believes that the heroes among men are doomed to bitter defeat. Dominique observes that it is her father—a phony, second-rate designer—who is acclaimed, and that Henry Cameron—the world's greatest builder—is rejected. Later, she observes the obsequiously dishonest Peter Keating on the fast track to success, while Howard Roark is scorned. She also knows that Gail Wynand—the most egregious panderer of all (as she initially construes him to be) has gained

an enormous commercial success, and that the viciously malignant
Ellsworth Toohey is held by millions to be a saint. Based on such observations, Dominique concludes that human society is corrupt and neither
admires nor rewards greatness. Only the debased succeed; the noble have
no chance.

In answer to one of moral philosophy's perennial questions—what is the
relation between virtue and success, between morality and practicality?—
Dominique holds initially that the two stand in inverse proportion to each
other: the more assiduously an individual pursues one, the more he necessarily disassociates himself from the other.

It is this conjunction of beliefs that forms the essence of Dominique's
complex character and explains her actions. Why does she destroy the Greek
statuette? Because there is no world for the vision of man's greatness that it
projects. Why does she pursue no career? Because success would require the
corrupt methods of Keating and Guy Francon. Why does she join forces
with Ellsworth Toohey to wreck Roark's career? As an act of mercy killing,
on the premise that Roark must be destroyed quickly, painlessly, and at the
hand of one who understands and reveres his work—not slowly, agoniz-
ingly, by a society that neither understands nor cares about his greatness—
so as to avoid the fate of Henry Cameron.

Similarly, why, at the very moment of fulfillment she has dreamed of,
does she resist the advances of the man she loves and has pursued? Because
of the man he is and his relationship to the world as she conceives it. Observe a strikingly positive feature of Dominique's character. Although she
meets Roark at the lowest ebb of his career, she recognizes *at one glance* that
his face is "the abstraction of strength made visible" (205). Later, at Kiki
Holcombe's party, she thinks that his "is the face of a god" (263). At the
quarry, she knows consciously neither that Roark is a genius nor a moral
paragon. As far as she knows, he may be an ex-convict, like some of the
other workers. But at a sense-of-life level, she recognizes strength—*moral
strength*, the face of a god—when she sees it. Roark's noble demeanor, his
confident economy of motion, his direct gaze, his upright posture—these
things may be unrecognizable to others. But Dominique observes it and, at
an emotional level, knows its moral meaning. And seeing it, she cannot remain unmoved. At a subconscious level deeper than her conscious understanding at that moment, Dominique recognizes Roark as a supreme example of Aristotle's "great-souled man." Her own greatness of character is
such that, spiritually, she gives herself to Roark in that moment, immediately and forever.

Though Dominique does not yet conceptually understand the data (later
she will), her subconscious comprehends the meaning of the physical qualities she observes. It has been famously pointed out that "The eyes are the
windows of the soul"—and in this scene Ayn Rand elaborates: the eyes, the

gaze, the facial expressions, the set of the jaw, the small physical manner-isms, the posture, the way of standing, walking, holding oneself, etc., rep-resent more than insignificant bodily details. They are clues, for a sensitive observer, to a man's deeper moral character. And Dominique Francon is an exquisitely sensitive observer.

But observe Dominique's agonizing moral dilemma. She is in love with the only kind of man who could move her, an exalted hero. But on her premises, a hero will inevitably be crushed by a malevolent society. If she permits herself to love him, what will be the result for her when the world destroys him? What, in fact, *is* the result when others condemn and tear down his magnificent Stoddard Temple? She suffers unendurable agony, a pain vastly worse than his. This is the essence of Dominique's emotional conflict at the quarry. Because of the hero he is, she must have him—but because of the immense consequent suffering when society inevitably de-stroys him, she cannot permit herself to do so. Therefore, her existential conflict: She pursues him aggressively, but resists him in the moment of her triumph.

Dominique's conflict is fundamentally intellectual, generated by her clashing premises of idealistic hero worship and a malevolent view of the world. But there is an important psychological concomitant. A clue to it is provided by something she says to Toohey. Though she works diligently to wrest commissions from Roark, she says, on hearing that Roark will build the Aquitania Hotel, that "I'm so happy, I could sleep with this Kent Lansing . . ." (314).

Though she believes that Roark will be defeated like Cameron, at the deepest level of her soul she desires Roark to be an unconquerable hero who will triumph over all. She yearns for a man whose will is stronger than society's—and stronger than her own. In Dominique's character, and above all, in her response to Roark, Rand dramatizes the essence of her view of femininity: the worship of masculine strength and the desire, in the sexual act, to be overpowered by it. There can be no question in her mind regard-ing the physical strength of the taut, lean worker she observes, but the only man she will accept is one who demonstrates, in action, that he has a strength of purpose, of character, of will to match. She shows him at the quarry both that she strongly desires him and that she will strongly resist. If he is to possess her body and her love, he must be willing to overpower her. She feels weak with pleasure at the recognition that his hands can break rocks. She feels weaker with a greater pleasure at the realization that his will can break her resistance.

Similarly, over years of struggle, he shows her that society's resistance is powerless to prevent him from reaching his goals. She worships him at first sight, but it is only when he demonstrates that his strength of character can-not and will not be conquered by the world—for example, that he will

never lapse into bitter drunkenness like Cameron—that she gives herself to
him in practical terms as fully as she does spiritually. It is only then that she
marries him. Dominique desires all or nothing.

This is the reason that Dominique continues to refer to their first encounter, in her own mind, as a rape (219, 671). In part, the term is a
metaphor for the violence of the sex. Observe in this regard Ayn Rand's description of their first act of lovemaking in New York, after the Holcombe
party: "her mouth on his, in a surrender more violent than her struggle had
been" (273). But it is more. The term "rape" connotes for Dominique the
dominant strength of her hero overpowering her—and all—resistance. It is
not that Dominique takes some neurotic pleasure in her degradation. It is
that there is no element of degradation in their sexual encounter. It is undi-
luted exaltation for her because her deepest desire has been fulfilled: She
has found the overpowering hero she craves, and he is hers. Her resistance
is a test—and her lover has passed it with the highest possible score, as she
prayed he would.

Does Roark know all this about Dominique? He does not know it all consciously until later. But even in their first meetings he knows several important facts. The first is that this beautiful woman desires him deeply. In addition to the blatant nature of her pursuit, he repeatedly tests her feelings.
The best example is when Roark sends Pasquale Orsini to repair the fireplace instead of coming to do it himself. Dominique's uncontrollable
rage—and the violence of her action—serve to underscore what she has already shown him regarding the intensity of her attraction.

But there is a second, more subtle fact that Roark knows about her. We
need to keep in mind that much of what transpires between human beings
is unstated, especially regarding romantic relations. The scene is narrated
from Dominique's perspective, so we know what she identifies about his
face, his eyes, his carriage and posture, his movements and mannerisms, his
hands—and the meaning of such observations. But what does Roark identify about her?

He observes that her glance and her bearing are aristocratic and proud.
There is a genuine, unpretentious haughtiness about Dominique. Such authentic nobility can only be the product of a profoundly pure moral character. Just as she sees in his face the abstraction of moral strength made real,
so he sees the same thing in hers. Further, for such a virtuous person sexual
attraction is a serious matter, solemn, even sacred. Roark understands that
this woman's deep attraction to him could never be a light, unserious affair.
Dominique is not a society girl slumming with her proletarian lover. Roark,
a man of artistic genius and sensitivity, would ask himself the question:
Why, of all the workers at the quarry, does this aristocratic woman choose
me? Roark would not be the only man there who is tall, lean, and powerful, whose hands are capable of breaking rocks. Her attraction, he knows, is

based on factors far deeper than that. He knows, though she does not, that she has chosen the one man there who is a great innovative thinker and a man whose moral character matches his intellect. Her attraction to him is based on these deeper qualities and says everything he will ever need to know about her.

Additionally, he knows she wants him in a particular way. Her flaunting of her name, her beauty, her ownership, and her power is presented in a manner that is challenging, not deterring. He knows that her actions state, loud and clear: "You can have me, but you must be ready to overcome every threat, obstacle, and resistance I will place in your path." Roark does not know the deeper reasons yet, but he knows that this is a woman who seeks to match her strength of will against his—and her deepest desire is to be overpowered by a man of superlative strength. Roark recognizes and finds irresistible the essential femininity of Dominique's character: her desire, in the sexual act, to be conquered and possessed by a dominant masculinity—above all, by a man whose moral strength is at least a match for his physical strength.

That Dominique's character stands in utter contradiction to the philosophy of feminism helps to explain why many readers find the "rape" scene inexplicable. Feminism essentially constitutes a war against metaphysical reality.[4] It holds that males and females should be equal, not just in moral and legal rights, but in their biological nature and physical abilities. Thus, according to feminists, women should be firefighters, combat marines, and Navy SEALs, even though few women can meet the demanding physical requirements of these professions. Psychologically, feminism leads to two related phenomena: hatred for, and a desire to undercut, a confident masculinity, and a similar hatred for femininity, the admiration of—and the desire to surrender sexually to—just such confident masculinity.

On these premises, the sexual relationship between Roark and Dominique is not merely incomprehensible, it is repugnant. Thus, for example, one prominent feminist intellectual condemns Ayn Rand as "a traitor to her sex."[5] And it is no wonder that men and women who hold such premises find it difficult to understand the "rape" scene.[6]

But those willing to question the feminist ideology and look objectively at the facts of the story can understand the truth about this scene. At an unspoken level, Roark and Dominique understand each other and the nature of their bond. As Ayn Rand writes at the end of the scene: "They had been united in an understanding beyond the violence. . . . The unrepeatable exultation was in knowing that they both understood this" (218). Dominique thinks of and describes their lovemaking later as rape—but she knows better than anybody that Roark's overwhelming of her defenses was not against her consent, but was, as Ayn Rand would later describe it, "by engraved invitation."[7]

NOTES

1. This scene occurs in Part 2, chapter 2 (215–18).

2. Michael S. Berliner, ed., *Letters of Ayn Rand* (New York: Dutton, 1995), 631.

3. Robert Mayhew, ed., *Ayn Rand Answers: The Best of Her Q&A* (New York: New American Library, 2005), 191.

4. See Mayhew, *Ayn Rand Answers*, 106.

5. Susan Brownmiller, *Against Our Will: Men, Women, and Rape* (New York: Bantem Books, 1975; Ballantine Books edition, 1993), 313–15.

6. Feminists are not the only ones who have had such a negative reaction. For example, the religious conservative Phyllis Schlafly says she stopped reading *The Fountainhead* on encountering the "rape" scene. See her *Feminist Fantasies* (Dallas: Spence Publishing Company, 2003), 23.

7. It is rumored that Ayn Rand said this following a lecture in the early sixties, in answer to a question about the "rape" scene, though I have been unable to locate the actual source. In any case, it's an excellent description.

This essay is a revised version of an article originally published in *The Intellectual Activist* (October 2000).

10

Humor in *The Fountainhead*

Robert Mayhew

"Howard Roark laughed." These opening words of *The Fountainhead* might momentarily suggest to a first-time reader that the novel is comic and/or that humor is an important part of Roark's character. But neither is the case. As Ayn Rand stated emphatically, humor does not play a major role in her novels nor in the lives of the heroes in them.[1] This is certainly true of *The Fountainhead*, her first presentation of an ideal man. Its theme and tone are serious; it is an earnest work of reverence for man the hero. And as one character in *The Fountainhead* puts it: "One doesn't reverence with a giggle" (636). Further, among the notes she made on Roark in preparing to write *The Fountainhead*, she wrote: "Laughs seldom. Does not joke. When he does—it is merely a quiet, indifferent kind of sarcasm."[2]

Nevertheless, there is a lot of humor in *The Fountainhead*, which is Ayn Rand's most satirical novel,[3] and the humor is directed at the unoriginal, the ugly, the non-heroic, the evil. Here are five examples: When Mrs. Keating informs Roark that the Dean has called, she adds, "The Dean himself through his secretary" (17). The Peabody Post Office "was the only structure anyone had ever known Professor Peterkin to have erected, before he sacrificed his practice to the responsibilities of teaching" (30). A similar humorous remark is made at the end of this description of one of Guy Francon's buildings:

> The Frink National Bank Building displayed the entire history of Roman art in well-chosen specimens; for a long time it had been considered the best building of the city, because no other structure could boast a single Classical item which it did not possess. It offered so many columns, pediments, friezes, tripods, gladiators, urns and volutes that it looked as if it had not been built of

white marble, but squeezed out of a pastry tube. It was, however, built of white marble. . . . The Frink National Bank Building . . . was a great success. It had been so great a success that it was the last structure Guy Francon ever designed; its prestige spared him the bother from then on. (43)

Another architect has an entire paragraph devoted to his physical appearance:

Ralston Holcombe had no visible neck, but his chin took care of that. His chin and jaws formed an unbroken arc, resting on his chest. His cheeks were pink, soft to the touch, with irresilient softness of age, like the skin of a peach that has been scalded. His rich hair rose over his forehead and fell to his shoulders in the sweep of a medieval mane. It left dandruff on the back of his collar. (113)

We are told that Eve Layton, the wife of multimillionaire Mitch Layton, "had the special faculty of making satin and perfume appear as modern as an aluminum table top. She was Venus rising out of a submarine hatch. . . . [She] believed that her mission in life was to be the vanguard—it did not matter of what" (555).

This is merely a sample. The aim of this essay is to examine (and further illustrate) the humor in *The Fountainhead*.

THE OPENING OF *THE FOUNTAINHEAD*, AND AYN RAND ON HUMOR

"Howard Roark laughed." At what was he laughing? A few paragraphs later, Ayn Rand tells us: "He laughed at the thing that had happened to him that morning and at the things which now lay ahead" (15). We later learn: "That morning he had been expelled from the Architectural School of the Stanton Institute of Technology." So he laughs at his expulsion. But then he stops laughing.

He did not laugh as his eyes stopped in awareness of the earth around him. . . . He looked at the granite. To be cut, he thought, and made into walls. He looked at a tree. To be split and made into rafters. He looked at a streak of rust on the stone and thought of iron ore under the ground. To be melted and to emerge as girders against the sky. (15–16)

There are things an Ayn Rand hero will laugh at, and things he will not laugh at.

These lines from the opening chapter of *The Fountainhead* illustrate Ayn Rand's conviction that "Humor is the denial of metaphysical importance to that which you laugh at."[4] It involves the denial of that which contradicts what she calls one's metaphysical value-judgments—one's appraisal of reality and man's relationship to it.[5] Laughter comes (at least in part) from an awareness of that which does not fit your view of reality; it is the response that accompanies the recognition of the insignificance of something and the consequent dismissal of it.

This conception of humor becomes clearer when we consider the distinction Ayn Rand makes between the metaphysical and the man-made.

> It is the metaphysically given that must be accepted: it cannot be changed. It is the man-made that must never be accepted uncritically: it must be judged, then accepted or rejected and changed when necessary. Man is not omniscient or infallible: he can make innocent errors through lack of knowledge, or he can lie, cheat and fake. The man-made may be a product of genius, perceptiveness, ingenuity—or it may be a product of stupidity, deception, malice, evil.[6]

The metaphysically given is not to be evaluated but accepted. Since humor involves an evaluation, the metaphysically given is not what we laugh at. What we laugh at—what we negate the metaphysical importance of—must be man-made, i.e., certain human ideas, actions, creations, and institutions that contradict one's view of the nature of reality and man's relation to it. This is one reason why Roark, at the beginning of *The Fountainhead*, does *not* laugh at the earth around him. (Of course, another reason is his love for this earth.)[7]

Howard Roark can laugh at "the thing that had happened to him that morning and at the things which now lay ahead," because he regards his expulsion from the university, the dean and the "principle behind the dean," and the unpleasant experiences that most likely "lay ahead," as inconsequential. They are not metaphysically important. (This is especially true for Roark, who is particularly unaffected by other people and by evil.) But this earth—and most of all, what *he* can transform this earth into—are not to be laughed at.

Not all humor is morally equivalent. In "Bootleg Romanticism," Rand writes: "Humor is not an unconditional virtue; its moral character depends on its object. To laugh at the contemptible, is a virtue; to laugh at the good, is a hideous vice."[8] If one is rational and moral, she argues, one will laugh at what is absurd or (in some cases) what is evil; if one is irrational or immoral, one will laugh at what is good and rational.[9]

To illustrate the distinction between morally proper and improper humor—that is, between benevolent and malicious humor—she sometimes referred to this passage from *Atlas Shrugged*:[10]

> Watching them, Dagny thought suddenly of the difference between Francisco and her brother Jim. Both of them smiled derisively. But Francisco seemed to laugh at things because he saw something much greater. Jim laughed as if he wanted to let nothing remain great.[11]

Humor in *The Fountainhead* takes both forms: Ayn Rand employs the proper kind of humor, to laugh at the contemptible; and to characterize Ellsworth Toohey and other villains, she has them make use of the improper form. In what follows, I discuss both uses.

KILL BY LAUGHTER

Ellsworth Toohey, the archvillain of *The Fountainhead*, is an explicit advocate of selflessness—and in fact, as he describes himself to Peter Keating, "the most selfless man you've ever known" (638). But his advocacy of selflessness is a corollary of his hatred of all values. To complete her portrayal of this central aspect of Toohey's character, Ayn Rand makes him a master at the malicious kind of humor.

She once said that "The worst evil that you can do, psychologically, is to laugh at yourself. That means spitting in your own face."[12] So it is no surprise that Toohey should advocate precisely this. In *The Art of Fiction*, Rand says that "One of Ellsworth Toohey's most evil lines in *The Fountainhead* is his advice that 'we must be able to laugh at everything, particularly at ourselves.'"[13] In the novel itself, she writes: "People admired [Toohey's] sense of humor. He was, they said, a man who could laugh at himself" (307).

But Toohey does not merely or especially laugh at himself. He applies his malicious laughter to others, to undercut every person's sense of self. And Toohey does not merely laugh "as if he wanted to let nothing remain great." He is more calculated and methodical. As Ayn Rand described him in her notes for *The Fountainhead*:

> Sarcasm is his pet weapon—as natural to him as smell to the skunk—as a method of offense and defense. He is magnificently, maliciously catty. He does not fight his opponents by straight argument or logical refutation—he disqualifies them from the game, dismisses them by mockery.[14]

Towards the end of *The Fountainhead*, Toohey explains his recipe for achieving power (including political power) over others. One ingredient is laughter:

> Kill by laughter. Laughter is an instrument of human joy. Learn to use it as a weapon of destruction. Turn it into a sneer. It's simple. Tell them to laugh at everything. Tell them that a sense of humor is an unlimited virtue. Don't let anything remain sacred in a man's soul—and his soul won't be sacred to him. Kill reverence and you've killed the hero in man. One doesn't reverence with a giggle. He'll obey and he'll set no limits to his obedience—anything goes—nothing is too serious. (636)

In contrast to Rand's conviction that humor is a conditional virtue, Toohey contends that one should laugh at everything, especially at the good. Laughter directed at the good aims to wipe out, to deny the importance of, to "kill" anything serious, sacred, heroic, reverential.

Here's an instance of this. After Keating tells Toohey that he loves Catherine, Toohey replies:

> How pretty. . . . Young love. Spring and dawn and heaven and drugstore chocolates at a dollar and a quarter a box. The prerogative of the gods and the movies. . . . I understand. And I approve. I'm a realist. Man has always insisted on making an ass of himself. Oh, come now, we must never lose our sense of humor. Nothing's really sacred but a sense of humor. Still, I've always loved the tale of Tristan and Isolde. It's the most beautiful story ever told—next to that of Mickey and Minnie Mouse. (232)

A little later, Keating tells Toohey that he and Catherine met seven years ago. Toohey replies:

> "And it was love at first sight of course?" "Yes," said Keating and felt himself being ridiculous. "It must have been spring [said Toohey]. It usually is. There's always a dark movie theater, and two people lost to the world, their hands clasped together—but hands do perspire when held too long, don't they? Still, it's beautiful to be in love. The sweetest story ever told—and the tritest. Don't turn away like that, Catherine. We must never allow ourselves to lose our sense of humor." (236)

After leaving Toohey's place, Keating and Catherine are walking hand and hand. "Then [Peter] thought suddenly that hands did perspire when held too long, and he walked faster in irritation. He thought that they were walking there like Mickey and Minnie Mouse and that they probably appeared ridiculous to passers-by" (239).

Toohey killed by laughter: he killed this moment, and he contributed to killing Keating's relationship with Catherine—one of Keating's few genuine values.[15]

Ayn Rand once said: "If you're laughing at the evil in the world—provided you take it seriously but occasionally permit yourself to laugh at it—that's fine."[16] Malicious laughter is an essential feature of Toohey's evil, and Rand takes it seriously. But she gets the last laugh, for Toohey and his followers are also the objects of her laughter. (More on this shortly.)

LAUGHING AT THE CONTEMPTIBLE

In *The Fountainhead*, as I point out above, Ayn Rand makes use of proper humor. As an illustration, I focus in this section on two kinds or cases: her use of narrative that is sarcastic or ironic, and her humorous treatment of the members and fellow-travelers of the Council of American Writers.

Writing Like Dominique

At the beginning of *The Fountainhead*, Dominique Francon, the heroine of the novel, writes a regular newspaper column entitled "Your House." Here is a passage on the Ainsworth house.

> You enter a magnificent lobby of golden marble and you think that this is the City Hall or the Main Post Office, but it isn't. It has, however, everything: the mezzanine with the Colonnade and the stairway with a goitre and the cartouches in the form of looped leather belts. Only it's not leather, it's marble. The dining room has a splendid bronze gate, placed by mistake on the ceiling, in the shape of a trellis entwined with fresh bronze grapes. There are dead ducks and rabbits hanging on the wall panels, in bouquets of carrots, petunias and string beans. I do not think these would have been very attractive if real, but since they are bad plaster imitations, it is all right. . . . (112)

Dominique is clearly employing sarcasm: she does not believe that the lobby is magnificent, the bronze gate splendid, the bad plaster imitations all right.[17] Dominique is also sarcastic in the interview she grants Sally Brent and (shortly thereafter) in the description she gives Gail Wynand of the critical praise received by Ike the Genius' play *No Skin Off Your Nose*.[18]

Ayn Rand wrote like this—i.e., sarcastically or ironically—in certain narrative passages in *The Fountainhead*.[19] There is one noteworthy difference, however, between Dominique's article and Ayn Rand's similar narrative: Dominique is mocking her readers as much as she is the Ainsworth House and its architect. But Ayn Rand's scorn or laughter is *not* directed at her audience.

Here are seven examples from the many instances of narrative sarcasm in *The Fountainhead*:

> It [the Stanton Institute of Technology] looked like a medieval fortress, with a Gothic cathedral grafted to its belly. The fortress was eminently suited to its purpose, with stout, brick walls, a few slits wide enough for sentries, ramparts behind which defending archers could hide, and corner turrets from which boiling oil could be poured upon the attacker—should such an emergency arise in an institute of learning. (20)

> When he [Keating] glanced at his [Stengel's] plans again, he noticed the flaws glaring at him from the masterpiece. (39)

> Pettingill was a cousin of the Bank president's wife and a famous authority on the ruins of Pompeii; the Bank president was an ardent admirer of Julius Caesar and had once, while in Rome, spent an hour and a quarter in reverent inspection of the Colosseum. (74)

> These things were permitted to him [Ralston Holcombe] because he was a genius. (113)

They had discovered a boy genius; Cosmo-Slotnick adored boy geniuses; Mr. Slotnick was one himself, being only forty-three. (187)[20]

That winter the annual costume Arts Ball was an event of greater brilliance and originality than usual. Athelstan Beasely, the leading spirit of its organization, had had what he called a stroke of genius: all the architects were invited to come dressed as their best buildings. It was a huge success. (322–23)

Sixty-five children, their ages ranging from three to fifteen, were picked out by zealous ladies who were full of kindness and so made a point of rejecting [for placement into the Hopton Stoddard Home for Subnormal Children] those who could be cured and selecting only the hopeless cases. (385)

Ayn Rand did not believe that an armed attack could arise at an institute of learning; neither she nor Keating thought Stengel's plan was a masterpiece; she did not consider Ralston Holcombe or Mr. Slotnick to be geniuses (nor the latter a boy); in her view, the Arts Ball was not—according to any objective standard—a huge success; and finally, she did not consider these zealous ladies on the subnormal-children selection committee to be full of kindness.

Why then did she write this way? Did the fact that she made sarcasm Toohey's pet weapon suggest that this was something she should not have employed? No. It fits Toohey perfectly that sarcasm is his pet weapon, but that's because of the *amount* of sarcasm he uses, and at *what* he directs it: it is his normal way of dealing with people and the world, and he directs it at everything, especially the good. But as Ayn Rand would later state in *The Art of Nonfiction*:

Sarcasm . . . should be used sparingly. The general principle is to prepare the ground for what you want to treat sarcastically. Make sure it is clear why you are making a sarcastic remark. . . . When you have prepared your ground . . . , a touch of sarcasm can be stylistically brilliant.[21]

The reason Ayn Rand added touches of sarcasm in her narrative is clear: she wished to mock, to criticize, to underscore the insignificance of the objects of her sarcasm, and she did this without overdoing her use of it. That the Stanton Institute of Technology was built to resemble a medieval fortress deserves criticism, but not a serious critique—at least not in *The Fountainhead*. The same is true of the annual costume Arts Ball, Mr. Slotnick's evaluation of himself as a boy genius, and so forth.

The Council of American Writers

Ayn Rand continues the above passage from *The Art of Nonfiction* as follows:

There are some subjects which one can discuss only sarcastically, e.g., the hippies or modern art. There the *subject* gives you the necessary ground. It is a caricature in itself, and therefore you cannot evaluate it except in sarcastic terms (though you *can* discuss its psychological and philosophical roots seriously).[22]

It is no surprise that in a novel in which an architect with integrity clashes with mediocrities and second-handers who draw solely on tradition in designing their buildings, the author would include comic presentations of some architectural works. We have seen some examples of that. But I think *The Fountainhead* is most satirical in its presentation of a group known as the Council of American Writers. This "Council" consists of writers who are even worse in their field than the bad architects of the novel are in theirs. They are modern artists and their fellow travelers, who can be treated only humorously or sarcastically, as their real-life counterparts are caricatures of themselves.

Ellsworth Toohey was the organizer (though not a member) of the Council of American Writers. Lois Cook was its chairman and "only famous member."

> The rest included a woman who never used capitals in her books, and a man who never used commas; a youth who had written a thousand-page novel without a single letter o, and another who wrote poems that neither rhymed nor scanned; a man with a beard who was sophisticated and proved it by using every unprintable four-letter word in every ten pages of his manuscript; a woman who imitated Lois Cook, except that her style was less clear. . . . There was also a fierce young man known only as Ike the Genius, though nobody knew just what he had done. . . . The Council signed a declaration which stated that writers were servants of the proletariat. . . . (306)[23]

The critic Jules Fougler is a fellow-traveler, but not a member ("I am an individualist. . . , I don't believe in organizations" [468]), and foreign correspondent Lancelot Clokey is probably a member.

Lancelot Clokey's first book was an account of his adventures in foreign countries. Here is Fougler's description of Clokey's book:

> You've written a remarkable collection of bilge—yes, bilge—but morally justified. A clever book. World catastrophes used as a backdrop for your own nasty little personality. How Lancelot Clokey got drunk at an international conference. What beauties slept with Lancelot Clokey during an invasion. How Lancelot Clokey got dysentery in a land of famine. (470)

Lois Cook complains that Clokey's "life wasn't worth living, let alone recording" (470).

Note that Clokey represents a definite type of writer whom Ayn Rand had encountered. (Perhaps she included in this type the quasi-autobiographical novels of Ernest Hemingway.) In a letter to Channing Pollock dated June 8, 1941, she writes:

I have read, appalled, the kind of autobiographies that are being published to-day. Autobiographies of nobodies full of nothing at all. Great big life stories of second-rate newspapermen *who use world events as a background for their nasty little personalities.* Like this: "And when I saw the fall of Vienna, it reminded me of a day seven years earlier when I met Jimmy Glutz in a dive in Singapore, and over a glass of absinthe I said: 'Jimmy, what is the meaning of life?' and Jimmy answered: 'Hell, who knows, you old bastard?'" You see what I mean? Is there any point, reason or excuse for this sort of thing? Yet it is being published every day and blown up into bestsellers.[24]

Ayn Rand made use of the description of these "second-rate newspaper-men" in *The Fountainhead*: "world events as a background for their nasty lit-tle personalities" became "World catastrophes used as a backdrop for your own nasty little personality."

Lois Cook was based not only on a *type* of writer, but on one particular "novelist." Elsworth Toohey describes her as "the greatest literary genius since Goethe." She writes, he says, "not exactly novels . . . No, not collec-tions of stories either . . . that's just it, just Lois Cook—a new form of liter-ature entirely" (232).[25] Ayn Rand's journals make it clear that her model for Lois Cook was Gertrude Stein. In the notes she made while writing *The Fountainhead*, Lois Cook's name was originally Gertrude, and at one point Ayn Rand refers to Stein explicitly.[26] The Cook-Stein connection is evident in a passage she gives us from Lois Cook's *Clouds and Shrouds*, "a record of Miss Cook's travels around the world": "toothbrush in the jaw toothbrush brush brush tooth jaw foam dome in the foam Roman dome come home home in the jaw Rome dome tooth toothbrush toothpick pickpocket socket rocket" (233). Here is a line from "Americans," an "essay" from Gertrude Stein's *Geography and Plays* (1922): "Never sink, never sink sinker, never sink sinker sunk, sink sink sinker sink."[27]

Ayn Rand would certainly regard this kind of "literature" as a subject that could be treated only sarcastically. She would claim, not that the writing of Lois Cook is a parody of Stein, but that Stein's writing is itself a joke (at whose expense, we shall see shortly). It is irrational and unintelligible, and as such incapable of evoking any genuine esthetic response, only boredom and disgust.

I do not know if Ayn Rand had anyone in particular in mind in creat-ing the character Ike the Genius, but no doubt he represents some aspect of the absurdist *avant-garde* theatre that was fashionable in the twenties and thirties.

We discover that Ike the Genius is a playwright who, at 26, had written eleven plays, though none of them had been produced. In one scene, he's reading his newest play to his friends from the Council of American Writ-ers, and their consensus is: "it's awful." Ike responds: "If Ibsen can write plays, why can't I? . . . He's good and I'm lousy, but that's not a sufficient reason." Against the general consensus, however, there is a dissenting voice: "'This is a great play,' said [Jules Fougler]. . . . He wore a suit, beautifully tailored, of a color to which he referred as *'merde d'oie.'*[28] He kept his gloves on at all times and he carried a cane. He was an eminent drama critic" (467–68). Ike the Genius says: "To write a good play and to have it praised is nothing. Anybody can do that. Anyone with talent—and talent is only a glandular accident. But to write a piece of crap and have it praised—well, you match that." Jules Fougler adds, in the same spirit: "What achievement is there for a critic in praising a good play? None whatever. . . . I have a right to wish to impress my own personality upon people." Shortly thereafter, we discover the title of this play in a humorous exchange between Fougler and Ike—a vulgar bit of wordplay in the spirit of Abbott and Costello's famous "Who's on First?" skit:[29]

> "Therefore, I shall make a hit out of—what's the name of your play, Ike?"
>
> "No skin off your ass," said Ike.
>
> "I beg your pardon?"
>
> "That's the title."
>
> "Oh, I see. Therefore, I shall make a hit out of *No Skin off Your Ass.*" (469)

Later, we discover that the play *is* a success. Jules Fougler says to Keating:

> It is the kind of play that depends upon what members of the audience are ca-
> pable of bringing with them into the theater. If you are one of those literal-
> minded people, with a dry soul and a limited imagination, it is not for you. But
> if you are a real human being with a big, big heart full of laughter. . . , you will
> find it an unforgettable experience. (473)

What kind of laughter does Jules Fougler expect this play to evoke? Mali-
cious laughter. Ayn Rand's humorous presentation of the nature of *avant garde* literature also serves as an illustration of the malicious kind of humor discussed in the previous section. Artists and critics such as Lois Cook, Jules Fougler, and Ellsworth Toohey do not take themselves or anything else seriously. They laugh at all values. To paraphrase the line about James Taggart quoted earlier, they laugh as if they wanted to let no art remain great. This becomes clearer in another literary project Toohey is promoting:

> I'm pushing the autobiography of a dentist who's really a remarkable person—
> because there's not a single remarkable day in his life nor sentence in his book.
> . . . Can you imagine a solid bromide undressing his soul as if it were a revela-
> tion? . . . When the fact that one is a total nonentity who's done nothing more
> outstanding than eating, sleeping and chatting with neighbors becomes a fact
> worthy of pride, of announcement to the world and of diligent study by mil-

lions of readers—the fact that one has built a cathedral becomes unrecordable and unannounceable. A matter of perspective and relativity. The distance permissible between the extremes of any particular capacity is limited. The sound perception of an ant does not include thunder. (471)

In a sense, Toohey is dead serious. But in another sense everything here is said tongue in cheek. There is laughter behind his words. We see this again in another part of the same scene, in a conversation between Toohey and Ike the Genius.

"Ibsen is good," said Ike.
  "Sure he's good, but suppose I didn't like him. Suppose I wanted to stop people from seeing his plays. It would do me no good whatever to tell them so. But if I sold them the idea that you're just as great as Ibsen—pretty soon they wouldn't be able to tell the difference. . . . And then it wouldn't matter what they went to see at all. Then nothing would matter—neither the writers nor those for whom they write. . . . (472)

Ike the Genius's play is Toohey's (and Ike's) joke on Ibsen, the theater, and theater-goers. Toohey has a very conscious purpose: he "kills by laughter." This is malicious laughter—the laughter of *modernism*. As Louis Sass puts it in *Madness and Modernism*, "it is only in the modernist era that we find artworks whose most central attitude is not to communicate or to celebrate, but to pour scornful laughter on the whole of existence."[30]

We have come full circle. In laughing at modern *avant-garde* literature (and its major advocate in the novel, Ellsworth Toohey), Ayn Rand laughs at malicious laughter. Further, laughing at modern literature, besides being unavoidable, serves to remind us that the universe is benevolent, that in the end, the evil and the insipid do not matter; what matters is great art—which, of course, has the central place in *The Fountainhead*.

CONCLUSION

I have shown that *The Fountainhead* is in some respects a satirical novel, and discussed the nature of its satire. In conclusion, I want to examine why Ayn Rand chose to write *The Fountainhead* in this way, but not *Atlas Shrugged*. Why is there much more humor and sarcasm in the former than in the latter?[31]

One reason may be that in writing *The Fountainhead*, Ayn Rand was influenced to some degree by Sinclair Lewis (somewhat in the way, and to the extent, that she was influenced by Victor Hugo in writing *We the Living*[32]), and that no such influence was exerted on her when she wrote *Atlas Shrugged*. In 1936, completing a questionnaire for Macmillan's publicity campaign for *We the Living*, beside the heading "Favorite Author" she wrote

"Sinclair Lewis"—which I take to mean that he was at that time her current favorite.[33]

Sinclair Lewis's novels are full of the kind of sarcasm found (with less frequency) in *The Fountainhead*. Here are a couple of examples, from *Elmer Gantry* (1927):[34]

> He [Elmer] had, in fact, got everything from the church and Sunday School, except, perhaps, any longing whatever for decency and kindness and reason. (34)

> There had been some difficulty over his [Frank Shallard's] ordination, for he had been shaky about even so clear and proven a fact as the virgin birth. (154)

Here are another two, which resemble passages from *The Fountainhead*. First, in *Elmer Gantry*, a minor character is described as follows: "he was sixty-eight, to the dean's boyish sixty" (73). This is similar to the *Fountainhead*-passage about Mr. Slotnick, who was called a boy genius, "being only forty-three" (187). Finally, here's a passage that bears comparing to the description of the Bank president who admired Julius Caesar and "had once, while in Rome, spent an hour and a quarter in reverent inspection of the Colosseum" (74):

> The bishop and his lady were fond of travel. They had made a six months' inspection of missions in Japan, Korea, China, India, Borneo, Java, and the Philippines, which gave the bishop an authoritative knowledge of all Oriental governments, religions, psychology, commerce, and hotels. But besides that, six several summers they had gone to Europe. . . . Once they had spent three solid weeks seeing nothing but London—with side-trips to Oxford, Canterbury, and Stratford. (246)

It is possible, and even likely, that the novels of Sinclair Lewis did exert some influence on the form the satire took in *The Fountainhead*. But that alone cannot explain why *The Fountainhead* was satirical, while *Atlas Shrugged* was not. For every essential in an Ayn Rand novel is determined ultimately by the purpose for which the novel is written.

I think the primary reason that *The Fountainhead* is more satirical is that, *in a sense*, it is more naturalistic. *The Fountainhead* is set in the world as it was around the time that Ayn Rand wrote it. As we have seen, she even had some real-life villains in mind (e.g. Gertrude Stein), and though Howard Roark is certainly not Frank Lloyd Wright, Roark's struggles with Classicism were modeled after Wright's actual struggles.[35] And there are many more naturalistic touches. Take for instance Gordon Prescott's testimony at the Stoddard trial:

> The correlation of the transcendental to the purely spatial in the building under discussion is entirely screwy. . . . If we take the horizontal as the one-

dimensional, the vertical as the two-dimensional, the diagonal as the three-dimensional, and the inter-penetration of spaces as the fourth-dimensional—architecture being a fourth-dimensional art—we can see quite simply that this building is homaloidal, or—in the language of the layman—flat. The flowing life which comes from the sense of order in chaos, or, if you prefer, from unity in diversity, as well as vice versa, which is the realization of the contradiction inherent in architecture, is here absolutely absent. I am really trying to express myself as clearly as I can, but it is impossible to present a dialectic state by covering it up with an old fig leaf of logic just for the sake of the mentally lazy layman. (354)[36]

Compare this to the following passage from an article by Kurt Jonas, in *South African Architectural Record*, which Rand copied down in her notes for *The Fountainhead*:

Here we find, indeed, a four-dimensional composition of space enclosed by solids. Especially the north and north-west aspect of the house shows a dynamic balance of forms, such as it would be hard to surpass. At the same time, it is not lacking in that interpenetration of spaces which brings out the hollow character, full of fluctuating life, which is the expression of architecture as compared with sculpture. . . .

The sphere of architecture is space. We must define space. But we cannot. For space is defined by movement. And movement presupposes time. Therefore we should speak more correctly of spacetime. Architecture is a four-dimensional art. . . .

[T]his is a contradiction not due to the [average] man's poor logic, but to the higher logic, the dialectics of all life and art. To emphasize this I started that essay, *Towards a Philosophy of Architecture*, with the statement: "Modern Architecture is the realization of a contradiction in itself."

That not all things are so simple as some people believe, that there are inherent contradictions in life and in art, is no fault of mine. It is the task of the writer to show and to express this dialectic state, not to cover it with a torn fig leaf of simplifying logical construction, all for the sake of a mentally lazy layman.[37]

Clearly, Gordon Prescott is serving the same function in architecture that Lois Cook serves in literature. And as with Lois Cook, Ayn Rand borrowed directly from reality to create him.

What kind of world is presented in *The Fountainhead*? The United States was a relatively free society but one in grave danger of becoming much worse through an orgy of altruism and an ominous growth in collectivism. The theme of *The Fountainhead* is individualism versus collectivism *within a man's soul*. The focus is not primarily on the deteriorating culture. Further, against whom is Roark struggling? This is an Ayn Rand novel, so his biggest struggles are against other heroes—in this case, Dominique and Wynand. But what about the villains? Toohey of course is pure evil; but as early as the end of Part 2, he is revealed to be no threat to Roark. Further, much of Roark's conflict—if you can even call it that—is against mediocre conventionalists, like Peter Keating and Ralston Holcombe. And they don't stand a chance against him. In this context, there is much more room for humor.

Incidentally, this is related to the Sinclair Lewis connection. In writing *The Fountainhead*, Ayn Rand could feel free to be influenced by someone like Lewis (whose novels were fully naturalistic), which is something that would not (and did not) happen in the case of *Atlas Shrugged*.

In contrast to *The Fountainhead*, consider the society depicted in *Atlas Shrugged*. The novel is set in the not-so-distant future, when the United States is close to dictatorship and Western civilization is collapsing. Outside of the United States, dictatorship has already taken over everywhere. This cultural context is much graver than *The Fountainhead's*—it provides much less opportunity for humor. And consistent with the universe of the novel, the villains are much higher abstractions of different types of evil, which makes them much less easy to laugh at (though in some cases they are laughable). Finally, the main conflict philosophically is between life and death—or rather, between those who worship life and those who worship death. Again, in such a context, too much humor—even the level of satire found in *The Fountainhead*—would have been inappropriate.

None of this makes *Atlas Shrugged* a less benevolent novel. On the contrary, humor is by its nature destructive—it underscores the evil and irrational and inconsequential as it dismisses them. That *The Fountainhead* is more satirical might arguably give it—if not less benevolence—a touch of bitterness that *Atlas Shrugged* lacks. Given the cultural context of *The Fountainhead*, however, a more satirical approach was and is not only appropriate, but desirable.[38]

NOTES

1. See Robert Mayhew, ed., *Ayn Rand Answers: The Best of Her Q&A* (New York: New American Library, 2005), 141.

2. David Harriman, ed., *Journals of Ayn Rand* (New York: Dutton, 1997), 97. This is not the only kind of laughter Roark is capable of. Recall the description of the nights Mike Donnigan, Steven Mallory, Dominique, and Roark spent together in Mallory's shack, when the Stoddard Temple was being built:

> They did not speak about their work. Mallory told outrageous stories and Dominique laughed like a child. They talked about nothing in particular, sentences that had meaning only in the sound of the voices, in the warm gaiety, in the ease of complete relaxation. They were simply four people who liked being there together. . . . Roark laughed as Dominique had never seen him laugh anywhere else, his mouth loose and young. (336)

There is a similar kind of laughter in two scenes in which Roark is talking to Peter Keating, who is being honest (33, 581).

3. Note that the tone of some of her early short stories—especially "Good Copy," "Escort," and "Her Second Career"—is light and humorous. These were all first published in Leonard Peikoff, ed., *The Early Ayn Rand: A Selection from Her Unpublished Fiction* (New York: New American Library, 1984; paperback edition, Signet, 1986; revised edition, Signet, 2005). On humor in her first novel, *We the Living*, see Robert Mayhew, "Kira Argounova Laughed: Humor and Joy in *We the Living*," in Robert Mayhew, ed., *Essays on Ayn Rand's* We the Living (Lanham, MD: Lexington Books, 2004).

4. See Mayhew, *Ayn Rand Answers*, 140–42, which contains Rand's most extensive discussion of humor. Similar statements can be found in Ayn Rand, *The Art of Fiction: A Guide for Writers and Readers*, ed. Tore Boeckmann (New York: Plume, 2000), 165, and in Ayn Rand, *The Art of Nonfiction: A Guide for Writers and Readers*, ed. Robert Mayhew (New York: Plume, 2001), 126. For a lengthier discussion of Ayn Rand's conception of humor, see Robert Mayhew, "Ayn Rand Laughed: Ayn Rand on the Role of Humor in Literature and Life," *The Intellectual Activist* 16, no.1 (January 2002).

5. See Harry Binswanger, ed., *The Ayn Rand Lexicon: Objectivism from A to Z* (New York: New American Library, 1986; Meridian paperback edition, 1988), s.v. Metaphysical Value-Judgments.

6. Ayn Rand, "The Metaphysical versus The Man-Made," *Philosophy: Who Needs It* (New York: Bobbs-Merrill, 1982; Signet paperback edition, 1984), 27.

7. In literature, exceptions can be used to great effect. For instance, in *The Fountainhead*, after the Cortlandt explosion and its injury to her, Dominique, losing consciousness, is described as "laughing at the law of gravity" (616).

8. Ayn Rand, *The Romantic Manifesto: A Philosophy of Literature*, revised edition (New York: Signet, 1975), 133.

9. Rand does not believe it is appropriate to laugh at *all* evil. In the *Art of Nonfiction*, she writes:

> When I say it is proper to laugh at evil, I do not mean all evil. It is improper . . . to write humorously about tragic and painful events or issues—about death, cemeteries, torture chambers, concentration camps, executions, etc. This is called "sick humor," and the designation is correct, because although it is possible to laugh at such things, one should not consider them funny. For example, take comedies about the Nazis. I have a strong aversion to war comedies. War *per se* is bad enough, but war and dictatorship combined are *a fortiori* not a subject for comedy. (126)

She provides an example of the kind of evil that *is* a proper object of laughter:

> Take the passage on Hegel in the title essay of *For the New Intellectual*. Describing Hegel's philosophy, I write that "omniscience about the physical universe . . . is to be derived, not from observations of the facts, but from the contemplation of [the] Idea's triple somersaults inside his, Hegel's, mind." The reference to triple somersaults is meant to be light or humorous. I am not denying the seriousness of the subject (the history of philosophy), but I am indicating that I do not take Hegel seriously and that we need not worry about this particular monster. (126–27)

10. See Rand, *Art of Fiction*, 166, and Mayhew, *Ayn Rand Answers*, 141.

11. Ayn Rand, *Atlas Shrugged* (New York: Random House, 1957; Signet thirty-fifth anniversary paperback edition, 1992), 96.

12. Mayhew, *Ayn Rand Answers*, 141.

13. Rand, *Art of Fiction*, 166; cf. *The Fountainhead*, 362.

14. Harriman, *Journals of Ayn Rand*, 109.

15. In a letter of June 3, 1944, Rand wrote: "As to Keating—no, he didn't love anybody. Catherine is the nearest he ever came to it—but even then it wasn't much, because—being actually selfless—he was not capable of any real and complete emotion." Michael S. Berliner, ed., *Letters of Ayn Rand* (New York: Dutton, 1995), 137–38.

16. Mayhew, *Ayn Rand Answers*, 141.

17. *The Oxford Pocket Dictionary and Thesaurus*, American Edition (New York: Oxford University Press, 1997), defines "sarcasm": "1. bitter or wounding remark. 2. taunt, esp. one ironically worded." Its entry under "irony" includes: "humorous or sarcastic use of language of a different or opposite meaning."

18. This is from the interview she grants Sally Brent:

> Oh yes, Miss Brent, I'm very happy. I open my eyes in the morning and I say to myself, it can't be true, it's not poor little me who's become the wife of the great Gail Wynand who had all the glamorous beauties of the world to choose from. You see, I've been in love with him for years. He was just a dream to me, a beautiful, impossible dream. And now it's like a dream come true. . . . Please, Miss Brent, take this message from me to the women of America: Patience is always rewarded and romance is just around the corner. (488)

And this is from her description of the praise for *No Skin Off Your Nose*:

> Why, Gail, it's the biggest hit in town. Your own critic, Jules Fougler . . . said it was the greatest play of our age. Ellsworth Toohey said it was the fresh voice of the coming new world. Alvah Scarret said it was not written in ink, but in the milk of human kindness. Sally Brent—before you fired her—said it made her laugh with a lump in her throat. Why, it's the godchild of the *Banner*. I thought you would certainly want to see it. (490–91)

19. She could also write like this in private, when confronted with something she regarded as contemptible. For example, see her architectural research notes on David Gray's *Thomas Hastings, Architect*, which she called "The most disgusting book that I have read to date." (Her notes on this book are dated July 12, 1937, and are found in Harriman, *Journals of Ayn Rand*, 135–42.) She copied out a story about Hastings (part of which I quote here):

> Shaking with laughter, Hastings went on to explain to [his female guest] that no dentist could have the anxieties of an architect; that when he was a beginner he was always afraid that his houses were going to fall down but now when he saw them again he was afraid that they weren't.

Her comment—"Such wit!"—is clearly sarcastic. (See also the following note.)

20. Cf. the passage in her essay "The Left: Old and New," in which she refers to Buckminster Fuller as "a bright young man of 75," calls Harvard sociologist Pitirim Sorokin "Another youthful authority," and writes: "The youngest of these rebels and trend-setters for youth is Marshall McLuhan, aged 59." Ayn Rand,

Return of the Primitive: The Anti-Industrial Revolution, ed. Peter Schwartz (New York: Meridian, 1999), 163.

21. Rand, *Art of Nonfiction*, 125.

22. Rand, *Art of Nonfiction*, 125.

23. Compare her description of the Council of American Artists:

The Council of American Artists had, as chairman, a cadaverous youth who painted what he saw in his nightly dreams. There was a boy who used no canvas, but did something with bird cages and metronomes, and another who discovered a new technique of painting: he blackened a sheet of paper and then painted with a rubber eraser. There was a stout middle-aged lady who drew subconsciously, claiming that she never looked at her hand and had no idea of what the hand was doing; her hand, she said, was guided by the spirit of the departed lover whom she had never met on earth. Here they did not talk so much about the proletariat, but merely rebelled against the tyranny of reality and of the objective. (306)

24. Berliner, *Ayn Rand Letters*, 49 (emphasis added).

25. Compare this description of Howard Roark's work early in the novel: "The buildings were not Classical, they were not Gothic, they were not Renaissance. They were only Howard Roark" (19).

26. Harriman, *Journals of Ayn Rand*, 210–11. For more on Rand's view of Stein, see *Art of Fiction*, 11–12; *Journals of Ayn Rand*, 44, 107, 153; and Berliner, *Letters of Ayn Rand*, 50.

27. Gertrude Stein, *Geography and Plays* (Boston: Four Seas Company, 1922), 45.

28. According to the *Dictionnaire de L'Académie française* (6th ed., 1835), s.v. *merde, merde d'oie* (i.e., "goose shit") is a color *"entre le vert et le jaune"*—between green and yellow.

Cf. Schiller's *Intrigue and Love*, act 1, sc. 6, in which the Chamberlain says: "His Highness is wearing a *merde d'oye* coat today." (Trans. by Charles E. Passage, in *Friedrich Schiller, Plays*, Walter Hinderer, ed. [New York: Continuum, 1983], 17.) The line has the following editor's footnote: "Goosedung green (*merde d'oye*) was the fashionable color of the 1782 Paris season, as Mercier's *Tableau de Paris*, published that year, shows." My thanks to Tore Boeckmann for bringing this to my attention.

29. I learned from Leonard Peikoff that Ayn Rand did know of the "Who's on First?" skit.

30. Louis Sass, *Madness and Modernism* (Cambridge, Mass.: Harvard University Press, 1995), 36.

31. The kind of sarcasm found in *The Fountainhead* is rare in *Atlas Shrugged*. I have come up with merely four (possible) examples:

1. Mrs. Vail is described as "a lady of noble breeding and unusual loveliness" (*Atlas Shrugged*, 71); it's possible that "unusual loveliness" is not an accurate description.

2. The "disinterested" in the last line of the following is somewhat sarcastic: "A group that called itself 'Committee of Disinterested Citizens' collected signatures on a petition demanding a year's study of the John Galt Line by government experts before the first train was allowed to run. . . . The consideration it

received was respectful, because it came from people who were disinterested" (214–15).

3. The use of "bright" in this line, and in the next example, may be sarcastic: "a new profession practiced by bright young boys just out of college, who called themselves 'defreezers'" (327).

4. "a bright young boy just out of college had been sent to him [Rearden] from Washington, as Deputy Director of Distribution" (336).

Although it is not narrative, this line from Eddie Willers is worth mentioning: "Clifton Locey [is] a bright, progressive young man of forty-seven" (524). On the sarcasm of "young man of forty-seven," see p. 215 (and n. 20) above.

32. See Shoshana Milgram, "*We the Living* and Victor Hugo: Ayn Rand's First Novel and the Novelist She Ranked First," in Mayhew, *Essays on Ayn Rand's* We the Living.

33. See Jeff Britting, *Ayn Rand* (New York: Overlook, 2004), 48.

34. Sinclair Lewis, *Elmer Gantry* (New York: Harcourt, 1927). Pagination refers to the 1967 Signet Classic edition. I want to thank Tore Boeckmann for not only providing me with a couple of the examples from Sinclair Lewis, but also for insisting that I consider Lewis in connection with the satirical nature of *The Fountainhead*.

35. On the naturalistic elements in *The Fountainhead*, see Tore Boeckmann, "*The Fountainhead* as Romantic Novel," in the present collection, 128–33, and Mayhew, *Ayn Rand Answers*, 200. On Roark's struggles with Classicism being modeled after Wright's struggles, see Michael S. Berliner, "Howard Roark and Frank Lloyd Wright," in the present collection, 51.

36. See also Prescott's speech at a meeting of the Council of American Builders (292–93).

37. Harriman, *Journals of Ayn Rand*, 152–53 (ellipses and brackets in the original).

38. Some of this material appeared earlier in "Ayn Rand Laughed: Ayn Rand on the Role of Humor in Literature and Life," *The Intellectual Activist* 16, no. 1 (January 2002). I would like to thank Rob Tracinski, the editor of *The Intellectual Activist*, for his comments on an earlier version of that essay. I also want to thank my fellow participants in the March 2005 Anthem Foundation Consultancy at the University of Texas, Austin (Harry Binswanger, Allan Gotthelf, and Tara Smith) for discussion of this paper, which led to many improvements. I am also grateful to Tore Boeckmann and Greg Salmieri for their comments on a later draft.

11

The Fountainhead and the Spirit of Youth

B. John Bayer

> *Whatever their future, at the dawn of their lives, men seek a noble vision of man's nature and of life's potential.*
>
> —Ayn Rand, Introduction to the twenty-fifth anniversary edition of The Fountainhead (xi)

According to Ayn Rand, young men's quest for a "noble vision of man's nature and of life's potential" helps to explain the enduring success of *The Fountainhead*. She identifies this "noble vision" as the "sense of life dramatized in *The Fountainhead*," what she calls *"man-worship"* (ix). Man-worshippers, she holds, are those who "see man's highest potential and strive to actualize it," those who are "dedicated to the *exaltation* of man's self-esteem and the *sacredness* of his happiness on earth" (x).

Ayn Rand thought it possible to grasp one's own potential introspectively, from one's own soul. But to *maintain* this sense of reverence for man's highest potential—especially in the face of a culture of mediocrity—more is often needed. To begin with, one also wants to know that someone else wants and *succeeds* in achieving the highest possible. One wants this, not to be reassured by others' approval, but to see that the values one seeks are real, and can be achieved. For this reason, Ayn Rand claims that without the inspiration of her husband, Frank O'Connor, she herself would not have been able to maintain her sense of life or complete the novel "over a long span of years when there was nothing around us but a gray desert of people and events that evoked nothing but contempt and revulsion" (vi).

But she also observes that the ideal of man-worship is one that has "rarely been expressed in human history" and which is "virtually non-existent" in contemporary culture (x). So portrayal of the ideal is in short supply, but heavily demanded—especially by the young.

The Fountainhead has enduring appeal because it virtually corners the literary market in portraying this man-worshipping sense of life. It does this through the character of Howard Roark, whom Ayn Rand describes in her introduction as an ideal man. She remarks that in a young person's quest to find the "noble vision" of man and life,

> There are very few guideposts to find. *The Fountainhead* is one of them.
>   This is one of the cardinal reasons of *The Fountainhead's* lasting appeal: it is a confirmation of the spirit of youth, proclaiming man's glory, showing how much is possible. (xi)

This essay will explore how *The Fountainhead* confirms the "spirit of youth," which Ayn Rand describes as a "sense of enormous expectation, the sense that one's life is important, that great achievements are within one's capacity, and that great things lie ahead" (xi). In essence, the spirit of youth is the spirit of *man*, i.e. the man-worshiping sense of life—but experienced by those who have not been corrupted by a society that works to oppose it.

The Fountainhead embodies a spirit of man-worship by giving us a portrait of a man worthy of such worship: Howard Roark. But in order to articulate for herself the nature of an ideal man, Ayn Rand tells us that she "had to define and present the kinds of premises and values that create the character of an ideal man and motivate his actions" (vii). In order to show how *The Fountainhead* succeeds in portraying Roark as ideal, this essay will, therefore, identify these premises and values.

Identifying them will also put a common criticism in its place. Critics of *The Fountainhead* often explain its popularity as resulting from "teen infatuation," a kind of rebellious "Ayn Rand phase" young readers eventually grow out of.[1] One critic writes that the book's "sub-Nietzschean assertiveness" is appealing mainly to "somewhat eccentric youngsters."[2] Another cynically urges that *The Fountainhead* is "better read when one is young enough to miss the point." This same critic confesses to having missed the point herself by "skipping over all the pages about egotism and altruism," and thinking the book was about an architect and his love life. She recounts that she lost interest in the book when she went to college and learned that "architects were, for the most part, not like Howard Roark" and that "altruism was not bad in moderation."[3]

It is fascinating that the attitude embraced by these critics bears a striking resemblance to that of the *villains* in the very book they regard as so unrealistic. We can imagine Ellsworth Toohey himself scoffing at the ambitions of his niece, Catherine Halsey, with much the same attitude. But, as we shall see, Toohey's influence does not correct foolish errors of the young—it works to destroy their ambitions and their happiness.

The critics may not always seek this destruction in the way that Toohey does, but even so their attitude results from the acceptance of Toohey's pernicious ideals. While these ideals are destructive of the spirit of youth, this spirit need not be destroyed—not so long as Roark's ideals exist as an alternative, especially not if Roark's ideals are understood explicitly.

ROARK'S EMBODIMENT OF THE SPIRIT OF YOUTH

Ayn Rand's most explicit statement about the spirit of youth was formulated in a nonfiction essay published a quarter-century after *The Fountainhead*: "The 'Inexplicable Personal Alchemy,'" which first appeared in *The Objectivist* in 1969. The essay is a commentary on a *New York Times* account of a sudden but limited outburst of political dissent in the Soviet Union in the wake of the "Prague spring" of 1968.[4] Five young Russian dissidents had spoken out against the Soviet invasion of Czechoslovakia, in the face of certain prosecution and exile. Impressed by the strength of their conviction, she named three hallmarks of the spirit of youth: idealism, independence, and goodwill. I will draw on Ayn Rand's discussion of each of these hallmarks to show how the spirit of youth is exemplified by Roark. Each represents one of the important premises or values motivating Roark, which make him an ideal man.

Roark's Seriousness about Ideas

Ayn Rand states that the first trait, seriousness about ideas, explains the otherwise "inexplicable" willingness of the young dissidents to fight for their ideals in the face of the opposition they encountered:

> There is a fundamental conviction which some people never acquire, some hold only in their youth, and a few hold to the end of their days—the conviction that *ideas matter*. . . . That ideas matter means that knowledge matters, that truth matters, that one's mind matters. And the radiance of that certainty, in the process of growing up, is the best aspect of youth.[5]

"Idealism" has long been associated with youth, but usually as a lofty, impractical naiveté. Ayn Rand, by contrast, characterizes idealism more precisely as "taking ideas seriously," or "intending to live by, to *practice*, any idea you accept as true."[6]

One of the first scenes in the novel, Roark's meeting with the Dean, introduces the reader to his seriousness about ideas. Roark's self-described "insubordination"—submitting assignments in his own style, rather than the assigned, conventional styles—has led to his expulsion from Stanton. The Dean offers to readmit Roark if he agrees to take a year off to "grow up," but Roark declines and states his intention to find work in architecture on his own. When the Dean criticizes him for wishing to improve upon the standards of the past, Roark says that he has no concern for other people's standards, but sets his own (23–24). Roark clearly treats knowledge, truth, and the judgment of his mind seriously, displaying the "radiance" of certainty that Ayn Rand describes as the "best aspect of youth."

The Dean, of course, thinks Roark's attitude is "childish," "naïve," "silly," and insists that because Roark is only twenty-two, he will "outgrow all that" (22–25). (He is the first negative character in *The Fountainhead* whom the critics will come to mimic.) Roark, of course, does *not* "outgrow all that." Against the Dean's advice, he goes to work for the unpopular Henry Cameron, only to lose the job after Cameron loses commissions and becomes ill. He is fired from the job he takes with Francon and Heyer when he refuses to design in a conventional style. He is fired again by John Erik Snyte when he breaks rank to reveal his unadulterated design for the Heller house. Roark even refuses the commission from the Manhattan Bank building—his last hope at keeping his office open—when he is told he must compromise his design to conform to classical sensibilities. Instead of taking the money and publicity the job might have brought, he opts to work as a day laborer in a quarry. So radiant is Roark's certainty here that he is willing to stake his career on it.

From these examples, one might conclude that Roark's idealism requires renunciation. Indeed, several characters in *The Fountainhead* get just this impression. The Dean characterizes Roark's ambition as a kind of impractical childish rebelliousness. Weidler, the middleman for the Manhattan Bank commission, says Roark's rejection of the bank job is "fanatical and selfless" (197). And Peter Keating wonders why Roark has to be "so damn serious"— even "so old" (!)—suggesting that Roark's "fighting and renunciation" makes him surrender all that is "simple and pleasant" (89).

But this impression is false. Roark explains to the Dean that if he does not derive personal joy from his work, he will be condemning himself to "sixty years of torture." Responding to the claim that his rejection of the Manhattan Bank commission was "fanatical and selfless," he tells Weidler that "that was the most selfish thing you've ever seen a man do" (197). Roark clearly *denies* that he is renouncing anything.

There is a basis for his denial. Responding to the Dean's claim that adhering to personal standards would be "impractical," Roark explains that *what* he intends to practice is building his own way (the way that allows him to take joy in the work itself), and that those clients who want his designs will come to him. And indeed they do. The Heller House serves as a beacon to attract Roark's kind of men, such as Roger Enright. The Enright House then precipitates a series of commissions, culminating in Roark's achievement of steady success after the Monadnock Valley affair.

Interestingly, *Keating's* impression that Roark's idealism involves renunciation is not simply a result of observing Roark's initial struggle. What he means by renunciation is revealed in the following exchange:

> "Oh, you'll never renounce anything! You'd walk over corpses for what you want. But it's what you've renounced by never wanting it."
> "That's because you can't want both." (89)

Here Keating and the Dean exhibit profound agreement, even while they differ on the question of whether Roark seems too old or too childish. In their view, society's standards of value—not one's own—are the only standards worth considering, and one's only choice is to accede to them in comfort, or to renounce them and fight a desperate and impractical battle.[7]

Roark's youthful idealism, then, is far from the cliché of mindlessly embracing—and then outgrowing—some transient, hopeless cause. As Keating observes, all that Roark renounces is the need for social approval—by never wanting it in the first place. His attitude exhibits the second hallmark of youth: independence.

Roark's Independence

Commenting on the *Times'* claim that the Russian dissidents had rejected their society's standards through "an inexplicable personal alchemy," Ayn Rand writes that

> Young persons who hold [the conviction of the supremacy of ideas, of truth] do not have to "throw off the leading conformity of the only society they have known." They do not conform in the first place: they judge and evaluate; if they accept any part of the prevalent social trends, it is through intellectual agreement (which may be mistaken), not through conformity.[8]

Just as serious young people do not conform in the first place, Roark has "renounced" social approval "by never wanting it" in the first place. Indeed all the previous examples of Roark's seriousness about ideas are examples of his independence.[9] Roark's architectural standards are the products of his own thinking, not of tradition or fashion: "The buildings were not Classical, they were not Gothic, they were not Renaissance. They were only Howard Roark" (19). His pursuit of work in accordance with these standards is motivated by pursuit of his own joy, not by society's approval through money or fame. As he tells the Dean, he doesn't care about the opinions of men on the street or of the Dean (23, 26). In other words, his judgment and values are his own: he is *independent*.

Furthermore, those like the Dean and Keating who engage in pragmatic compromise are thereby dependent on the judgment of others. In a later conversation with Wynand, Roark observes that while most consider men like Keating to be selfish, Keating's only aim has been to achieve "Greatness—in other people's eyes" (605). Keating wants to be a great architect, not in order to build great buildings—but to be admired and envied by others. He wants money, not to support his own personal luxury, but to impress or stun others.

By ceding their independent judgment to others, these allegedly "practical" men come to embody actual selflessness. As Roark observes, second-handers like Keating lose all concern with what they desire and what they think is true: they literally lose their self, their ego. In a discussion with Wynand, Roark notes that it is impossible for men to achieve the altruistic goal of "absolute humility," of surrendering every form of self-esteem. As a result, they accept altruism the only way they can: "By seeking self-esteem through others" (607). By substituting the desires of their neighbors for their own, it comes as no surprise that they complain of never finding happiness: "Every form of happiness is private," says Roark (607).

The anticonformists of *The Fountainhead*—like Lois Cook, Ike the Genius, Gus Webb, and the other avant-garde artists Toohey collects in his various art councils—have also abandoned their independence. Since they define their standards in opposition to society's, it is society that sets the terms. Some anticonformists are simply "exhibitionists trying to attract attention," to use the Dean's inapt description of Roark. Others gain a sense of nihilistic glee by defiling society's standards, enjoying the recognition that comes from *disapproval*. In either case, their motivation is social recognition of one kind or another.

But Roark knows that not all men are or need be second-handers. Waiting patiently to find his own "kind of people" (159), he projects a sense of goodwill toward men.

Roark's Goodwill

Considering the peculiar fact that the Russian dissidents sought to debate political issues with an unlikely audience—the secret police—Ayn Rand observes that their willingness was a further consequence of their seriousness about ideas:

> The dedication to ideas leads, in practice, to an almost involuntary goodwill toward men—or rather to something deeper and more important, which is the root of goodwill: *respect*. It leads to the attitude, in individual encounters, of

treating men as rational beings, on the unstated premise that a man is innocent until proved guilty, that he is not evil until he has proved himself to be; "evil," in terms of this attitude, means closed to the power of ideas, i.e., of reason.[10]

Like the Russian dissidents, Roark sometimes extends benevolence to those who do not deserve it (like Keating). But before discussing this, it is instructive to examine his benevolence toward friends and comrades.

Consider Roark's first meeting with Mike Donnigan. Supervising the construction of a building for Francon and Heyer, Roark finds Mike installing conduits inefficiently and offers advice. Mike responds incredulously, objecting that a "punk" like Roark, one of the "college smarties," has the audacity to give advice on how to do a man's work (92). Roark doesn't flinch but proceeds to demonstrate the task he has recommended, easily and with confidence. Mike is impressed and concedes victory, which Roark acknowledges with a good-natured smile. On their next encounter, Mike offers to buy Roark a beer, and he agrees. When they discover that they each worship competence and ability, a new friendship is born. Roark's benevolence toward Mike has allowed him to find one of his kind of men.

Roark's goodwill toward Mike is rooted in his other youthful traits. First and most importantly, Roark's independent idealism leads him to a confidence in his own efficacy, demonstrated in this scene by his proficiency in demonstrating the skill. When relating with others, he experiences this confidence as a kind of overflowing of his own potential, from which he is happy to see others benefit. We see the same quality in Roark's interaction with his staff in Clayton, Ohio, where Dominique observes a worker asking for advice. Roark responds with an easy competence ("That's easy"), and in the interaction, Dominique feels "the quality of Roark's relation to that man, to all the other men in that pit, and odd sense of loyalty and of brotherhood, but not the kind she had ever heard named by these words" (464).

Second, and as a consequence, Roark is happy to grant the benefit of his efficacy to any man when he recognizes the same efficacy (or the potential for it) in them. An earlier scene, also featuring Roark's staff, demonstrates that Roark related to them not by inquiring about their personal lives, but by responding to their creative capacity. If men demonstrate this capacity, Roark grants his benevolence "not as a gift, but as a debt . . . not as affection, but as recognition." This outlook "bred an immense feeling of self-respect within every man in the office" (309).

Roark's self-confidence is so profound—and the benevolence that results, so natural—that he extends his assistance even to those, like Peter Keating, who would not otherwise warrant it. Throughout college and his career, Roark helps Keating with assignments and design problems. Even toward the end, Roark agrees to design Cortlandt Homes for Keating. While Roark's primary motivation is the pleasure of solving the design problem involved in the project, he deals with Keating encouragingly. He understands that Keating's confession of reliance on Roark represents a moment of honesty and a chance to do "something wonderful," "starting from the beginning" and collaborating as partners in the authentic way (581). Keating is puzzled about why Roark is "the most egotistical and the kindest man" he knows. He does not realize that Roark is kind *because* he is "egotistical": his own supreme self-confidence precludes feeling threatened or aggrieved by others in any serious way.

A final example of youthful benevolence is found in a minor but memorable character, who interacts with Roark but once: the boy on the bicycle. The scene, set in the woods outside of Roark's Monadnock Valley homes, provides Ayn Rand's entire view of youth in microcosm. The boy has just graduated from college and does not fully recognize that he has come to the woods to "decide whether life was worth living" (503). He thinks it must be if the earth can look as beautiful as it does—but that he only feels this way at present because he has "seen no sign of men for hours" (503). In particular he has found no inspiration in the message of service and self-sacrifice he has been taught in college. He is angry that he should find inspiration only by escaping from men, because he does not want to have to despise them. He wants to "love and admire them"—but dreads the vulgarity he has come to expect from men (504). But he does not give up hope:

> He had always wanted to write music, and he could give no other identity to the thing he sought. If you want to know what it is, he told himself, listen to the first phrases of Tchaikovsky's *First Concerto*—or the last movements of Rachmaninoff's *Second*. Men have not found the words for it nor the deed nor the thought, but they have found the music. Let me see that in one single act of man on earth. Let me see it made real. Let me see the answer to the promise of that music. Not servants nor those served; not altars and immolations; but the final, the fulfilled, innocent of pain. Don't help me or serve me, but let me see it once, because I need it. Don't work for my happiness, my brothers—show me yours—show me that it is possible—show me your achievement—and the knowledge will give me courage for mine. (503-4)

The boy on the bicycle symbolizes not only the spirit, but the *struggle* of youth surrounded by a world of mediocrity and evil. Like the Russian dissidents in "The 'Inexplicable Personal Alchemy'," the boy's ambitions are opposed by his elders. Like these dissidents, the boy also takes his elders' ideals seriously, but is tortured in the attempt to practice them. And like the dissidents, who saw hope for man "abroad," it is also true for the boy that "the mere knowledge that a nobler way of life is possible somewhere, redeems the human race in one's mind."[11] The boy finds this knowledge when he stumbles upon Monadnock Valley—and meets Roark, its creator. Through this encounter, he acquires "the courage to face a lifetime" (506).

The boy is not (yet) in Roark's position. Still unsure of what he is to make of his life, he does not yet have Roark's degree of self-confidence. Thus he needs Roark's example in a way Roark doesn't need from others. He wants to see the achievement of his brothers, to give him courage for his own. Without Roark's inspiration, it is possible that the boy would be run down by society and the ideals of his elders. As Ayn Rand remarks in her Twenty-fifth Anniversary Introduction,

> Some give up at the first touch of pressure; some sell out; some run down by imperceptible degrees and lose their fire, never knowing when or how they lost it. Then all of these vanish in the vast swamp of their elders who tell them persistently that maturity consists of abandoning one's mind; security, of abandoning one's values; practicality, of losing self-esteem. (xi)

Roark, however, is the heroic exception, one of the few who "hold on and move on, knowing that that fire is not to be betrayed, learning how to give it shape, purpose and reality" (xi). His example inspires not only the boy, but Cameron, Mallory, Wynand, and most significantly, Dominique.[12]

Not every young person is fortunate enough to meet men like Roark. What happens when youth are deprived of such examples and presented ideals—like the ideals of selflessness offered by the boy's elders—which repudiate the very spirit of youth? To see the effects that they have on young people—and thus on man in general—we must now turn to Roark's antithesis, Ellsworth Toohey.

TOOHEY'S DESTRUCTION OF THE SPIRIT OF YOUTH

There is no point in detailing the variety of ways in which Toohey has abandoned the spirit of youth in his own soul. They are too obvious (and too uninspiring) to dwell on. Here we can follow Toohey's own advice: "Don't bother to examine a folly—ask yourself only what it accomplishes" (636). The example of Toohey's character is relevant for our purposes insofar as it sheds light on the nature of the ideals to which the boy on the bicycle is struggling to find an alternative.

Toohey is the foremost advocate in *The Fountainhead* of the ideal of a "life of service and self-sacrifice." Aside from being a prominent cultural critic who spreads these ideals publicly, Toohey dispenses vocational advice directly to the young. He counsels the "grown-up" renunciation of "hysterical" passions and the embrace of promiscuous lust. We can even imagine that it was the boy on the bicycle who received the following advice from Toohey:

> No, I wouldn't advise you to continue with your music. The fact that it comes to you so easily is a sure sign that your talent is only a superficial one. That's

just the trouble—that you love it. Don't you think that sounds like a childish
reason? Give it up. Yes, even if it hurts like hell. (301–2)

Given advice like this, we are told that "some of his protégés did quite well,
others failed. Only one committed suicide" (302).

The record of Toohey's attempted destruction is too vast to catalogue
here. Most obviously, he seeks to destroy Roark by pitting Dominique
against him. But Roark's heroic ability and idealism enable him to prevail
over Toohey. Toohey's niece, Catherine Halsey, does not possess Roark's
ability and does not fare so well. The example of Toohey's destruction of her
thus illustrates the normal consequences of his ideals.

When we first meet the young Catherine, stepping off the train in New
York, her face projects a momentary beauty suggesting that

> . . . the future were opening before her and its glow were already upon her fore-
> head, as if she were eager and proud and ready to meet it. It was one of those
> rare moments when the humblest person knows suddenly what it means to
> feel as the center of the universe, and is made beautiful by the knowledge, and
> the world—in the eyes of witnesses—looks like a better place for having such
> a center. (303)

Toohey had not planned on keeping Catherine at his home after the death
of her mother, but when he sees her for the first time, projecting this attitude, he changes his mind. He will not have anyone feeling as the center of
the universe. Catherine is to be another of his victims.

Toohey's measures against Catherine range from short-term tactics to
long-range strategy. Tactically, he slowly chips away at her life's ambitions—
both professional and romantic—through subtle disparagement and overt
humor. Strategically, he teaches Catherine altruistic ideals.

From early on, Toohey discourages Catherine from getting her own job
or going to college. When she insists on a job, he reluctantly pays her for
menial work to be done at home. Later when he does arrange a job for her,
it is as a social worker, a career which soon leads to her frustration, as we
shall see momentarily.

Likewise, Toohey belittles Catherine's open affection for Keating, calling
him her "T-square Romeo" (60). Reacting to Keating's delay of their wedding, and recalling how "Uncle Ellsworth laughed so much" at the prospect
of the marriage, she suggests that perhaps Toohey was correct: "perhaps we
were being foolish, we're both so young" (157). Toohey keeps on laughing
in the presence of both Catherine and Keating, mocking the idea of marriage as mundane and domestic, child-rearing as a "nuisance" (235), and
stories of young love as the "tritest" ever told (236).

Meanwhile, Toohey revels in subtle jokes that diminish Catherine's looks
and manners. His sense of humor is used unsparingly against *any* manifes-

tations of serious reverence: "Kill reverence and you've killed the hero in man," he later says to Peter Keating (636).[13]

Catherine might have withstood her uncle's disparagement. She might have overcome even the obstacles he had erected to her career and romance, especially if Keating had gone through with their wedding. But Toohey's long-term strategy of instilling altruistic ideals made overcoming these obstacles exceedingly difficult. He knows that with this strategy, he can harness Catherine's own idealism and use it against her. As he tells Keating, no man has achieved or will ever achieve the ideal of altruism, and preaching it as an ideal instills in a man a sense "of guilt, of sin, of his own unworthiness." Because the ideal cannot be achieved, one therefore "gives up eventually all ideals, all aspiration, all sense of his personal value" (635).

Having been taught selflessness for years—and without any idea of an alternative moral code or the genius to discover one for herself—Catherine *does* begin to give up her sense of idealism, and the resulting decline is noticeable. Earlier in the story, Keating had observed that Catherine, at the time almost twenty, "looked no older than she had looked at seventeen" (83). Later, after years of social work and Toohey, we are told that at twenty-six "she looked like a woman trying to hide the fact of being over thirty" (359).

At the age of twenty-six, Catherine presents Toohey with the very dilemma he had intended altruism to engender in her. She says that from an early age, she had always "wanted to do right," while acknowledging that it might look "terribly childish" to Toohey (361). She observes that the question of *what* is right is one that is too big for her to answer, but that her uncle and men for centuries have been claiming that the ideal is selflessness (361–62). So she strove for this ideal, but now finds that she is unhappy. She finds that she wants to be thanked for her service to the poor, that she only likes the poor who are servile toward her. She resents those who find lives for themselves, as they remind her of her own abandoned college ambitions. Even in her devotion to selfless ideals, there is still this mangled remnant of her self-esteem (362–63).

Toohey responds to Catherine's dilemma by announcing that her problem is that she is practicing the ideal of altruism as if *it* were a selfish goal. Her problem is *wanting* to be virtuous. Instead, "she must stop wanting *anything*" (364)—in effect, she must stop pursuing ideals of any kind. As a further bit of fictitious rationalization, Toohey again plays on the idea that the pursuit of ambitions—even *moral* ambitions—is childish. He says that even her sense of guilt is an expression of egoistic concern for her own virtue, that these feelings are "growing pains," but that "[a]ll growth demands destruction" (364–65). Only when Catherine cares no more, when she has lost her self-identity, will she paradoxically "know the kind of happiness" or "spiritual grandeur" that Toohey has promised (365).

Even after this onslaught, Catherine retains an element of her original dignity. When Keating finally proposes that they elope together, she reasserts herself against Toohey, declaring that she is not afraid of him (368). But at this point the odds are stacked against her. Almost immediately Keating leaves Catherine to marry Dominique (in no small part because of Toohey's own scheming). Catherine is now at the peak of her vulnerability—and at the mercy of Toohey. She surrenders to him, and her decline is precipitous.

The death knell sounds for Catherine's spirit when she is put in charge of occupational therapy at the Stoddard Home for Subnormal Children. When the most hopeless of the subnormal children achieves some ordinary task, Catherine reveals how much she has lost by confessing to what she now regards as valuable "self-expression":

> Isn't it wonderful and moving! There's no telling how far the child will go with proper encouragement. Think of what happens to their little souls if they are frustrated in their creative instincts! It's so important not to deny them a chance for self-expression. (386–87)

This revelation is ironic on several levels. Catherine is celebrating the "self-expression" of the lowest of the subnormal children—while slum children with agile bodies and intelligent eyes "gaze wistfully" at the facilities of the Stoddard Home—while Steven Mallory is relegated once again to poverty—while Roark's Stoddard Temple has been defiled—and, of course, while Catherine *herself* has now quelled her last gasp of self-expression.

This irony reminds us of a passage from "The 'Inexplicable Personal Alchemy,'" in which Ayn Rand condemns advocates of selflessness who claim to be motivated by "compassion," noting the fate of the young idealistic men of ability who never benefit from any such compassion:

> They perish gradually, giving up, extinguishing their minds before they have a chance to grasp the nature of the evil they are facing. In lonely agony, they go from confident eagerness to bewilderment to indignation to resignation—to obscurity. And while their elders putter about, conserving redwood forests and building sanctuaries for mallard ducks, nobody notices those youths as they drop out of sight one by one, like sparks vanishing in limitless black space; nobody builds sanctuaries for the best of the human species.[14]

When we last see Catherine, in her final meeting with Keating, she has morphed into a miniature, humorless version of her uncle. When Keating expresses his sorrow for how he treated Catherine, she confesses that of course she suffered. Now, however, she says this was "foolish," and that now that she and Keating are "grown-up, rational people, nothing is too serious" (597–98). "Nothing is too serious" is Toohey's expression to a letter (636). Catherine *has* forgotten her identity and the name of her soul—only no gates of spiritual grandeur seem to have opened. Such is the dead end of the ideal of selflessness.

Fortunately, no one needs to share in Catherine's fate. The popularity of *The Fountainhead* bears witness to the possibility of an alternative.

UNCHANGING YOUTH

We are now in a position to understand fully *The Fountainhead*'s enduring popularity.

In the above, I have shown how Roark's character embodies youthful idealism, independence, and benevolence. Ayn Rand described the spirit of youth, the view with which most men start out in life, as "a sense of enormous expectation, the sense that one's life is important, that great achievements are within one's capacity, and that great things lie ahead." We can now see that the reason men hold this view is that their independent idealism gives them confidence in their own capacity—and the resulting benevolence gives them an expectation to find it in others. This is why they believe great things lie ahead.

But why do young readers so desperately want to see a fictional character who displays these traits? The answer is: to experience what the boy on the bicycle experiences by seeing Monadnock Valley and meeting Roark. Whereas it is primarily the architectural beauty of Monadnock that inspires the boy, it is Roark himself who inspires the young reader. And, whereas architectural beauty has universal esthetic appeal, the contemplation of Roark is particularly relevant to a young reader, because Roark's story is *about* the very struggle the young reader undergoes on a daily basis: the struggle with elders and a society that enshrines mediocrity at the expense of excellence.

As I claimed in the introductory section, *The Fountainhead* offers hungry readers a commodity in short supply: the sense of uplift that comes from contemplating an ideal man. We have now seen that what makes Roark ideal is independent adherence *to* his ideals. But why does the contemplation of such a man provide a sense of uplift? The answer derives from the particular nature of the literary art.

Ayn Rand discusses the role of Romantic literature in a young person's development in her essay "Art and Moral Treason." In particular, she notes that a child cannot learn the concept of moral values from the "chaotic, bewildering, contradictory evidence offered by the adults in his day-by-day experience," as he lacks the ability to sift through this evidence and abstract the good from the bad. Therefore the child's major "source and demonstration" of morality is Romantic art, especially literature. This literature provides not moral rules, but "the image of a moral *person—i.e.,* the *concretized abstraction* of a moral ideal, . . . a concrete, directly perceivable answer to the very abstract question which a child senses, but cannot yet conceptualize: What kind of person is moral and what kind of life does he lead?"[15]

The sense of uplift derived from contemplating the character of Roark is not a result of being swept away in some emotional torrent. Instead the reader is presented with a specific image, selected for its role in presenting the essence of certain moral values. In this way, the child learns not abstractions, but "the pre-condition and the incentive for the later understanding of such principles: the emotional experience of admiration for man's highest potential, the experience of *looking up* to a hero."[16] The reader does not necessarily know that he is examining the traits of idealism, independence, and benevolence, but his attention is drawn to actions that in fact express them and make their nature accessible. The emotional response is a consequence of the reader's *own* conviction that his life and ideas are important—and the rare opportunity of seeing these values clarified so crisply, when he is otherwise offered only the "chaotic, bewildering, contradictory evidence" of the rest of the world. Perhaps the reader shares the same sense that the young photographer in *The Fountainhead* experiences when *he* sees Roark:

> [H]e had always wondered why the sensations one felt in dreams were so much more intense than anything one could experience in waking reality . . . and what was that extra quality which could never be recaptured afterward. . . . He thought of that because he saw that extra quality for the first time in waking existence, he saw it in Roark's face lifted to the building. (307–8)

Roark's story is particularly inspiring to the young reader because it helps to demonstrate that this dreamlike quality can be made real—that the struggles of youth can be *won*. Presented with Roark's idealism, and the impotence of the second-handers who oppose him, the reader is shown that youthful ideals do not need to be abandoned, that man's youthful state is his natural and proper state. Steven Mallory sees this when he says of Roark that

> I often think that he's the only one of us who's achieved immortality. . . . I think he is what the conception really means. You know how people long to be eternal. But they die with every day that passes. When you meet them, they're not what you met last. In any given hour, they kill some part of themselves. They change, they deny, they contradict—and they call it growth. At the end there's nothing left, nothing unreversed or unbetrayed. . . . But Howard—one can imagine him existing forever. (452)

Even Keating realizes this, when he realizes in a moment of honesty that Roark is "a creature glad to be alive." It is in the same moment that he recants his original criticism of Roark and says, "You're . . . so young, Howard. . . . You're so young. . . . Once I reproached you for being too old and serious" (581).

Who is it that, in Mallory's words, calls denial and contradiction "growth"? The same people who think idealism is foolish—the same critics who think the readers who respond to the idealism of *The Fountainhead* are going through a "phase." They share the same attitude—and error—of the compromisers and villains of *The Fountainhead*. It is Toohey who says that "all growth demands destruction." The Dean and Keating do not speak so self-consciously, but they concede society's (Toohey's) standard of maturity and of the morally ideal. Earlier, Keating sees Roark as too old and serious because he associates the seriousness of his idealism with *renunciation*—the same ideal encouraged by the conventional morality of selflessness. But Roark's ideals are not conventional—or selfless. The Dean sees Roark precisely as critics see readers of *The Fountainhead*, as foolish or childish. He *also* must associate idealism with renunciation, except that, being older and "wiser," he sees the ideal of selflessness as impossible to achieve. But Roark is not selfless, so neither he, nor readers of *The Fountainhead*, are embracing an impossible ideal. There is no reason to accuse them of foolishness. The accusation is merely a confession of the Dean's and the Dean-like critics' own foolish surrender to conventional standards.

Of course it is impossible to appreciate the possibility and practicality of enduring youthful idealism unless one examines the ideals that make it possible, the ideals that offer an alternative to conventional ideals of selflessness. One must, as Ayn Rand puts it in "Art and Moral Treason," *translate* one's sense of life "into adult, conceptual terms."[17] Ayn Rand held that a sense of life was a preconceptual grasp of life's deepest questions about the nature of man and the universe, i.e., an implicit *philosophy*. To translate the man-worshipping sense of life into conceptual terms, therefore, is to validate Man's life as the standard of value, philosophically. For this, readers of *The Fountainhead* are encouraged to consult *Atlas Shrugged*.

But even after one acquires a philosophic understanding, one still requires a concretization of one's ideals. The appeal of Romantic art, and of *The Fountainhead*, is therefore truly *enduring*. Youth of every new generation will continue to read and find inspiration in it—and those originally inspired by it (such as this author) will continue to *re*-read it, again and again: "If man is to gain and keep a moral stature, he needs an image of the ideal, from the first thinking day of his life to the last."[18]

Or, as Ayn Rand writes in *Atlas Shrugged*, "To hold an unchanging youth is to reach, at the end, the vision with which one started."[19]

NOTES

1. Phil Kloer, "Author's philosophy, influence still hold weight with masses," *Cox News Service*, 1 February 2005.

2. Allan Bloom, *The Closing of the American Mind* (New York: Simon and Schuster, 1988), 62–63.

3. Nora Ephron, "A Strange Kind of Simplicity," *The New York Times Book Review*, 5 May 1968, BR8.

4. Henry Kamm, "'For Three Minutes I Felt Free,'" *The New York Times*, 13 October, 1968, E7. Reprinted with Ayn Rand, "The 'Inexplicable Personal Alchemy,'" in Ayn Rand, *Return of the Primitive: The Anti-Industrial Revolution*, ed. Peter Schwartz (New York: Plume, 1999), 119–21.

5. Ayn Rand, "The 'Inexplicable Personal Alchemy,'" 122.

6. Ayn Rand, "Philosophical Detection," *Philosophy: Who Needs It* (New York: Signet, 1982), 16.

7. Throughout the novel, Roark is concerned to answer the question of *why* the Dean and Keating adhere so slavishly to society's standards. He works to learn the "principle behind the Dean," the "central impulse" in other men that accounts for "some important difference between his actions and theirs" (27), the difference between the "creator" and the "second-hander." This shows that his seriousness about ideas is not only an ambition to abide by his architectural standards, but also the commitment to evaluate the ideas that make men like the Dean and Keating possible.

8. Ayn Rand, "The 'Inexplicable Personal Alchemy,'" 123.

9. It is not an accident that the examples of Roark's seriousness about ideas are the same as the examples of his independence. The two traits are closely related. Being serious about ideas means the willingness to *act* on one's own best judgment; independence means acting on *one's own* best judgment. So seriousness and independence refer to the same character traits, but from a different perspective.

10. Ayn Rand, "The 'Inexplicable Personal Alchemy,'" 124.

11. Ayn Rand, "The 'Inexplicable Personal Alchemy,'" 126.

12. Of course Wynand—unlike the others listed here—does not succeed in following Roark's lead to the end. He gives in to the board of the *Banner* and ceases his defense of Roark. But even after giving in, Wynand realizes Roark was right after he is acquitted in the Cortlandt trial.

13. See Robert Mayhew, "Humor in *The Fountainhead*," in the present volume.

14. Ayn Rand, "The 'Inexplicable Personal Alchemy,'" 128.

15. Ayn Rand, "Art and Moral Treason," *The Romantic Manifesto*, revised edition (New York: Signet 1971), 146.

16. Ayn Rand, "Art and Moral Treason," 146.

17. Ayn Rand, "Art and Moral Treason," 147.

18. Ayn Rand, "Art and Moral Treason," 147.

19. Ayn Rand, *Atlas Shrugged*, 35th anniversary edition, (New York: Signet, 1996), 669. I wish to acknowledge the kind assistance of the following individuals: Robert Mayhew, for offering invaluable advice on how to transform an extremely rough idea into a serious paper; Greg Salmieri, for advice on the execution of Robert's idea, and for offering insightful commentary on both philosophic content and on the clarity and accuracy of my writing; and Marc Baer, whose keen editorial eye helped to exorcise numerous devils from my details.

12

The Basic Motivation of the Creators and the Masses in *The Fountainhead*

Onkar Ghate

In religion, the existence of the moral ideal, God, requires no cause, no action, no effort, no achievement. It is beyond account or explanation, to be taken on faith. The existence of evil, then, also becomes unintelligible. How can God, a supposedly omnipotent and supremely good being, permit evil? Although theologians have long tried to give a rational answer to this question, to solve "the problem of evil," the attempt is hopeless. Religion's monopoly in ethics actually leaves man with the following alternative: either abandon reason by dismissing evil as, somehow, justified by a mysterious divine purpose or as nonexistent, and the good as beyond human comprehension—or abandon belief in the ideal.[1]

For Ayn Rand, the ideal is neither to be relegated to an irrational dimension nor to be discarded. It *can* exist, here on earth, but its existence is an achievement; it demands much of man. The focus of Rand's thought is fundamentally on the good: to discover it, to rationally define its nature and causes, and to give it form. "[T]he motive and purpose of my writing," she said, is "*the projection of an ideal man*. The portrayal of a moral ideal, as my ultimate literary goal, as an end in itself" (vii). In the character of Howard Roark, *The Fountainhead* gives us her first complete presentation of the ideal.

Although it is only a secondary issue, there are, she thinks, important things to learn about the nature of evil. Evil does exist in the world: it results when men default on the responsibility to achieve the ideal. And there *is* an actual problem of evil. In the presence of evil men, can the good survive and prosper? And if so, how? This question occupied Rand from early in her life to its end. One can see her thinking about the question in her first philosophic notes to herself.[2] Each of her four novels, *We*

243

the Living, Anthem, The Fountainhead, and *Atlas Shrugged,* deals with some aspect of the issue: each contains a hero (or heroes) acting in a world in which significant numbers of men are indifferent or hostile to the good. She returns often to the question in her nonfiction writing, analyzing different aspects of it, as for instance in her article "How Does One Lead a Rational Life in an Irrational Society?"[3] And the question is crucial to the envisioned theme of an unwritten fifth novel, *To Lorne Dieterling.*[4]

Rand's final conclusion is that the good can and (ultimately) must win; evil is impotent.[5] Prior to *The Fountainhead,* however, there was a streak in Rand's thought that considered the possibility that the great man could exist only by trying to rule the corrupt masses, masses who could (and perhaps eventually would) destroy him. These thoughts are most pronounced in her 1928 notes for the planned novel *The Little Street.*[6] The young protagonist is Danny Renahan. "The boy is a perfectly straight being, unbending and uncompromising. . . . He shows how impossible it is for a genuinely beautiful soul to succeed at present; for in all [aspects of] modern life, one has to be a hypocrite, to bend and tolerate. This boy wanted to command and smash away things and people he didn't approve of." The opposition he faces, and which the story was to be a condemnation of, is the mob: "Show that the mob determines life at present *and show exactly who and what that mob is.* Show the things it breaks. . . . Show that all humanity and each little citizen is an octopus that consciously or unconsciously sucks the blood of the best on earth and strangles life with its cold, sticky tentacles." Renahan's fate in the story? "He is surrounded by a mob and lynched. Torn to pieces, beaten to death on the pavement with the water of the gutter running red."[7]

This view of life is blasted away in *The Fountainhead.* Rand's conception both of what greatness demands and of what the "masses" are has changed. Individual greatness is not identified with ruling others, but with the absence of the desire to rule or be ruled; the great man is motivated by the desire to create. A creator, if he is armed with the proper understanding and motivation, is beyond the reach of the "masses"; he has nothing to fear from them or, more generally, from evil.[8] As we shall see, if he achieves complete independence, his life and soul are untouchable and incorruptible. He becomes god-like. Roark achieves this independent state; Henry Cameron, Dominique Francon (until the end), and Gail Wynand, in different ways, do not. In the world of *The Fountainhead,* the creator only has to fear destroying himself.

And the man of average ability is not viewed as intellectually or morally corrupt, though the "masses" remain so. There is potential dignity in any man, in man the individual, even if he possesses only average ability. The sole question, as we shall see, is whether the average man is motivated by a desire to realize his ability and practice the virtue demanded of him.

THE CREATORS

Roark is beyond the reach of the "masses." He is the independent individual: independent in thought, in judgment, and in action. But Cameron, Dominique, and Wynand all *also* exercise their independent thought and judgment; their conclusions, like Roark's, are formed from their own first-hand thinking. What, then, is the root of Roark's uniquely untroubled and untouched soul—an existence "so healthy that" he "can't conceive of disease" (331)? The root is that Roark's basic *motivation* in life is completely unconcerned with and unaffected by other people. His goal and his pursuit of it are purely independent and selfish. Roark stresses this point in his courtroom speech. "The egotist in the absolute sense," he says, ". . . is the man who stands above the need of using others in any manner. . . . He is not concerned with them in any primary matter. Not in his aim, not in his motive, not in his thinking, not in his desires, not in the source of his energy" (681). "His moral law is never to place his prime goal within the persons of others" (682).

Roark's goal is to build. He wants to transform, for himself, the earth into his vision of a more uplifting, more human place (49). This desire would remain even on a desert island; only its implementation would change: he would not build gas stations and skyscrapers but, say, a hut or a cabin. His basic aim is unconnected to other people. As an architect, he must have clients in order to build (26, 160), but they do not supply him with his motive. They are simply part of the necessary materials from which he builds, like bricks or steel. The type of building the client requires and the specific functions the client needs the building to perform, are, like the site itself, elements which shape the nature of the building Roark designs (578). But the client is not why Roark builds. When Roark sits, alone, at his drafting table, sketching and re-sketching the new structure, bringing his creative vision into existence, the client does not enter his mind.

The focus of Roark's consciousness is on the building: he must make it as great as he can, he must make the building worthy of the site and of its intended function, he must bring his idea of a better world into existence. The client's particular needs and feelings are irrelevant. If Roark accomplishes his primary goal, to design a great building, it is the client's responsibility to appreciate and live up to the structure. Roark designs the building not as another architect would, but as it should be designed: his focus is not client-centric but building-centric; what Roark expects of the client is that the client will use the building not as he would use any other building, but as the building should be used. Roark thereby immensely enriches his client's life—precisely because his primary focus was not on the client "as he is," but on what should be. Austen Heller tells Roark that when he moves into the house Roark designed for him, "I'll have a new sort of existence, and even my simple daily routine will have a kind of honesty or dignity that I can't quite define. Don't be astonished if I tell you that I feel as if I'll have to live up to that house." "I intended that," Roark replies (136). When Heller tells Roark that Roark has been so considerate of him because the house is so functional and so suited to Heller's genuine needs, Roark says that he did not think of Heller at all, only of the house. "He added: 'Perhaps that's why I knew how to be considerate of you'" (137).

Roark is thus essentially alone when he creates; other people are irrelevant to the process and to the failure or success of its outcome. Fundamentally, they can neither enrich the experience nor interfere with it. What fuels Roark's creative process is his thought, his judgment, and his vision of what can be. When that fuel is transformed into a completed structure, the achievement is his and the joy is his. His standard for determining whether his goal has been reached is independent of other people; they do not enter into the equation. What matters is only whether he has succeeded in creating something that is objectively valuable. Any fame or social standing that he might thereby obtain is insignificant; any wealth he earns or benefit he brings to the client is but a secondary, relatively unimportant, consequence (605, 578). The essence of the creator's motivation is this: he knows that his new idea is true and that it is good—he passionately wants to see it made real, here on earth—he dedicates himself to achieving it. What others may do in response to what he creates is irrelevant. "The creator," Roark states in his courtroom speech, "faces nature alone" (679). The "whole secret of [the creator's] power" is that it is "self-sufficient, self-motivated, self-generated" (678).

The joy that comes from the creator's successful dedication to his aim has a similar quality of self-sufficiency. When Roark agrees to design Cortlandt Homes but to allow Peter Keating to put his signature on it, he tells Keating that he, Roark, will gain what no one can give another: he will have built Cortlandt (581). No one can give this to a man—and no one can take it from him. Although Keating, Gordon L. Prescott, John Erik Snyte, and Gus Webb disfigure Roark's Stoddard Temple and turn it into the Hopton Stoddard Home for Subnormal Children (385), the fact remains that Roark built it. "Nothing else," he tells Dominique, "can seem very important" (344).

Roark's standard of self-respect is derived from his fundamental goal. He reveres himself if he knows that he has striven to give expression to the knowledge and vision within him, if he has spared no part of himself in the process—think of Roark sprawled on the floor of Cameron's office, asleep, a coffee pot knocked over, and the completed design resting on the drafting table (74–75). Roark respects himself if he has remained true to his truth—true to the creative best within him. How and where he stands in relation to other people is irrelevant. "I don't make comparisons. I never think of myself in relation to anyone else" (582). His own achievements will not be diminished if others have achieved more than he has; nor will his own achievements be enhanced if others have achieved less than he has. Roark does not measure himself against other people; he measures himself against nature. If he has worked to make himself as competent as he can be, then he knows he is good; self-respect must follow. Roark is earnest when he tells Cameron, a man of similar fire and acquired competence, but now almost forgotten by society, that if he ends up as Cameron does, he will "consider it an honor that I could not have deserved" (64).

The core of Roark's being is untouched and untouchable by others. Their hands cannot reach into his motivation, his joy, or his self-respect. No matter the specific frustration and pain in his life, he knows that he is competent, that he has achieved a human stature, and that he is right for reality. This is the source of Roark's serenity and quiet exaltation. "I'm not capable of suffering completely," he tells Dominique. "I never have. It goes only down to a certain point and then it stops. As long as there is that untouched point, it's not really pain" (344).[9]

A consequence of Roark's fundamental way of facing the world, and the fact that he knows "the source of his actions" (27), is that he does not feel fear of or hatred toward other people. Indeed, he does not notice other people, even when he stands on trial, alone, in a courtroom (17, 64, 348–49, 677). A person fears the destruction of his values and hates the cause. Roark explicitly knows that his success or failure is up to him. Others cannot occasion the destruction of his basic values. Only he can. Other people, therefore, are not possible objects of fear or hatred. In the sense of a *characteristic* emotion, both fear and hatred are directed primarily at oneself, no matter how they may be projected outward. A person experiences fear when he senses that *he* is in some fundamental way inadequate to cope; he experiences hatred when he senses that *he* is the cause: he has defaulted on the responsibility to achieve competence and self-respect. Since Roark is firmly dedicated to his values and to his ability, and he is aware of this fact, fear and hatred are emotions unknown to him. "Have you always liked being Howard Roark?" Wynand asks him. Roark's amused, involuntary smile gives the answer (521).

The closest Roark feels to hatred is when he witnesses harm done to those he loves—a hatred for Wynand and his papers because of the despair they cause Cameron (178), a hatred of those who would have Mallory sculpt dimpled babies (329), a hatred for those who make Dominique think that she must become Mrs. Peter Keating and then Mrs. Gail Wynand (374, 463, 515). But even here Roark knows that the actual cause of the harm to those he loves is not other people but the errors and inability to understand on the parts of Cameron, Mallory, and Dominique; they have granted to other people a power those people do not in fact possess.

But that Roark does not feel fear of or hatred toward other people does not mean that he expects his path to be easy. He knows it will be difficult (15, 98). He has seen Cameron's life and knows he is taking a risk in opening his own office after landing the commission to build Heller's house (131). He knows too that the opposition he will face stems from far more than just a reaction to his innovative way of building. Although he does not yet have the words for its cause, Roark senses that he engenders in many people a nameless fear, resentment, and hatred. He knows, for instance, what happened between him and the Dean at Stanton. Roark's existence reminds people that they have betrayed their own souls; in his presence, their fear and hatred of themselves oozes to the surface of their consciousness—and gets projected onto him.

But the fact that many people respond to Roark and his work not with respect and admiration but with resentment and hostility does not concern him. He does hate incompetence, but not incompetent people; he dismisses them without further thought. Their antipathy is a reflection not of Roark and his prospects for success, but of themselves and their own inner emptiness. He consequently has no desire to gain power over such men in order to protect himself from them, and he certainly has no desire to rule them: What possible value could ruling them bring him (529)? Their opposition to him is *their* loss, not his.

When people fail to appreciate one of Roark's designs, the loss is theirs, not Roark's. When people do not hire Roark but instead contract with Keating for a home with Classic façades, with Ralston Holcombe for a Renaissance villa, or with John Erik Snyte or Gus Webb for a bare box, the loss is theirs, not Roark's. In the lead-up to the Stoddard trial Roark tells each person to go and see the Temple for himself. If people are unable to appreciate its beauty, to experience a sense of self-respect and uplift within it, and to stand erect in reverence—if they allow the Temple to be disfigured and turned into a home for subnormal children—the principal loss is theirs, not Roark's. Roark can and does experience a sense of reverence and uplift from his own life and work in creating structures like the Stoddard Temple; most other people, however, can get such a concrete, esthetic experience only from Roark.[10]

Roark has no desire to force his ideas on others because he knows the attempt is futile. As Roark tells Heller, "I don't like people who have to be handled" (159). Roark can show men his buildings and can explain to a prospective client, and often does, the principles by which he builds, but he cannot make them understand. That requires a spark of thought and of first-hand judgment, a desire to see through their own eyes, which only they can supply. If they do not supply it, the loss is theirs.

Roark does feel pain when he cannot build in his own way—he feels pain during the time he spends employed in the offices of other architects (90,

124), during the months of idleness in his office (175), and, perhaps worst of all, during the period when he must leave the profession to work in a granite quarry, uncertain when or if he will return (203–4). But his pain comes *only* from the fact that he is not erecting, for himself, the world that he wants to create. He is not doing what *he* loves to do: build. The cause of his pain is not fundamentally other people. They have taken nothing from him, and they have nothing they could grant him. What he wants, they cannot give. Their money and second-hand recognition have no meaning to him. If Roark cannot do his work done his way (579), any secondary consequences lose their significance.

This is why there is in Roark's consciousness no experience of being "beaten" by other people. "But I don't think of you," Roark memorably replies when Toohey asks him what Roark thinks of him (389). Roark laughs when Mike Donnigan is outraged by the idea of Roark taking a building trades job in the city and of other architects gloating over Roark's fall. These architects have taken nothing from Roark. What he has, they never can have. And Roark experiences no jealousy toward them: the concept of gain is not applicable to them; to gain, there must be a self that is doing the gaining. Roark's only pain—Mike sees "something in Roark's eyes which he knew Roark did not want to be there" (199)—comes from the fact of not being able to build.

But even this pain of inactivity cannot penetrate deep within Roark, because he also knows that his fundamental course of action is right: there is no other way to achieve his goals, and no other goals worth achieving. He expected it to be difficult and knows that he must wait; he must be patient. He regards his pain as unimportant, detached from the essence of his person, and works to quell it (90, 203–4).

Roark knows it will take time for him to find his "kind of people" (159). He is an innovator. It will take time for his kind of person to first see his buildings, to learn to understand, to learn to desire, and then to come ask him for what only he can give.[11] He knows that his kind of person exists because he knows that he is not a freak, that the rule and method of his functioning is open to anyone to attain. And he sees "so many products of man's genius around us today" (577)—he who knows the source of such products. "I can tell my kind of people by their faces," he says to Heller. "By something in their faces. There will be thousands passing by your house and by the gas station. If out of those thousands, one stops and sees it— that's all I need" (160). Even when Roark dynamites Cortlandt, he thinks he has a chance to be acquitted. (I discuss the topic of Roark's "kind of people" in much more detail in the next section.)

And in any event, Roark knows that he must fight for what he wants, even if the price may be the disfigurement of the Stoddard Temple or ten years in jail. To refuse to fight for his work done his way would be *already* to have lost—to have lost, without the knowledge that he did all he could for his highest value. To renounce his goal to build because the "masses" are indifferent or opposed to him would be to surrender his most basic motivation—and the meaning of his life.[12]

Roark is the ideal, and the fate of the ideal is not defeat at the hands of the "masses." If one remains consistent and whole, fully independent in one's basic motivation, one will achieve joy, self-respect, and success in life. "Success" here does not mean universal fame or fortune, but doing one's own work one's own way on whatever scale possible, and in cooperation with the only kind of people it is worth cooperating with—whether it be Roark designing a five-story department store in Clayton, Ohio, or erecting the Wynand Building in New York City.[13] There are reasons, as we will see in the next section, why the latter scenario for Roark is more likely than the former, but that forms no essential part of Roark's aim.

The possibility of actual defeat enters only when a creator permits other people to cloud his basic motivation or his assessment of the feasibility of, or the means to, his goal. This is what explains Cameron's downfall.

Cameron and Roark share a fundamental similarity: a first-hand passion for their work. Both are innovators. Cameron decides that "no building must copy any other" as he gives form to a new kind of architecture; he designs skyscrapers as they should be designed, flaunting rather than apologizing for their height (44). A newspaper interview of Cameron captures his attitude: "It said: 'Architecture is not a business, not a career, but a crusade and a consecration to a joy that justifies the existence of the earth" (80). This is Roark's attitude toward architecture as well.

And like Roark, Cameron never compromises his fundamental goal. He never erects buildings that he judges to be flawed and never makes any alterations to his designs to satisfy a client's second-hand demands.

Yet their careers are not parallel. Cameron does rise to the top of the profession and has his pick of clients; but when "an orgy of Classicism" takes place after the Columbian Exposition of Chicago, and "the architect with the best library" comes to be considered best (45), Cameron's firm shrinks, his clients disappear, and he eventually turns to drink, broken by society. Why does he break when Roark does not?[14]

The crucial difference between the two men is that for Cameron, unlike for Roark, the world is *not* divided into "my kind of people" and the others, who do not matter. Cameron does not understand people. In part, this is because Cameron does not have the same self-awareness that Roark has of his own motivation. Cameron tells Roark that Roark will find the words for what Cameron could not (76–77). Cameron does not fully grasp that any person can attain his essential stature, whatever the person's level of ability, so long as the person dedicates himself to the task. Cameron does not actually understand what "his kind of people" would be, let alone have Roark's conviction that they do in fact exist. Revealingly, he tells Roark that "I've lost the habit of speaking to men like you. Lost it? Maybe I've never had it" (63). He sees the incompetence, the indifference, and the meanness of soul of those around him, and silently concludes that *all* people are impossible to communicate with.[15]

But he still needs clients in order to build. As a consequence, there is an impatience and willfulness in Cameron's character that has no counterpart in Roark's. Cameron burns with the desire to build his kind of buildings, but there is no real possibility of his kind of people coming to grasp the functional beauty that he uniquely has to offer. His only recourse seems to be to force them, somehow, to accept it, to in effect shove it down their throats for their own good—as if he could, by a sheer act of will, make others see what he has seen and value what he values. "He demanded of all people the one thing he had never granted anybody: obedience. . . . People called him crazy. But they took what he gave them, whether they understood it or not, because it was a building by 'Henry Cameron'" (44). Toward his clients he is contemptuous and even belligerent, calling them "unprintable names"; he behaves "like a feudal lord and longshoreman" (44).

It cannot work. He is able to keep clients mostly because of his "astute business manager, a mild, self-effacing little man of iron, who, in the days of [Cameron's] glory, faced quietly the storms of Cameron's temper and brought him clients; Cameron insulted the clients, but the little man made them accept it and come back" (46). But his manager dies—and Cameron "had never known how to face people"; he "had never learned to give explanations, only orders" (46).

He had never known how to face people or learned to give explanations, because he thought it was futile. And this mistaken premise forms a vicious circle. He has concluded that people cannot be reached, and so he treats them contemptuously and offensively; this causes people to misunderstand and to shun him, which reinforces his original conclusion.

Because Cameron senses that he cannot compel people to see the truth of his buildings—but thinks that he *must* do this in order to bring his vision of what could be built into existence—he grows fearful that his gifts will be rejected. He tries to hide this fear by *welcoming* opposition against him: he deliberately fans the hatred against him (44), he curses the Columbian Exposition, he throws an inkstand at a distinguished banker who asks him "to design a railroad station in the shape of the temple of Diana at Ephesus" (45); as his clients become rarer, he grows more overbearing (46).

But his fear of people remains. He confesses to Roark: "Do you ever look at the people in the street? Aren't you afraid of them? I am" (63). Cameron thinks that to build he will have to *beg*. He could not force them to see, so the only alternative is to plead for life from those who are unreachable. He tells Roark that Roark's fate will be to be reduced to begging a man,

> pleading, your voice licking his knees; you'll loathe yourself for it, but you won't care, if only he'd let you put up that building, you won't care, you'll want to rip your insides open to show him, because if he saw what's there he'd have to let you put it up. But he'll say that he's very sorry, only the commission has just been given to Guy Francon. And you'll go home, and do you know what you'll do there? You'll cry. You'll cry like a woman, like a drunkard, like an animal. (65)

Like Roark, Cameron has long periods of waiting, his hands idle. "There will be days," he tells Roark, "when you'll look at your hands and you'll want to take something and smash every bone in them, because they'll be taunting you with what they could do, if you found a chance for them to do it" (64). But the waiting consumes Cameron in a way that it does not Roark, because Cameron has *nothing* to wait for. There is no such thing as his kind of person. He waits, he is forced to wait, but it eats him up inside—and he turns to drink for an escape.

Cameron and Roark are at root the same. Both are creators whose basic motivation is personal and completely independent from others. For Roark, the motivation is that he loves the earth. "That's all I love. I don't like the shape of things on this earth. I want to change them. . . . For myself" (49). To Cameron, it is a "crusade . . . to a joy that justifies the existence of the earth" (80). This basic aim neither ever compromises or betrays, which is why Cameron can say at the end what Wynand cannot: that it was worth it (178).

But Roark has the strength to persevere to the end, while Cameron does not. Cameron does not because he is mistaken about the means necessary to achieve his end. He has allowed the "masses" to dictate the possibilities: either to force people to see or to plead with the blind. He has precluded from his view of the world the possibility that his, and Roark's, kind of people exist.

Cameron, however, learns from Roark. He senses that Roark can carry the battle to the end, in a way that he could not. "I have no answer to give them, Howard. I'm leaving you to face them. You'll answer them" (76–77). Cameron lives to see Roark's first buildings, he sees Roark's method of gaining clients and of patiently carrying out the battle for their vision, and he loses his hatred for people. "I don't . . . hate anybody anymore," he tells Roark just before he dies (178). He comes to understand at the end that those who cannot see what he and Roark have to offer are penalized by their own default. And he at last understands that another kind of response from people is possible and even to be expected. Hatred remains only for

Wynand—a man who pours his energy into the triumph of "overbearing vulgarity" (178); this is the man Cameron thinks Roark will have to fight.

Cameron is the creator mistaken about the proper means of achieving his goal; Dominique Francon, on the other hand, is the stillborn creator. We get a glimpse of her ability in the savage, brilliant writing of some of her newspaper columns; and, during the strike of the Union of Wynand Employees, as she and Wynand struggle to keep the *Banner* going, we get a glimpse of her almost exhaustless energy, greater even than Wynand's (652). But she never acquires the fundamental motivation that is Cameron's and Roark's: to re-shape, for *oneself*, the earth into a place of joy. Until the end of the story, she does not fully comprehend the nature and possibility of such a motivation.

Like Cameron, Dominique wants perfection—in a world that accepts only the half-way and the in-between (143, 375). And in essence Dominique shares Cameron's view of humanity. "You know," she tells Alvah Scarret,

> it's such a peculiar thing—our idea of mankind in general. We all have a sort of vague, glowing picture when we say that, something solemn, big and important. But actually all we know of it is the people we meet in our lifetime. Look at them. Do you know any you'd feel big and solemn about? There's nothing but housewives haggling at pushcarts, drooling brats who write dirty words on the sidewalks, and drunken debutantes. Or their spiritual equivalent. . . . That's your mankind in general. (143–44)

Dominique also believes, like Cameron, that mankind seethes with hatred toward the man who desires to reach great things through his love for his work. "You love your work," Cameron tells Roark. "God help you, you love it! And that's the curse. . . . You love it, and they know it, and they know they have you. Do you ever look at the people in the street? . . . The substance of them is hatred for any man who loves his work" (63–64). "[I]t would be terrible," Dominique tells Scarret, "if I had a job I really wanted" (143).

Dominique senses that the option of trying to force other people to see and to want what is good, as Cameron at first tries, is hopeless. The only real option is the option Cameron finds himself reduced to: to plead with those who hold power over you. "You want a thing and it's precious to you," she explains to Scarret. "Do you know who is standing ready to tear it out of your hands? You can't know, it may be so involved and so far away, but someone is ready, and you're afraid of them all. And you cringe and you crawl and you beg and you accept them" (143).

To escape this fate, Dominique resolves to desire nothing; her desire is to resist all desires (144).[16] What she seeks is freedom, freedom from any attachment to the world. From early in life she suppresses any creative drive within her, before it can take shape and tie her, through her love of her work, to the "masses."

When she meets Roark, she therefore both loves and struggles against him. She loves him, because he gives her her first real desire in the world. But she hates him for this, because she now has something at stake in the world; her freedom is gone (242–43). And when she discovers that the man in the quarry is Howard Roark, creator of the Enright House, she is close to despair. He is a man who loves his work. He will be tortured by the world and forced to beg and crawl for commissions—a fate Toohey graphically spells out for her.

> [T]o start by the side of this mediocrity [Keating] and to watch it shoot up, while he [Roark] struggles and gets nothing but a boot in his face, to see the mediocrity snatch from him, one after another, the chances he'd give his life for, to see the mediocrity worshiped, to miss the place he wants and to see the mediocrity enshrined upon it, to lose, to be sacrificed, to be ignored, to be beaten, beaten, beaten—not by a greater genius, not by a god, but by a Peter Keating—well, my little amateur, do you think the Spanish Inquisition ever thought of a torture to equal this? (268)

When Dominique hears Toohey say this, she takes away, that evening, the first of many commissions from Roark, Joel Sutton's office building (269–71).

She does it to spare Roark his looming torture, to starve, near the beginning, his desire to create—as she has long since strangled hers. She does it in self-protection, to remove from her sight the unbearable spectacle of having to watch the man she loves being tortured at the hands of the "masses." She prays without hope—"I believe in nothing and have nothing to pray to" (272)—that she will fail and that Roark will succeed, that Roark cannot be destroyed. But she must follow her actual conviction.

Doubts begin to surface, however, when she sees Roark starting to succeed despite her active opposition and Toohey's deliberate silence. "I'm so happy," she tells Toohey after Roark gets the contract for the Aquitania hotel, "I could sleep with this Kent Lansing, whoever he is." She continues: "I shall try to stop any job that comes [Roark's] way. . . . It's not going to be so easy as it was, though. . . . The Enright House, the Cord Building—and this." She wonders: "Ellsworth, what if we were wrong about the world, you and I?" (314).

The Stoddard trial obliterates Dominique's doubts.

She sees what she had feared: that Roark will face torture because of his love for his work, that he will even walk into the hands of his torturers in order to build—Dominique tells him that Toohey made Hopton Stoddard hire Roark, but Roark just laughs (333–34). She cannot bear to witness any more of such torture. To kill the pain, she plans to efface herself out of existence through marriage to Peter Keating. "Roark, you won't win," she tells him, "they'll destroy you, but I won't be there to see it happen. I will have destroyed myself first. That's the only gesture of protest open to me. What else could I offer you?" (375). The plan fails. To accomplish the same goal, she picks (with Toohey's encouragement) an even more loathsome object, Gail Wynand. But she soon realizes that he is not suitable for her purpose because he seems to be a man from her own world, not theirs (448–49). In the last act open to her, she intends revenge: she will make Wynand pay for the Stoddard trial and for the *Banner*.

What Dominique must grasp, in order to be able to return to Roark and to enter her own world for the first time, is the basic motivation of those she despises and of those she loves. She must grasp the motivation and resulting smallness of soul of those whom she thinks can harm her and Roark. And she must grasp the motivation and resulting untouchable sense of joy of a creator like Roark. She does not understand either. She is mistaken about the nature of evil and, in part because she has silenced within herself her own desire to create, does not fully understand the nature of the good.

Dominique must see that she has grossly exaggerated the power of the "masses" to control and to destroy. Their primary victim is themselves. Evil, she is beginning to realize during her marriage to Wynand, is not "single and big," it is "many and smutty and small" (492). She has seen the best kind of man that the "masses" have to offer, Peter Keating; she has seen him when he is at the top of the architectural profession; and she has seen the utter emptiness of his life. He controls nothing and has power over nothing. He is a marionette whose strings are pulled by Toohey. And Toohey, too, is petty and small. He is an envy-ridden creature leading a life even more empty than Keating's. His leitmotif, like Keating's, is fear (230). He fears Roark, he fears Wynand, he even fears her; she rightly becomes more and more dismissive of him. When she sees Toohey at her and Wynand's wedding reception, and he quickly turns away from her, she wants to laugh aloud, "but the matter of Ellsworth Toohey caught off guard did not seem important enough to laugh about now" (480).

Toohey's illusion of power comes from Wynand. Wynand creates the *Banner* and turns its voice over to Toohey. And *only* Wynand could create the *Banner*: its source is the warped creator within him. It is Wynand's error and treason (494) that give power to the "masses" and the men, like Toohey, who lead them. And the primary victim of Wynand's treason is himself. She had wanted to make Wynand pay for the *Banner*; she realizes that "It can't be paid for" (494). Wynand's case is tragic; tragic for him and tragic for all creators: he is a potential creator who has turned against his own species. But the tragedy is not inevitable: Wynand can resist. "He could have closed the paper," she tells Roark at the end (666).

But, above all, what Dominique must grasp is the motivation of the true creator. She believes that "Everything has strings leading to everything else. We're all so tied together" (143). She does not yet realize how radically independent is the creator's aim, how unconcerned he is with other people, how irrelevant those people are to the failure or success of his goal, and so how his joy and suffering are unaffected by them. She is haunted by windows and streets and lunch wagons and cocktail shakers (287, 463), by the undeserving people who might look at or touch elbows with Roark (243), by women who "will hang diapers on his terraces" and men who "will spit on his stairways and draw dirty pictures on his walls" (244). At the Stoddard trial she condemns Roark for sacrilege toward his own values.

> In what kind of world did Roark build his temple? For what kind of men? Look around you. Can you see a shrine becoming sacred by serving as a setting for Mr. Hopton Stoddard? For Mr. Ralston Holcombe? For Mr. Peter Keating? . . . When you see a man casting pearls without getting even a pork chop in return—it is not against the swine that you feel indignation. It is against the man who valued his pearls so little that he was willing to fling them into the muck and to let them become the occasion for a whole concert of grunting, transcribed by the court stenographer. (356)

What Dominique must come to learn, which she does in part from Roark's own example, is the independence of the creator's motivation. She is wrong to think that Roark builds in order to offer his creations to other men, wrong to think that he is casting pearls in hope of a return. Roark's goal is the building, which he builds for his own sake. His return *is* the pearl—which he made. For what kind of men, Dominique asks, did Roark build his temple? For none. He built it for himself, to experience and express his concept of exaltation. Who might benefit from the temple, or even who might come along to destroy it, is not his focus. It might be destroyed, but that does not erase the fact that he built it.

This is the explanation of their differing reactions to the disfigurement of the Stoddard Temple. Dominique's focus is on what vermin dared smash; she thinks they are draining from Roark his very lifeblood. Roark's focus is on the fact that he built the temple—his primary goal realized, something that never can be taken from him. Dominique cannot believe that Roark is not in agony; she cannot understand how the pain can go down only to a certain point. It goes down only to a certain point because the essence of Roark's goal and the core of the experience its achievement brings are devoid of relation to other men.

Dominique must grasp the truth of Roark's words in the courtroom: "The creator lives for his work. He needs no other men. His primary goal is within himself. . . . He is not concerned with [others] in any primary matter. Not in his aim, not in his motive, not in his thinking, not in his desires, not in the source of his energy" (679–81). She must understand what Roark tells Wynand, that the meaning of life is "The material the earth offers you and what you make of it" (551). When she visits Roark in Clayton, Ohio, at the site of the Janer Department Store, she says "it's the quarry again." Roark smiles. "If you wish. Only it isn't. . . . I love doing it. Every building is like a person. Single and unrepeatable" (462). She must grasp that she is wrong here and he is right. She must grasp that the creative act itself—and the effort, struggle, and dedication it demands—is what brings meaning to life. And this remains so, whether other people turn a blind eye to one's achievement, as happened to Cameron, or disfigure it, as happened to Roark with the Stoddard Temple, or even imprison one for it, as may happen to Roark after Cortlandt.

She has to reach the point where she can declare, with full understanding and certainty,

> Howard . . . willingly, completely, and always . . . without reservations, without fear of anything they can do to you or me . . . in any way you wish . . . as your wife or your mistress, secretly or openly . . . here, or in a furnished room I'll take in some town near a jail where I'll see you through a wire net . . . it won't matter. . . . Howard, if you win the trial—even that won't matter too much. You've won long ago. . . . I'll remain what I am, and I'll remain with you—now and ever—in any way you want. (667–68)

And when she reaches this point, she will be able to see that Roark has a real chance to triumph in the world as it is. Her pessimism about mankind is unwarranted. Roark's "kind of people" can and do exist. Dominique has always known this at one level. She knew that men like Enright and Heller existed and that they were successful and untouched (259). But she dismissed such people, like herself, as "freaks" (Toohey calls any real individual a "lone freak," 223); she did not understand the basic motivation of such men and the fact that this motivation is open to anyone to achieve. She believed that such freaks existed only by accident and by courtesy of the "masses," who could not yet be bothered to crush them. She now knows better. "They own nothing. They've never won. . . . One cannot hate the earth in their name. The earth is beautiful. And it is a background, but not theirs" (665–66). Whatever their number, it is the creators who move the world. There is no reason to conclude that Roark must end up in a granite quarry or a jail cell or even doing only five-story buildings in Clayton, Ohio.[17]

Henry Cameron, as we have seen, is the creator who undermines himself by allowing the "masses" to decide the *means* of achieving his basic goal. Dominique Francon is the would-be creator, who defeats herself by allowing the "masses" to dictate that her basic goal is *impossible* to achieve. Gail Wynand, in contrast, is the creator who destroys himself by allowing the "masses" to *set* his basic goal.

From an early age, Wynand develops a searching, ambitious, and life-aspiring mind. In each crucial area of life, he is met with other people's indifference, incompetence, and resentment. This inhuman opposition leads him to alter his life's ambition.

The young Wynand has a tremendous thirst to learn, to understand and to acquire the traits necessary for success. He teaches himself to read and write at age five and learns his first mathematics and geography from engineers and sailors in his neighborhood. He never accepts anything on another's say-so: it must make sense to him. At age twelve, he enters a church and hears his first sermon on "patience and humility"; he never goes back (403). Into the best streets of the city he ventures in order to discover what makes people successful. "He felt no bitterness against the world of wealth, no envy and no fear" (403). People glare at him, but it has no effect. "He wanted nothing, for the time being, except to understand" (403). When he decides that what makes the people on the streets of Manhattan different from those of Hell's Kitchen are books, he begins to read voraciously, savagely. He even directs his gang to steal books from the Public Library. He must understand. "He could not tolerate the inexplicable. . . . The emblem of his childhood . . . was the question mark" (402–3).

But when he enrolls himself in public school, he feels revulsion for its unwillingness to prize his intelligence and effort. At first his teacher takes great pleasure in calling on him, because he always knows the answers; and when Wynand "trusted his superiors and their purpose, he obeyed like a Spartan" (403). But soon the teacher's attention shifts: "she had to concentrate on the slower, duller children" (403). Wynand cannot understand why they matter more than he does, why he is made to suffer boredom for their sake, why he is being penalized for his ability. "'Why,' he asked, 'should I swill everything down ten times? I know all that.' 'You're not the only one in the class,' said the teacher'" (403). He utters a profanity and quits school in disgust.

In the world of work, which he enters at a very young age, Wynand is eager to improve each business where he is employed. The response he encounters is similar to that of the teacher's. He sells newspapers on street corners and explains to the pressroom boss that they could boost circulation by delivering the paper to the reader's door each morning. He is answered not with an argument but with indifference: "Yeah? . . . Well, you don't run things around here" (402). Working in a grocery store, underutilized, Wynand one day explains to the owner why it would be good to sell milk in bottles. He's met not only with indifference but with outright hostility: "You shut your trap . . . don't you tell me nothing I don't know about my business. You don't run things around here" (402).

Met with this ceaseless refrain, Wynand learns to loathe people. "He felt many emotions toward his fellow men, but respect was not one of them" (402). With great effort, however, Wynand learns "to keep silent, to keep the place others described as his place, to accept ineptitude as his master— and to wait" (402). To wait for what? To wait for the time when he, not incompetence, would be in command and could achieve his vision of the world. At his favorite job, bootblack on a ferry boat, he loves to look at Manhattan when he has no customers, to look "at the yellow boards of new houses, at the vacant lots, at the cranes and derricks, at the few towers rising in the distance. He thought of what should be built and what should be destroyed, of the space, the promise and what could be made of it" (402).

At its deepest root, Wynand's motivation is like Roark's (and Cameron's). Both hate incompetence and both want to erect, for themselves, their vision of a better world.

But Wynand allows the smug incompetence and indifference of other people to warp his motivation. Underlying Wynand's fierce desire to learn and to work is a profound will to live. One of his most significant memories, when he looks back on his life, is himself, at age twelve, back against a wall, ready to fight three gang members for his life (399–401). When people turn a blind eye to that will to live, Wynand cannot stomach it. Age fifteen, severely beaten by a drunken longshoreman, Wynand manages to crawl, his blood smearing the pavement, to the door of a saloon. It was the only time Wynand ever asked for help. The saloonkeeper looks at Wynand, "a glance that showed full consciousness of agony, of injustice—and a stolid, bovine indifference" (404); he slams the door in Wynand's face.[18]

In a world where his will to live is resented by incompetents, the teenage Wynand concludes that it is rule or be ruled, kill or be killed. "Did you want to scream," the adult Gail Wynand asks Roark,

> "when you were a child, seeing nothing but fat ineptitude around you, knowing how many things could be done and done so well, but having no power to do them? Having no power to blast the empty skulls around you? Having to take orders—and that's bad enough—but to take orders from your inferiors! Have you felt that?"
>
> "Yes."
>
> "Did you drive the anger back inside of you, and store it, and decide to let yourself be torn to pieces if necessary, but reach the day when you'd rule those people and all people and everything around you?"
>
> "No."
>
> "You didn't? You let yourself forget?"
>
> "No. I hate incompetence. I think it's probably the only thing I do hate. But it didn't make me want to rule people. Nor to teach them anything. It made me want to do my own work in my own way and let myself be torn to pieces if necessary." (529)

Roark's and Wynand's differing conclusions here explain the meaning of what Wynand, age sixteen, does after his father has died and he stands atop the roof of his tenement, alone against the city. The time "had come to decide what he would make of his life" (405). To Wynand, that question now means: What must he do in order to rule? "He asked himself a single question: what was there that entered all those houses, the dim and the brilliant alike, what reached into every room, into every person? They all had bread. Could one rule men through the bread they bought? They had shoes, they had coffee, they had. . . . The course of his life was set" (405).

Against the hatred of the "masses," Cameron had seen only two possibilities: by a sheer act of will, somehow to force them to see and accept the good and, if that fails, to beg. Dominique thinks the first possibility is hopeless and the second shameful: she renounces begging by renouncing desire. Wynand too will not beg. Nor will he try to force the good on people. But he sees another possibility. To rule them: to control them and keep them at bay by catering to their depraved desires.

Wynand is losing grip of his original motive. That motive had been to create, to build that which should be built and destroy that which should be destroyed, and to thereby fulfill the promise of what could be made of the world. His original motivation was Roark-like. But people's indifference to the good and to justice is warping that motivation—he is permitting it to be warped. In an act that would be unimaginable to Roark, Wynand allows others to determine what career he will choose. Wynand will still create—but the "masses," and not his own vision, will dictate what he creates and why.

Why does he want to rule? Wynand has no real answer to this question. He would say that at *some* point he will have the power necessary to stop catering to depravity and instead to erect his kind of world. But that point is undefined and *indefinable*. It is an abstraction that can never be made concrete. He still loves the city and its skyscrapers, he loves the possibility they represent, and he would throw his body over the skyline to protect it (446); but he never actually does anything to improve that which he loves.[19]

This is the deep significance of the Wynand Building to him. The envisioned building represents his original motivation and aim: to sweep aside what should not exist and build what should. But his whole career does precisely the opposite. Wynand wants to believe that his basic goal is still to rebuild his city and that he will in the end make his goal concrete, in the form of the Wynand Building. But by the logic of his life, he never will. And so, although he himself does not know why, he never feels ready to erect the Wynand Building (499). He comes to feel ready only when he comes to feel "as if I had been forgiven" (592–93).

Wynand's actual motivation has turned defensive. He is not on a crusade for his values and vision of existence, as Cameron was and Roark is. He is on a crusade to protect himself and his values from destruction at the hands of a belligerent mob. But what of his self will there be left to protect, once he abandons the essence of self: the motivation of a creator?

Wynand pours his energy into his chosen goal, and by eighteen is an associate editor of a fourth-rate newspaper, the *Gazette*. At twenty he falls in love with a woman and offers his creative energy to her in support and protection of this supreme personal value. "Sitting at her feet, his face raised to her, he allowed his soul to be heard. 'My darling, anything you wish, anything I am, anything I can ever be. . . . That's what I want to offer you—not the things I'll get for you, but the thing in me that will make me able to get them. That thing—a man can't renounce it—but I want to renounce it—so that it will be yours" (406). Her reaction is moronic indifference. He renounces love.

In the two most important areas of life, creative ambition and romantic love, Wynand has now barred his soul from expressing itself. What good then is the power he seeks? What will he accomplish with it, when he gains it? What is there left to defend? This is the contradiction of Wynand's life, which he confronts for the first time a year later.

He faces a crucial test because, in the fate of Pat Mulligan, his goal to rule comes into conflict with his prior vision of what the world should be. Wynand "was twenty-one when his career on the *Gazette* was threatened, for the first and only time. . . . [W]hen Pat Mulligan, police captain of his precinct, was framed, Wynand could not take it; because Pat Mulligan was the only honest man he had ever met in his life" (406).

Mulligan is being framed by the people who control the *Gazette*—and Wynand wants to fight for him. This will mean the destruction of the *Gazette* (and more), Wynand knows, but he still wants to fight. "His decision contradicted every rule he had laid down for his career. But he did not think. It was one of the rare explosions that hit him at times, throwing him beyond caution, making of him a creature possessed by a single impulse to have his way, because the rightness of his way was so blindingly total" (406). Wordlessly and subconsciously, Wynand still wants to see his vision of the world made real, protected, and defended, and he will act for it despite his chosen goal to rule. That goal still remains subordinate to his vision of what should be.

In order to bring down the *Gazette*, Wynand seeks as his ally the famous editor of a great newspaper who had written "the most beautiful tribute to integrity" Wynand had ever read (406). The editor is shocked that anyone could take so seriously the swill he writes. His glance is one Wynand "had seen before: in the eyes of the saloonkeeper who had slammed the door" (407).

Wynand now makes his fateful choice. He renounces integrity not because it cannot be achieved—there is no question of Mulligan actually being a corrupt policeman, unworthy of defending—but because it is not *worth* achieving. Why is it not worth achieving integrity, fighting for his vision, and even going to jail in its cause if necessary? Because then the "masses" will be ruling over Wynand, snickering at him. His standard of what is worth having is now intimately tied to the "masses" and their corrupt leaders. To achieve integrity, he thinks, is to embrace victimhood. Wynand walks back to the *Gazette* "feeling . . . only a furious contempt for himself, for Pat Mulligan, for all integrity; he felt shame when he thought of those whose victims he and Mulligan had been willing to become. He did not think 'victims'—he thought 'suckers'" (407). And what makes power worth having? It will prevent one from being other people's sucker. Wynand reverses course and writes an editorial for the *Gazette* denouncing Mulligan.

Although he is not yet aware of the full meaning of his choice, Wynand has chosen the emptiness of ruling: ruling without purpose or goal, ruling for the sake of ruling, ruling as an end in itself. Wynand is not building an empire to defend the few men of integrity who may exist in the world; he has used his incipient empire to destroy such a man. He is not building his empire to protect those he loves; he has renounced personal love. He is not building his empire to protect himself; he has now abandoned the fundamental goal that made up his self, his desire to erect his kind of world. Wynand no longer has any real answer to the questions: To rule—for whom? To gain power—for what? His goal is now to *not* be a sucker, which irrevocably ties him to others. To avoid being a sucker is *not* to achieve anything.

This is the cause of Wynand's inner emptiness, which he feels, at age fifty-one, a gun raised to his temple (390). Only the dread of discovering the unanswered in his life keeps him going. "The thought of death gave him nothing. The thought of living gave him slender alms—the hint of fear" (415). The emblem of his childhood, the question mark, remains, but it now hangs solely over his own life.

The editor of the great newspaper knew that there was something very wrong in the way the twenty-one year old Wynand thanked him. But he "did not know"—as Wynand did not know then—"that it had been an obituary on Gail Wynand" (407).

Wynand's life thereafter is a quest for power. By twenty-two he owns the *Gazette* and changes its name to the *Banner*. The majority of the public prefers to help a chambermaid with a "tragic expression and disarranged clothes" (408) rather than a starving scientist, and this is therefore the mentality the *Banner* is designed to appeal to. Wynand delivers "the paper, body and soul, to the mob" (408). He does the same for his personal life. "Every bastard in the country," he observes, "knows the inside of my icebox and bathtub" (413). Devoid of a real end, he pursues the means passionately and unscrupulously: "All the drive, the force, the will barred from the pages of his paper went into its making" (409). By age forty he has erected his empire.

But Wynand begins to sense the meaninglessness of his quest. He creates the art gallery as a refuge and an escape. He goes there, occasionally, to experience both joy and suffering (413). Joy, because he can contemplate the existence of integrity—but an existence that can never be made concrete, real. Suffering, because his power is useless if there is nothing that can exist in life worth using it for.

Outside of this refuge, Wynand must convince himself that there is no other road open but the one he took. "You can't escape depravity, kid," he gently tells a talented young reporter who, unlike most, will not work for Wynand. "The boss you work for may have ideals, but he has to beg money and take orders from many contemptible people. I have no ideals—but I don't beg. Take your choice. There's no other" (412).

Confronted with individuals who seem to have reached financial success by some other means, Wynand sets out, "coldly and with full intention," to ruin them (411). By deliberately taking a loss on his investments, he destroys, among others, a bank president, a head of an insurance company, and an owner of a steamship line. "The men were not his competitors and he gained nothing from their destruction" (411).

Confronted with the possibility that some may experience real, discriminating personal love, which he has renounced, Wynand sets out to prove the phenomenon illusory. "It was said that he never enjoyed a woman unless he had bought her—and that she had to be the kind who could not be bought" (413).

Through a "long process" and toward a result for which there "had been premonitory signs," these desires crystallize into a need to break men of integrity (413).

Wynand himself does not know the cause of his desire (496–97). But faced with the—to him—contradiction of a man of integrity who is not a victim, Wynand must prove to himself that the man does not actually possess integrity. These men, many of whom were able to withstand the indifference and hostility of the "masses," cannot withstand the ferocious ability that Wynand directs against them. But their destruction does not and cannot bring Wynand joy: the desire to crush them is his life's basic meaninglessness coming to the surface.

If integrity cannot exist in anyone, what is the point of gaining power? To achieve what and protect whom? But, much more obviously, if integrity can exist, what is the point of Wynand's life? Wynand therefore wants the person to break, but even this outcome cannot validate his life. When, against Alvah Scarret's expectation, he manages to break the first of the men of integrity, Dwight Carson, Wynand laughs almost uncontrollably. The "laughter had an edge of hysteria" (414). Wynand's inability to control his emotion "contradicted everything [Scarret] knew of Wynand; it gave Scarret a funny feeling of apprehension, like the sight of a tiny crack in a solid wall; the crack could not possibly endanger the wall—except that it had no business being there" (414).

The crack is blasted open when Wynand meets Dominique and Roark.

Wynand falls in love with Dominique. He responds to her integrity and thinks that, if integrity could exist at all, it could exist only in such a mangled form. Its bearer would have to be a profound victim. He tells her, "Do you think I could believe any purity—unless it came to me twisted in some such dreadful shape as the one you chose?" (448). But even this much is hard for Wynand to admit, since he is at the stage where he cannot acknowledge the existence of *any* embodiment of integrity, and Dominique's life is superior to his. His love, like all love he thinks, is exception-making (496). "Why didn't you set out to destroy me?" Dominique asks him (497). "The exception-making, Dominique. I love you. I had to love you. God help you if you were a man" (497).

For the first time, the adult Wynand loves something in the world. His love for Dominique is an expression and recapturing of his true self, of that within him which thinks and judges and says "Yes" and "No"—of that which he has never permitted expression before.

> I've never really wanted anything. Not in the total, undivided way, not with the kind of desire that becomes an ultimatum, "yes" or "no," and one can't accept the "no" without ceasing to exist. That's what you are to me. But when one reaches that stage, it's not the object that matters, it's the desire. Not you, but I. The ability to desire like that. Nothing less is worth feeling or honoring. And I've never felt that before. (502)

His love for Dominique becomes his salvation: a justification of his pursuit of power. Although his power has in a sense protected him from the mob—in a glass cage atop a skyscraper—the price was his soul; in his person, there exists nothing worth protecting. But Dominique's soul remains intact. Wynand has an overwhelming desire to shield her from the "masses." He orders all the Wynand papers to destroy every picture of her and to never write about her (459); he does not even want her to leave the penthouse (487). "I must put her out of reach—where nothing can touch her, not in any sense," he tells Roark when asking him to design their new home outside the city; the "house is to be a fortress" (519).

Wynand knows that Dominique does not love him (495–96), but his consecration to her will validate his own life. He rededicates himself to the *Banner*. He "worked with a new energy, a kind of elated, ferocious drive that surprised the men who had known him in his most ambitious years" (487). "Nothing changed," however, "in his methods and policy" (487). Nothing essential changes in his policy because he thinks the *Banner*, the vehicle for appeasing and controlling the "masses," is what gives him the power to protect Dominique from them. His newfound joy causes him only to try to eliminate the worst excesses of the *Banner* and to let Dwight Carson go (523). Wynand views himself as a great alchemist who takes "the worst refuse of the human spirit" and makes "of it this necklace on [Dominique's] shoulders" (489).

Now that he has Dominique and his love for her, real in the world, he experiences for the first time the only kind of experience "worth feeling or honoring"; he is no longer much interested in learning—nor afraid of facing—the unanswered in his life (502).

But one thing does still haunt Wynand, and that is the fact that the *Banner*—and so his life—served as an instrument to torture Dominique. "FIRE THE BITCH" read the cablegram he sent when Dominique wanted to print, in her column in the *Banner*, what she had said on the stand during the Stoddard trial. Dominique pins the cablegram to her dressing room mirror; when he holds her, his eyes often move to it (490). An unanswered question remains: Is the *Banner* really Dominique's protector or her tormentor?

He must face the full implications of this question when he meets Roark. At first, Wynand helplessly responds to Roark's integrity: the integrity of his buildings and the integrity of his person. "I never meet the men whose work I love," he tells Roark. "They're an anticlimax to their own talent. You're not" (518). But when Wynand learns that the full power of the *Banner* was unleashed against Roark during the Stoddard trial, Wynand senses the question he cannot escape. Alone at his desk, after reading the file on Roark, Wynand hears the presses of the *Banner*. He "had always liked that—the sound of the building's heart beating." But now he wonders. "He listened. They were running off tomorrow's *Banner*. He sat without moving for a long time" (525).

When Wynand realizes that Roark is through with the Stoddard trial, but he is not—that it is Wynand who will have to face and forgive himself for the Stoddard trial and, he dimly senses, for his pursuit of power—Wynand feels the danger to himself (526–30). He looks for the easier way out: to crush Roark in order to reaffirm his conclusion that a man like Roark is impossible. But though Wynand does not yet know this, it is not, as we have seen, really a way out. And it is only comparatively easier, since it is a form of self-torture. Roark sees what "Dwight Carson had been the first [to see]. Wynand's lips were parted, his eyes brilliant. It was an expression of sensual pleasure derived from agony—the agony of his victim or his own, or both" (532). The fate Wynand wants to sentence Roark to is the fate that Wynand *chose* for himself. "You'll create in your sphere," he tells Roark, "what the *Banner* is in mine" (532). But if this fate would empty Roark's life of meaning, does this not imply that Wynand's is *already* empty of meaning? Wynand cannot escape the basic contradiction of his life's motivation.

Roark, of course, does not give in. Wynand is not happy about this fact, but he does not fight further, since he senses that Roark would survive the battle while he would not (533). In another act of love as exception-making, Wynand submits to his reverence for Roark. It is both penance and atonement. Penance, because he "is punishing himself for what he has done—by bowing before what he should have done."[20] When Dominique asks Wynand what Roark is to him, Wynand answers: "a hair shirt" (552). But it is also atonement, because it is Wynand's "first acceptance of an ideal."[21]

Through Roark, Wynand begins to learn the true nature of the creator's motivation and the fact that that motivation is radically unconcerned with and unaffected by other men. "I always look at the men in the street," Wynand tells Roark. "I used to hate them and, sometimes, to be afraid. But now I look at every one of them and I want to say: 'Why, you poor fool!' That's all" (547).

But if this is the correct attitude toward other men, it means that Wynand's life is beyond redemption.

His redemption, Wynand thought, would come first in the form of using the *Banner* to protect Dominique and, now, in the form of promoting Roark. Wynand does not have to face the "unthinkable"—closing the *Banner* (589)—because he can use it to plug Roark. There are now days when he loves the *Banner* (589). But Wynand is beginning to get a glimpse of the nonexistence of his power; his readership remains indifferent to Roark's achievements and the people who frequent intellectual circles begin to sneer at Roark, "the genius of the yellow press" (590). "We'll see," Wynand says in contemptuous response, and continues "his private crusade" (590).

In the aftermath of Cortlandt's destruction, the *Banner* rises to Roark's defense—and readership plummets, employees rebel and strike, Wynand's editorials and arguments go unheeded, and the mob grows contemptuous of him and of Roark. Three weeks into the strike, he goes to Roark to admit that the *Banner* is not helping but actually hurting Roark. Roark tells him it does not matter. This is a battle between Wynand and God—as Dominique put it (618)—a civil war for Wynand's soul. "I knew that something like that had to happen, when I saw you for the first time," Roark tells him. "You knew it long before that" (654). "If you stick to the end," Roark tells him, "you won't need me any longer" (653).

But to stick to the end, Wynand realizes, means to close the *Banner*. It means that the goal of Wynand's life was worse than useless: his basic motivation placed his life in the service of the destruction of that which he loved, integrity. He is back to the beginning of his career. He is back to the choice of defending Pat Mulligan by destroying the *Gazette*, or of preserving the *Gazette* and sacrificing the only honest man he knows. Only now the choice is writ large—Howard Roark versus the *Banner*—and its meaning is fully clear to Wynand.

Wynand now grasps his moral treason and the cause of his inner emptiness. He cannot forgive himself; he must be the one to pay for his sin.[22] He surrendered to the mob even before selling out Pat Mulligan; he surrendered to the mob by allowing it to dictate his basic goal in life: to rule. "Howard," Wynand thinks to himself, "I wrote that editorial [denouncing Roark] forty years ago. I wrote it one night when I was sixteen and stood on the roof of a tenement" (662). Wynand will not try to evade responsibility: "I had no right to kneel and seek redemption," he thinks to himself (658). "I'll pay—I signed a blank check long ago and now it's presented for collection—but a blank check is always made out to the sum of everything you've got" (656). By placing his incredible creative power in the hands of the "masses," he gave expression to their souls and allowed them to direct his ability toward the destruction of that which he loved. "Anything may be betrayed, anyone may be forgiven. But not those who lack the courage of their own greatness" (663).

His last solace is to return to Dominique, now as a beggar. He is again back at the beginning. At age twenty, Wynand had bared his soul to an unworthy woman; by allowing such experiences to warp his aim in life, it is now *his* soul that is unworthy of the woman *he* loves, and it is he who must seek a relationship he cannot deserve. In their final meeting, Wynand accepts the full pain his life has caused his highest value, Dominique, and that which she loved: Howard Roark. "I think I should have understood," he says in the manner of "a bank teller balancing a stranger's account that had been overdrawn and had to be closed." "You married Peter Keating. Right after the Stoddard trial" (671). When Dominique cries that he had no right to become what he became, if he can take it like this, he replies: "That's why I'm taking it" (671). He allows the *Banner* to smear Dominique and receives letters "generous in their condolences, unrestrained in the indecency of their comment on Dominique Francon"; he forces himself to read every letter; it "was the worst of the suffering Gail Wynand was to know" (673).

His final act is to commission the Wynand Building—the symbol of his original and deepest motivation, which he now knows he betrayed. "I told you once," Wynand says to Roark in their last meeting, "that this building was to be a monument to my life. There is nothing to commemorate now. The Wynand Building will have nothing—except what you give it. . . . Build it as a monument to the spirit which is yours . . . and could have been mine" (692).

THE AVERAGE MAN AND THE MASSES

The creator is mistaken to give sway to other people. In his view of how to reach his goal, of whether it is possible to reach his goal, and of what goal he should therefore be trying to reach, he must not allow the specific choices or actions of other men to enter. To his basic goal of building the things he knows to be valuable, in order to reshape for himself the earth that he loves, he must hold fast. If he does, the evil of the "masses" and of their intellectual molders and agitators will have no power to touch him. If he does, the ideal of creative productivity and joy is reachable—here, now, on this earth. In *The Fountainhead*, individual greatness does not consist in ruling others, but in being radically independent from them.

When the creator grasps the nature and meaning of his actual motivation, he will also understand that the idea that others form a mob eager to tear him to pieces is mistaken. In essence, *anyone* can share the motive of the creator. As Roark explains in his courtroom speech: "Degrees of ability vary, but the basic principle remains the same: the degree of a man's independence, initiative and personal love for his work determines his talent as a worker and his worth as a man" (681). The masses do not represent a fact of nature; membership in their ranks is *self-made*, by a chosen default, and does not indicate the essence of man, not even of the man of average ability (hereafter, the "average man"). It is wrong, as the notes for *The Little Street* suggest, that "all humanity and each little citizen is an octopus that consciously or unconsciously sucks the blood of the best on earth and strangles life with its cold, sticky tentacles." Some men lower themselves to the state of an octopus—or to that of a swine grunting in the muck, in the more accurate imagery of *The Fountainhead*—and some do not. The creator's attitude should be to ignore those who debase their own souls, however many their number, and to seek out those who do not.

In the world of *The Fountainhead*, average men are divided into two categories, inclusion in which is determined by their singular response to the greatness in man. Do they admire competence and look up to the creator? Or are they indifferent to, even resentful of, the presence of both? The indictment of the masses in *The Fountainhead* is the indictment of the average man who is not roused by the sight of greatness. Even if such a man cannot match the enormous creativity of the pathbreakers in his society, he can appreciate and give thanks for what they bring into existence that he could not; he can acknowledge his intellectual debt to them; he can resolve to equal their creative dedication in his own life and on his own scale, with whatever creative spark he possesses and has managed to fan; and he can defend and support them when they come under attack. Average men who refuse to do this—average men who, in Toohey's words, "have not risen in fury when we called you average" (638)—are condemned.[23]

Most of the opposition Roark (and the other creators) faces comes from those indifferent or hostile to achievement. From the Dean, who neither approves of criminals nor great men and therefore concludes that Roark is a dangerous man, not to be encouraged (25–26)—to the architects who will not consider hiring Roark, not because they thought he was worthless but because they "simply did not care to find out whether he was good" (99)— to Gordon L. Prescott, an architect who bemoans "the hardships placed in the way of [the profession's] talented beginners" but who, when he meets Roark and sees Roark's drawings, tells him that the "genius is the one who knows how to express the general" (100)—to Mrs. Wayne Wilmot, who resents that Roark is trying to teach her something about buildings (162)—to those who "did not know whether his buildings were good or worthless" but who think they are nevertheless fit to judge Roark because "they knew only that they had never heard of these buildings" (175)—to Ralston Holcombe, who, in a moment of "complete sincerity," can say before his fellow architects that we "are only men and we are only seekers. But we seek for truth with the best there is in our hearts" (200), and yet who can, when he sees the Heller house, denounce it and declare that there "ought to be a law" (137)—to Joel Sutton, who tells Roark that "I think you're a great architect" but that "that's just the trouble, greatness is fine but it's not practical" (271)—to the wretches who criticize the Stoddard Temple (342–43)—to those who attack Roark as "an egomaniac devoid of all moral sense" (622) because he deprives them of the idea that charity is an "all-excusing virtue" and exposes the social worker as deriving "an unearned respect from all, by grace of his fingers on the wounds of others" (622)—the sum and essence of people's opposition to Roark is their unwillingness to try to match his achievement and stature of soul. These are the average men who see greatness—and do not want it. These are the men who form Mallory's beast (331–32, 511).

In the character of Peter Keating we see the basic cause of this rejection of greatness. Keating can recognize Roark's greatness, and one of Keating's most appealing aspects is that he occasionally responds to it. Early in the story, for instance, in a conversation with Roark, Keating remarks: "'You know,' said Keating honestly and unexpectedly even to himself, 'I've often thought that you're crazy. But I know that you know many things about it—architecture, I mean—which those fools never knew. And I know that you love it as they never will'" (33). But to match Roark's dedication and effort is too demanding. "When I'm with you," Keating tells Roark, "it's always like a choice. Between you—and the rest of the world. I don't want that kind of a choice" (89).

What Keating wants is a borrowed greatness: greatness, without the effort it entails; self-respect, without the bother of having to achieve it. He flocks to those who make him feel that this is possible. Prescott gives a speech about the meaning of architecture: "The architect is a metaphysical priest dealing in basic essentials, who has the courage to face the primal conception of reality as nonreality—since there is nothing and he creates nothing. If this sounds like a contradiction, it is not proof of bad logic, but of a higher logic." Keating listens attentively, with "thick contentment"; he thinks to himself: "One could not worry about one's value or greatness when listening to this. It made self-respect unnecessary" (292). At Toohey's meetings for young architects, Keating finds "a feeling of brotherhood, but somehow not of a sainted or noble brotherhood; yet this precisely was the comfort—that one felt, among them, no necessity for being sainted or noble" (245).

To men like Keating, the presence of a great man can topple their moral rationalizations and fraud. A man like Roark stands as a constant reminder of what they are not, and as a reproach. They need to feel superior to a man like Roark, so they ignore him and oppose him and hate him and denounce him—and seek an escape from him. For all of this, Toohey supplies them the means.

Toohey helps manufacture the masses by appealing to the worst in the average man. His racket is to convince men that it is wrong to admire greatness and, even more, to kill in their minds the very conception of greatness (635). He helps deprive men of genuine self-respect, which they must then replace with the illusion of self-respect (605–7, 635). It is an illusion that requires, as Keating's example shows, the spiritual slop of irrationalism, altruism, and collectivism that Toohey continuously feeds them. But Toohey's racket cannot exist without the basic default of a man like Keating: Keating's refusal to exert the effort required to work and to rise. A man who retains a core of competence and so of self-respect is immune to Toohey's machinations. "I can't understand why people of culture and position like us understand the great ideal of collectivism," declares Mitchell Layton, "while the working man who has everything to gain from it remains so stupidly indifferent. I can't understand why the workers in this country have so little sympathy with collectivism." "Can't you?" answers Toohey (556).[24] Toohey knows the source of his power; he knows that he is a dependent seeking power over dependents, a life even more empty than Keating's (638–39).

The average man enters the rank of the masses only by his own default. It is neither his fate nor indicative of his nature. How can he achieve the moral stature of a Howard Roark? Only by practicing the opposite of compassion: the demanding virtue of admiration. "Compassion is a wonderful thing," Dominique explains to Mrs. Jones.

> It's what one feels when one looks at a squashed caterpillar. An elevating experience. One can let oneself go and spread—you know, like taking a girdle off. You don't have to hold your stomach, your heart or your spirit up—when you feel compassion. All you have to do is look down. It's much easier. When you look up, you get a pain in the neck. Compassion is the greatest virtue. It justifies suffering. There's got to be suffering in the world, else how would we be virtuous and feel compassion? . . . Oh, it has an antithesis—but such a hard, demanding one. . . . Admiration, Mrs. Jones, admiration. But that takes more than a girdle. (282)

To practice the virtue of admiration *does* demand much of a man. He must respect and nurture the best within himself and within any man: his ability to produce and create on whatever scale he is capable of. His God must be man's competence. He must be willing to look up and to exert the effort to learn from those of superior knowledge and ability. He must be willing to acknowledge the intellectual gifts that he receives from those more productive than him, which he can become worthy of in part by showing his gratitude. He must judge the world scrupulously, deciding for himself what deserves his "Yes" and his "No" (539). And then he must further and fight for that which he sees to be good, for that to which he has granted his "Yes." To practice the virtue of admiration is to stand, head lifted, and give thanks for the greatness of another man and all that it, and its sight, will make possible in one's own life. It is to be *motivated* by the best possible to oneself and to man.

This is the virtue that Mike Donnigan exemplifies—and why he represents the best of the men of average ability. When Roark first meets him, Mike is struggling to bend some conduits around a beam. Impatient with the know-nothing architects normally sent to the building site, Mike dismisses Roark when Roark tells him that he is wasting his time. But when Roark demonstrates to Mike a more efficient way, by cutting a hole in the beam and running the pipes straight through, Mike's attitude changes. He stares with *reverence* at the hole that Roark's expert hands have burned: "Jesus! . . . Do you know how to handle a torch!" (92). Mike is not, as many people would be, resentful of the fact that Roark has "shown him up"; Mike, rather, is appreciative of the fact that he has learned a better way to do things. He later seeks out Roark's company and tells Roark of the only thing he worships: "expertness of any kind" (93). As to what counts as expertness, Mike judges that first-hand; Mike despises all other architects, but profoundly admires one, Cameron, for whom he once worked. When Roark tells Mike that he too has worked for Cameron, and indicates the same admiration for Cameron as Mike's, their friendship is sealed.

Thereafter Mike supports and fights for Roark in whatever way he can, knowing that he is the lucky one for being able to participate in the erection of Roark's buildings and the progression of Roark's career. Mike works on every one of Roark's buildings (336). When Roark discovers him at the construction site of his first building, the Heller house, Roark is shocked that Mike would bother with a small private residence. "Why such a come-down?" Roark asks him. Mike knows better: "you think it's a come-down? Well, maybe it is. And maybe it's the other way around" (134). Mike is properly outraged when Roark is fired from Francon and Heyer (97) and, later, when Roark must close his office because he cannot find enough clients (197); Mike helps land Roark the job he needs in the granite quarry. He stands by Roark's greatness despite the abuses hurled at Roark by the hostile crowd: he is in Roark's camp of supporters at both the Stoddard and Cortlandt trials. And he takes inspiration from Roark, who helps Mike sustain his conviction that the good is worth striving for and will prevail: "I told you not to worry," he tells Mallory at one point during the construction of Monadnock Valley, "at the [Stoddard] trial that was. He can't lose, quarries or no quarries, trials or no trials. They can't beat him, Steve, they just can't, not the whole goddamn world" (508).

This virtue of admiration is shared by all of Roark's friends and forms the bond between them. Cameron hires Roark over his own reluctance, because he recognizes Roark's incredible talent. Austen Heller responds to Roark's greatness when he sees it in Snyte's office, offering Roark the commission on the spot. He then works to bring Roark clients and praises Roark's buildings in print. Roger Enright picks Roark as his architect based on his own judgment of good architecture; persists in locating Roark, who is working in the granite quarry; and fires from his employ the bored secretary who could not be bothered to properly assess Roark as a potential builder of the Enright House (251); he also wants to bring Roark clients. Both Heller and Enright confront Dominique when they think she is attacking Roark's buildings in her columns. Kent Lansing fights savagely for Roark. He tells him: "I want a good hotel, and I have certain standards of what is good, and they're my own, and you're the one who can give me what I want. And when I fight for you, I'm doing—on my side of it—just what you're doing when you design a building. Do you think integrity is the monopoly of the artist?" (313). And of course Roark acts in the same way. He respects the work of Enright and Lansing, he praises Heller's articles, he profoundly admires Cameron.

After Heller in his writings defends Monadnock and Roark's other buildings by putting "into words the things Roark had said in structure. Only they were not Austen Heller's usual quiet words—they were a ferocious cry of admiration and anger," Lansing names the quality all these men share: "It takes two to make a very great career: the man who is great, and the man—almost rarer—who is great enough to see greatness and say so" (512).

To cultivate the ability to recognize greatness reaps immediate benefits. Mike learns from Roark and gets to participate in the construction of buildings he could never have designed himself. Heller gets his house; Enright, his apartment building; Lansing, the Aquitania Hotel.

But the virtue should be cultivated for more than this. To practice the virtue of admiration is how men of less than supreme ability play their role in creating a human world. As Toohey notes, looking out over the lights of the city, "Think of the thousands who worked to create this and of the millions who profit by it. . . . it is said that but for the spirit of a dozen men, here and there down the ages, but for a dozen men—less, perhaps—none of this would have been possible" (281). These few men, Roark observes in his courtroom speech, were usually made to suffer for the great gift they brought. Imagine if they had *not* been made to suffer. Imagine if the creators sensed that they faced not a drooling beast—masses indifferent, even hostile, to achievement—but a group of *individuals* eager to rise and meet the demanding task of looking upward. What then might have been possible?

Imagine what Cameron might have created, if he had not turned, in despair of finding another human face, to drink. Imagine what Dominique might have done, if she had not been paralyzed by people who settle for the half-way and the in-between. Imagine what Mallory might have created, if he had not sensed that he was ignored and hated for his ability. Imagine what Wynand might have built instead of the *Banner*, if in childhood he had been admired and encouraged for his tremendous intellect and drive.

A creator like Roark will hold out to the end. The creator who is fully conscious of the nature and moral rightness of his motivation knows that he is beyond the grasp of evil; the pain can go down only to a certain point. But men of lesser ability have no right to demand such moral endurance of the Roarks, and no interest in doing so.[25]

The crucial difference between the virtue of admiration and of compassion is captured in the scenes dealing with the disfigurement of the Stoddard Temple (383–87). Built, as Dominique says, as a "temple to the human spirit," in which one can experience exaltation though the contemplation of man "as strong, proud, clean, wise, and fearless" and the consciousness of "living up to one's highest possibility" (355)—it is transformed into the Hopton Stoddard Home for Subnormal Children. It goes from a building dedicated to man's greatness to one dedicated to cases of congenital incompetence. The ladies who pick the Stoddard House's occupants make "a point of rejecting those who could be cured and selecting only the hopeless cases" (385). The children enter "their new home, their eyes staring vacantly, the stare of death before which no world existed" (385). Outside, children from the slums "gape wistfully" at the Home (385). "These children had filthy clothes and smudged faces, agile little bodies, impertinent grins, and eyes bright with a roaring, imperious, demanding intelligence. The ladies in charge of the Home chased them away with angry exclamations about 'little gangsters'" (385–86).

One can only wonder how many Wynands are among those "little gangsters," and how badly they have been mangled inside.

Men of greatness, as already indicated, must also practice the virtue of admiration. In regard to a man of equal ability, this means mutual admiration, as exists between Roark and Cameron. In regard to a man of lesser ability, this means that they should appeal to, deal with, promote, and accept nothing less than the man's best; great men will thereby play a role—beyond creating their life-giving products—in creating a human world. This is Roark's policy.

Roark patiently waits for clients: for his kind of men. He offers them the very best of himself—his work—and in the name of that value often explains to them the meaning of buildings and what they should be seeking from architecture. We see Roark doing this with the very first of his potential clients, with Wayne Wilmot, with Robert L. Mundy, with Nathaniel Janss, and with the Sanborns (161–70). As Roark begins to build, choosing to erect only uncompromised structures of incomparable value, individuals who may not be able to equal Roark's achievements, but who have retained the capacity to respond to them, see Roark's buildings and do respond. Jimmy Gowan sees Heller's house, likes it, and hires Roark to build his filling station (158). John Fargo hires Roark to build his department store after walking through the Gowan Service Station and the Heller house (167). This is the pattern by which Roark gets almost all his clients.

Roark knows that such men, though comparatively rare, are not freaks.[26] They have simply achieved their human stature, the basic independence that anyone can attain. It will take patience to find them and for them to see and to learn—as Lansing says to Roark, "men like you and me would not survive beyond their first fifteen years if they did not acquire the patience of a Chinese executioner" (336–37). But it is possible, and they are the only kind of people worth dealing with.

And the better people do learn from Roark—they come to see the logic, the purpose, and the functional beauty of his buildings, and they respond. Roark designs the Enright House "as a rising mass of rock crystal . . . so that the future inhabitants were to have, not a square cage out of a square pile of cages, but each a single house held to the other houses like a single crystal to the side of a rock" (234). It rents "promptly. The tenants . . . did not discuss the value of the building; they merely liked living there. They were the sort who lead useful, active private lives in public silence" (308). The Stoddard Temple also attracts patrons to experience its unique conception of exaltation. "There were a few who came, and saw, and admired the building in silence. But they were the kind who do not take part in public issues" (342). Monadnock Valley—for which Roark had argued that "people of good taste and small income had no place to go, if they found no rest or pleasure in herds. . . . Why not offer these people a place where, for a week or a month, at small cost, they could have what they wanted and needed?" (506–7)—also proves a success. It is rented out within a month of opening and by the end of the summer leased for the following year. It attracts a "strange mixture" of people: "society men and women who could have afforded more fashionable resorts, young writers and unknown artists, engineers and newspapermen and factory workers. . . . The place became news; but it was private news" (510).[27]

In his day-to-day work Roark also seeks to deal only with the best within each man. In the sunlight of Roark's office, each man's irrelevancies are stripped away.

[Roark] did not smile at his employees, he did not take them out for drinks, he never inquired about their families, their love lives or their church attendance. He responded only to the essence of a man: to his creative capacity. In this office one had to be competent. . . . But if a man worked well, he needed nothing else to win his employer's benevolence: it was granted, not as a gift, but as a debt. It was granted, not as affection, but as recognition. (309)

Rather than feeling vulnerable or insignificant, each man feels that, for once, he is being seen for whom he really is, for what really matters about him and for what is truly important in life. Although their friends and family say that Roark's office must be cold and inhuman, the employees know, without having the ability to put the knowledge into words, that for the first time in their lives they are in a *human* environment. They experience self-respect toward themselves and loyalty and love toward Roark (309).

When a creator like Roark ceaselessly strives for the best within himself, and then offers that in trade to those who can see and appreciate it, he gives courage and inspiration to those willing to enter the same battle. Mallory might not have the breadth of vision and conviction, and the moral strength and endurance, to persevere alone, as Roark does, but he will work to earn the lifeline Roark's very existence throws him (329–32). During the construction of Monadnock Valley, Mallory thinks to himself: "Battle . . . is a vicious concept. There is no glory in war, and no beauty in crusades of men. But this was a battle, this was an army and a war—and the highest experience in the life of every man who took part in it"; those working on the project do their part to deserve the experience that Roark makes possible for them, with the unstated knowledge that their leader will keep them from harm—"the architect who walked among them . . . the man who had made this possible—the thought in the mind of that man—and not the content of that thought, nor the result, not the vision that had created Monadnock Valley, nor the will that had made it real—but the method of his thought, the rule of its function—the method and rule which were not like those of the world beyond the hills" (508).

By his life, Roark does what George Washington advised: he raises a standard to which the wise and the honest can repair. As Part Four of *The Fountainhead* opens, the boy on the bike is searching for real "joy and reason and meaning in life." "Don't work for my happiness, my brothers," he thinks to himself, "show me yours—show me that it is possible—show me your achievements—and the knowledge will give me courage for mine" (504). He sees Monadnock Valley. "Who built it?" he asks Roark. "I did." "Thank you," the boy replies. Roark inclines his head, in acknowledgement; he "did not know that he had given someone the courage to face a lifetime" (505–6).

But there is even more than this to Roark's benevolence. Roark knows that the good has never had a voice. Recall those who can respond to the Enright House, to the Stoddard Temple, and to Monadnock Valley: good people, but without public voice. Remember his employees, who can find no name for the feeling that represents the best within themselves. Remember that even exemplary men like Roger Enright think they have no abstract ideals (251). And remember the task Cameron charges Roark with:

> I have no answer to give them, Howard. I'm leaving you to face them. You'll answer them. All of them, the Wynand papers and what makes the Wynand papers possible and what lies behind that. It's a strange mission to give you. I don't know what our answer is to be. I know only that there is an answer and that you're holding it, that you're the answer, Howard, and some day you'll find the words for it. (76–77)

Roark will find the words, primarily for himself—"I wished to come here and state my terms," Roark says at the Cortlandt trial. "I do not recognize anyone's right to one minute of my life. . . . I am a man who does not exist for others" (684)—"and for every creator whose name is known—and every creator who lived, struggled and perished unrecognized before he could achieve" (685). But Roark's words are also addressed to the jury, and he thinks that he has a chance of winning (654).

Roark selects as jurors those with the "hardest faces," "attentive and emotionless" (675). The twelve men—executives, engineers, factory workers, a mathematician, a truck driver, a brick layer, an electrician, a gardener—are precisely the type of men who would choose to live at the Enright House, to come to the Stoddard Temple to experience uplift, and to vacation in the peaceful solitude of Monadnock Valley. These are good, average men, who live honorable lives, without public acknowledgment or voice. These are men who are unable to equal Roark's creative genius, unable to find the words that name Roark's achievement and the forces that oppose Roark, and unable to express their understanding and gratitude (though they probably should do more in regard to this last, as Mike does). But if the words and the case are presented to them, they will make the right choice. Roark explains to them the conflict between creators and second-handers, the immorality of their existing moral concepts, the fact that he was not paid for Cortlandt, and the reason why he had to dynamite it. The jury acquits him (685).[28]

There is in *The Fountainhead* a tremendous rift between the honest average man, represented by Mike, and the intellectuals, represented by Toohey and his avant-garde of nihilistic writers, architects, and critics. True, to the extent that the average man is not motivated by his work, by developing his competence and earning his self-respect, he needs the moral rationalizations the intellectuals provide him. This is Keating's dependence on Toohey: Toohey preys on a person's insecurities and immoralities, and drives a wedge between a person and his soul. But to the extent that what motivates the average man is commitment to creative work and genuine self-respect, he is in no need of the intellectuals. This is why the workers—who would contain men in varying degrees similar to Mike—do not go for Toohey's collectivism. But even the best of them remain vulnerable, unable fully to understand themselves, unable consistently to identify the good, unable to explain and defend it against those who attack it. To all the good men whom the intellectuals deprive of voice—from honest men of average ability to, most importantly, creators like Cameron and Mallory and Wynand—Roark provides a voice in his courtroom speech.

Gail Wynand's course of action in this regard is the opposite of Roark's. Wynand appeals to the worst in men (which is the reason Roark's friends hate Wynand). Wynand does not look for his kind of reader; he designs his papers for the man who "lacked even the positive distinction of a half-wit" (409). He does not address the minds of the public, but instead, through "enormous headlines, glaring pictures and oversimplified text," helps relieve them of the responsibility of thought, of "any necessity for an intermediary process of reason, like food shot through the rectum, requiring no digestion" (409). He does not offer his creative best to the world and thereby inspire fallen creators to rejoin the battle or nascent ones to take it up; he offers the spectacle of an "exceptional talent . . . burned prodigally to achieve perfection in the unexceptional" (409). His work helps drive a man like Cameron to despair and an average man to spiritual bankruptcy. Wynand does the opposite of raising a standard to which the wise and the honest can repair: he creates a pool of slime in which the dishonest can frolic. Is it any wonder, then, that he comes to loathe the sight of the men around him?

During the strike of the Union of Wynand Employees, as Wynand tries to use the *Banner* to defend Roark, he thinks to himself

> that men had been willing to work for him when he plugged known crooks for municipal elections, when he glamorized red-light districts, when he ruined reputations by scandalous libel, when he sobbed over the mothers of gangsters. Talented men, respected men had been eager to work for him. Now he was being honest for the first time in his career. He was leading his greatest crusade—with the help of finks, drifters, drunkards, and humble drudges too passive to quit. The guilt, he thought, was not perhaps with those who now refused to work for him. (650)

Worst of all, Wynand has the intellect to explain and defend greatness. We see this in his conversation with Roark aboard the yacht and in his articles defending Roark. But Wynand chose to turn his voice over to others. He does not present to men the actual alternatives, in clear, explicit, graspable terms. He never allows them the possibility of making an honest, informed choice. He presents them only the *Banner's* and Toohey's intellectual corruption. When Wynand tries to argue Roark's case with minds that have been constantly fed such corruption, he is met with "indifferent silence, half boredom, half-resentment"—and with pronouncements quoted from the *Banner* (628–29).[29]

Wynand has helped create Toohey; without him, Toohey is powerless. Toohey's first mention in the story is in connection with the magazine *New Frontiers*, which has "a following that described itself as the intellectual vanguard of the country; no one had ever risen to challenge the description" (50). Wynand's crime is not only that he did not challenge this vanguard—he who, like Roark, could have found the words "for something that should win" (133)—but that he built Toohey his platform. Wynand has unleashed Toohey and the masses:

> I released them all. I made every one of those who destroyed me. There is a beast on earth, dammed safely by its own impotence. I broke the dam. They would have remained helpless. They can produce nothing. I gave them the weapon. I gave them my strength, my energy, my living power. I created a great voice and let them dictate the words. The woman who threw the beet leaves in my face had a right to do it. I made it possible for her. (663)

At the end of the Cortlandt trial, when Wynand and Roark both rise to face the jury, it is the final verdict on Wynand's life. At this point, there is no question in Wynand's mind that, whether or not Roark is acquitted, Roark's way of life is right and Wynand's is wrong. In this sense, Wynand is simply awaiting formal sentencing. But one outstanding issue remains. Was Wynand right that the average man is inherently corrupt and impervious to reason? This would not justify, but it would at least mitigate, his quest for power. But the jury's acquittal of Roark, without need of further deliberation upon hearing Roark's speech, reveals that even on this issue Wynand is mistaken. Offered clear alternatives, the best among average men will choose the rational one.

In her 1945 letter "To the Readers of *The Fountainhead*," Rand observes:

> The success of *The Fountainhead* has demonstrated its own thesis. It was rejected by twelve publishers who declared that it had no commercial possibilities, it would not sell, it was "too intellectual," it was "too unconventional," it went against every alleged popular trend. Yet the success of *The Fountainhead* was made by the public. Not by the public as an organized *collective*—but by single, individual readers who discovered it of their own choice, who read it on their own initiative and recommended it on their own judgment. . . . To every reader who had the intelligence to understand *The Fountainhead*, the integrity to like it and the courage to speak about it—to every one of you, not in mass, but personally and individually, I am here saying: *Thank you*.[30]

At a deeper level, however, it is the *existence* of *The Fountainhead* that demonstrates its own thesis. It took a mind like Roark's, a mind whose *motive* was its own truth, a mind which wanted to see, for itself, this kind of story and characters made real, a mind which understood that meaning in life comes from what one creates, not from how others respond or fail to respond to it—it took such a mind to create *The Fountainhead*. For a reader who cherishes the sense of exaltation that comes from entering *The Fountainhead*'s world, and who has been inspired by Ayn Rand's achievement to have the courage to revere the best within himself and within man, to say "thank you" hardly seems enough.[31]

NOTES

1. In her "Introduction to the Twenty-fifth Anniversary Edition" of *The Fountainhead* (v–xi), Rand discusses some consequences of religion's monopoly in the field of ethics.

2. David Harriman, ed., *Journals of Ayn Rand* (New York: Plume, 1999), 66–74.

3. Ayn Rand, *The Virtue of Selfishness: A New Concept of Egoism* (New York: New American Library, 1964), 82–86.

4. For Rand's notes on the unwritten novel, see Harriman, *Journals of Ayn Rand*, 704–16. In an editorial comment on these notes, Harriman writes: "So AR has come full circle. She returned at the end to a problem that had concerned her from the beginning: how does one maintain a view of life as it could be and ought to be, while living in a culture that is predominantly hostile to rational values. At this stage, however, she knows the solution" (715–16).

5. The best single source to read to understand her final view on the power of the good and the impotency of evil is *Atlas Shrugged*. However, apart from a few endnotes in which I mention later places where Rand dealt with a point I am discussing, my focus is going to be strictly on *The Fountainhead*. There is much more to say about Rand's later elaborations on some of the general issues I discuss, elaborations contained both in *Atlas Shrugged* and in some of her nonfiction articles. For instance, I think her full analysis of Mallory's beast is her analysis of the phenomenon of hatred of the good for being the good. But all this later material would require an essay of its own; I have, however, already touched on one aspect of it in "The Death Premise in *We the Living* and *Atlas Shrugged*," in Robert Mayhew, ed., *Essays on Ayn Rand's* We The Living (Lanham MD: Lexington Books, 2004), 335–56.

6. Harriman, *Journals of Ayn Rand*, 20–47. These notes are fascinating from the perspective of how many issues they contain that she returned to in *The Fountainhead* and of how her views on those issues developed by the time she wrote *The Fountainhead*.

7. Harriman, *Journals of Ayn Rand*, 27, 24, 29; square brackets in original.

8. The context of *The Fountainhead*, as well as of the discussion in this chapter, is that of an essentially free society, not of a dictatorship. I do not mean to suggest by this qualification, however, that Rand thought evil is potent in a dictatorship; the

point is only that (somewhat) different considerations are relevant when applying her principles about the efficacy of the good and the impotency of evil to the case of a dictatorship. The political conditions in *Atlas Shrugged* are close to those of dictatorship; a central theme of the novel, nevertheless, is the impotency of evil and the power of the good.

9. Leonard Peikoff offers a penetrating analysis of Rand's philosophic point here, distinguishing between "metaphysical pleasure" and "the more specific pleasures of work, friendship, and the rest." See Leonard Peikoff, *Objectivism: The Philosophy of Ayn Rand* (New York: Meridan, 1993), 335–343; the quotation is from 340.

10. In a 1937 note to herself, Rand writes: "If a genius passes unnoticed, the loss is humanity's, more than his. There must have been many great innovators that never influenced culture because they were not recognized in time. So much the worse for culture." In a 1944 note, she writes: "[Fools] cannot stop the inventor or the invention. It is the history of every great innovation that it [overcame] fools. And it's the fools who suffered—not the inventor, nor society. *Provided* the social system is *free*, and the inventor has a chance to fight." Harriman, *Journals of Ayn Rand*, 124, 267; second set of square brackets in original. And in a 1948 letter to a fan, she writes: "I wrote [*The Fountainhead*] for the same reason Roark built his buildings. How people would react to it was not my primary concern. If they are not brave enough, it is their tough luck, not mine. I have found, however, that a great many of them are brave enough for it." Michael S. Berliner, ed., *Letters of Ayn Rand* (New York: Dutton, 1995), 417.

11. In a 1962 letter to a fan, Rand writes that "if your achievement is rationally valuable, you will find people who will appreciate it—as you should have learned from the story of Howard Roark. No man can expect to be an innovator and, simultaneously, expect to find a ready-made audience sharing in advance the values he has not yet produced." Berliner, *Letters of Ayn Rand*, 593.

12. In that same 1962 letter to a fan, Rand writes: "You say that you want to quit. How can you quit what you have never started? If you do not fight for your own ideas, you have no right to blame the ideas of others, nor to complain." Berliner, *Letters of Ayn Rand*, 594.

13. In a 1940 synopsis of *The Fountainhead* (then still provisionally titled *Second-Hand Lives*) written for prospective publishers, Rand writes "[Roark] never achieves universal recognition—which he never sought. But he wins the freedom to work as he believes, he fights through to the chance of creating great buildings." Harriman, *Journals of Ayn Rand*, 231.

14. Rand says of Cameron: "Cameron is an independent man who has been broken by [an inimical] society; he is a man who could have been like Roark, but his premises and confidence were not strong enough." Ayn Rand, *The Art of Fiction: A Guide for Writers and Readers*, ed. Tore Boeckmann (New York: Plume, 2000), 80; square brackets in original.

15. Unsurprisingly, Rand possessed Roark's conviction, not Cameron's. And I suspect her conviction came from the same source: her own understanding of her basic motivation and method of functioning. In a 1944 letter to Gerald Loeb, she writes: "all my life I have been troubled by the fact that most people I met bored me to death and I wondered where and how one can meet interesting people. I knew such people existed, I didn't believe that all of humanity was like the dreadful,

wishy-washy, meaningless specimens I saw around me—but I seemed to have terrible luck in meeting the kind I could have liked. . . . but I do like people—when they are really human beings—I love to meet interesting minds and exchange ideas and feel an interested affection, not contempt, for those around me." Berliner, *Letters of Ayn Rand*, 153.

16. Rand states Dominique's motivation this way in her 1940 synopsis of *The Fountainhead*. See Harriman, *Journals of Ayn Rand*, 229–30.

17. In a 1943 letter to Archibald Ogden, her editor, Rand writes: "It will be my fate, like Roark's, to seek and reach the exceptions, the prime movers, the men who do their own thinking and act upon their own judgment. The Tooheys . . . don't count—and may God damn them. One man out of thousands is all I need—all any new idea needs—and these men, the exceptions, will and do move the world. Whatever I do in my future career, I will always have to seek and reach an Archie Ogden. You were the first and the most eloquent symbol of what I mean." Berliner, *Letters of Ayn Rand*, 104.

18. Tellingly, the adult Wynand does nothing to the longshoreman but drives the saloonkeeper to suicide (405).

19. And so, at the end, he knows that he betrayed his city and that the skyscrapers stands in judgment of him (662–63).

20. Harriman, *Journals of Ayn Rand*, 233.

21. Harriman, *Journals of Ayn Rand*, 233.

22. In Berliner, *Letters of Ayn Rand*, Rand calls it "moral treason" (644) and an "unforgivable sin" (224).

23. In her 1947 "Screen Guide for Americans" Rand writes:

In the American doctrine, no man is *common*. Every man's personality is unique—and it is respected as such. He may have qualities which he shares with others; but his virtue is not gauged by how much he resembles others—*that* is the Communist doctrine; his virtue is gauged by his personal distinction, great or small. In America, no man is scorned or penalized if his ability is small. But neither is he praised, extolled and glorified for the *smallness* of his ability. America is the land of the *uncommon man*. It is the land where man is free to develop his genius—and to get its just rewards. It is the land where each man tries to develop whatever quality he might possess and to rise to whatever degree he can, great or modest. It is *not* the land where one is taught that one is small and ought to remain small. It is not the land where one glories or is taught to glory in one's mediocrity. No self-respecting man in America is or thinks of himself as "little," no matter how poor he might be. *That*, precisely, is the difference between an American working man and a European serf. Harriman, *Journals of Ayn Rand*, 362.

24. In her article "Don't Let Go," Rand writes:

The innocence and common sense of the American people have wrecked the plans, the devious notions, the tricky strategies, the ideological traps borrowed by the intellectuals from the European statists, who devised them to fool and rule Europe's impotent masses. There have never been any "masses" in America: the poorest American is an individual and, subconsciously, an individualist. Marxism, which has conquered our universities, is a dismal failure as far as the people are concerned: Americans cannot be sold on any sort of class war; American workers do not see themselves as a "proletariat," but are among the proudest of property owners. It is professors and businessmen who advocate cooperation with Soviet Russia—American labor unions do not. *Philosophy: Who Needs It* (New York: Signet paperback edition, 1984), 212.

25. In her article "The Establishing of an Establishment," Rand writes:

We shall never know how many precociously perceptive youths sensed the evil around them, before they were old enough to find an antidote—and gave up, in helplessly indignant bewilderment; or how many gave in, stultifying their minds. We do not know how many young innovators may exist today and struggle to be heard—but we will not hear of them because the Establishment would prefer not to recognize their existence and not to take any cognizance of their ideas. So long as a society does not take the ultimate step into the abyss by establishing censorship, some men of ability will always succeed in breaking through. But the price—in effort, struggle and endurance—is such that only exceptional men can afford it. Today, originality, integrity, independence have become a road to martyrdom, which only the most dedicated will choose, knowing that the alternative is much worse. A society that sets up these conditions as the price of achievement, is in deep trouble.

The following is for the consideration of those "humanitarian" Congressmen (and their constituents) who think that a few public "plums" tossed to some old professors won't hurt anyone: it is the moral character of decent average men that has no chance under the rule of entrenched mediocrity. The genius can and will fight to the last. The average man cannot and does not. In *Atlas Shrugged*, I discussed the "pyramid of ability" in the realm of economics. There is another kind of social pyramid. The genius who fights "every form of tyranny over the mind of man" is fighting a battle for which lesser men do not have the strength, but on which their freedom, their dignity, and their integrity depend. It is the pyramid of moral endurance."

Rand, *Philosophy: Who Needs It*, 171.

26. Note that Mallory puts the percentage of men who understand and respond to Monadnock Valley at one tenth of one quarter of the population (512).

27. In her article "What is Capitalism?" Rand explains the progress of innovation under capitalism: without sacrifice of anyone to anyone, the creator raises the intellectual standards and judgment of other people by demonstrating to them what is possible. In *Capitalism: The Unknown Ideal* (New York: Signet, 1967), 11–34.

28. In her article "Altruism as Appeasement," Rand writes:

When intellectual leaders fail to foster the best in the mixed, unformed, vacillating character of people at large, the thugs are sure to bring out the worst. When the ablest men turn into cowards, the average men turn into brutes. No, the average man is not morally innocent. But the best proof of his non-brutality, of his helpless, confused, inarticulate longing for truth, for an intelligible, rational world—and of his response to it, when given a chance he cannot create on his own—is the fact that no dictatorship has ever lasted without establishing censorship. No, it is not the intelligent man's moral obligation to serve as the leader or teacher of his less endowed brothers. His foremost moral obligation is to preserve the integrity of his mind and of his self-esteem—which means: to be proud of his intelligence—regardless of their approval or disapproval. No matter how hard this might be in a corrupt age like ours, he has, in fact, no alternative. It is his only chance at a world where intelligence can function, which means: a world where he—and, incidentally, they—can survive.

Ayn Rand, *The Voice of Reason: Essays in Objectivist Thought*, ed. Leonard Peikoff (New York: Meridan, 1989), 39.

29. The sentence before Washington's famous words is apt in regard to Wynand: "If to please the people, we offer what we ourselves disapprove, how can we afterwards defend our work? Let us raise a standard to which the wise and the honest can repair."

30. Berliner, *Letters of Ayn Rand*, 672–73.

31. I would like to thank my fellow participants in the March 2006 Anthem Foundation Consultancy at the University of Texas, Austin—Harry Binswanger, Allan Gotthelf, Robert Mayhew, and Tara Smith—for preliminary discussion of some issues pertaining to the subject of this essay.

13

Unborrowed Vision

Independence and Egoism in *The Fountainhead*

Tara Smith

Ayn Rand is well known as a champion of egoism, the view that individuals should act to promote their own self-interest.[1] *The Fountainhead* offers a dramatic portrait of independence. Through its fiercely independent hero, Howard Roark, as well as characters who reflect several varieties of dependence, Ayn Rand reveals the symbiotic relationship between independence and egoism. Egoism (and the achievement of rational interest and happiness that it makes possible) requires independence, and independence requires egoism. For the sacrifice of one's interest that is enjoined by other moral codes is incompatible with the exercise of independence. It is *The Fountainhead*'s portrayal of this two-way relationship that I shall explore in this essay.

In the first part, by focusing on Roark, Keating, and Wynand, we will observe the way in which egoism depends on independence. Then, by considering Toohey (including the practical effects of his philosophy on Katie), we will see how altruism smothers independence. Finally, we will probe the most puzzling character in the book, Dominique, whose transformation relies on her realizing that she had underestimated the power of the independent egoist.

Ayn Rand writes that independence is "one's acceptance of the responsibility of forming one's own judgments and of living by the work of one's own mind."[2] Independence is a function of the fundamental method by which a person leads his life. In order to acquire knowledge and to gain values, to answer questions and to make decisions, where does a person direct his attention: to what other people think about reality, or to reality itself? Does he seek intellectual sustenance from the opinions of others or from his own judgment? Does he seek material sustenance from the labor of others or through his own productive work? Whereas the independent person's "concern is the conquest of nature," Roark observes, "the parasite's concern is the conquest of men" (679).[3]

The alternative to the independent person is the second-hander, who "regards the consciousness of other men as superior to his own and to the facts of reality."[4] Rand sometimes refers to this type of person as a "social metaphysician," which vividly conveys such a person's premise that what is real and important is dictated by society's beliefs.[5] While such parasitism can assume many forms (freeloader, dictator, social climber, sycophant, and so on), the shared essence in all its incarnations is the attempt to replace the sovereignty of reality with other people.

In commending independence, Ayn Rand is not endorsing the subjectivist view that any of a person's beliefs or desires or actions is valid, so long as it his. "One's own independent judgment is the *means* by which one must choose one's actions," she explains, "but it is not a moral criterion nor a moral validation."[6] Because independence consists in the orientation to reality, it requires *rational* judgment. The independent person's attitude is not "me first," but "reality first." Nor is Ayn Rand suggesting that the independent man is a nonconformist or antisocial. A deliberate effort at nonconformity would merely be an inverted form of subservience to others, a reverse game of Simon Says in which one still takes one's cues from others. And relationships with others can add inestimable value to one's life. Roark readily acknowledges that he needs people to give him work; he is "not building mausoleums" (160). What prevents this from compromising his independence is that it does not involve sacrificing his judgment to theirs. "An architect needs clients," he explains, "but he does not subordinate his work to their wishes. They need him, but they do not order a house just to give him a commission." Moreover, while "an architect requires a great many men to erect his building . . . he does not ask them to vote on his design" (682).[7]

The essence of independence, again, consists in the primary orientation to reality rather than to other men.[8] The independent man does not filter his thoughts, values, or actions through the attitudes of other people. He is, in Roark's resonant phrase, the man of "unborrowed vision" (678).[9]

EGOISM REQUIRES INDEPENDENCE

While many readers are emotionally drawn to Roark's independence, it is important to appreciate that his independence is at the core of his egoism. Independence is indispensable to a person's ability to actually serve his interest and achieve happiness. A full demonstration of this point depends on a thorough explanation of the origin and objectivity of value, a far more involved issue than we can go into here.[10] For our purposes, however, a few points are telling.

Happiness results from the achievement of values—of those things that advance one's life. Values encompass a vast range of things, from food and shelter through recreation and art to a rewarding marriage or a challenging career. Values, however, are objective. While individuals may differ in the specific things that they *consider* valuable and while certain things can be valuable for some people but not others, it is a matter of fact whether a given thing carries a positive or negative impact on an individual's life. Value is not relative to different people's perspectives; value is not created by individual or group will, belief, or attitude.[11] The achievement of values, accordingly, requires rationality (the deliberate adherence to reality in the use of one's mind).[12] Since we live in reality, it is only through respect for reality (i.e., rationality) that we can take the actions necessary to attain life-sustaining ends. By its nature, however, rationality is a first-handed enterprise. "Thinking is something one doesn't borrow or pawn," as Kent Lansing remarks (313). "The mind is an attribute of the individual," Roark explains in his Cortlandt defense. "There is no such thing as a collective thought. An agreement reached by a group of men is . . . drawn upon many individual thoughts. It is a secondary consequence. The primary act—the process of reason—must be performed by each man alone" (679).

To fail to think for oneself is, truly, to fail to think. The repetition of the say-so of others—whether that represents rationally arrived at conclusions, on their part, or mere noises—without one's own first-handed confirmation of its validity, is not rational thought. It is the behavior of a parrot.[13] All of which points to man's need for independence. To see this more vividly, consider Roark.

The Man Who Does Not Exist for Others

Roark is the only character who is happy, from start to finish. Only he consistently serves his interest. Although he confronts serious obstacles, he gets to build, he wins Dominique, and he is true to himself throughout.

We meet Roark in solitude, laughing at his expulsion from school (15). This reaction to adversity is a recurring motif: he laughs when he learns that Dominique was behind his losing the commission from Sutton (271), that Toohey arranged his selection for the Stoddard Temple (334), and that Monadnock Valley was a hoax intended to lose money (511). His laughter does not signify nervous denial, but the folly of these adversaries' schemes. Utterly at peace with himself and with the world, Roark brushes off others' efforts to thwart him, confident that they cannot succeed. This is not cockiness about the odds of his winning a particular battle. Rather, it reflects his consummate self-esteem. Because he lives rationally and because he knows that this is the only course by which human beings *can* achieve values, he is confident that his values will ultimately prevail. He knows that the world is conducive to human happiness and that he is living in the requisite manner. Roark's attitude reflects what Ayn Rand labels the benevolent universe premise, the conviction that the world is fundamentally hospitable to man's prosperity and that human beings' success and happiness are the norm rather than the exception.[14]

Unlike Keating, who suffers continuous inner turmoil as he ceaselessly struggles to decide whom to please, Roark matter-of-factly proceeds by his own rational judgment. His independence is the basis of his calm confidence and serene self-esteem.

We see Roark suffer pain only rarely, as when he learns that Dominique has married Keating (373–75). Clearly, he experiences serious setbacks: losing commissions, losing his practice, defeat at the Stoddard trial, separation from the woman he loves. Yet life's worst kind of pain results from letting oneself down (as Wynand poignantly illustrates). As long as Roark does not do that, external blows carry a limited sting, hurting "only down to a certain point" (344). Blows inflicted by others cannot hurt *him*, in the sense that they cannot damage his character. (During the Stoddard Temple imbroglio, he tells Dominique that what matters is not others' reactions to the building, but that he built it [344].)

Much of what is attractive about Roark is his integrity. He repeatedly refuses to compromise his convictions.[15] His integrity consists not in stubborn adherence to socially sanctioned ideals, however. Roark adheres to *his* principles, based on the verdict of his rational judgment. When Heller chastises him for declining a compromised commission by remarking, "you've got to live," Roark replies: "not that way" (164). Roark lives on *his* terms. His independence comes through even more starkly in his refusal to accept the Manhattan Bank project, a job he desperately needs. He responds to incredulity at his "selflessness" in turning it down by saying, "that was the most selfish thing you've ever seen a man do" (197). The money he would have acquired from the job would have been of no value to *him*—to his goals and happiness. Only by declining could Roark preserve himself.

While Roark does not care what others think of him and does not compare himself to others (26, 72–73), his disposition toward other people is entirely benevolent. He is respectful in his meeting with the Dean and frequently generous with Keating and Wynand. Roark is perfectly willing to help others; he is not willing to sacrifice for them—to surrender greater values for lesser values or non-values.[16] Roark does not view human relations as adversarial, such that one person's well-being can come only at the expense of others (681). When Keating asks Roark why he hates him, Roark innocently asks, "why should I?" (89). At his trial, the crowd realizes that "no hatred was possible to him" (677; also see 515). When Toohey asks what Roark thinks of him, his response is: "but I don't think of you" (389). (In simply asking the question, we see Toohey's opposite orientation.)

Roark enjoys close friendships with Mike, Mallory, and Wynand—bonds built on the values that each, individually, brings to these relationships. He is glad that Wynand likes him not because Wynand is a "VIP," but because he respects Wynand. Roark candidly acknowledges his need and love of Dominique, going so far as to say that she "owns" him—as much as he can be owned (311). Roark loves select individuals and is prepared to die for them, but not to live for them (608). This again reflects his independence. To love another person is not to subordinate oneself to him. It is to recognize the objective value that he offers to one's happiness.[17]

Roark's independence is not an idiosyncratic personality quirk. He appreciates the importance of independence—for others as well as himself. Early on, when Keating solicits his career advice, Roark points out that even to ask for it is a mistake (33). When Dominique tells him that she would annul her marriage to Keating if Roark told her to, he knows that such submission would destroy any chance for their happiness. He does not dictate to people because he realizes that dependence on "the right people" offers no more value than any other form of dependence. Notice how he waits for Dominique to learn her error for herself, rather than attempting to impose the lesson before she is ready. Similarly, Roark makes Keating explain why Roark should design Cortlandt rather than simply dictating the reasoning (578–81). Roark realizes that rationality demands that individuals understand proper principles for themselves. "Yes men"—in any relationship— offer no objective value.[18]

Roark is his own man *par excellence* and he wishes others to be the same. He does not regard the thoughts or actions of other people, as such, as important. Other people have no standing in his mind *simply because* they are other people. He articulates his attitude at the Cortlandt trial, when he declares that the egoist is not concerned with others in any primary manner— in his aim, motive, thinking, desires, or as the source of his energy (681–82). The egoist does not exist for others (681, 684). And this independence is critical to his happiness. Its role emerges more fully when we consider two characters who mean to serve their own interests, but fail, because of their second-handed methods.

The Self Betrayed

Keating represents a commonplace type of second-hander, the shameless conformist. He is introduced, fittingly, as a member of a crowd, barely distinguishable within "a soft, shivering aspic made of mixed arms, shoulders, chests and stomachs" (28). From the outset, he is keenly aware of others' eyes on him (28). For it is others who give Keating a feeling of his own value (72–73). He was as "great as the number of people who told him so," as "right as the number of people who believed it" (188). As Roark describes it, "others dictated [Keating's] convictions . . . others were his motive power and prime concern. He didn't want to be great, but to be thought great" (605). Keating advises Roark that the shrewd policy for success in life is to "always be what people want you to be" (261). Whereas Roark's orientation to reality is apparent from his passion for building, Keating has difficulty concentrating on the work in front of him and cannot even remember his projects (72, 172–73, 30). While craving success as an architect, Keating "hated every piece of stone on the face of the earth" (72; also see 172–73).

Keating is selfish—in the conventional sense. He is a social climber "looking out for number 1," ruthlessly seeking career advancement at any price (witness his manipulation of Tim Davis, Claude Stengel, and Lucius Heyer). Yet what is searingly exposed, over the course of the story, is Keating's utter lack of self. "It's his ego that he has betrayed and given up," Roark observes (605)—every time he acquiesced to the preferences of his mother, a client, Toohey, society. He would do anything to get ahead—by others' standards of what that meant. Correspondingly, he was willing to *be* anything, which meant that *his* identity was dissolved in the process.

In contrast to the serenity of Roark, Keating is at war with himself throughout. His life is littered with acts of self-betrayal. He pursues a career in architecture despite his preference for painting. He hates Dominique for her failure to respond to his kiss but doesn't let that get in the way of their relationship's strategic utility (180–81). He never marries Katie, the one woman he truly loves. During an uncharacteristically honest, penetrating conversation with Dominique about the way he has led his life, he leaps at the escape offered by Toohey's phone call (427). At every decision point at which he could assert *his* judgment, Keating defers to others, treating their will as master. (The pattern is set at the outset in a seemingly trivial incident: though Keating wants his mother to leave him alone with Howard, he tells her the opposite [34–35].)

Frequently, Keating does struggle, before abdicating. He initially tells Katie that he doesn't want to meet her uncle, for instance, because he fears he might use her to get on her uncle's good side (60). Yet he quickly reverses himself, making light of his previous reservations (84). Similarly, when Wynand proposes to buy Dominique for the Stoneridge commission, Keating indignantly refuses—momentarily. He quickly succumbs, further burying *his* will (450). The erosion of Keating's identity is evident not only in his repeated failures to stick to his guns, however. He also routinely has trouble in even forming his will. When Dominique proposes marriage, he is unnerved by the need to make up his mind and longs "to escape the responsibility of consciousness" (369). He never brings himself to decide that he wants to marry Katie. Rather, he tentatively ventures at one stage, "we're engaged, aren't we?" (85). He later tells Katie to insist on their marrying, instead of insisting on it himself (157). No definite, firm values are possible to Keating, because he recedes in the face of others' desires.

After selling Dominique to Wynand, Keating feels as if he has sold himself (455). This is exactly what he has done—as he has on numerous previous occasions, this being simply one of the most grotesque. By doing so, he has forfeited all identity of his own. Far from serving himself, Keating has immolated himself on the altar of others' standards. The result is not the happy life that a self-interested person seeks. Indeed, we increasingly observe the hollowness of Keating's satisfactions. At the opening of his Cosmo-Slotnick triumph, he feels no joy (320). The gratification from gaining the Stoneridge commission is "faded and thin" (476). Even late in the story, when he has succeeded spectacularly by conventional measures (head of an important firm winning prestigious commissions, boasting a trophy wife and the patronage of Toohey), his days are plagued with boredom and disquiet, indifference to his work and panicky insecurity in his desperate quest for others' reassurance. Despite having attained everything he'd ever wanted, Keating is not happy (479). The reason is that *he* didn't want those things. Keating attempted to obtain his values, his self-esteem—his very identity—from others. They could not supply it.

Over the course of their marriage, Dominique has deliberately served as a mirror to Keating, exposing the hollowness of his being. His description, one night, of how she has behaved actually reveals what he has been, his entire life. Keating laments that Dominique has not expressed her own desires, during their marriage. "There's no real *you* any more," he observes, and her soul—"the thing that thinks and values and makes decisions"—has been dormant. When he finally asks, "Where's your I?" she responds, with devastating effect, "Where's yours, Peter?" (425; the scene begins on 418).

Eventually, Keating himself realizes that his greatest guilt is his betrayal of his own wants (598).

The other prime case of a mistakenly betrayed self is Wynand. By conventional images of egoism, Wynand has amassed what any selfish person might want: wealth, fame, power. Yet what is he doing when the reader first meets him? Contemplating suicide (390). His flirtation with suicide is only casual, we learn, yet that makes it all the greater an indictment of the state of his life. That he could toy with the thought of killing himself indicates how bereft of values his life has become. All his "success" has hardly won him happiness.

Wynand is not a textbook conformist. Unlike Keating, who compliantly marches to others' tunes, Wynand seemingly calls the tune. Yet his quest for power amounts merely to a different form of second-handedness. Wynand seeks his happiness from standing on top—from attaining a certain relationship *to other people*. He seeks to rule not because he has an independent vision of the good that he benevolently thinks he can rationally lead other people to realize. Rather, he simply lusts after others' submission.

Wynand chooses journalism as a career because it promises the widest possible influence. "What was there that entered all those houses?" he asks himself, when deciding. "What reached into every room, into every person?" (405). What, in short, would allow him to rule? Later, by training the *Banner*'s staff to identify the news not as objectively significant events but as "that which will create the greatest excitement among the greatest number" (409), Wynand hitches his success to the fickle tides of popular tastes. Although his yacht's name, *I do*, is intended as a bold declaration of Wynand's supremacy over others ("I run things around here"), the attitude it conveys confesses his abiding subservience. He remains consumed by his relationship to other people. Bristling under the orders he receives from others as a youth, Wynand erroneously concludes that the only alternative to being ruled lies in ruling (400–401). He assumes that men's interests are in perpetual conflict and that life is a competition for social position: what is most important is not the achievement of objective values, but the domination of other people.[19]

Though Wynand aspires to a seemingly different position than does Keating, his second-handed path is equally barren. Even his prize accomplishment, his power, is an illusion. This is painfully revealed when he attempts to mobilize the *Banner* for a cause that *he* believes in, the defense of Roark from prosecution for the Cortlandt explosion. He discovers that his empire is a house of cards and that he has actually been a slave to the people, all along, able to exert only as much power as they were willing to grant (603; also see 656). While Wynand might wish, as he tells Toohey, not to be confused with his readers (396), he has relinquished the independence that would have preserved the basis for that distinction. All he has been is whatever they wanted him to be.

Through Wynand, Ayn Rand is illustrating that the person who seeks to dominate others is still dependent on others. By treating the conquest of others as the means to happiness, Wynand has actually created the power that destroys him (663). He gave others the power to control his success and it is he who is crushed, in the process. Wynand's pursuit of power is destined to fail because, as he himself ultimately realizes, "a leash is only a rope with a noose at both ends" (660). The man intent on ruling makes himself a slave.

In many respects, Wynand is far superior to Keating. My point here, however, is that whatever their differences, Keating and Wynand both abide by Keating's policy of being whatever people want you to be. Keating is simply more self-aware on this score. Whereas we observe Keating selling his soul piecemeal over the course of the story, Wynand sells his soul wholesale, early on, when he charts the course for conquest from which he rarely de-

viates. The exceptions—his private art collection, his relationships with Dominique and Roark—offer glimpses of the glorious soul he has sacrificed.
(They reveal, as Roark puts it, that he was not "born to be a second-hander,"
608; also see 663, where Wynand himself thinks the same.) Yet Wynand af-
firms his second-handedness by caving in to the strikers' demands and
abandoning the fullest assertion of self he had ever ventured.

Both Keating and Wynand mean to be egoists; they seek to advance (what
they think is) their self-interest. Because of the second-handed methods
that each adopts, however, their happiness remains miserably unrealized.
Egoistic intentions are not sufficient. Independence is essential for achieving one's interest. Man cannot succeed in reality by erecting any sovereign
above reality, and a person cannot achieve self-interest through means that
destroy his self.[20]

INDEPENDENCE REQUIRES EGOISM

Through Roark, Keating, and Wynand, then, we have seen that rational egoism requires independence. Egoism and independence are entwined even
more intimately, however. Primarily through Toohey, Ayn Rand reveals the
way in which altruism destroys independence. Independence can be sustained only through the consistent practice of rational egoism.[21]

Like all second-handers, Toohey's life revolves around other people. Yet
Keating and Wynand seem amateurs, in comparison—easily forgivable children. Toohey brings second-handedness to profoundly more sinister
depths. Both Keating and Wynand experience some attraction to the good
and exert some element of egoism, however quickly suppressed or com-
partmentalized. Toohey does not.

Like Wynand, Toohey seeks power (634).[22] Whereas Wynand's attitude is
to give people whatever they want and cash in from doing so, Toohey has a
distinct vision of what people *should* want and he methodically schemes to
make them conform. Toohey does not merely practice second-handedness,
in other words; he preaches it, systematically planting seeds so that it will
take root and rule. The specific moral code that Toohey spouts is altruism,
which crucially depends on second-handedness.

Literally, "altruism" means other-ism.[23] "The basic principle of altruism is
that man has no right to exist for his own sake, that service to others is the
justification of his existence, and that self-sacrifice is his highest moral duty,
value and virtue."[24] Wynand believes (albeit mistakenly) that he can gain
genuine value from attaining power over others. Toohey, in contrast, seeks
power purely as a means of destruction. Toohey's motive in promoting altruism is not a sincere, if misguided, love of his fellow men. He seeks only
to bring others down. His basic attitude is crystallized in the episode in

which, at age seven, he turns a hose on Johnny Stokes in his new Sunday suit (293–94). Over the course of his life, Toohey turns that hose on everyone.[25] Toohey's campaign is importantly different from Wynand's effort to hire writers of talent on the condition that they henceforth publish only shlock. For Wynand, this is part of an ill-conceived attempt to prove that integrity is impossible—and thereby excuse his own breach of integrity. Wynand needs to prove it because he doesn't truly believe it (as evidenced in his response to Roark and his buildings). Toohey, in contrast, has no doubts that integrity *is* possible. That is why he sets out to destroy it.

Toohey knows exactly what he is doing, as his explanations of his methods to Dominique and to Keating, at various stages, make clear (281, 567–68, 634–39). He recognizes great achievements, such as the brilliance of Roark's buildings (281). Yet he thirsts to see Roark following orders (633). Nor does he doubt the unvarnished joy that creative achievement makes possible. He despises the photo of Roark's face lifted to the Enright House with an air of "utter rapture" (308) precisely because he grasps what it signifies. Toohey doesn't want that, for himself or for anyone else. (This is what drives Mallory to shoot him [225–26].)

Roark's description, in his climactic courtroom speech, of the basic alternative between the parasite and the creator is not news to Toohey. Toohey realizes that he is a parasite. This occasions no internal conflict or self-reproach, as it does, sporadically, for Keating and for Wynand. A parasite is what he wants to be. Toohey is willfully committed to sucking life from those who create values and to training others to do the same. He fully realizes that altruism offers no genuine value to human life.[26]

It is important to appreciate that Toohey reflects not merely an exotic, virulent strain of altruism, or strange distortions introduced by a perverse man. Toohey represents the essence of altruism. He exhibits a masterful understanding of its fundamental character and full implications. By its nature, altruism destroys. This is not to say that every person who embraces altruism realizes its destructive repercussions and intends them, as Toohey does. These are what the practice of altruism inescapably delivers, however. The only way to practice altruism is to subvert one's own mind. Subservience to others—to their needs, their desires, their beliefs—is the paramount imperative. This way lies only destruction, however, insofar as independence is prerequisite to the creation of objective, life-sustaining values. It is only through an unwavering respect for reality as one's touchstone (rather than any person's opinions about reality) that human beings can create the values that propel our lives. (The damage inflicted by altruism is often minimized by the diluted form in which it is typically practiced. The more consistently a person obeys altruism's command and sacrifices objective values, the more destructive its effects.)[27]

To fully understand altruism's assault on independence, it is worth examining the relationship a little more closely.

Altruism instructs people to sacrifice their good for the good of others. It is only a short step from the idea that a person should surrender his interest to the idea that he should surrender his judgment. For altruism's repudiation of the self is all-encompassing. Altruism does not leave a person half a loaf; it does not say: "keep your soul, your mind, but give us your physical labors and their material fruit." Rather, altruism claims all of a person, spiritually as well as materially. It does so because the only way it can reliably draw from people materially is by claiming people spiritually (that is, by subduing their minds). A whip will suffice to enslave a person's body; no acceptance of altruism is needed for that. Altruism seeks a person's voluntary enlistment in the service of others, however. And the only way to entice people to voluntarily adopt such a code is to dismantle their rational capacity. All moral codes must appeal to minds, of course, if they are to be voluntarily adopted. What Toohey realizes is that since the prescriptions of altruism make no sense, people cannot rationally embrace them. The only way to win converts, therefore, is to make people abandon their rational, independent judgment.

If a person were to think about altruism honestly, for himself, and judge it by the yardstick of reality rather than by its widespread approval by others, he would easily see its basic contradictions and unanswerable questions. Ayn Rand poses some of these in Galt's speech in *Atlas Shrugged*:

> Why is it moral to serve the happiness of others, but not your own? If enjoyment is a value, why is it moral when experienced by others, but immoral when experienced by you? If the sensation of eating a cake is a value, why is it an immoral indulgence in your stomach, but a moral goal for you to achieve in the stomach of others? Why is it immoral for you to desire, but moral for others to do so? Why is it immoral to produce a value and keep it, but moral to give it away? And if it is not moral for you to keep a value, why is it moral for others to accept it? If you are selfless and virtuous when you give it, are they not selfish and vicious when they take it? Does virtue consist of serving vice? Is the moral purpose of those who are good, self-immolation for the sake of those who are evil?[28]

Given the absence of logical reason to practice self-sacrifice, for people to accept that self-sacrifice is nonetheless what they *must* practice; what is needed is the stifling of their exercise of reason. Because independent judgment threatens to expose the absurdity of the altruist doctrine, independent judgment is the enemy of altruism.[29]

The antagonism between altruism and independence runs still deeper, however. Independent judgment is anathema not only as a means of

exposing altruism's irrationality. An individual's independent judgment is a
central part of what altruism's basic directive of self-sacrifice includes.

Rational action requires rational evaluation of one's options.[30] For a person to have reason to do something is for him to have an understanding of
why he should do it, of the good (within his hierarchy of values) that it will
accomplish. There can be no such thing as understanding why one should
sacrifice a value, however, or why one should surrender a greater value for
a lesser or non-value. Consequently, in demanding sacrifice, altruism demands that a person disregard his judgment of reality. Altruism essentially
instructs a person to *stop caring* about whether he has reason to do something. He should shut down his mind and turn himself into an obedient,
unthinking serf. By sacrificing his values, therefore, he *is* sacrificing his independence. This is why Ayn Rand observes:

> It is your *mind* that they want you to surrender—all those who preach the creed
> of sacrifice. . . . Those who start by saying: "It is selfish to pursue your own
> wishes, you must sacrifice them to the wishes of others"—end up by saying: "It
> is selfish to uphold your convictions, you must sacrifice them to the convic-
> tions of others."[31]

Toohey understands all of this completely. He astutely recognizes what it
takes for altruism to prevail, and he conducts his campaign accordingly. Notice that his efforts are not focused on great benefits that can allegedly come
about through altruistic offerings. Instead, he targets all those who create
values. The soul cannot be ruled, he believes; therefore, it must be broken
(635). In his final speech to Keating, Toohey explains his principal techniques: kill aspiration and integrity (by making men feel small and guilty);
kill man's sense of values (by enshrining mediocrity); kill reverence (by
laughter); kill happiness and joy in living (by taking "away from them
whatever is dear or important to them. . . . Make them feel that the mere
fact of a personal desire is evil" (635–36). The altruist goal is a world in
which "no man will hold a desire for himself, but will direct all his efforts
to satisfy the desires of his neighbor who'll have no desires except to satisfy
the desires of the next neighbor who'll have no desires—around the globe,
Peter. Since all must serve all" (638).

Toohey's employment of these techniques is on display throughout. From
his youth, Toohey befriends all comers and proceeds to talk each out of his
intended career path (301–2); he discourages Katie from attending college
(59). He eventually advises Katie that she must stop wanting anything—that
is, to become a complete second-hander, devoid of personal desires (364).
(More savvy than he expects, Katie wonders: when she attains this lofty status, *who* will enter the pearly gates? [365].) Toohey's characteristic response
to anyone's expression of concern about some weighty matter is to trivial-

ize, to mock, to leaven with humor (e.g., 232, 236). He identifies love with drugstore chocolates and reduces marriage to the domestic comfort of cream of wheat (232). He admonishes Katie's request for his approval of her engagement "as if the whole thing were important enough to disapprove of" (236) and wearily dismisses happiness itself as "so middle class" (257). When Katie seeks his counsel about her unhappiness, he makes light of her "cosmic tragedy" and ridicules her for caring so selfishly about *her* happiness (364).[32] Nothing is ever serious with Toohey; he declares a sense of humor to be the only thing that's sacred (232, 236). His superficially above-it-all posture is itself carefully calculated, because he knows that the things he casually dismisses as insignificant are actually anything but.

The destructiveness of Toohey's course could not be more plain. All of Toohey's targets—aspiration, integrity, values, reverence, happiness—are selfish; they are expressions of individual thought and will and thus of individual identity. Toohey does not advocate integrity, contending simply that it should be directed into the service of altruistic ideals. Rather, he expressly seeks to "direct [integrity] toward a goal destructive of all integrity. Preach selflessness" (635). He recognizes, in other words, that integrity is incompatible with altruism and that altruism is a fraud. "Tell men that altruism is the ideal. Not a single one of them has ever achieved it and not a single one ever will" (635). In acknowledging this, Toohey is acknowledging that his aim is destruction. Altruism is only a means to the end of breaking men's souls and men's capacity for happiness.

Toohey's methods *are* lethal, as Katie's trajectory tragically illustrates. When we meet her, Katie is a bright-eyed idealist who wants to do what is right. (See p. 361 for her own later account of this.) Telling Keating about her uncle, she gushes with sincere admiration, describing Toohey as "really wonderful," "amazing," "so kind, so understanding" (58–59). She is utterly without pretense and candid about her feelings for Keating (so much so that he comments on her poor flirtation technique); she suggests no trace of second-handedness. Katie sets out to be an independent altruist; by the nature of altruism, however, she is steadily pulled into parasitism. The demand for self-sacrifice gradually crushes her independence and swallows her self.

Late in the story, when Katie encounters Keating for the first time in several years, she sounds eerily like her uncle in dismissing her pain at Keating's earlier breach of their engagement (597–98). She is indifferent to Keating's admission of his unhappiness and worse, seems beyond concern even with her own, treating her feelings as childish and inconsequential.[33] This is Toohey's ideal. This is the model person he strives to make of everyone. (It is also noteworthy that by leading the life of an altruist, Katie's initial benevolence is replaced by hatred and resentment. The Toohey-designed "humanitarian" berates a beneficiary who is not sufficiently appreciative of

Katie's sacrifices as "trash," is "sore as hell" at someone who manages to solve a problem without her help, and discourages a boy from attending college out of envy for his pursuing the path that she had abandoned [363].)

To summarize this section, let me reiterate the two primary ways in which altruism is in conflict with independence. First, a policy that calls for sacrifice of the values that sustain one's life and happiness is a policy of suicide. Since no one could rationally embrace such a policy (other than some of those who wish to commit suicide), rationality and the independent judgment it rests on are the enemy of altruism.[34] Altruism condemns independent judgment not only because such judgment threatens to expose altruism's irrationality, however. Independent judgment is actually part and parcel of what altruism demands that individuals surrender. Altruism's command that a person act in defiance of his rational judgment by choosing lesser values over greater values is the command to abandon rationality. Altruism's dictate of self-sacrifice, as we have seen, is total. Anything that is yours—your thoughts, your values, your dreams, as much as your material possessions—is to be sacrificed to others. Altruism decrees it wrong to hold onto any element of *you*. Independence, therefore, which is the virtue of directing one's life by one's own judgment of reality, is anathema.

DOMINIQUE

At the other end of the spectrum from Katie, the figure who undergoes significant change for the better, thanks to the influence of Roark's philosophy, is Dominique. She is also the character who is most difficult to understand. Dominique recognizes creative achievement and reveres it, yet she acts to oppose it and seems to adopt, in many respects, the course of a second-hander. She casts the statue that she adores down the air shaft; she lobbies to thwart Roark's career; she writes bromidic pabulum, praising derivative architecture and smarmy planks of conventional morality, for a journalistic rag; she marries a social climber and then a power-luster who represent everything that she despises. What explains this behavior?

Dominique is rent by an inner conflict between idealism and pessimism.[35] Dominique is an idealist insofar as she prizes the very best that human beings can create. She recognizes the unique value in first-handed achievement and is unwilling to reconcile herself to the prevailing mediocrity (and worse) around her. Dominique wants perfection or nothing, she explains to Alvah Scarret; she cannot accept the halfway, she tells Roark (144, 375; also see 288). Alongside this idealism, however, uneasily rests a deep-seated belief that values cannot be achieved, long-term. The good is doomed to fail. To want something, Dominique believes, would be to make her happiness dependent on the "whole world"—a world too filled with second-handers to expect success (143). Dominique reflects the malevolent universe premise: the belief that the world is not fundamentally conducive to man's success and happiness; failure and frustration are the norm.

Clearly, her premises are in tension. It makes sense to aspire to ideals only if one believes that their realization is possible. To escape the contradiction, Dominique withdraws from the pursuit of values. Her attitude is essentially: why bother? "What is the use of building for a world that does not exist?" she asks in her Stoddard testimony (356). She has no desire to wage futile battles or to suffer the indignity of defeat by such unworthy opponents (see 375). The idealist in Dominique roots for Roark, believing—at least, hoping—that he will succeed. The pessimist in her works against Roark, to spare them both the greater pain of what she considers inevitable, eventual defeat.[36]

Just as Dominique's deliberate deference during her marriage to Keating exposes Keating's lack of self, Dominique's marriage to Wynand (a man strikingly similar to her in certain respects) sheds an illuminating light on her. Wynand and Dominique both admire objective values intellectually, but neither pursues those values practically in a rational, healthy manner. Wynand seeks to protect his art collection (and later, Dominique herself) in a private sanctuary, secure from the gaze of others; Dominique longs to protect Roark from the rest of mankind, resenting passersby who so much as lay eyes on him. Dominique and Wynand share a bleak assessment of the prospects for men of integrity, agreeing that they cannot ultimately succeed. In the face of this belief, each fights such men: he, any writer with a voice of his own; she, most conspicuously, Roark. Whereas Wynand tries to break men of integrity and hopes to win, however (since "the man I couldn't break would destroy me" [497]), Dominique fights to "tear every chance" away from Roark and hopes that she will lose. "I'm going to pray that you can't be destroyed," she tells him (272). When Dominique first sees Wynand's art gallery, she thinks the worse of him because his impeccable judgment shows what he is capable of and all that he has betrayed (442). Over the course of their marriage, Dominique comes to recognize her own analogous mistake. Wynand and she have committed the same treason, she realizes, against themselves, against the convictions of their independent judgment. And they are the losers, for it (491–94).

It would be inaccurate to describe Dominique as a second-hander. Her beliefs and values are not hand-me-downs from others. While many of her actions could lead one to think otherwise, what is crucial is that her course does not stem from doubts about her own judgment or worth. (Contrast Keating in this regard.) Why does she work for the *Banner*? It is the quintessential embodiment of the second-handed culture that she believes cannot be defeated, so she immerses herself in its dreck to dull its power to hurt her. Why does she marry Keating? To punish herself, she says (apparently, for the "foolish" idealism of valuing things [181]). Why does she marry Wynand? As a means of self-destruction (448). His career makes a mockery of all true values; by becoming "Mrs. Wynand Papers" (449), Dominique thinks she can kill her own capacity to value. Why does she fight Roark? The answer here is more complex. Dominique's overarching desire is to protect the good from desecration. (She destroys her statue of Helios, for instance, to save it from the worse fate of degradation at the hands of others.) Her crusade against Roark is but the most dramatic example of this. Believing that he cannot succeed in the long run, Dominique thinks that she can hasten his defeat by deflecting commissions and thereby spare him greater suffering (310, 375). At one level, Dominique is attempting to convince herself that her idealism is not viable; Roark's failure would reinforce her malevolent universe premise. At the same time, however, the part of Dominique that prays that he cannot be destroyed seeks to be proven wrong and to have her idealism vindicated.

What is salient is that Dominique at no point concedes the propriety of the second-handers' ways. Others' views do not shake her certainty about what is real or what is valuable one inch. She simply miscalculates the power of false ideas. Through first-handed methods, she reaches a false conclusion about the efficacy of those methods. This is a serious mistake, carrying significant consequences, but it is not a reflection of second-handedness.

Dominique's admission that to want something would make her dependent on other people (143) reveals her central mistake. In fact, by denying herself *for that reason*, she unwittingly gives others power and makes herself dependent on them. She thinks that she attains "freedom" by wanting nothing (144), yet this abandonment of her values only shackles her course to the parameters set by others. Unlike Keating, who credits others' opinions as the definitive standard of value, Dominique openly loathes them. The intensity of her distress at others' attitudes, however, reveals that she accords undue significance to their views. Dominique's Stoddard testimony, condemning Roark for "casting pearls without getting even a pork chop in return," implies that creators need something from second-handers (356). They do not. She may be right that most men are not worthy of Roark's building, but he does not build *for* them, at root. Their worthiness is beside the point.

Roark, of course, realizes this from the outset. Eventually, Dominique learns it as well. "You must learn not to be afraid of the world," he tells her when she informs him of her marriage to Keating. "Not to be held by it as you are now" (376). When she visits Roark at his worksite in Ohio, she likens it to his exile in the quarry (462). Whereas she cannot bear to watch him reduced to such pedestrian projects, he accepts them without resentment, for he simply loves the work, the designing and building. He realizes in this encounter that Dominique is not ready to be with him because, having inquired closely about his most incidental contact with strangers, she remains consumed with others' response; she is "still afraid of lunch wagons and windows" (463). They cannot be together, he explains, gesturing to indicate the streets, "Until you stop hating all this, stop being afraid of it, learn not to notice it" (483). When Dominique asks, "What are you waiting for?" Roark replies simply that he is not waiting (466). The reader observes that he is quietly but persistently doing all he can, every day, to shape the world to his liking. The real question is: what is Dominique waiting for? She is the one who has postponed pursuing her values (including Roark) and thereby prevents her own happiness.

Though Dominique tries for a long time to adopt some of the methods of second-handers, suppressing her own judgment to accede to others' standards, this course does not numb her pain and does not bring her happiness.[37] Her marriages do not extinguish her capacity to value. Try as she might to resist it, her idealism is undiminished. Moreover, Dominique observes Roark succeeding—flourishing despite tremendous external obstacles: indifference, hostility, even organized campaigns mounted to defeat him. He is as uncompromising an idealist as one could imagine, yet he is happy, succeeding *on his terms*. Roark is a walking refutation of the malevolent universe premise.

Dominique learns, from her own experience and from Roark, that she is the one who has miscalculated. Happiness does not depend on the world's endorsement, and the independent person *can* succeed. The action that signals her liberation is her complicity in carrying out the Cortlandt explosion. Here, she unequivocally allies herself with Roark against the standards of society and takes action in pursuit of *her* values. While in the past, Dominique was afraid of sharing Roark with others, she now advertises their relationship to the press (668–69). Even her anger at Wynand for yielding to the strikers reflects her finally full and unqualified recognition that integrity *is* possible and should be demanded.

Dominique learns that happiness does not require the surrender of one's ideals and that no good can come from such surrender. What Roark's independence and integrity and success demonstrate is that idealism and reality are not in conflict.

*   *   *

When the boy on the bike sees Monadnock Valley, he gains the "courage to face a lifetime" (506). Roark does not seek to inspire anyone.[38] He simply leads his life. By doing so in a first-hand, fully human way, however, he confirms the spirit of youth (which is what Ayn Rand once identified as the source of her novel's enduring appeal).[39] This spirit is "a sense of enormous expectation, the sense that one's life is important, that great achievements are within one's capacity, and that great things lie ahead" (xi). Through his unwavering independence, Roark shows that all great things are possible. Indeed, for Roark himself, the riches of happiness are not merely possible; they are realized. It *is* a benevolent universe. And independence is essential to reap its boundless rewards.[40]

NOTES

1. See Ayn Rand, "Introduction," *The Virtue of Selfishness* (New York: Signet, 1964), vii–xii, and "The Objectivist Ethics," *The Virtue of Selfishness*, 13–39.

2. Rand, "The Objectivist Ethics," 28.

3. For more on the nature and various types of second-handedness, see Leonard Peikoff, *Objectivism: The Philosophy of Ayn Rand* (New York: Dutton, 1991), 253 and 258. Also see Tara Smith, *Ayn Rand's Normative Ethics: The Virtuous Egoist* (New York: Cambridge University Press, 2006), chapter 5.

4. Rand, "The Argument from Intimidation," *The Virtue of Selfishness*, 165.

5. See Rand, "The Argument from Intimidation," 165, and David Harriman, ed., *Journals of Ayn Rand* (New York: Dutton, 1997), 678.

6. Rand, "Introduction," *The Virtue of Selfishness*, xi, emphasis in original.

7. For more on the independent person's proper relationships with others, see Smith, *Ayn Rand's Normative Ethics*, chapter 5.

8. Peikoff, *Objectivism*, 251.

9. In his final courtroom defense speech, Roark says a good deal that clarifies Rand's view, 677–85. For discussion of the ballyhooed notion of man's interdependence, see Peikoff, *Objectivism*, 257–58, and Smith, *Ayn Rand's Normative Ethics*, chapter 5.

10. See Rand, "The Objectivist Ethics," Peikoff, *Objectivism*, 206–49, and Tara Smith, *Viable Values: A Study of Life as the Root and Reward of Morality* (Lanham, MD: Rowman & Littlefield, 2000), 83–151.

11. Strictly, a thing does need to be recognized by a person as a value in order to be a value, for him. See Peikoff, *Objectivism*, 241–43. For discussion of the optional values that can objectively vary for different individuals, see Smith, *Viable Values*, 99–101, 127–28.

12. For more on the basic nature of rationality, see Peikoff, *Objectivism*, 116–21, 152–63, and Smith, *Ayn Rand's Normative Ethics*, chapter 3.

13. The necessary first-hand confirmations do not require that a person attempt to become a jack of all trades and eschew the knowledge of experts. For more on this aspect of independence, see Peikoff, *Objectivism*, 257–58, and Smith, *Ayn Rand's Normative Ethics*, chapter 5.

14. For discussion of this principle, see Peikoff, *Objectivism*, 342–43. Rand uses this term in journal entries pertaining to *Atlas Shrugged*. See Harriman, *Journals of Ayn Rand*, 425, 555–56. The benevolent universe premise is reflected, among many places in *Atlas Shrugged*, in Ragnar's response to Dagny's question about the risks he takes, in Galt's explanation of his attitude toward pain, and in Dagny's realization

that "we never had to take any of it seriously." *Atlas Shrugged* (originally published 1957), 35th anniversary edition (New York: Dutton, 1992), 759, 959, 702.

15. Independence and integrity are both major virtues, in Rand's moral theory. Along with honesty, justice, productiveness, and pride, they are reflections of the fundamental virtue of rationality; each, to be fully practiced, requires each of the others. See discussion of all the virtues in Peikoff, *Objectivism*, 250–324, and Smith, *Ayn Rand's Normative Ethics*.

16. Rand, "The Ethics of Emergencies," *The Virtue of Selfishness*, 50. Also see Galt's speech in *Atlas Shrugged*, 1028.

17. For explanation of how an egoist can be willing to die for another person, see Rand, "The Ethics of Emergencies." Related discussion is also in Smith, *Viable Values*, 143–45. On friendship more generally, see Smith, "Egoistic Friendship," *American Philosophical Quarterly* 42, no. 4 (October 2005): 263–77.

18. *Atlas Shrugged* includes several passages that emphasize the necessity of seeing for oneself. See especially the exchanges between Dagny and Akston and between Dagny and Mulligan, concerning her decision about whether to remain in the valley, 735, 802.

19. His view is akin to the philosopher Thomas Hobbes' brand of egoism.

20. It is because conventional notions of selfishness do not truly advance a person's self-interest that Rand titles one of her books *The Virtue of Selfishness*, rather than adopting some more palatable label for her view and surrendering the term "selfishness" to those who do not understand its true nature and requirements. She unqualifiedly advocates each person's pursuit of his happiness and she argues that only true selfishness—the rational selfishness of the independent individual—actually advances that end.

21. A full defense of this last claim is beyond the scope of this paper. Since altruism is not the only alternative to egoism (sacrifice for its own sake or for the sake of God, for instance, are also possible), the fact that altruism destroys independence does not by itself entail the stronger claim that independence requires egoism. Any call for sacrifice is equally incompatible with independence, however, as should become clear as we focus on the conflict between independence and altruism.

22. In her journals, Rand describes Toohey as having an "insane will to power." Harriman, *Journals of Ayn Rand*, 102.

23. The word's French and Latin roots are given in the *Oxford English Dictionary* (New York: Oxford University Press, 1971).

24. Rand, "Faith and Force: The Destroyers of the Modern World," *Philosophy: Who Needs It* (New York: Bobbs-Merrill, 1982), 74. Also see "The Objectivist Ethics," 37–38. This characterization is hardly peculiar to Rand. See, for instance, among contemporary academic ethicists, Thomas Nagel, *The Possibility of Altruism* (Oxford: Clarendon Press, 1970), 79; E.J. Bond, "Theories of the Good," *Encyclopedia of Ethics*, ed. Lawrence C. Becker (New York: Garland, 1992), vol. 1, 410; Burton F. Porter, *The Good Life* (New York: Ardley House, 1995), 283; Lawrence Blum, "Altruism," *Encyclopedia of Ethics*, ed. Becker vol. 1, 35.

25. This way of couching Toohey's attitude was suggested to me by Allan Gotthelf.

26. Toohey bears an obvious resemblance, in his deepest motivation, to James Taggart in *Atlas Shrugged*. In essays, Rand observes that "The advocates of altruism are motivated not by compassion for suffering, but by hatred for man's life" and that

"Altruism holds *death* as its ultimate goal and standard of value." "An Untitled Letter," *Philosophy: Who Needs It*, 123; "The Objectivist Ethics," 38, emphasis in original.

27. An egoist can sometimes choose, consistently with his self-interest, to do things for others. Kindness and charity, for instance, do not contradict rational egoism so long as they do not involve self-sacrifice. See Rand, "The Ethics of Emergencies," Smith, *Ayn Rand's Normative Ethics*, chapter 10, and "Virtues or Vices? Kindness, Generosity, and Charity," lecture, audio available from Ayn Rand Bookstore (www.aynrandbookstore.com).

28. Rand, *Atlas Shrugged*, 1031.

29. For discussion of the threat that independent judgment poses to collectivist political ideals, see Onkar Ghate, "Breaking the Metaphysical Chains of Dictatorship: Free Will and Determinism in *Anthem*," in Robert Mayhew, ed., *Essays on Ayn Rand's* Anthem (Lanham, MD: Lexington Books, 2005), 225–54.

30. This paragraph is indebted to Darryl Wright's lecture on "Reason and Selfishness," audio available from Ayn Rand Bookstore.

31. Rand, *Atlas Shrugged*, 1030. Because human action is volitional and because a person's mind and body are an integrated, indivisible whole, no moral code could call for the performance of certain physical actions (such as giving money to the poor) without correlatively (at least implicitly) calling for the performance of certain kinds of mental actions (such as putting one's faith in god, dispensing with logical priorities, etc.).

32. Rand observes elsewhere that "Guilt is altruism's stock in trade, and the inducing of guilt is its only means of self-perpetuation." "Moral Inflation," Part II, *Ayn Rand Letter* III, 13, 2.

33. Rand identifies, among the principal consequences of altruism, lack of self-esteem and lack of respect for others. "The Ethics of Emergencies," 49.

34. This is not to say that anyone who chooses to commit suicide is altruistic or has reason to be altruistic. In certain circumstances, suicide can be a rational, egoistic choice. The point is simply that for a person who truly does not value his life, the suicidal nature of altruism would not render altruism irrational. For further discussion of the status of suicide in the Objectivist ethics, see Smith, *Viable Values*, pp. 143–45.

35. For a brief discussion of this, see Peikoff, "The Art of Thinking," lecture # 3, audio available from Ayn Rand Bookstore. (This topic occupies only a portion of that lecture.)

36. I employ "pessimism" here only as a convenient shorthand; strictly, pessimism is not the equivalent of the malevolent universe premise. See Peikoff, *Objectivism*, 343.

37. We should note, however, that her suppression of judgment is different from that of the typical second-hander, who has no independent judgment *to* suppress. Dominique judges continually, if often silently. Thanks to Greg Salmieri for pointing this out.

38. At one point, he remarks that he does not wish "to be the symbol of anything" (602).

39. Rand, "Introduction" to 1968 edition (xiii).

40. Thanks to Harry Binswanger, Allan Gotthelf, and Robert Mayhew for helpful discussions of my early ideas for this essay, and to Robert Mayhew, Greg Salmieri, and Ann Ciccolella for helpful comments on a draft of it.

14

Roark's Integrity

Dina Schein

". . . make your own adaptation of the Classic motive to the façade. . . ."

"No," said Roark. . . .

"It's sheer insanity," Weidler moaned. "I want you. We want your build-ing. You need the commission. Do you have to be quite so fanatical and selfless about it?" . . .

Roark smiled. He looked down at his drawings. . . . He said: "That was the most selfish thing you've ever seen a man do." (196–98)

Since integrity is loyalty to one's values, Roark is a perfect model of a man of integrity. His refusal of the Manhattan Bank Building commission on the Bank committee's terms is a particularly dramatic illustration of his in-tegrity: due to his desperate financial situation, not accepting this commis-sion makes it necessary for him to close down his office and to become a manual laborer in a granite quarry, perhaps never again to work in the ca-reer he passionately loves. Because Roark is willing to pay this price instead of accepting a seemingly minor alteration to his design, many readers of *The Fountainhead* might wonder whether he is being foolishly obstinate and might be tempted to agree with Weidler's assessment of his decision as "fa-natical and selfless." Roark's rebuttal that he acts in his own interest may ap-pear baffling.

Young readers of *The Fountainhead* are often confused about what exactly Roark gains by his refusal to compromise his convictions. As a veteran judge in the Ayn Rand Institute's essay contest on *The Fountainhead* for high school students, I have read many essays that state or imply that Roark is a failure as an architect, as his high standards drive away potential clients, but that his compensation for adhering to his principles is a feeling of inner satisfaction.

Even more knowledgeable students of Objectivism might accept to some extent the premise that life requires a trade-off between material success and spiritual fulfillment. Ayn Rand, however, rejects this premise, and so do her heroes. The events of Roark's life provide evidence that integrity is the recipe for both spiritual and physical well-being.

The purpose of this chapter is to show that Roark's refusal to compromise is a matter of self-preservation. I will show why the gain from staying loyal to one's rational convictions is inestimably greater than the alleged gain derived from betraying them or from not having any, and indicate that there is no rivalry between material and spiritual success. In the process the uniquely Objectivist identification of the nature and value of integrity will come to light.

In order to understand why Roark is loath to compromise his convictions, it is imperative to grasp what he is fighting for and how his values differ from those of conventional people. Roark becomes an architect because he wants to build things of beauty and to create comfortable and convenient buildings. What Roark loves about his work is the design, the solving of structural problems. This is the standard directing the jobs he takes. He goes to work for Cameron in order to complete his education in architectural design. Later he takes a job with Snyte, even though he wouldn't see his buildings erected, because "he would be free to design as he wished and he would have the experience of solving actual problems" (104). Clients are only the means to Roark's ultimate end: erecting functional and beautiful buildings (26).

By contrast, other architects believe that an architect's ultimate goal is not to build but to uphold traditions and to kowtow to clients. Architects such as Francon and Holcombe venerate Classical and Renaissance building styles simply because they are traditional. Snyte's eclecticism of architectural styles does not stem from his judgment that his buildings would be better were he to adopt selected features from various eras, but from the wish to get as many clients as he can by catering to many tastes. A few architects reject traditional styles, though not because they have found a better way to build. For example, Gus Webb negates the conventional, whatever it happens to be—from structural principles whose validity accounts for their longevity to good manners. The architectural avant-garde declares war on standards as such.

Roark's focus in his career is on the work of designing buildings. The joy he derives from his career comes from his work done his way. The other architects' focus in their profession is not on building but on pleasing other people—or displeasing them, in the case of the avant-garde.

This difference in focus is not confined to the realm of earning a living. The same orientation guides each man in his private life. Roark wants to find a soulmate with whom he would have an ecstatic lifelong romance. For friends Roark seeks similar-minded people whose company he could enjoy. At first glance, Roark's friends appear to have nothing in common. They range from a member of high society (Austen Heller) to a plain workman (Mike Donnigan), from one of the wealthiest men in America (Gail Wynand) to one of the poorest (Steven Mallory). What unites all these men is their professional competence and independent judgment. This is what attracts Roark to them. He seeks out a romantic partner and friends for his own enjoyment, rather than for show.

By contrast, the conventional men want the kind of spouse and friends whom their associates and society at large would expect and approve of, or whom they could manipulate for their own advancement. Keating gives up Catherine Halsey, the woman he loves, because his mother and society disapprove of her. Even though he fears Dominique, he seeks to marry her in order to advance in Francon's firm and because her beauty would make his colleagues jealous. Unlike Roark, Keating would never cultivate a friendship with a man like Mike Donnigan: Donnigan lacks wealth and prestige, has no connections of which Keating could take advantage, would not ask Keating for favors, and is contemptuous of Keating's incompetence and pretentiousness. Instead he cultivates friendships with men like Tim Davis, whom he does not respect and whom he chooses at the beginning of his career in order to take Davis's place in Francon's office. He derives little pleasure from the company of his friends, for he does not pick them for his own enjoyment. He marries Dominique not to be happy, but to garner the envy of other people.

What is the difference between Roark's values and the pursuits of second-handers? Roark is committed to identifying and embracing the things that would bring him happiness. Second-handers pursue what other people want them to pursue. Instead of identifying their own preferences, they sniff out other people's desires and imitate them. Imitation governs even their choice of housing and recreation. Keating wants to move to the country not because he would enjoy the quiet of the surroundings or the beauties of nature, but because "everybody that's anybody" lives in the country (423). He wants to take up horseback riding, even though he dislikes it, in order to imitate Gordon Prescott (423). The second-handers have no values of their own. They substitute mimicry for valuing. Because the purpose of their pursuits is not their own enjoyment, none of their pursuits genuinely matters to them.

This is the key to the difference between the depth of Roark's emotions and those of the second-handers. Roark loves the entire process of designing and erecting a building. He is hard at work at each of his construction sites. His joy in his work is visible to everyone from his employees to his clients. What he feels for his work is "the combination of holy sacrament, Indian torture and sexual ecstasy" (252). Roark loves Dominique and so needs her as selfishly as he needs oxygen (376). He greatly respects his first employer and teacher Cameron. He loves Wynand as another self. Both his work and the special people in his life are profoundly important to him.

By contrast, Keating regards architecture as "a business like any other. . . . What's so damn sacred about it?" (352). After Francon establishes his professional reputation, he never bothers to design another building. Instead he spends his time entertaining clients and basking in his colleagues' admiration and envy. Clearly, what attracts the conventional architects to architecture is not the work. The design itself is for them simply an unpleasant chore. Despite being focused on other people, the second-handers do not love anyone. Emotions between spouses in the few conventional marriages presented in the novel are predominantly negative: Eve Layton despises her husband, Mitch; Keating fears Dominique; Ralston and Kiki Holcombe do not exchange a single affectionate word or gesture (254–65).

Roark is passionate; the second-handers do not care deeply about anything. The presence or absence of strong emotions stems from a person's being value-oriented, or failing to be so. Roark has values of his own, which are intimately connected to his happiness. This is why he is unwilling to surrender them. The second-handers do not have any genuine values of their own, so they are not committed to any of their particular pursuits or pastimes. They willingly change their preferences—e.g., put up a modernistic building instead of a Classical one to please a client—because neither the former nor the latter selection is their own first-handed choice.

While readers of *The Fountainhead* admire Roark for remaining true to his values, some might be amazed that he is not tempted to compromise his principles, even when the stakes are high. The reason for Roark's lack of temptation may be found in his explanation to Stanton's Dean: "I have, let's say, sixty years to live. Most of that time will be spent working. I've chosen the work I want to do. If I find no joy in it, then I'm only condemning myself to sixty years of torture. And I can find the joy only if I do my work in the best way possible to me" (24). Building Renaissance villas (à la Ralston Holcombe), Victorian mansions (à la Peter Keating), and skyscrapers that look like ancient Greek temples would be torture for Roark, because such buildings lack artistic integrity. Similarly Roark would derive no pleasure from having a showcase wife, a house to make the neighbors jealous, or membership in elite country clubs, for he considers such objects and activities to be of no value to himself. He is not tempted to live like the others because he knows that he has nothing to gain by doing so.

Roark staunchly supports his convictions in the face of opposition. But the mere fact that a man refuses to yield is not yet proof that he has good reasons for standing his ground. Children often stubbornly cling to range-of-the-moment desires. How does Roark's resolve to uphold his principles at any price differ from childish obstinacy? To answer this question we need to look at the origin of his values. Roark does not adopt them at random.

In his work he wishes to erect the best buildings he can. In order to become a competent architect, Roark has to give a great deal of thought to what makes a building structurally and esthetically good. At age twenty-two, during his interview with Stanton's Dean, he explains to the Dean what is wrong with imitating traditions of the past (22–25). Roark's knowledge and argument are strikingly deep for a young person; they required years of concerted thinking. He identifies the correct architectural standard, "form follows function," and figures out how to achieve it. The same depth of thought characterizes Roark's approach to other issues. He thinks about what motivates people in their approaches to life and formulates what he calls the Principle Behind the Dean. This allows him to judge people well and to pick out the ones whom he can respect and love. Roark identifies what he wants and what makes these things objectively good. His values are products of his own judgment.

We can now fully answer the question that befuddles some readers of *The Fountainhead*: why does Roark not agree to the demands of the Manhattan Bank committee, perhaps risking never working as an architect again? To those who regard affixing a Classical façade onto a skyscraper as a matter of mere cosmetic detail, Roark's decision might indeed appear to be foolish obstinacy. However, what is actually at stake is something far greater. Because the purpose of a skyscraper is different from the purpose of an ancient Greek temple, its look should be different, too. Roark knows how to erect a functional and beautiful building. Agreeing to the Bank committee's demands to put a Classical façade on a skyscraper, when he knows that such construction is worthless, would be a declaration that his judgment is irrelevant, that it cannot distinguish truth from falsehood. Roark is not quibbling over unimportant detail but facing the choice to rely on or to negate his own mind. This is a fundamental choice. A reader must grasp this if he is to understand that Roark's refusal to compromise his principles is a matter of self-preservation.

A person would not be tempted to eat a mushroom he knew to be poisonous, because the consequences of ignoring his judgment would be death. It is just as important for Roark not to jettison his convictions, for he knows that the result would be the kind of living death that second-handers experience.

This is why Roark is married to his ideals. His reasoned judgment is invested in his work. His independent thinking and evaluation are the cause of the passion he feels for all his values.

By contrast, Keating, Francon, Snyte, etc. compromise readily because they have no independent judgment.[1] They do not identify what makes a building sound, how to have a rewarding marriage or a stable friendship;

instead they try to please other people. Thus they have no objective standards in their work or in their private lives. Because they have no standards, they are not committed to anything. If a person pursues a goal merely to impress the neighbors, his self is not invested in the pursuit. Hence he would lack the fire for it, which would sap his motivation to fight for it. Why fight for something if you do not know whether it is valuable or worthless? Independent judgment is a precondition both of having solid convictions and of the strength to defend them.

Roark fights for his values and eventually wins. He is acquitted in the Cortlandt trial and penetrates the barrier of professional opposition. But suppose that circumstances had turned against him and he had not broken through professionally? Even in such a case Roark would have been better off than Keating, Holcombe, Francon, Webb, et al. are at the peak of their careers. Any enjoyment Roark has in life—from the challenge of solving architectural problems, to the rapture of his love affair with Dominique, to the hours he spends with his friends, to the pleasure he finds in contemplating a good work of art—stems from the conclusions of his mind. In a quarry or in jail, he would have something the second-handers could never have: the exercise of his own judgment, a correct identification of what success requires, genuine values, and consequently an efficacy at dealing with the world and a strong sense of self. Whether or not Roark succeeds at a particular endeavor, he has the roots of such success: his own reasoning mind. The riches and prestige of conventional architects are worthless without this foundation.

Roark has the preconditions of success, yet the conventional architects surpass him in wealth. So it may still seem as though life requires a trade-off between spiritual fulfillment and material success. By remaining true to his principles, however, Roark maximizes his chances of having material prosperity as well. To make his work remunerative, he needs to find people who recognize its value and are willing to hire him. For this to happen, it must be clear what sort of work Roark does, so that those who value it would know that he provides it and could contract with him for his services.

He explains to Heller his strategy for acquiring clients: "What can I tell people in order to get commissions? I can only show my work. If they don't hear that, they won't hear anything I say. . . . I'm waiting [for my] kind of people. . . . There will be thousands passing by your house and by the gas station. If out of those thousands, one stops and sees it—that's all I need" (159–60). His statement turns out to be prophetic. Roark gets his third commission, the Fargo store, after Fargo drives by the Gowan station and sees the Heller house, then bribes Heller's cook to see its interior (167). Even after Roark is obliged to close his office due to lack of commissions, Enright hunts him down after Enright sees the Fargo store and Roark's other buildings (219). He gets commissions for the Norris house, the Cord Build-

ing, the Aquitania Hotel, and Wynand's private country residence as a result
of these men seeing his previous buildings (308, 311–13, 517–18). The
competence of his construction serves to advertise his services.

Because Roark has objective value to offer his clients, he benefits from
those clients who can identify that value. Other people's first-handed judgment is thus good for him. Kent Lansing states to Roark what he seeks in an
architect: "I want a good hotel, and I have certain standards of what is good,
and they're my own, and you're the one who can give me what I want"
(313). Because Lansing is a man of independent judgment, he fights for
Roark and eventually secures the Aquitania Hotel commission for him. As
long as Roark is able to find enough clients of that type, he will prosper.
That is why Roark seeks to convince, not to flatter or bully, appealing only
to his potential clients' reason instead of to their desires to impress their
neighbors, and why he seeks only reason from them.

In order to attract his kind of client, it is in Roark's interest not to compromise the purity of his work. Were he to jettison the principles of
proper construction and esthetics, the clients who want functionality and
beauty in their buildings—the only kind of clients who could make it
possible for him to make a living by designing buildings the way he wants
to—would pass him by. Compromising his artistic integrity would be utterly impractical.

This is also why the solid wall of opposition raised against him has no
power to throttle his career. How much harm can Roark's enemies cause
him? At worst, the disapproval of the AGA, of the Wynand papers, and of
Toohey would deter a great number of potential clients from seeking his
services. But Roark would have nothing to gain from such clients anyway:
those who regard the AGA, the Wynand papers, and Toohey as architectural
authorities do not exercise their own judgment, and therefore could not see
the value that Roark has to offer. Were Roark to get their commissions, they
would stop his work by involving him in endless debates trying to make
him change his designs for invalid reasons or even bringing lawsuits against
him, as the cases of the Sanborn House and the Stoddard Temple make
clear (167–70, 38–40).[2] But not even Toohey's most concerted effort can
drive away from Roark those clients who do think for themselves and who
see the value of his services. Men of independent judgment, such as Heller,
Enright, and Lansing, will seek him out, because Toohey's opinions have no
power to sway them.

The only way in which Toohey et al. could destroy Roark would be by
making it impossible for people to contract with Roark for his services,
which could be accomplished only if they had the power of governmen-
tal decree behind them.[3] But as long as men live in a free society, they can
act on their judgment, and the machinations of such evil people as
Toohey can have no long-lasting or fundamental effects. This is why Ayn

Rand regards political freedom as an essential of human life. In a free society, she argues, a man's

> success depends on the objective value of his work and on the rationality of
> those who recognize that value. When men are free to trade, with reason and
> reality as their only arbiter, when no man may use physical force to extort the
> consent of another, it is the best product and the best judgment that win in
> every field of human endeavor, and raise the standard of living.[4]

Roark's ultimate success is not due to Ayn Rand's fondness for her hero
and happy endings. Rather it is the necessary outcome of Roark's allegiance
to rational principles. Roark wishes to succeed, so he identifies the principles of action that lead to success and adheres to them, recognizing that betraying them would cause him to fail. Rand rejects all forms of the mind/
body dichotomy, a view entrenched in the history of philosophy, that forces
a man to choose between the necessities of self-esteem and material well-
being. In a revolutionary identification, she argues that integrity is the allegiance to the only guide to success of both mind and body.[5]

   The real choice confronting Roark—and each of us—is: a fulfilling life of
spiritual and material values versus an existence characterized by emptiness,
boredom, and self-invisibility. Integrity, one's loyalty to rational principles,
is the means of gaining the former. The man who understands this would
not be tempted to stray from his convictions, because there are no values of
any kind to be gained by it.[6]

NOTES

   1. Some readers may wonder if Holcombe, who refuses to build in any other style
but Renaissance (114), has integrity. His preference for this style, however, is merely
stubborn adherence to a certain tradition, not the result of independent judgment.

   2. Roark's client for the Sanborn house, Mr. Sanborn, is a man of independent
judgment. The trouble comes from his wife, who wishes to impress her neighbors.

   3. If Toohey had been commissar in charge of building, with absolute political
power to determine which architects were allowed to design what buildings, Roark
would have been a tragic hero, like Edmund Rostand's Cyrano de Bergerac or Ayn
Rand's Kira Argounova. He would have failed to achieve his values existentially but
kept his integrity intact.

   4. Ayn Rand, *For the New Intellectual* (New York: New American Library, 1961), 26.

   5. For an excellent discussion of the virtue of integrity and of the practicality of
virtue, see Leonard Peikoff, *Objectivism: The Philosophy of Ayn Rand* (New York: Dutton, 1993), 259–67 and 326–35.

   6. I wish to thank Tore Boeckmann and Robert Mayhew for their comments on
an earlier draft of this chapter.

15

A Moral Dynamiting

Amy Peikoff

> *I agreed to design Cortlandt for the purpose of seeing it erected as I designed it and for no other reason. That was the price I set for my work. I was not paid.* (684)
>
> —Howard Roark

In the climax of *The Fountainhead*, architect Howard Roark dynamites Cortlandt Homes, a housing project that he designed. This climax has, not surprisingly, created a huge controversy. Some readers find it difficult to understand why Roark is justified in his action. Others attribute his behavior to Rand's Romanticism, and therefore do not think it is necessary for Rand to offer a fully plausible justification. These latter are, however, forgetting that Rand is a Romantic *Realist*. This means that for Rand to succeed, she must show why her heroes are morally justified, and also—to use Rand's term—"psychologically justified"[1] in doing what they do.

The basic moral justification for Roark's dynamiting Cortlandt consists in the fact that the government destroys the artistic integrity of Cortlandt in violation of its contract with Peter Keating, thereby stealing Roark's intellectual property while permitting him no legal recourse. The result is that Roark is forced to act as an altruist, to sacrifice his creative work to the need of those who would live in Cortlandt. "They took the benefit of my work and made me contribute it as a gift. But I am not an altruist. I do not contribute gifts of this nature" (684). Roark properly[2] rejects the altruist claim that others have an unearned right to his time, energy, or achievements, "No matter who makes the claim, how large their number or how great their need" (684). When the State forcibly appropriates his design on others' behalf, he is justified in acting so as to both defend the integrity of his own work and withdraw from others the benefits of that part of his design which has been left intact.

> [Cortlandt] was a double monster. In form and in implication. I had to blast both. The form was mutilated by two second-handers who assumed the right to improve upon that which they had not made and could not equal. They were permitted to do it by the general implication that the altruistic purpose of the building suspended all rights and that I had no claim to stand against it. (683–84)

That Roark is morally justified in dynamiting Cortlandt does not mean, however, that he is morally required to do it. The virtue of integrity—"never sacrific[ing] one's convictions to the opinions or wishes of others"[3]—demands that Roark never voluntarily agree to changes that desecrate his design. It does not demand that he break the law when others make such changes without his knowledge or consent. This is why Rand must show why Roark is also psychologically justified in dynamiting Cortlandt.

Rand builds her case throughout the novel, showing that Roark is willing to endure tremendous hardships—forgoing his degree in architecture, living in poverty, working in a granite quarry—in order to preserve his ability to do his work his way.[4] She also shows that Roark has an enduring interest in the problem of low-cost housing (576), an interest that goes back at least as far as his discussions with Henry Cameron about the efficient use of new materials. In other words, she shows that Cortlandt is not just a tremendous achievement, but also an achievement of importance to him. Rand's summation comes in the form of Roark's reaction upon seeing building one of Cortlandt.

> Roark stood across the space of the future road before the first house of Cortlandt. He stood straight, the muscles of his throat pulled, his wrists held down and away from his body, as he would have stood before a firing squad. (609)

Roark does not want to live in a world in which that building is allowed to exist, both because of what it is, and because of what it demonstrates about his ability to pursue his values in the world as it might become. In addition, while Roark is willing to go to jail if necessary, as "[his] act of loyalty [to his country], [his] refusal to live or work in what has taken its place" (685), he does not believe that this is the inevitable outcome. He thinks he has a chance of winning (654) and thereby demonstrating that it is possible to preserve a world in which he can achieve his values.

In light of this, it is interesting to learn that, for at least one day, Rand considered writing a different climax in which Dominique Wynand kills Ellsworth Toohey. In this alternative scenario Roark still must defend himself in court (and presumably make a powerful courtroom speech), because he takes responsibility for the murder and forces Dominique to remain silent. Why would Rand entertain such an alternative? Perhaps it was because "Many years [after writing *The Fountainhead*] she remembered hesitating over her original idea for the climax. . . . She was concerned that it might be difficult to make 'plausible objectively' why Roark would be justified in such a dynamiting."[5] After doing some more thinking about her idea, and trying it out on a friend whom she described as an "arch enemy of Romanticism," Rand decided she could "sell it," i.e., "justify it psychologically."[6] While at first she found the task "formidable," she says that, "As [she] progressed with the book, it became easier and easier."[7]

The moral justification for Roark's dynamiting Cortlandt depends on the fact that he has no *legal* recourse available to him. Accordingly, I will spend much of the rest of this chapter discussing what should be Roark's legal case against the government. I will present the legally relevant facts, explain why a proper court would grant Roark an injunction for the destruction or modification of Cortlandt, and show that, in fact, Roark could get no such remedy from a United States court, either at the time Rand was writing *The Fountainhead* or today.

In Part 4, chapter 8 of *The Fountainhead*, Roark enters into a contract with Peter Keating: Roark will design a low-rent housing project according to certain specifications. Keating will have the right to represent the design as his own and offer it to the government, which has been reviewing designs for such a project. If Keating convinces the government to adopt the design, he may keep any monies or honors for himself. In exchange, Keating promises that the housing project, Cortlandt Homes, will be built exactly as Roark designs it.

During their negotiations, Roark ensures that Keating understands the nature of their bargain. He asks Keating to make him an offer, to name something that will persuade him to design Cortlandt. Roark then rejects, in turn, a few of the usual enticements—money, saving another's (Keating's) life, helping the poor—which would persuade another architect to work on such a project. Finally Keating realizes the one thing that would motivate *Roark* to work on Cortlandt. "You will love designing it," he says (577). Keating insists that he understands with his "whole mind" that the only thing he can offer Roark is a guarantee that the project will be built exactly as designed; he agrees that he has "no right to [Roark's design] except on these terms" (580). Roark realizes that it will not be easy for Keating to keep his end of the bargain. Just before the two sign the deal, he advises Keating, "get yourself an ironclad contract with your bosses and then [be prepared to] fight every bureaucrat that comes along every five minutes for the next year or more" (580). To the extent that this is possible, Keating understands his contractual obligation.

As readers of *The Fountainhead* know, Keating succeeds in getting the government to accept Roark's design and to sign a contract limiting the terms of its use. He also does his best to fight his government employers "against every possible objection" to the design (594). Nonetheless, Cortlandt is not built as Roark intends it to be. When Roark returns to New York after a vacation, he finds the first building nearly completed.

> The building had the skeleton of what Roark had designed, with the remnants of ten different breeds piled on the lovely symmetry of the bones. He saw the economy of plan preserved, but the expanse of incomprehensible features added; the variety of modeled masses gone, replaced by the monotony of brutish cubes; a new wing added, with a vaulted roof, bulging out of a wall like a tumor, containing a gymnasium; strings of balconies added, made of metal stripes painted a violent blue; corner windows without a purpose; an angle cut off for a useless door, with a round metal awning supported by a pole, like a haberdashery in the Broadway district; three vertical bands of brick, leading from nowhere to nowhere; the general style of what the profession called "Bronx Modern"; a panel of bas-relief over the main entrance, representing a mass of muscle which could be discerned as either three or four bodies, one of them with an arm raised, holding a screwdriver. (609)

The changes are the work of "associate designers" Gordon L. Prescott and Gus Webb. Toohey uses his connections to have them added to the payroll for the purpose of "building up their reputation" (609). Prescott and Webb, however, are not content with a mere boost to their reputations. When asked by Keating to defend their proposed changes, Prescott answers, "We want to express our individuality too" (610). The two associate designers, along with an "amused" Toohey and an incomprehensible "entanglement of responsibility" among the government officials assigned to the project, manage to sap whatever is left of Keating's strength. "He went from office to office, arguing, threatening, pleading," all to no avail (610). Soon, he is unable to fight any longer.

In a proper society, the laws of contract and copyright would offer Keating and, more importantly, Roark the legal right to demand the building be torn down and, if it was to be rebuilt, for it to be rebuilt exactly as Roark designed it. The law would recognize Roark's right to specify the conditions on which others may use his intellectual property, because it would recognize that the very possibility of Cortlandt is a result of Roark's design. Roark's design, in turn, would not have existed but for his knowledge, skill, creativity, and effort. This is true of all intellectual property; in *The Fountainhead* Rand shows how this applies to the case of Cortlandt.

Only Roark is able to solve the technical problem of low-cost housing presented by Cortlandt. By the time Keating comes to see Roark, we are told, several architects have already tried—and failed—to solve it (571–72).

Moreover, Roark is able to solve the problem precisely because he is the only architect who rejects the practice of copying elements from historical structures; he instead creates entirely new structures that are designed so as to best exploit the unique features of each site and capacities of available building materials. Thus, while it is debatable when and to what extent a second-hander's work deserves to be called "intellectual property,"[8] Rand makes it clear that this is not true of Roark's work. His design for Cortlandt, although an abstract entity, is just as much his property as is any piece of land or physical object.

> [W]hat [a] patent or copyright protects is not [a] physical object as such, but the *idea* which it embodies. By forbidding an unauthorized reproduction of the object, the law declares, in effect, that the physical labor of copying is not the source of the object's value, that that value is created by the originator of the idea and may not be used without his consent; thus the law establishes the property right of a mind to that which it has brought into existence.[9]

For bringing the value of Cortlandt into existence Roark deserves to have absolute control over the use of his design, as he demands.

Any intellectual property right that Keating has to offer the government is subject to the condition under which he acquired it: that Cortlandt be built exactly as Roark designed it. Once the government mangles Roark's design and begins to build, therefore, it breaches its contract with Keating and loses the right to use the design. As a consequence, either Keating or Roark (as third-party beneficiary) should be able to sue for breach of contract or, in the alternative, for copyright infringement.

However, neither the United States as depicted in *The Fountainhead*, nor as it existed at the time Rand wrote the novel, nor even as it exists today, would offer the legal relief to which Roark is entitled. "All right, go ahead, try to sue the government. Try it" (610). This is what Keating is told when he tries to invoke the terms of his contract. In the 1940s, when Rand was writing *The Fountainhead*, it was, in fact, unlikely that the case would ever have been heard. Just because one made a contract with the government did not mean that one could sue the government for breach of contract. For the federal government to be subject to lawsuit—i.e., for courts to have jurisdiction over such a case—it had to waive its sovereign immunity. Thus if Keating were to sue for breach of contract in a court of law, all the government would need to do is refuse to waive its sovereign immunity, and the case would be dismissed.

Note that Rand does not mention explicitly the possibility of suing for copyright infringement.[10] This may have been because, at the time she was writing, suing the government for infringement of copyright in an architectural work was even more hopeless than suing it for breach of contract. Of course the issue of sovereign immunity would apply to suits not only under contract law, but also under copyright law. In addition, in the 1940s—and for several decades thereafter—the law did not treat the act of erecting a building as constituting an infringement of copyright in an architectural design.[11] One could infringe a copyright in an architectural work only by making a copy of the design itself, where the copy was made in the same medium as the one in which the author first physically embodied the design. So, for example, if an architectural design were embodied in a two-dimensional drawing, only a two-dimensional copy of that drawing would be held to infringe one's copyright in the work. Thus, even though the Cortlandt building was clearly taken from Roark's original design, the act of building it would be held not to violate his copyright.

Today's legal system would treat Keating's and Roark's claims more favorably. With respect to the breach of contract claim, Keating would have a better chance of having his case heard in court. In 1978, Congress passed the Contract Disputes Act,[12] a generalized waiver of federal sovereign immunity with respect to cases arising from breaches of certain government contracts. Whether the Act applies to a particular contract, however, turns on factors like (1) whether the funds used to pay the contractor are "appropriated" or "nonappropriated" and (2) if nonappropriated, whether the contract was made with certain agencies within the military or NASA.[13] While readers are no doubt thankful that Rand omitted such mind-numbing details from *The Fountainhead*, the fact that she did so means we cannot know whether Keating would have been able to sue the government for breach of contract in today's courts. One can nonetheless be sure that Keating, even if allowed to sue, would not have been able to obtain the proper remedy—the tearing down or rebuilding of Cortlandt—even today. A court might grant an injunction which would prevent the government from using Roark's design in building the rest of the project.[14] On a purely contract-based claim, however, it is likely that the best Keating could get for the desecration of Roark's design would be monetary damages.

In order for Roark to have any chance of obtaining the relief to which he is entitled, he would have to raise a claim under copyright law. Such a claim could be made today, thanks to Congress's passing the Architectural Works Copyright Protection Act,[15] which became effective in 1990. The Act provides that erecting a building using a copyrighted design, without permission, does constitute copyright infringement. Accordingly, Roark could argue that, due to its breach of contract with Keating, the government did not have the right to use Roark's plans, and therefore its building of Cortlandt infringed his copyright. Alternatively, he could invoke the concept, now recognized in many areas of copyright law, of an author's "moral right" to the artistic integrity of his creation, which the government clearly violated.

It is, however, doubtful whether either of these claims would result in Roark's being awarded the proper remedy. First, with respect to the *federal government's* taking of a copyrighted design, a court would probably treat the act as it would any other government taking of private property, and hold that Roark would be entitled solely to "just compensation."[16] Moreover, it is unlikely that even a private party who erects a building in violation of copyright would, in today's courts, be ordered to destroy or rebuild the building. Writes one commentator, "Once construction has begun, determining the appropriate remedy is much more complex. Destruction should be available only when it would not cause unreasonable economic waste."[17] The commentator goes on to say that destruction of even a single-family home would likely be seen as unreasonable economic waste. One federal district court refused to grant an injunction that would require "destruction or modification of [an] infringing building" because, in its view, "the plaintiff's injury can be adequately remedied by monetary compensation, and . . . there is no danger that additional infringements will occur."[18] Note that in that case, both litigants were private parties and the building at issue was a computer center for the defendant's business. Thus it seems that, even when the building has no apparent "altruistic purpose" (683), a federal court will refuse to grant the relief an architect deserves. Surely, then, the destruction of a nearly completed building that is intended to provide low-cost housing for the poor would be considered unreasonable economic waste, and therefore Roark, even if allowed to sue, could never obtain such a remedy. Recall the sentiment expressed by the prosecutor in the Cortlandt trial who says, in his remarks to the jury, "Had it been some plutocrat's mansion, but a *housing project*, gentlemen of the jury, a housing project!" (675).

With respect to the issue of Roark's moral right to the integrity of his work, note that his unique architectural style, in which the arrangement of spaces and use of materials constitute a structure's primary ornamentation, might actually work against him in a court of law. One element of the current legal test determining whether a work will be protected is "whether the original, artistic elements are functionally required."[19] One commentator remarks, "By its very nature, this test implies that a building using un-functional decoration is a work of art and thus, protected while a building that is completely functional is unprotected."[20] In addition, note that there is language in the 1990 Act requiring an architect who wants to retain the right to make "derivative works"—i.e., buildings based on an alteration of the architect's original design—to include in his contract a provision stating this.[21] The making of an unauthorized derivative work could constitute an infringement of an author's moral rights. The Act's language might therefore be interpreted as denying architects any statutory protection for such rights. The Act's cautionary language, however, has been held to apply only to existing buildings.[22] It seems that Congress assumed that a building will, at least originally, be built as designed, and was concerned only with the right to make modifications later. In the case of Cortlandt, the government modifies

Roark's design before beginning construction on the first building. For this reason, and also because a provision prohibiting modification was included in the government's contract with Keating, perhaps Roark could succeed in his moral rights claim. Even so, it is unlikely that he would get the relief he deserves, due both to the doctrine disfavoring economic waste and to Cortlandt's being a housing project.

Thus neither in fiction nor in reality is Roark offered a proper legal remedy.

Today's readers of *The Fountainhead* may be less receptive to Rand's justification for Roark's action, because of changes in the culture that have occurred over the last several decades. First, with respect to the moral justification, note that while legal protection of copyright has in many respects improved popular support for that protection, both among intellectuals and in the culture more broadly, has declined. Intellectuals at top universities have launched an attack on the moral foundations of copyright as such.[23] They argue, for example, that authors do not really create anything alone; instead they simply "build upon the creativity that went before and that surrounds them now."[24] They argue that exercising one's right to free speech requires more "access" to copyrighted works than is allowed under current law,[25] and that copyright law that is "too restrictive" hinders precisely what the Constitution's Copyright Clause was designed to promote: "Progress of Science and useful Arts."[26] Rand seems to predict these developments when she writes about the popular speculation as to Roark's motive:

> Some said it was professional jealousy. Others declared that there was a certain similarity between the design of Cortlandt and Roark's style of building, that Keating, Prescott and Webb might have borrowed a little from Roark—"a legitimate adaptation"—"there's no property rights on ideas"—"in a democracy, art belongs to all the people"—and that Roark had been prompted by the vengeance lust of an artist who had believed himself plagiarized. (621)

A reader who accepts these ideas—that creativity is a myth, that one's free speech requires the use of others' original expression, and that the sole justification for protection of copyright is utilitarian—will be loath to agree that Roark was justified in doing what he did.

The same is true of certain attitudes toward copyright and patent that exist among members of the general public. For example, based on informal polls I have conducted, most college students do not believe it is morally wrong to download copyrighted music without paying for it. To them, copyright law is a nuisance that keeps them from enjoying the music they want to hear. Popular musicians are, after all, quite wealthy, while most students are on limited budgets; therefore the musicians should not complain when students "share" their music. A similar view is held by government officials, workers for nonprofit organizations, and those concerned individuals whose efforts are geared toward preventing or curing diseases in third-world countries. The target of these individuals is not copyright, but rather patent law. They believe that a pharmaceutical company should be forced to relinquish its patent in any life-saving medication, simply on the grounds that those in third-world countries need the medication and cannot afford it. Such individuals, if they wished to be logically consistent, would oppose Roark's dynamiting of Cortlandt, especially considering the building's purpose.

Unfortunately, the decline in popular support for copyright protection is but one symptom of a more general degradation of the culture that has occurred in the decades since Rand wrote *The Fountainhead*. I think it is this more general degradation that makes it more difficult for contemporary readers to understand why Roark was psychologically justified in dynamiting Corlandt. In the 1940s people still expected the government to protect, not violate, their rights. Readers living in such a culture, it seems, could more easily empathize with the outrage experienced by Roark, who values his right to his own life and the integrity of his work above all, and has his work stolen and its integrity violated by his own government! Such readers could therefore more easily imagine and applaud Roark's willingness to take an illegal action in retaliation, and to accept the consequences.

Today, however, after a century or more of the American government inventing new ways to initiate force against its citizens, it is often difficult even to muster outrage at a new rights violation—one might spend his life constantly enraged—much less the initiative required to do something about it at the risk of going to jail. Moreover, because so many people not only support the expansion of government that has taken place, but also ask for ever more government programs and rights violations, one might understandably conclude that civil (or not-so-civil) disobedience, as a method of effecting cultural change, has become futile.

In his courtroom speech Roark states, "[T]he integrity of a man's creative work is of greater importance than any charitable endeavor. Those of you who do not understand this are the men who're destroying the world" (684). Unfortunately most men today do not understand this, and they and their predecessors have been working slowly to destroy the world for over a century. If we succeed in reversing this trend, it will be due not only to the hero who defends himself so eloquently in the Cortlandt trial, but also and primarily to the philosopher-novelist who created that hero.[27]

NOTES

1. Biographical interviews (Ayn Rand Archives).

2. See Ayn Rand, "The Objectivist Ethics," *The Virtue of Selfishness: A New Concept of Egoism* (New York: New American Library, 1964), 13–39.

3. Rand, "Objectivist Ethics," 28.

4. The same can be said of his relationship with Dominique: He is willing to live without her for years—and even to design a house for her and her husband—in order to make sure that when he does have her, it will be on his terms.

5. David Harriman, ed., *Journals of Ayn Rand* (New York: Dutton, 1997), 214.

6. Biographical interviews (Ayn Rand Archives).

7. Biographical interviews (Ayn Rand Archives).

8. For example, Keating's design of the Cosmo-Slotnick Building was in "the style of the Renaissance" and required that he borrow "from all of [Ralston] Holcombe's favorite Italian palaces" (173).

9. Ayn Rand, "Patents and Copyrights," *Capitalism: The Unknown Ideal* (New York: New American Library, 1967), 130.

10. This may have been implicit in Keating's and Roark's discussion of Roark's (nonexistent) prospects for suing the government (611), as copyright infringement is presumably the strongest claim he could make.

11. See Baker v. Selden, 101 U.S. 99, 104 (1879). Until 1990, courts interpreted *Baker* "to allow copyright protection only to the original architectural plans and technical drawings of a building and not to the building itself." Antoinette Vacca, "The Architectural Works Copyright Protection Act: Much Ado About Something?" 9 Marq. Intell. Prop. L. Rev. 111, 113 (2005).

12. 41 U.S.C. § 602.

13. 28 U.S.C. §§ 1346(a)(2), 1491(a)(1).

14. But see Balsam/Olson Group, Inc. v. Bradley Place Limited Partnership, 966 F. Supp. 757, 764 (C.D. Ill. 1996) (refusing to grant preliminary injunction to prevent a private-party defendant from completing construction of admittedly infringing buildings, where buildings at issue constituted a low-income housing project for senior citizens).

15. 17 U.S.C. §§ 101–102, 120.

16. See 28 U.S.C. § 1498 (b) (providing for "reasonable and entire compensation as damages" for infringement of a copyright by the government); Eugene Volokh, "Sovereign Immunity and Intellectual Property," 73 So. Cal. L. Rev. 1161 (2000).

17. Andrew S. Pollock, "The Architectural Works Copyright Protection Act: Analysis of Probable Ramifications and Arising Issues," 70 Neb. L. Rev. 873, 895–96 (1991).

18. Bonner v. Dawson, 2003 WL 22432941 *8 (W.D. Va.).

19. Vacca, "Architectural Works Copyright Protection Act," 127.

20. Vacca, "Architectural Works Copyright Protection Act," 127; Trek Leasing, Inc. v. United States, 66 Fed. Cl. 8, 16 (2005) (holding that those elements of the design of a USPS building that are "dictated by efficiency, necessity, or external factors" are not "deserving of copyright protection").

21. Pollock, "Architectural Works Copyright Protection Act," 888.

22. Guillot-Vogt Assoc., Inc. v. Holly & Smith, 848 F. Supp. 682, 687 (1994).

23. See, e.g., Lawrence Lessig, *Free Culture: How Big Media Uses Technology and the Law to Lock Down Culture and Control Creativity* (New York: Penguin 2004).

24. Lessig, *Free Culture*, 29; Vacca, "The Architectural Works Copyright Protection Act," 120 (noting that acclaimed architect Michael Graves said, in hearings before Congress, that "architecture, by its very nature, is a 'transformative' rather than an 'inventive' process").

25. Lessig, *Free Culture*, 128–73.

26. In fact, some scholars have come to call the clause of the Constitution granting power to Congress to enact legislation protecting intellectual property the "Progress Clause," to emphasize the clause's utilitarian roots. See, e.g., Lessig, *Free Culture*, 131.

27. Thanks to Robert Mayhew and Leonard Peikoff for many helpful comments on earlier drafts of this chapter and to Adam Piergallini for research assistance.

Epilogue

An Interview with Leonard Peikoff

On October 12, 2005, I interviewed Leonard Peikoff on The Fountainhead *for more than an hour. Dr. Peikoff read the transcript, which I edited, but he has not read all of the essays in this collection, so the inclusion of this interview in it should not be taken to imply his approval of any of the other contributions.*

—Robert Mayhew

RM: When did you first read *The Fountainhead*?

LP: I think it was the summer of '49, in which case I was 16 at the time.

RM: What was your initial reaction?

LP: I was spellbound. I had a date to meet someone and I'm usually very reliable about showing up on time. But when reading Roark's trial it was impossible for me to care about the hour. I knew he was waiting for me on a downtown street and would be angry, but I just could not put the book down until I finished it.

Of course, I was just a kid at the time and did not understand the novel's deeper meaning. I didn't know it contained a whole philosophy of life. I thought only that it was a wonderful novel that made some important points.

RM: How long after that did you first meet Ayn Rand?

LP: I met her in the spring of '51.

RM: I assume you discussed *The Fountainhead* with her?

LP: Oh, absolutely. I went with one burning question: Is Roark an idealist or a realist? My father had told me for years that you can't be both, which tortured me because he seemed to be right. But I couldn't determine which one Ayn intended Roark to be: he was obviously an uncompromising idealist; yet I could also see that in long-range terms he was the practical man, whereas Keating had to fail. I was completely baffled. You can imagine how she reacted, because the issue went to the heart of her conception of morality. Moreover, when I met her, she had earlier that day begun Part Three of *Atlas Shrugged*, so morality was very much on her mind. She gave me a lengthy answer—15 or 20 minutes—without interruption. She told me in detail what the answer to my question was, why it was a crucial issue, and what thinking-errors had led me to hold the wrong view. It was a breathtaking performance. The other main question I asked that evening was: Is there nothing wrong with pursuing only your own happiness? Of course, that's self-evident in the novel, but it wasn't to me at that age. And she replied: "More than that, you are *obligated* to pursue your own happiness, that's the purpose of life." That astonished me. She was so powerful intellectually, and so eloquent; if you showed the slightest frown—any indication of not understanding her—she would provide further elaborations, or question you about what wasn't clear, so that by the time she finished, it was as if you grasped the point through sense perception; you couldn't imagine a time when you didn't know it.

RM: Was there much of a gap between your first meeting and when you saw her again? Did you return to her with other questions about *The Fountainhead*?

LP: I saw her a week later. I was visiting Los Angeles, where she lived at the time, and staying with relatives. I started to espouse her ideas—ineptly, because I did not know what I was talking about—and my relatives buried me with objections, which I dutifully copied down. I got an appointment with Ayn for the following week (which amazed me, because I thought I'd never see her again). I went over every objection with her, and she gave me the answers, and told me how to figure out these issues on my own, and what I should read in order to be clear on certain points. It's been over 50 years, so it's hard to recall all the questions I asked then. I know we discussed reason and emotion, and whether intuition is a source of knowledge. I had a completely wicked cousin-by-marriage, who said the essence of life is dying: you start to die the moment you're born, and get closer to death with each passing moment. I asked Ayn what was wrong with this, and she was indignant and tore it to shreds. But I can't remember any details. By the way, as I was leaving, she asked me if I believed in God. When I replied that I didn't know, she told me to find out, because "it's an important issue."

RM: Aside from the question of whether Roark was moral or practical, were you confused about any of the other characters at that first reading, and did that come up in conversation?

LP: I was confused about some characters, but for the most part simply eager to discover more about them. We discussed Dominique, who, incidentally, was the character with whom I most closely identified when I first read the novel. If you remember the scene where she tells Alvah Scarret about her dropping a classical sculpture down the airshaft—I had much the same attitude in essence: the idea that in life it's everything or nothing. She couldn't accept compromise, but, she thought, one can't succeed in this world without it. So she gave up the world. That aspect of Dominique was a lot like me. In essence, we were both idealists embittered by the belief that ideals are impractical.

I also asked about Wynand, because I wanted to separate out what was good about him and what wasn't. I was also interested in Toohey and whether such a person was possible—somebody who was that conscious of the evil of his philosophy and nevertheless acted on it.

RM: What did she say about that?

LP: She said that her characterization of Toohey involved a certain degree of poetic license—that in real life, Toohey would have had to evade more and be less explicit to himself about his corrupt ideas. He couldn't act on them, she noted, if he said to himself: "All I want is destruction, as an end in itself; I am depraved." This *is* what Toohey thought, but she brought it out into the open, without evasions and defenses; so in that sense it was a literary device. Her view is that if you know the good, you do have to act on it—*unless* you evade it.

I also wanted to hear how the different strands of the story were brought to a climax in the dynamiting of Cortlandt—how that single event was the culmination of the life-courses of Roark, Wynand, Dominique, Toohey, and Keating. We discussed this stunning feat of plot-construction, and I remember that she said that she had found it difficult, because she needed a *physical event* that would integrate all the different storylines and characters. It couldn't be a speech or mere conversation; as a Romanticist, she needed a dramatic, physical action. She told me that for quite some time she couldn't get anywhere with the problem. All I recall now of what she said about reaching the solution is this: she was in a diner, sitting at the counter eating lunch, and the climax suddenly struck her, and she rushed out to get it on paper. That one integrating flash came to her after a long, seemingly futile struggle.

I wish I could remember more of our discussions of *The Fountainhead*. Part of the problem is that when I met her, she was in the midst of writing

Atlas Shrugged. So after some general discussion of *The Fountainhead*, my focus shifted with her to *Atlas Shrugged*. I began reading her new writing on *Atlas*, with her in the same room or nearby, and we would discuss my reactions, questions, etc. For the first few chapters of *Atlas*, *The Fountainhead* was still my frame of reference. I would say to her about some scene she had just written: "Isn't that just like such-and-such in *The Fountainhead*?" And she would smile and reply: "Yes, there's a similarity." But after I read the scene with Rearden and Dagny riding on the John Galt Line, she asked me: "Do you see a parallel to *that* in *The Fountainhead*?" I replied that it was definitely a different novel. She was pleased with that.

RM: I heard that you used to read the novel repeatedly, to the point where you pretty much knew every line. Could you talk about that?

LP: I had virtually memorized the entire book. Some of us used to play a game in which someone would read any line from *The Fountainhead* (with the exception of "he said" or "she said"), and the others would try to say, e.g., which character said it and in what context. I could rarely be stumped. Give me even only a clause, or sometimes a single word, and I could usually quote the entire line.

RM: How many times do you think you've read *The Fountainhead*?

LP: It's been 56 years since I first read it. I'll take a wild guess and say 30 to 40 times. I haven't read it for 5 or 6 years now, because I got to the point where I *couldn't* read it anymore. I knew it inside out.

RM: I heard you say in a lecture that you went back to *The Fountainhead* when you were having trouble with the section on integrity in your book *Objectivism: The Philosophy of Ayn Rand* [*OPAR*], and that that proved to be very helpful. Is that correct?

LP: Yes, but it's misleading to single out integrity. In *OPAR*, I tried to reproduce exactly Ayn Rand's essential thought on everything relating to philosophy. So I steeped myself in her work, including *The Fountainhead*, for every topic. *The Fountainhead* doesn't offer an explicit epistemology, but I certainly returned to it many times for the sections in *OPAR* on independence, sex, selfishness versus altruism, physical force, and the like. I milked *The Fountainhead* of everything I thought essential. For instance, at the end of the section on productiveness, I quote from a scene with Austin Heller and Roark, which contains one of my favorite lines in the novel. Heller says: "After all, it's only a building. It's not the combination of holy sacrament, Indian torture and sexual ecstasy that you seem to make of it." Roark answers: "Isn't it?" That's a wonderful way to describe in condensed form the three components of genuine creative work—the three essential elements of the inner state of a creator. I just wish that in my work I'd had less Indian torture and more sexual ecstasy.

RM: What other scenes and lines are your personal favorites?

LP: It's hard to say, because there are far too many. But at random, without claiming that this is exhaustive or in any order of importance: I liked the scenes with Wynand and Roark on the yacht, because it gave me an idea of what it would be like to have a real friend. I love the section on the strike against the *Banner* and Wynand's holding out. The single line in *The Fountainhead* which had the greatest suspense for me was during the strike, when the Board of Directors says to Wynand that they can save the paper if he gives in to the union's demands, but if not, it's over; and then they say to him: "Yes or no?" When I first read *The Fountainhead*, I hoped so intensely for Wynand, and I put my hand over the page and was afraid to go on and read what she wrote. This is one of my top scenes, and now I see why it had to end as it did.

Of course, the "rape" scene—who could omit that? I suppose that should be number one. I like all the love scenes. I reacted strongly to the scene where Dominique visited Roark in Clayton, Ohio, and he was walking her back to the train, and a piece of old newspaper blew against her legs, and she picked it up and started to fold it, and he said, "What are you doing?" "Something to read on the train," she said. Then he grabs the paper and throws it away, because it was clear that she wanted something, anything, that pertained to him, even trash—that it would take on the glow of a supreme value because of its connection to him. I loved both characters as impassioned valuers. Of course, he wouldn't allow an empty symbol, such as trash.

Another scene I like is the first time Roark and Dominique meet again after the "rape" scene, at a cocktail party, and Ayn writes that he knew how brutal it was for her, and admired her strength. Then she describes how Dominique felt: "as if there were no floor around her but the few square inches under her soles and she were safe so long as she did not move or look down"—as though there was a precipice everywhere else. I thought it was such a vivid way of communicating her paralyzed, astounded inner state.

I love the way Dominique fought for the newspaper during the strike, and of course I love her columns. I also think Toohey's columns were excellent—very witty, very vicious. I could go on forever. But the implication I want to avoid is that because I mentioned *these* scenes, therefore I don't like many other scenes just as much. That's not true.

RM: With the understanding that the same disclaimer applies to this next question, what are some of your favorite lines?

LP: I can quote a couple, but it's like asking about a symphony, "What's your favorite bar?" If I re-read the book from the point of view of my favorite lines, and had to underscore them, there would be thousands. But here are a few that occur to me now: When Dominique and Peter are at home alone and she never expresses an opinion on anything, and he explains that the essence of being a person is judging and valuing, and asks her: "Where's your I?" She replies: "Where's yours, Peter?" It's so powerful. He made a speech that focused on her external behavior—on home decoration and going to parties and so on—and then in three words she said to him all the same things, but on a deeper, psychological level, and one which he could not help but see. That is brilliant writing.

Here's another line, which I think of whenever I hear a typical professor of philosophy, especially linguistic analysts, dismiss Ayn Rand's ideas: "The sound perception of an ant does not include thunder." This helps me to keep in proper perspective the kind of people in the intellectual world today; there's no use arguing with them, because they're ants and can't hear and that's it.

I love the fact that the novel starts and ends on the words "Howard Roark": "Howard Roark laughed" and "Then there was only the ocean and the sky and the figure of Howard Roark." That emphasizes that he is the core of the novel.

I once took a course in creative writing and was told that it's important to give some single touch to a lesser character that will stick in the reader's mind as: *this* is the type of person he is. Not a speech or whatever, but some little touch. Ayn did that perfectly.

Offhand, Ralston Holcombe comes to mind. She described his wonderful mane of hair that "rose over his forehead and fell to his shoulder" and then "left dandruff on the back of his collar." That touch made him memorable—and killed him, no matter what he did thereafter. Another one here pertains to Gus Webb. The touch I always remember is: Gus Webb at a party at Lois Cook's, with Jules Fougler saying that he doesn't like Gus Webb; when asked why, Fougler replies: "Because he doesn't wash his ears." Ever since, Gus Webb to me is the one who doesn't wash his ears— with all the dirt of soul this implies. The book is full of lines like that, where one touch or estimate after another is brilliantly expressed. Her descriptions are always so great—so clever or witty or economical or sarcastic (in the good sense).

RM: What is distinctive about *The Fountainhead*, compared to *We the Living* and *Atlas Shrugged*?

LP: It has a distinctive focus. The emphasis of *The Fountainhead* is that idealism is possible and practical on earth. Its focus is on man's capacity to

achieve and succeed as an individual. *We the Living* is denunciatory: its focus is on those who *destroy* man's capacity to achieve and succeed—on the
enemies of this capacity, rather than on its existence and glory. *Atlas
Shrugged* is on a higher level, because it takes for granted that men of
achievement and success are possible on earth, and then shows how they
are making their own destroyers possible. So all three books are centered in
one way or another on man's capacity to achieve values, but each with a different emphasis and perspective.

The Fountainhead is the most intimately personal of the three novels. *We
the Living* is a social novel, in the sense that it describes Russia under Communism and how that system destroys the best among men. *Atlas Shrugged*
is also, in its own way, a novel about the decay and collapse of a society. But
The Fountainhead does not involve government, except at the very end, in regard to the Cortlandt project. The assumption of *The Fountainhead* is: we're
living in a free (and for now politically safe) society, and these are the
choices men make in it. The novel is concerned with the good choices and
the bad choices. So it's on a personal level, not focused on society as a
whole. It has political implications, of course, but that's not part of the
theme, in the way politics *is* essential to the other novels.

Another difference is that in *We the Living*, Ayn was still on the premise
of making the woman the protagonist. With *The Fountainhead*, however, a
man is the hero, and the woman is essentially someone in love with him.
In *Atlas Shrugged*, of course, Galt is the supreme hero.

If you could imagine the characters of *The Fountainhead* in *Atlas Shrugged*
for a moment, I think Roark would be one of the strikers, like Rearden, but
he would not be on the level of Galt. He's too young, he's learning throughout the novel what people are like, he doesn't have the philosophic mastery
or understanding that Galt has. Even towards the end, he is naive enough
to work with Keating on the Cortlandt project; Galt wouldn't have tolerated
such an idea.

I think all this parallels Ayn's own growth. I hold, as a hypothesis, the
view that any (or at least many) creative persons who work across time go
through three stages in writing. The first stage is denouncing, ridding your
subconscious of the evil background from which you sprung. That's *We the
Living*. For the next stage, your mental slate is now clear, and you present
without obstruction your positive vision of life, but in simple, essentialized
terms, without any "higher mathematics": here's the hero, here's the villain,
here's the conflict. That's *The Fountainhead*. Then, in the final stage, you take
the totality of the knowledge you've gained and present the positives in
your *magnum opus*, synthesizing all of your knowledge of good and of evil,
identifying fundamentals that are much more complex than was possible to
you earlier. That's *Atlas Shrugged*.

RM: Let's move to the characters that give a lot of readers a hard time: Wynand and especially Dominique. Can you say something about what they have in common, and how they're different?

LP: Yes I can. But I want to start by saying, without giving offense, that Ayn Rand felt a particular indignation against people who said they didn't understand Dominique's psychology. She could accept that they might have problems with Wynand or Toohey, but if they couldn't understand Dominique, then she concluded that they had no concept of idealism—because the essence of Dominique, as I said earlier, is an embittered idealism.

Dominique wants the ideal, she's in love with the good, she won't settle for anything less—however, she's convinced that, by the nature of people as she observes them, the good simply cannot be achieved. Since she won't settle for less, she chooses to want and take nothing from the world. To appreciate her character, you must be able to understand her passionate idealism and her complete despair.

Both Dominique and Wynand are valuers in despair; so far they are alike: they're both idealists who believe that ideals cannot be achieved in a world filled with rotten people. So he and Dominique were similar. On this point, Ayn has Dominique say to him: "I think we have a great deal in common, you and I. We've committed the same treason somewhere." But the difference between Wynand and Dominique is profound, because of how each acts in the face of his malevolence. Dominique withdraws from the world: she says people are irrational, so values are impossible, so I want nothing to do with the world. Wynand says: if that's the way people are, I'm going to become one of them, in effect, a super-powerful one, who can force them to obey *my* values instead of the other way around. She chooses in effect to enter a convent rather than to corrupt her soul; he chooses to enter a brothel in order to become a dictator, who survives by having power over people who sicken him. That is quite a difference between them!

RM: Why does Wynand have to fail, while Dominique can be redeemed?

LP: Because Wynand betrays and destroys his values *in action*. For example, whatever his motivation or rationalization, in actual fact his power-lust is the only thing really hurting Roark—both professionally and personally. Whereas Dominique can be redeemed because, given her moral purity, all she needed was knowledge—that she was wrong about the universe being malevolent. She did give a few commissions to Roark's competitors, but that was more symbolic than practically significant.

Dominique loved Roark and devoutly wished he could survive unbroken. But Wynand set out to prove that Roark *could* be broken; and when Roark shows that he can't, Wynand says: "Don't think it was one of those temptations when you tempt just to test your victim and are happy to be beaten.

. . . Don't make that excuse for me. . . . I'm not glad and I'm not grateful to you for this." And that was true, for Wynand the power-luster—and thus Wynand the unredeemable.

RM: Why does Roark say that the man who seeks power is the worst second-hander?

LP: Ayn answers that in the book. She says that the other second-handers, such as Peter Keating, want to submit or live through others, at least for what they can get for themselves, like money, fame, etc. They have to sacrifice their soul and minds to do it, so that the things they get are no source of value or pleasure to them; but nevertheless, to that extent they are concerned with desires of their own. Whereas the man who seeks power, she explains in the novel, is living entirely through and for others—Toohey says this in his speech—for what he can do to others. His whole life is in others and how he can affect them. He doesn't care about money, he doesn't even care about titles, he doesn't care if he's poor and anonymous. What he wants is only the ability to shape the lives of others. So he is selfless in the most profound and all-inclusive way.

RM: Isn't Toohey a much worse second-hander than Wynand?

LP: Of course, because Wynand does hold ideals, however perversely he acted on them. Toohey does not. Now you could say that Wynand is worse precisely *because* he has values, and then betrayed them by going after power. But Wynand does not really understand the nature of power lust, and would not have chosen it if he had, as Toohey explains to him: "So you were after power, Mr. Wynand? . . . You poor amateur! You never discovered the nature of your own ambition or you'd have known that you weren't fit for it." Toohey is incomparably worse.

RM: Here's another question on Wynand: Ayn Rand once described Wynand's feelings for Roark as romantic love, an expression she usually reserved for a certain relationship between a man and a woman. What did she mean by this?

LP: Ayn distinguishes three types of relationships—friendship, love, and sexual love—and we're speaking now in the context of your question relating to two men. In the case of friendship, the other person is a value—perhaps even a great value, but is not irreplaceable in your life. If something were to happen to them, or they moved to Brazil, you would miss them and want to talk to them, etc., but you could go on with your life ultimately just as happily, and make another friend, with whom you were also extremely close. This is not to say you would forget the lost friend, but he wouldn't be an ongoing reality in your life.

Her definition of "love" is what you feel for the irreplaceable: the person loved is of such personal value to you that if lost, you could never again find someone of that value. You could never get your life back to the way it was. You could go ahead with your life, work creatively, meet other people, but there would always be a void and an ache in your person, because you so valued the uniqueness of this person, the combination of qualities that no one else has. That is what she calls love. This relationship, she holds, can exist between two men who are both healthy; it would not include sex—because, she thought, they won't have the desire for that form of expression of their love. But such love can include admiration of the other's body, and that's why she included Roark standing naked on the deck of the yacht and Wynand commenting that Roark's body should have been the model for the statue, not Dominique's.

Finally there is sexual love, between a man and a woman, in which the same irreplaceability exists, but with the additional and crucial form of expression of the sexual relationship.

RM: Let's turn briefly from the novel to the film version of *The Fountainhead*: What is your opinion of it, and did you ever discuss it with Ayn Rand?

LP: I would say the film is okay, about 7 or so out of 10. The script was excellent—Ayn wrote it. But there were other aspects that left something to be desired. It was not Romantic enough in style; in fact, Ayn's major objection was that the direction was Naturalistic and clashed with the novel. She also thought Gary Cooper's acting was pretty shaky. She told me that she had been on the set throughout the filming, and she had tried to help him, repeatedly going over Roark's speech with him, and he sort of got its meaning in the end, but not entirely. According to Ayn, after he saw the final cut, he said to her: "Now I understand how I should have delivered it." Gary Cooper was a nice guy, but totally nonintellectual; he often played Westerns, for instance, and it was difficult for him to give a philosophical speech preaching unconventional ideas. He deserves a lot of credit, though, because I understand he was under tremendous pressure from his agent and other associates not to do the movie—on the ground that its politics would harm him in Hollywood; but he was adamant. He liked the novel and was going to do this film, no matter what the consequences. That's a rare phenomenon. Patricia Neal took the role of Dominique not out of courage, but because this was her entry into the big time—to star in a role like that with Gary Cooper (and, so it was said, have an affair with him at the same time). I thought she did very well—better than Cooper. On the whole, though, I didn't like the casting. Greta Garbo, I should add, was Ayn's choice for the part: but Garbo flatly refused to appear with Cooper as her lover—he wasn't her type, she explained.

Ayn was moderately pleased with the film, though she thought the Italian version of *We the Living* was much better than the Hollywood version of *The Fountainhead*. It was more faithful to the book, and Alida Valli, she held, was *perfect* for the role of Kira. (She didn't like Rossano Brazzi that much as Leo.)

RM: One last set of questions: What did *The Fountainhead* mean to you when you first read it and continued to re-read it? What does it mean to you now?

LP: What I get from *The Fountainhead* is the experience of a universe in which I want always to live: a world of ideas, passion, values, drama, creativity—of people of stature, brilliance, achievement. It is the exact opposite of the world I grew up in—a small town with ordinary people who were uninterested in ideas, and would dismiss philosophical questions with the comment: "Nobody knows, and what's the difference?" There is no aspect of Winnipeg that I could consider heroic, with the possible exception of the fact that people regularly went out in –35 degree weather. Reading *The Fountainhead* was like going to another planet. That's why I kept steeping myself in it. Now once I was in New York and seeing Ayn regularly, I didn't need *The Fountainhead* as much; because Ayn in person radiated the same universe. But the book could still bring back my youth and what it meant to me, and the astonishment of finding out what was possible in life. Reading *The Fountainhead* always took me out of the routine—even after being an Objectivist for decades—and brought me back to my beginning and to what is still possible. I kept at it until I got to know it too well.

RM: You continued reading *The Fountainhead* regularly *after* the publication of *Atlas Shrugged*?

LP: Are you kidding? I continued reading it as long as I felt the need, and I felt it often. I have a much more personal relationship to *The Fountainhead* than I ever did to *Atlas Shrugged*. I love and admire *Atlas*. There's no question it's the greatest book Ayn wrote. But *The Fountainhead* was *to me* the opening up of reality. It was what hit me as a person, intellectually and emotionally, and changed my life. It was what made it possible for me to understand *Atlas*. *The Fountainhead* was always my ideal, my idealism, and my personal guide—and it has never lost that status.

Select Bibliography

This bibliography is limited to books by Ayn Rand—and books about Ayn Rand and her philosophy, Objectivism—cited in this collection.

Berliner, Michael S., ed. *Letters of Ayn Rand.* New York: Dutton, 1995; paperback edition, Plume, 1997.

Binswanger, Harry, ed. *The Ayn Rand Lexicon: Objectivism from A to Z.* New York: New American Library, 1986; paperback edition, Meridian, 1988.

Britting, Jeff. *Ayn Rand.* New York: Overlook Press. 2005.

Harriman, David, ed. *Journals of Ayn Rand.* New York: Dutton, 1997; paperback edition, Plume, 1999.

Johnson, Donald Leslie. *The Fountainheads: Wright, Rand, the FBI and Hollywood.* Jefferson, NC: McFarland, 2005.

Mayhew, Robert, ed. *Ayn Rand Answers: The Best of Her Q&A.* New York: New American Library, 2005.

———, ed. *Essays on Ayn Rand's* Anthem. Lanham, MD: Lexington Books, 2005.

———, ed. *Essays on Ayn Rand's* We the Living. Lanham, MD: Lexington Books, 2004.

Peikoff, Leonard, ed. *The Early Ayn Rand: A Selection from Her Unpublished Fiction.* New York: New American Library, 1984; paperback edition, Signet, 1986; revised version, Signet, 2005.

———. *Objectivism: The Philosophy of Ayn Rand.* New York: Dutton, 1991; paperback edition, New Meridian, 1993.

———. *The Ominous Parallels: The End of Freedom in America.* New York: Stein and Day, 1982; Meridian paperback edition, 1993.

Rand, Ayn. *Anthem.* Fiftieth anniversary paperback edition. Introduction by Leonard Peikoff. New York: Signet, 1995.

———. *The Art of Fiction: A Guide for Writers and Readers.* Edited by Tore Boeckmann. Introduction by Leonard Peikoff. New York: Plume, 2000.

———. *The Art of Nonfiction: A Guide for Writers and Readers.* Edited by Robert Mayhew. Introduction by Peter Schwartz. New York: Plume, 2001.

———. *Atlas Shrugged.* New York: Random House, 1957; Signet thirty-fifth anniversary paperback edition, 1992.

———. *Capitalism: The Unknown Ideal.* New York: New American Library, 1966; expanded paperback edition, Signet, 1967.

———. *For the New Intellectual.* New York: Random House, 1961; Signet paperback edition, 1963.

———. *The Fountainhead.* New York: Bobbs-Merrill, 1943; Signet fiftieth anniversary paperback edition, 1993.

———. *Night of January 16th.* Definitive edition. New York: Plume, 1987.

———. *Philosophy: Who Needs It.* New York: Bobbs-Merrill, 1982; Signet paperback edition, 1984.

———. *Return of the Primitive: The Anti-Industrial Revolution.* Edited by Peter Schwartz. New York: Meridian, 1999.

———. *The Romantic Manifesto: A Philosophy of Literature.* Revised edition. New York: Signet, 1975.

———. *The Virtue of Selfishness: A New Concept of Egoism.* New York: New American Library, 1964.

———. *The Voice of Reason: Essays in Objectivist Thought.* Edited by Leonard Peikoff. New York: New American Library, 1989; paperback edition, Meridian, 1990.

———. *We the Living.* Sixtieth anniversary paperback edition. Introduction by Leonard Peikoff. New York: Signet, 1996.

Schwartz, Peter, ed. *The Ayn Rand Column.* New Milford, CT: Second Renaissance, 1991; revised second edition, 1998.

Smith, Tara. *Ayn Rand's Normative Ethics: The Virtuous Egoist.* New York: Cambridge University Press, 2006.

———. *Viable Values: A Study of Life as the Root and Reward of Morality.* Lanham, MD: Rowman & Littlefield, 2000.

Index

About the Contributors

B. John Bayer holds an M.A. in Philosophy from the University of Illinois, Urbana–Champaign, where he is completing his Ph.D. dissertation and has taught Philosophy. He specializes in epistemology.

Michael S. Berliner holds a Ph.D. in Philosophy from Boston University. He was Executive Director of the Ayn Rand Institute for its first fifteen years and previously taught Philosophy of Education and Philosophy at California State University, Northridge. He created the first two catalogs of the Ayn Rand Papers at the Ayn Rand Archives and is currently compiling a definitive inventory. He is editor of *Letters of Ayn Rand* and Ayn Rand's *Russian Writings on Hollywood*. He has lectured throughout the United States and in Europe, Australia, and Israel on Ayn Rand's life.

Andrew Bernstein holds a Ph.D. in Philosophy from the Graduate School of the City University of New York and teaches at Pace University and SUNY Purchase. He is the author of the novel *Heart of a Pagan* and of *The Capitalist Manifesto: The Historic, Economic and Philosophic Case for Laissez-Faire*. He lectures widely on topics relating to both Ayn Rand's novels and her philosophy of Objectivism. His website is www.andrewbernstein.net.

Tore Boeckmann is a writer whose mystery short stories have been published and anthologized in several languages. He edited Ayn Rand's *The Art of Fiction: A Guide for Writers and Readers* and has lectured on Ayn Rand's literary esthetics in America and Europe.

Jeff Britting is Archivist of the Ayn Rand Archives, a collection of the Ayn Rand Institute. He is author of the short illustrated biography *Ayn Rand*. He developed and associate-produced the Academy Award–nominated documentary *Ayn Rand: A Sense of Life* and the feature film *Take Two*, and he co-produced the first stage productions of Ayn Rand's play *Ideal* and her novella *Anthem*. As a composer, he has written incidental music for eleven stage productions and three films, and is currently writing an opera based on an original libretto set in the Middle Ages.

Onkar Ghate holds a Ph.D. in Philosophy from the University of Calgary. He is a Senior Fellow at the Ayn Rand Institute, where he specializes in Ayn Rand's philosophy of Objectivism and teaches Philosophy in the Institute's Objectivist Academic Center. Recent publications include "Postmodernism's Kantian Roots" and (coauthored with Dr. Edwin Locke) "Objectivism: The Proper Alternative to Postmodernism" (both in *Postmodernism and Management: Pros, Cons and the Alternative*), and an entry on Ayn Rand in the *Encyclopedia of Science, Technology, and Ethics*.

Robert Mayhew is Professor of Philosophy at Seton Hall University. He is the author of *Aristotle's Criticism of Plato's Republic, The Female in Aristotle's Biology,* and *Ayn Rand and Song of Russia*. He has translated a play of Aristophanes (*Assembly of Women*), and edited three volumes of unpublished material of Ayn Rand: *Ayn Rand's Marginalia, The Art of Nonfiction,* and *Ayn Rand Answers*.

Shoshana Milgram [Knapp] holds a Ph.D. in Comparative Literature from Stanford University, and is Associate Professor of English at Virginia Tech. She has published articles on a variety of nineteenth- and twentieth-century figures in French, Russian, and English/American literature, including Napoleon Bonaparte, Victor Hugo, George Sand, Anton Chekhov, Fyodor Dostoevsky, Leo Tolstoi, Victoria Cross, George Eliot, John Fowles, W. S. Gilbert, Henry James, Ursula K. LeGuin, Vladimir Nabokov, Herbert Spencer, W. T. Stead, E. L. Voynich—and Ayn Rand. She is also the author of introductions to editions of *Toilers of the Sea* and *The Man Who Laughs*, by Victor Hugo, and *The Seafarers*, by Nevil Shute. Her current project is a study of Ayn Rand's life up to 1957.

Amy Peikoff is Assistant Professor of Philosophy at the United States Air Force Academy. She holds a J.D. from the University of California, Los Angeles, School of Law, and a Ph.D. in Philosophy from the University of Southern California. She has written articles on law and philosophy for academic journals and leading newspapers. Her current research interests include the "right" to privacy, theories of judicial interpretation, and Christian ethics.

Leonard Peikoff holds a Ph.D. in Philosophy from New York University and is the preeminent Rand scholar writing today. He worked closely with Ayn Rand for thirty years and was designated by her as heir to her estate. He has taught philosophy at Hunter College, Long Island University, and New York University, and lectures on Rand's philosophy throughout the country. He is the author of *The Ominous Parallels* and *Objectivism: The Philosophy of Ayn Rand*, and is currently writing a book entitled *The DIM Hypothesis*.

Richard E. Ralston received a B.A. in History from the University of Maryland after serving seven years in the U.S. Army. He then completed an M.A. in International Relations at the University of Southern California. He has been the Managing Director of the Ayn Rand Institute, and Circulation Director and Publishing Director of the *Christian Science Monitor*. He is the editor of two books, *Communism: Its Rise and Fall in the 20th Century* and *Why Businessmen Need Philosophy*. He is presently the Executive Director of Americans for Free Choice in Medicine.

Dina Schein holds a Ph.D. in Philosophy from the University of Texas at Austin and is Visiting Assistant Professor at Auburn University. She has translated Ayn Rand's *Russian Writings on Hollywood* and is currently translating the Russian correspondence written to Ayn Rand in the 1920s and 1930s. She regularly lectures on topics in ethics and in literature, and on Ayn Rand's years in Russia.

Tara Smith is Professor of Philosophy at the University of Texas at Austin, where she currently holds the Anthem Foundation Fellowship for the Study of Objectivism. A specialist in moral, political, and legal philosophy, she is the author of *Ayn Rand's Normative Ethics: The Virtuous Egoist, Viable Values: A Study of Life as the Root and Reward of Morality,* and *Moral Rights and Political Freedom*.